D1300631

1-20-69

1-20-69

WORSHIP IN THE NAME OF JESUS

Peter Brunner

WORSHIP IN

English Edition of a Definitive Work

THE NAME OF JESUS

on Christian Worship in the Congregation

Translated by M. H. Bertram

CONCORDIA PUBLISHING HOUSE | SAINT LOUIS   LONDON

Concordia Publishing House, St. Louis, Missouri
Concordia Publishing House Ltd., London, E. C. 1
© 1968 Concordia Publishing House
Library of Congress Catalog Card No. 68-30965

Translated by permission from the original German title,
Zur Lehre vom Gottesdienst der im Namen Jesu versammelten Gemeinde
in *Leiturgia, Handbuch des evangelischen Gottesdienstes,* Volume I,
edited by Karl Ferdinand Müller and Walter Blankenburg,
Johannes Stauda Verlag, Kassel, 1954

MANUFACTURED IN THE UNITED STATES OF AMERICA

CONTENTS

FOREWORD

In his *Formula of Mass and Communion for the Church at Witten-berg*, written in 1523, Martin Luther startled the world of his day with his brief remark: "Something must be dared in the name of Christ." [1] After 1517 the Reformer dared to say many things that had not been heard before. No one dared to consider that what Luther said should have been said before because the eternal welfare of the hearts of men, women, and children was involved.

In 1953 the ice was finally broken; in that year the Johannes Stauda-Verlag of Kassel, Germany, in Volume I of its *Leiturgia, Hand-buch des evangelischen Gottesdienstes*,[2] published the article *Zur Lehre vom Gottesdienst der im Namen Jesu versammelten Gemeinde*. Not until the second half of our 20th century, therefore, did an eminent theologian of the church venture to say in print what scholars and theologians had not dared to say before. Then it was Peter Brunner of Heidelberg University (b. April 25, 1900) who called attention to the fact that as yet nothing noteworthy had been said in theological literature to alert people to the situation that confronted them. Though throughout many ages Christians had worshiped and adored the Holy Trinity and on many occasions had discussed important issues of the Christian religion and its worship, no one had as yet produced a major literary opus devoted exclusively and profoundly to the significant doctrine of Christian worship.

Although Martin Luther had said that "something must be dared in the name of Christ" and had referred specifically to Christian wor-ship, had even based his entire Reformation on man's utter need for true Christian worship, he did not devote so much as a single volume of his many books wholly to the doctrine of Christian worship. He touched on these matters also in his explanations of the Third Commandment in his Small[3] and Large Catechisms,[4] in his explanations of the First[5] and Second[6] Petitions of The Lord's Prayer, and in numerous other passages of his writings,[7] but here, too, he passed up a wonderful opportunity to discuss the doctrine of worship in the holy catholic church in greater detail.

Luther dealt with the doctrine of Christian worship only in passing in his *Von ordenung gottis dienst ynn der gemeyne* ("Concerning the Order of Divine Worship in the Congregation"), 1523, in his *Formula missae et communionis pro ecclesia Wittembergensi* ("Formula of Mass and Communion for the Church at Wittenberg"), 1523, in his *Eyne Christliche vormanung von eusserlichem Gottis dienste unde eyntracht an die yn lieffland* ("Exhortation to the Christians in Livonia Concerning Public Worship and Unity"), 1525, and finally in his *Deudsche Messe und ordnung Gottis diensts* ("The German Mass and Order of Service"), 1526.[8] It may seem strange to some that Luther failed to see the need for discussing at length the theology of Christian worship in these great writings, which are among the most noteworthy items he wrote for his followers. However, one should not forget that they are among his earliest writings and were written about the same time that he wrote the overwhelming majority of his 37 hymns. On the whole, his hymns share the characteristics of his writings. Both types are strongly doctrinal and both treat the doctrine of Christian worship incidentally and casually rather than specifically. Luther's adherents followed his example, and to this day many Lutheran theologians and hymn writers say relatively little in their literature regarding the theology of Christian worship. To them the issue seems self-evident, and they prefer to treat the doctrinal word rather than the doctrine of worship itself. This applies also to such eminent Lutheran theologians as Johann Gerhard, Abraham Calov, Polykarp Leyser, and many others of the 16th and 17th centuries. It is well to recall, too, that many expert theologians lack the imagination which Martin Luther had in rich measure and are therefore not qualified to write theological literature that calls for imagination, especially when it is based on a worship approach.

Both Martin Luther and Peter Brunner received unique imaginative gifts from God. Luther was an exegete, Brunner a systematician. To discover the vast riches of each, one need but read their books. Peter Brunner's literature evinces clearly that its author is one of the most eminent and versatile theologians of 20th-century Protestantism. To this day he is a highly esteemed member of the theological faculty of the University in Heidelberg, Germany. He plays an important role in the Lutheran World Federation and is often called upon to read theological essays at noteworthy theological conferences and conventions. We are therefore not surprised to note that in 1965 he was honored through the publication of a *Festausgabe* prepared for him by his many friends and admirers of Europe and North America. Its title is *Zur Auferstehung des Leibes Christi* ("Regarding the Resurrection of the Body of Christ"). The volume was edited by Edmund Schlink and Abrecht Peters; it was published by the Johannes Stauda-Verlag in Kassel, Germany.

As a systematician Dr. Brunner wrote the two volumes of his *Pro Ecclesia — Gesammelte Aufsätze zur dogmatischen Theologie* ("For the Church—Collected Essays on Systematic Theology"), issued in 1962 and 1966 by Herbert Renner and the Lutherisches Verlagshaus of Berlin and Hamburg. These two volumes constitute a work of 399 and 380 pages respectively; the opus closes with a chapter on *Singen und Sagen* ("Singing and Saying"), pp. 352—380. These volumes give eloquent testimony to the theological knowledge, depth, and originality of their author.

In 1953 the *Johannes Stauda Verlag* printed as Chapter II of the first volume of its *Leiturgia, Handbuch des evangelischen Gottesdienstes,* edited by K. F. Müller and Walter Blankenburg, pp. 84—361, Peter Brunner's *Zur Lehre vom Gottesdienst der im Namen Jesu versammelten Gemeinde* ("The Doctrine of Worship in the Name of Jesus"). This work paved the way for future generations and gave to the church its first book on the theology of Christian worship. Discussions followed rapidly. Not a few theologians began to follow in Brunner's footsteps; others differed with him.

The publication of this important work in the English translation by Martin Bertram is a significant contribution to theological literature. The reader will find the work of Peter Brunner rich and poignant. He will enjoy following the thought of Brunner as he contrasts the worship of the pagans with that of the Christians, relates the universal plan of Christian salvation to the cross of Jesus Christ, compares the worship of the Old Testament with that of the New, speaks of eschatological facts and problems, the worship of the angels and other creatures, and the individual parts of the Lutheran liturgy.

WALTER E. BUSZIN

INTRODUCTION

The title of our essay intimates that it is difficult to find an appropriate term for the subject of our study. In a dogmatical essay, terminology is appropriate when it corresponds to the apostolic proclamation found in the New Testament. But New Testament diction does not permit us simply to use the word "worship" *(Gottesdienst)* to designate the subject of our investigation.

To be sure, in Rom. 9:4 Paul also mentions the word "worship" *(latreia — λατρεία)*,[1] meaning the rites instituted by God and regulated by the laws of the Old Covenant, among the marks that identify the people of Israel as the true bearers of God's revelation. Correspondingly Heb. 9:1, 6 applies the same term to the official acts of the priest in the tabernacle or in the temple [RSV uses "worship" in v. 1, "ritual duties" in v. 6]. However, in the New Testament the word "worship" *(latreia)* manifestly conveys an entirely different meaning; for here the Christians are told that their *latreia* is a "spiritual" worship — the undivided surrender of their entire physical existence to God (Rom. 12:1). On the other hand, the enemies of the Christians madly perverted the meaning of the word "worship" *(latreia)*, applying it to the execution of Christians; this was conceived as a service to God, as an act of *latreia*. (John 16:2)

The corresponding verb "to serve God" *(gottdienen — latreuein — λατρεύειν)* points in the same direction. In the New Testament it indicates the ritual veneration which the pagans render their gods, but also the ritual veneration which apostate Israel rendered astral idols (Rom. 1:25; Acts 7:42). In accordance with Rom. 9:4 and Heb. 9:1, 6, the ritual acts of the priests in the tabernacle or the temple are also designated with this term (Heb. 8:5; 9:9; 10:2; 13:10). Also the rigid, legal-ritual conduct of the Jews by which they hoped to pro-

11

cure the fulfillment of the Messianic promises is called "serving God" (*gottdienen — latreuein*); and perseverance in fasting and praying in the temple is stressed as a special mark of such worship among "the quiet in the land." (Acts 26:7; Luke 2:37)

But when the act of *gottdienen* relates to Christians, we are again faced with the fact that this *latreuein* has a new content and meaning. This is evident from Luke 1:74 f., and particularly from Heb. 9:14 and 12:28. In the instance of the Christians, to serve God through *latreia* implies that they have been transported into the new reality of salvation of the fulfilled Messianic era; that they are liberated from the might of the opposing powers; that they are freed from groveling fear; that they are purified by Christ's sacrifice from the dead works of their old being and thus liberated for the good work, for the new obedience to the new commandment of love, and filled with gratitude because they may already share in the ultimate, enduring kingdom of God. But simultaneously, conscious of the grave nearness of the Day of Judgment and its terrifying glory and confronting the God who will prove Himself a consuming fire in His approaching judgment, they are also filled with the fear and the awe of an ultimate responsibility. Such a Christ-given vitality before God in holiness, righteousness, gratitude, love, awe, and fear, thus a conduct and an activity that encompasses the entire practical life of the Christian in all its ramifications, constitutes the priestly service of the Christian with which he serves God in the New Covenant.

The fact that Paul in Acts 24:14 (similarly in 2 Tim. 1:3) calls his Christian estate "worship" conforms to this usage of the term. In Phil. 3:3 the apostle joins hands with the congregation in this action. "We," not the synagog, "are the true circumcision," the chosen people of God. "We" who serve God in spirit also have the "worship" now. The antiritual character of this service is very clearly discernible here where worship designates the total conduct of the Christian before God "in thought and prayer, in word and deed" (Lohmeyer). This conduct is made feasible and is effectuated solely through the miraculous gift of the Messianic end time: through the Spirit of God. But the Spirit has burst asunder the legal-ritual bonds to Torah and worship form. The Spirit touches the total existence of man. Thus to serve God in the Spirit through *latreia* must indeed be the Christians' "living sacrifice" described in Rom. 12:1 f. In Rom. 1:9 Paul may also call particularly his missionary and apostolic activity a service to God, a worship of God. Thus Paul views the entire activity of Christian life in general and his apostleship in particular as worship that must be accorded God.

Only in the perfection of heaven before God's throne will the service or worship of God divest itself of the "ethical" traits which characterize the earthly existence of the Christian and consist solely in hymnic adoration (Rev. 7:15; 22:3); in this life the adoration of God (*proskynein* — προσκυνεῖν) obviously does not yet coincide with the worship of God (*latreuein*), even if it is included in it. (Matt. 4:10; Luke 4:8)

Another term occasionally used for worship in the New Testament is *threskeia* (θρησκεία).[2] When this term is applied to non-Christian situations, it bears a strong ritualistic stamp. In Acts 26:5 it is used as it were for a category of religious history. The Vulgate translated it pertinently with *religio*. In this speech of Paul's it signifies the Jewish mode of adoring God, the Jewish religion, a recognizable entity distinguished in the multiplicity of other religions by its ordinances, rites, and observances. In Col. 2:18 the ritualistic hue of this term is especially perceptible. There it signifies the adoration of the elements as practiced by the heretics and viewed by these as personalized spiritual powers, as angels. The context demonstrates that this *threskeia* consisted in manifold legal-ritual celebrations and observances.[3] However, when this word refers to Christians in James 1:26 f., it again, in a veritable polemical thrust, casts off everything specifically cultic and ritual. The religion of him who cannot bridle his tongue is vain. The pure and undefiled and God-pleasing "religion" of Christians consists in providing for widows and orphans in their need and sorrow and in keeping oneself unspotted from the filth of the world. Thus we are here dealing with a very conscious "de-ritualization" of *threskeia*, a term originally replete with ritualistic content.

A third New Testament term which Luther reproduced with "to accord someone worship" (*Gottesdienst erzeigen*) is the word *sebesthai* (σέβεσθαι). This word refers to the worship connected with a certain holy place or an image of an idol (*sebasma* — σέβασμα). In Acts 19:27 this worship is rendered a pagan deity, likewise in Rom. 1:25, where the related word *sebazesthai* (σεβάζεσθαι) is used. Luther also translated the noun *sebasma* ("sanctuary," "image of an idol") with the word "worship" (*Gottesdienst* — Acts 17:23; 2 Thess. 2:4).[4] He envisages what happens in front of the idol in the sanctuary. But also the Jewish-Pharisaic ritualism is described by this term *sebesthai* in the New Testament as quoted from Is. 29:13 (Matt. 15:9; Mark 7:7). And,

13

conversely, the Jews in Corinth conceive of the conversion to the church of Christ as a defection to a worship *(sebesthai)* which runs counter to the Torah (Acts 18:13). However, the Christians themselves in the New Testament never call their worship a *sebesthai*.

Also the word *leiturgia* (λειτουργία) does not identify the subject of our investigation in the New Testament.[5] Originally, *leiturgia* was a term used in the realm of politics and constitutional law. It was current in the constitution of the Greek city-state, and it played an important role in the administration of the Roman empire.[6] In the interesting section *De vocabulis missae* of the Apology (XXIV, 78–83), Melanchthon elaborated this basic meaning of *leiturgia* with astonishing accuracy. Both with regard to its linguistic components ("pertaining to the people" and "work") and in view of its original use, this word might be translated "work done for the people" *(Volkswerk)* or "service rendered the people" *(Volksdienst)*. A service is being rendered the people as a political community by means of a work which the community itself should really perform. Affluent citizens may be obligated to the payment of special "liturgies," that is, to particular payments for the benefit of the community over and above the payment of their regular taxes. Occasionally these sums were paid voluntarily. In the Roman Empire these liturgies were expanded into a system of taxes and levies that affected all classes and conditions and were regarded as a most oppressive burden. It was of particular consequence that the term *leiturgia* was also used as a designation for the cultic service which was rendered the gods in sacrifices and hymns. The association between this usage with the political-constitutional one must not be overlooked. The worship accorded the gods is an eminently political matter insofar as "sacrifices and hymns are necessary for the preservation of city and country." [7]

It is at this usage of the word that the Old Testament through the Septuagint translation enters the picture.[8] There *leiturgia* and the related verb *leiturgein* (λειτουργεῖν) never refer to a service to man but exclusively to cultic functions. These are fixed expressions for the cultic service rendered the God of Israel in the tabernacle or in the temple. In isolated instances *leiturgia* also expresses the exercise of an intruding idolatry (Ezek. 44:12; 2 Chron. 15:16). When the New Testament views the Old Testament worship in retrospect, it consistently adopts the linguistic usage of the Septuagint. *Leiturgia* is the sacrificial service performed in the tabernacle (Heb. 9:21), the regular seven-day priestly service of Zechariah in the temple in Jerusalem (Luke 1:23); *leiturgein*

14

denotes the daily offering of sacrifice by the priest in the Old Covenant (Heb. 10:11). But this *leiturgia* and this *leiturgein* do not find a direct continuation among the Christians on earth. The "continuation" of the Old Testament *leiturgia* takes place in heaven in eschatological excellence, transcendence, and absolute perfection. *Leiturgia* is the eternal sacerdotal service performed by the Crucified, exalted to the right hand of God as the Liturgist of the true heavenly sanctuary. (Heb. 8:2, 6)

But the "liturgical" ministrations of the creatures are of an entirely different type than those performed in the Old Covenant. These services, to be sure, all relate directly or indirectly to God, or, more exactly, to the redemption offered during the time of salvation here on earth. But these services are astonishingly manifold. They are either not at all or only remotely related to what we commonly call congregational worship. The angels are dispatched to minister to those who are to be the recipients of salvation gained by Christ. And since the angels participate in the redemptive event through their proclamation of the Gospel on earth, they are called "liturgical," that is, "ministering spirits" (Heb. 1:14). The persons who exercise governmental powers and, within the confines of the law, in their official capacity assert themselves for the support of good and the suppression of evil are, by virtue of this activity, the authorized "ministers of God," "liturgists" of God. (Rom. 13:6)

The church itself seems to have adopted precisely this political-constitutional usage, with ecclesiological modification. If we substitute the new people of God of the end time, the *ekklesia* (ἐκκλησία), for the political commonwealth, then the profane meaning will immediately illustrate the usage of *leiturgia, leiturgein,* and *leiturgos* in a number of New Testament passages. Accordingly, a *leiturgia* is, in contradistinction to, let us say, a private charity or a private, personal devotion, a ministration undertaken vicariously by individuals or by congregations and performed publicly before the *ekklesia* for one and all. For example, the charitable gifts collected by the congregations in Macedonia and Greece for the congregation in Jerusalem as a token of gratitude for the receipt of the Gospel, gifts which were transmitted by Paul, present such a *leiturgia* (2 Cor. 9:22), or the gifts which were gathered for Paul's needs by the affections of the congregation of Philippi and delivered by Epaphroditus, who thereby became a "liturgist" for the apostle's wants (Phil. 2:25, 30). However, also the image of the priest's sacrificial offering might be involved, since the

Philippians' gift of love is called "a fragrant offering, a sacrifice acceptable and pleasing to God" (Phil. 4:18 RSV). As these gifts are presented to the apostle, they are, simultaneously, presented to God; this makes Epaphroditus' act of presentation a priestly service. The political-constitutional element of our term (rendition of service for the civil community) and the cultic-priestly element (administration of the sacrificial service) attract each other and blend, although here in the New Testament both spheres, the political and the cultic, are already transcendent in their pre-Christian particularity. Perhaps also the special praying and fasting of those five prophets and teachers in Antioch, which Acts 13:2 terms "worshiping the Lord" *(leiturgein),* may be viewed as a special, as it were a vicarious service of individuals for the *ekklesia.*[9]

In this connection thought will also have to be given to the fact that Paul in Rom. 15:16 and in Phil. 2:17 regards his apostolic service as a *leiturgia.* To be sure, this conception is filled with Old Testament content, which, however, has been very peculiarly modified. Indeed, the apostolic *leiturgia* includes a priestly offering of sacrifice. The sacrificial gifts presented to God are the converts from paganism or the faith of the Gentile Christian congregations, the fact of their being Christians. Through the Holy Spirit these groups, extricated from a paganism remote from God and hostile to Him, purified, and incorporated into the body of the *ekklesia,* became a sacrificial gift which the apostle presents to God through his service. Thus whenever a congregation anywhere comes into being through Paul's apostolic service, and it persists and grows in faith, a sacrificial gift, consisting concretely of these people united in the *ekklesia,* ascends to God.

But the cultic tool with which this sacrificial gift is prepared and presented is the proclaimed apostolic Gospel. In the manipulation of this tool, the apostle is the "liturgist" of Jesus Christ, and this manipulation is itself a priestly service of the Gospel (*hierurgein* — ἱερουρ-γεῖν), through which, by the power of the believed Gospel, the pagan peoples receive the Holy Spirit, are thus sanctified, and then are presented by the apostle as a God-pleasing sacrificial gift. The interpretation of the apostolic service as a sacrificial act becomes particularly vivid in Phil. 2:17 with an allusion to a possibly imminent martyrdom of the apostle. The sacrificial gift tendered to God by the apostle is the faith of the congregation.[10] The presentation itself is *thysia* (θυσία) and *leiturgia,* sacrificial act and priestly sacrificial service. The person performing this priestly sacrificial service is the apostle.

His apostolic service by which the faith of the congregation, the sacrificial gift, is engendered is viewed by him, simultaneously, as the sacrificial act which presents the gift. In the cited passage, Paul recognizes the possibility that, in the performance of this sacrificial act and, as it were, as the incidental crowning event of his apostolic service, his blood may be poured out in martyrdom as an accompanying drink offering.[11] (Cf. Num. 28:7; also 15:24.)

It is unnecessary to discuss the New Testament passages which express the service to God or to Christ with the word *duleuein* (δου-λεύειν). The Septuagint already uses this word "in the sense of a total devotion to the Godhead, not in the sense of a single act of worship." [12] Conforming to the basic meaning "to serve as a bondman," *duleuein* emphasizes that the whole man, like a bondservant, is pressed into service by his lord. Passages such as Matt. 6:24; Rom. 7:6; 12:11; 14:18; Col. 3:24; 1 Thess. 1:9 demonstrate that this service to God applies to the Christian's whole behavior.

We are confronted with a very significant fact. Not any of the terms used by the Greeks or those used in the Old Testament for the specific adoration of the Godhead in the worship service is able to express the experience of Christians assembled for worship. What happens in this worship of Christians is manifestly something radically new.[13] In its very essence, this phenomenon is radically different not only from the pagan cult but also from the worship of Israel. And it is a particularly conspicuous fact that the terms descriptive of the Old Testament worship are in part adopted to signify the redemptive work of Jesus and in part, after being peculiarly reinterpreted and stripped of their concretely ritualistic sense, are applied to Christian conduct in general or to special services within the church; but they are deliberately not used in speaking of the particular worship in which the congregation sings, prays, listens to the Word, and celebrates Holy Communion.

On the other hand, the New Testament shows us that these congregational meetings for worship were the focal point for the Christian's every thought and act.[14] That is evidenced not only by passages such as 1 Cor. 10—14, which deal thematically with these assemblies. But over and above this, the New Testament research of the last 30 years has demonstrated in increasing measure how the proclamation of the New Testament writings was again and again affected and determined by the prayers of the congregation, by its doxologies, its hymns, its confessions, and also by the views connected with the sac-

17

raments. If the conduct of the Christians as a whole is worship, this is closely linked to the fact that their temporal life has found a concrete focal point, a power station, so to say, which controls and directs their whole existence. This sustaining center is the occurrence through which they were implanted into the *ekklesia* and which lets them share in what happens when Christians assemble as *ekklesia*.[15]

Thus we come upon the term which in the New Testament expresses what we today, in a special sense of the word, call "service" or "worship" *(Gottesdienst)*. Among the New Testament terms, "to be assembled in the name of Jesus" (*synagesthai* — συνάγεσθαι; cf. Matt. 18: 20; 1 Cor. 5:4; in the same meaning Acts 4:31; 20:7 f.; and others) or "to convene in the *ekklesia* or as *ekklesia*" (*synerchesthai* — συνέρχεσθαι; cf. 1 Cor. 11:18, 20; 14:23; in the same meaning 11:17, 33, 34; 14:26) reproduces the common meaning of our word "worship" most aptly. At all events, "worship" is the essential event in those gatherings of the Christians. Therefore the worship with which our investigation deals is *ekklesia* — assembly.[16]

Indeed in two places the New Testament presents the term "assembly" (*synagoge* — συναγωγή: James 2:2, and the compound which emphasizes the locality of the assembly, *episynagoge* — ἐπισυναγωγή: Heb. 10:25) as a designation for the Christians' assembly for worship.[17] It can be proved that the term *synagoge* was used with reference to these assemblies in the early Christian era, indeed as late as the third century.[18] That this word was also used to designate the Jewish communion of faith (Rev. 2:9; 3:9) may account for the fact that it was not applied more extensively and that it did not survive.[19]

The same concrete idea that underlies the word *synagoge* is also mirrored by the word *synaxis* (σύναξις), which is formed from the same basic word "to assemble," although in a different manner.[20] Beginning with the fourth century, *synaxis* was for some time the prevailing designation for the Eucharist.[21] It is regrettable that this term failed to maintain itself in Christendom.[22] Viewed from the New Testament, it is the designation for the church's worship which not only is most closely related to the language of the New Testament but also conspicuously does justice to the novelty of character of the Christian worship, inasmuch as it stresses no other special content beyond that of the assembling of the people. Furthermore, the import of the word "assembly" is closely akin to that of the word *ekklesia*.[23] Worship in the sense of the assembly of the Christian congregation in the name of Jesus is virtually the dominant mode of the manifestation

18

of the church on earth. In such an assembly the epiphany of the church takes place. The church is such an assembly in the name of Jesus, and such an assembly in the name of Jesus is church. The popular expression "there is church today" *(es ist Kirche)*, and not "there is worship" *(es ist Gottesdienst)*, is indeed perfectly correct; it most closely approaches the New Testament situation and the early church's terms *synagoge* and *synaxis*.[24]

Outside of this, the only New Testament expression that comes into consideration as a designation for common worship is the term "the breaking of bread." This term poses its special problems.[25] It is a Palestinian term, which originally had no bearing at all on worship. It refers to the customary breaking of bread by the Jewish paterfamilias at the beginning of each meal. Occasionally it also includes the prayer of thanksgiving preceding the breaking of bread, without thereby losing its profane meaning. The early Palestinian congregation availed itself of this term as a designation for its fellowship meals (Acts 2:42, 46).[26] Within the compass of the Pauline missions, "breaking of bread" is obviously the term for the Eucharist, which Paul calls "the Lord's Supper" in 1 Cor. 11:20; this is evident from a comparison between Acts 20:7 and 1 Cor. 10:16 and 11:33. "The old Palestinian expression 'breaking of bread' has . . . very likely become the oldest name for early Christendom's new fellowship meal, partaken of in worship, namely the Lord's Supper." [27] Since the Christian assemblies for worship — aside from the meetings in which the Sacrament of Initiation was administered — were in all probability from the very beginning and without exception Holy Communion assemblies which included proclamation and instruction,[28] the term "breaking of bread" used in Acts 20:7 becomes the oldest designation for the early Christian worship service. In our connection it is important that here, too, a term is used which is borrowed from the sphere of everyday life and not from the area of worship. This very circumstance expresses the "newness" of this worship. The former cultic terms founder on this newness.

However, the expression "breaking of bread" did not prevail. Also the word *synaxis* failed to take root. The word which definitely replaced it in the East is the word with which we are already familiar — *leiturgia*. We noted that already in the New Testament, analogous to ancient usage, special services performed within the area of the *ekklesia* bear this name and that the performer of such services is accordingly called a *leiturgos*. As performers of such ecclesiastical services, bishops and deacons are mentioned already in *Didache* 15, 1; they render the entire congregation the service *(leiturgia)* of the prophets and teach-ers.[29] As late as the fourth century the word *leiturgia* is used to express the total activity of priests and deacons. But the most important service which these *leiturgoi* have to render the people of God is more and more regarded to consist in the administration of the Eucharist, and this is finally exclusively labeled as *leiturgia*. In the ninth century this linguistic-historical development is concluded.[30]

From the history of terms used for "worship" in the Latin church we note that no designation has come to the fore that absorbed the full meaning of *synagoge* or *synaxis*. The word *collecta* (cf. Vulgate, Heb. 10:25: *collectio*) is a translation of *synaxis,* but it was used only temporarily as a designation for Sunday worship.[31] Moreover, it was soon used to designate certain forms of prayer, namely the collects.

It is further significant that the obvious term *cultus* was manifestly avoided. This reserve is already clearly seen in the Vulgate. In the New Testament the verb *colere* is preferred to express pagan idol wor-ship (cf. Acts 17:23; 19:27; Rom. 1:25; Acts 17:25; also 18:13).[32] The noun *cultus* evidently is not used anywhere. Only the Old Testament sacrificial worship is called *cultura* in Heb. 9:1, and those who perform it are called *cultores* in Heb. 10:2. The basic meaning of the word "cult" is indeed unsuited to express the essence of the worship of the Christian church. *Cultus* is the attention and the care that may be directed to the fields (tilling and cultivating), to the body (nourishing and attending to its needs), to the entire external mode of life (furnish-ings, comfort), to the mind (education through instruction and the arts), but also to the gods. In the last-named instance, the care and attention consist in the presentation of sacrifices and prayers, in the observance of rites and of feasts.

However, we will have to guard against viewing the *cultus* activity of the pagan as a "cultivating" of the deity, which, similar to a field, may be induced by such cultivation to yield useful fruit to man.[33] The pagan cultus does not fit the rationalistic formula *do ut des;* it extends into essentially deeper dimensions. Those performances and sacrificial offerings release a mysterious and powerful current, which also encompasses the activity of the gods and on which, in the final analysis, existence in general depends. "The sacrifice preserves the cur-rent of power. The gifts' current of power insures not only the com-munion between man and man, between man and God, it can also be conducted through all sorts of obstacles and can, by absorbing these into the communion, eliminate them."[34] The genuine pagan cult which

20

has not yet degenerated into a "godless" magical work of self-assured man is, also according to the New Testament, no empty gewgaw, but it is charged with a weird reality (cf. 1 Cor. 8:5; 10:20; 12:2; Rom. 1:18 ff.). But for that very reason a great gulf separates it from Christian worship. It is an "abomination" from which the Christian can only recoil. That is already evident from the fact that even the word for this object, *cultus,* is shunned. Not until Humanism was it possible to divorce this word from the object indicated by it.

The word *liturgia* is but rarely found as a loanword in the Occident.[35] The word *munus* undoubtedly furnishes a relevant translation; it was used as a synonym of *leiturgia* even in the prayer texts themselves.[36] In addition, other terms of similar meaning appear, e. g., *officium.* Also the word "office" *(Amt)* for worship still lets us recognize the meaning of *leiturgia* clearly. The term "mass" has its own history; this cannot be elaborated here.[37] The immediate correspondence with our word *Gottesdienst* ("service") might be supplied by the term *servitium dei,* an expression which refers above all to the monastic life but also to the church's worship service in the sense of *officium ecclesiasticum.*[38] The Vulgate does not employ *servitium* or *servire* to designate the Christian worship service.[39]

Luther and the Lutheran confessional writings use the Latin word *cultus* quite naturally as synonymous with *Gottesdienst.* The French and especially the English language have adapted themselves to *servitium* without a genitive modifier ("service"). Although the simple word *dienst* without any adjunct was used in the Middle Ages for *Gottesdienst,*[40] the genitive case combination prevailed in the language of Luther. But the word *Gottesdienst* retains its wide and comprehensive meaning. Read, for example, Luther's explanation of the First Commandment in the Large Catechism. To be related to God as He, according to Luther's explanation, demands this in the First Commandment, namely "that the heart should know no other consolation or confidence than that in Him, nor let itself be torn from Him, but for Him should risk and disregard everything else on earth," that is "true honor and worship *(Gottesdienst).*"[41] Thus this true worship is nothing else than the faith which obtains the remission of sin in the Gospel and the love for God and man issuing from this faith.

But the word *Gottesdienst* is used simultaneously in the narrower sense of an assembly for divine worship: "to assemble in order to hear and to discuss God's Word, and then to praise God, to sing, and to pray." [42] Luther's *Von Ordnung Gottesdiensts in der Gemeine* (1523) uses the word *Gottesdienst* throughout in the sense of the everyday and Sunday assemblies for worship. His *Formula missae et communionis* (1523) uses the term *cultus dei* in the same sense. In the *Deutsche Messe* (1526) the term *Gottesdienst* is used collectively for all forms of assembly for worship in the congregation, and then again it approaches the meaning of "mass" very closely, becoming nearly synonymous with it.[43]

Here we break off our terminological reflections. They have demonstrated our inability to present an unmistakably concise and really relevant term for our subject. This subject is an event, an occurrence. To begin with, we shall indicate this event only with regard to its external manifestations. Men and women, baptized in the name of the Triune God, assemble on certain days at a definite time for an appointed meeting. The place of the meeting is situated so that everyone who is willing may reach it on time. This meeting is distinct from all others for which people convene. For in this assembly of Christians virtually everything is done with prayer. The characteristic feature of this gathering lies in the fact that it is a being-together in the name of Jesus, that it is marked by invocation of this name and takes place in the effectual presence of its Bearer. In view of this, one might call it a prayer meeting, not because an occasional prayer is spoken in it, but because all that happens there is embraced and supported by prayer.

That reflects the conviction of those gathered here that this meeting is taking place in the presence of God the Father, God the Son, and God the Holy Ghost. This does not refer to the general omnipresence of the Triune God but to a very special presence. The question regarding the particularity of this presence will have to make further claims on our attention later. But even here already we want to identify it under the aspect of prayer as that presence of God in which God is so immediately present to man that he, through the Spirit of God's working in him, addresses God the Father through Jesus Christ in intimate terms. No matter what the details of the assembly may be otherwise, it is certain that it will embody the reading from the sacred writings of the Christians. In the churches of the Reformation, the texts that are read on a Sunday or a holy day are also expounded in a "sermon" by a person commissioned for this purpose. Furthermore, hymns are sung in such an assembly. These hymns are in part prayers, in part laudations, but they are also forms of proclamation of the Sacred Scriptures. Furthermore, a particular celebration is associated with such assemblies — not necessarily with each one and not necessarily involving the participation of all present — in which bread and wine are used, and amid prayer and hymn of praise a meal is taken, even if only in an allusive form.

These assemblies of Christians are the subject of our investigation. As we designate these assemblies on the following pages with the collective term *Gottesdienst,* we are aware of the inadequacy of this term. To be sure, we are in this regard following the tradition created by Luther's Reformation. It was of great concern to Luther that these assemblies of Christians were called *Gottesdienst.* "It were fine indeed if it could become customary to call going to hear a sermon going to a "service of God" *(Gottesdienst)* and to call preaching "serving God" *(Gott dienen),* and to say of all assembled there that they are gathered in a truly sublime "service of God" *(Gottesdienst).*[44] As we retain this usage of language, we bear in mind that Christian worship encompasses far more than what is done in these assemblies. We will also have to remember that the New Testament writings manifestly do not wish to apply the specifically cultic terms of the Old Testament, such as *leiturgia* and *latreia,* to the Christian worship assemblies but are intent on relating these to the total inward and outward daily life of Christians or to special ministrations which are not confined to the framework of those assemblies.

And yet we might safely say that the Lutheran Reformation used the word "worship" as a collective term for these gatherings of Christians. Its chief reason for doing this was by no means merely a matter of following medieval usage of language; it was, rather, a kerygmatic-missionary and a reformational-polemical concern that found expression here. If these assemblies of Christians are "worship," then they must be so constituted as to correspond to the standards and guidelines that govern the entire Christian life as a service to God. An act of worship that is in conflict with the First Commandment as Luther expounded it is no longer worship but blasphemy. If what happens in those assemblies of Christians is to be a service to God, it must be bound over to judgment under the critical standard by which all our doing and life is judged — God's will as we find it revealed in God's Word. In consequence, there is no cultic sphere which is separated from a Christian's life of obedience and may lay claim to its own particular rules and norms. In consequence, there can also be no breach in the life of a Christian either when he returns

23

home or to his vocation from those worship services or when he repairs to them from his vocational duties. The entire service to God is already an internal unit in this temporal life, even though carried out in varying forms. That the form of serving God in these assemblies has a special significance because it is performed with a view to the eternally enduring service of God in ultimate perfection and is therefore already, in earthly forms, on its way to the eschatological particularity of worship, and thus is indeed the real worship, will become clear in the course of our investigation.

The Scope of This Study

The task of our investigation is to answer the question: What should be taught in the church of Jesus Christ relative to that assembly which we, in common with Luther's Reformation, call divine service (Gottesdienst)? It is obvious that what we teach is in a practical way decisive for the implementation of this service of worship, both with regard to the external form of this implementation and with a view to the spiritual, internal cooperation of the assembly itself. The church's doctrine on worship will determine which liturgical order it employs, which it leaves to freedom of choice, and which it rejects. This doctrinal question will also decide, in regard to worship, what the pastor proclaims to the congregation by way of assurance, promise, comfort, admonition, and instruction.

But the answer to this doctrinal question will be determinant, above all, for the most important factor, what the fathers of the Reformation termed the proper usus. In our context we may paraphrase this word as "the pneumatic application of that which takes place in the service." What does the person in the pew do with the words he hears? What does he do with the song or the prayer he voices? What does he do with the gift he receives at the Lord's table? What does the called servant of the Word do with the words that are printed for his use in the Agenda (service book)? How does he carry out the service of proclamation in the pulpit? What happens within him as a person, in his mind, in his heart, when he administers the sacrament?

Even before we begin our investigation, these questions have already impressed us with the fact that the implementation of worship involves a peculiarly critical event, an actual crisis. It is not the Word of God, not Christ's sacrament, that enters a crisis in the service, but man who here encounters God's Word and sacrament.

Will this encounter prove salutary? Will a pneumatic appropriation of the gift, a Spirit-filled consummation of the act, and therewith a proper *usus* of worship, result in this encounter? For after all, the proper spiritual implementation by the assembled congregation and its servants is and remains the most important factor in worship. To be sure, this most important factor never lies within our power. But without a correct doctrine of worship we will never arrive at the proper *usus,* especially not in our present situation, which is so confused in many respects. If error relative to what is done in worship is taught and preached to the congregations and their servants, or if they, perhaps, are told nothing at all, how can they arrive at a proper pneumatic application? The Spirit is dependent on the Word also in this instance. And doctrine exists to serve the Word.

This insight also outlines the only way in which we may attain such a doctrine of worship. We have already observed the kerygmatic-polemical definition, consisting in the fact that the Lutheran Reformation called those assemblies of Christians "worship." The basic requirement that must be made of everything called worship reads: God must be able to give assent to everything that happens there; it must be acceptable to Him. The worship of God depends on what is pleasing to Him. And whatever pleases God must be enclosed in His Word and commandment. God did not proclaim what He demands of us in vain. And he who would serve Him, disregarding this proclamation, must know that he can never please God. Only that worship which in its implementation is obedient to God's proclamation, God's communications, and God's institution is pleasing to God and is deserving of its name. Just as we can serve God in our whole life only by pursuing the ways He revealed to us, so the Christian worship assemblies are worship only if they consist of nothing other than what God Himself instituted.

If we remain faithful to this proposition of the Reformation, then everything that happens in worship will conform to the revelation that has already happened, the revelation witnessed and transmitted to us by the mouth of the prophets and apostles. Therefore our task must now be formulated thus: What happens in those assemblies of Christians by virtue of divine institution and as certified by the divine Word, and what must, in consequence, be done in such assemblies by us today? With this question we have formulated our task as a dogmatic one in the strictest sense of the word. It becomes dogmatic by reason of the fact that the answer to the posed question hinges unconditionally on the past revelation of God. Only in this dependence on the words of revelation, which disclose God's institution to us, is a doctrine on worship possible. Thus this doctrine does not find its norm in what happens in the present-day worship services of Christendom; its orientation is not empirical-descriptive. Nor does this doctrine rest on any experiences the congregation or individual members of the congregation may have in such assemblies; in this sense it is oriented neither psychologically nor anthropologically. Nor does this doctrine derive from the synthetic sum total of all of Christendom's teachings on worship in the course of the centuries. As surely as it is meet for us to give ear to the voice of the fathers and the brethren in the evolution of the doctrine on worship, so surely dare this doctrine never be a historicizing eclecticism. Inasmuch as we surrender our doctrine of worship unconditionally to past revelation, it will have to be oriented, along the entire line, to the living Word of God.

But if this is actually done, then this doctrine, to be at all practicable, must unavoidably be carried out in a concrete and historical place. This place is the physical phenomenon of the church of Jesus Christ, in which the past revelation is known, acknowledged, witnessed, and expressed by way of repetition in the words of the confessional writings. The ties to the past revelation are concrete and real only where they simultaneously include ties to a present attestation of this revelation. The dogmatic doctrine confronting us as our task can, therefore, be elaborated only in those circles in which a consensus on what constitutes the proclamation of the Gospel and the administration of the sacraments in accord with revelation has become an actual event. This event by no means justifies any of the many "confessions" which stand side by side as partial truths with more or less equal right. Rather, the event of such a consensus is possible only where the insignia of the one holy, apostolic church of Jesus Christ has appeared on the scene, that is to say, the unadulterated Gospel and the administration of the sacraments in conformity with Christ's institution.

Thus the ties of dogmatic doctrine to the concrete, historical place of the appearing church of Jesus Christ will be "confessionalism" only for the nonparticipating spectator. For the true participant there are, on the other hand, basically only two possible ways of judging a truly dogmatic doctrine: in it he will hear either a voice that belongs to the one holy, apostolic church of Jesus Christ or the voice of heresy. This does not exclude the possibility that important differences and varying patterns may arise in the dogmatic elaboration within the consensus of the one holy, apostolic church. But these differences and diversities remain within the consensus expressed in the dogma.

Particularly in the doctrine of worship will such differences and diversities become intense and conspicuous in the present situation. Precisely in this area will the question unavoidably arise whether certain doctrinal opinions still come within the *consensus doctrinae*. It is just this doctrine of worship that will compel us to scrutinize closely the boundaries drawn for us by this dogma. After all, it could be that traditional views which enjoy the repute of dogmatic orthodoxy are, in fact, questioned by the dogma that conforms to revelation and that other views, which at first glance appear suspect, perhaps occupy the very center of the consensus in which the one holy, apostolic church recognizes itself.

As we surrender our doctrine of worship to past and attested revelation, we do not lose sight of the present worship in which we ourselves participate. Our doctrine of worship may, by reason of its ties to the revealed Word, bring surprising, perhaps even disconcerting facts to light; but if the dogmatic statements do not simultaneously express what takes place in the concrete worship service in which we take part, this worship will find itself in a bad way. It would then cease to be the worship instituted by God and Christ. The fathers of the Reformation made this terrible discovery with regard to the worship in which they had been reared. Therefore reformation signified for them first of all a reformation of the worship service, a reformation of the service along the whole line and so also a reformation of the worship of the congregation assembled in the name of Jesus. Are we so sure that we may not be similarly tried and troubled by a recognition of the true essence of worship as instituted by God and Christ? Whoever involves himself in a dogmatic doctrine of worship must be aware of what he is doing. He delivers the heart of the church's life to the judgment of the apostolic Word. Fortunate is he who accepts this judgment, no matter what the deductions may be. Only the recognition of this judgment will save the church from a decay from which there is no escape.

27

PART I

THE PLACE OF WORSHIP

1

THE DOGMATIC DEFINITION OF THE PLACE OF WORSHIP

Our first task will consist in answering the question regarding the peculiar essence of worship. If one wishes to recognize an object in its peculiar essence, it is necessary above all else to define the place it occupies in the framework of reality. Such a definition of place must be aimed at a recognition of the lines which delimit the distinctive and peculiar object in question and thus make it recognizable to us. These delimiting lines which portray the object in its inherent features are commonly called its definition. Definition is delineation of place — and vice versa. We are here concerned with a theological, a dogmatic, definition of the place of worship. Therefore we cannot attempt to draw those defining lines of demarcation on the basis of an existential analysis of human existence. Our task also bars the method of a theological phenomenological analysis of cultus as a "phenomenon" in the world of religions, as was carried out by Gerhardus van der Leeuw.[45] In a dogmatic study, the definition of the place of worship will have to pursue its own course, because the Word of revelation itself pursues its own course in this matter.

The chief course which Holy Scripture follows in drawing the lines that delimit worship with regard to its peculiar and real essence consists in showing us how the worship of the church occupies a very definite "place" within the history which God initiated for our salvation with the creation of man and continues for our salvation until Christ's return. Following this way, we are led to a plan-of-salvation definition of the place of worship. We construe God's plan

31

of salvation as the sum total of the plans, the institutions, the interventions, the elections, the signs which God Himself has given and will still give in the course of the eons, beginning with creation and enduring into the eternity which dawns with Christ's return, in order to effect the salvation which He appointed for us men even before the foundation of creation was laid. As we glance at this plan of salvation of God, we must ask: To what extent are essence and peculiarity of worship determined by the place it occupies within the history of God's redemptive activity?

Reading the New Testament, we soon notice that the congregation, assembled for worship as *ekklesia,* in many respects stands at the center and intersection of all of God's plans and institutions for man's salvation. Retrospectively, the congregation and its worship are directly related to what took place in Jesus and through Jesus by the will of God. But thereby they are also peculiarly related to that institution of God which Heb. 8:13 calls the Old Covenant. But the Old Covenant stands in the midst of the world's nations, and it is election out of the paganized nations of the world. Thus a view is afforded of God's plan of salvation as it began to operate in the realm of time with the creation of man and his fall into sin. On the other hand, the New Testament takes no less cognizance of the fact that this worship of the *ekklesia* also points forward toward a future consummation that is already prepared in heaven with God. The worship performed in the temporality of this earth is already oriented to the worship before God's throne in eternity, in which the former already participates in a peculiar manner. What takes place in congregational worship can be understood correctly only when perceived in its bidirectionally oriented incorporation into God's plan of salvation.

This plan-of-salvation definition of the place of the church's worship is its fundamental dogmatic "definition." All other possible theological definitions of place are included in its plan-of-salvation orientation, which of course simultaneously implies a plan-of-salvation emphasis and a special position. Therefore every other theological definition of the place of worship can be but a certain reflection of the plan-of-salvation definition. Holy Scripture lets us perceive a twofold reflection of this plan-of-salvation definition of the place of worship.

In the first place, every individual is embraced and affected by God's plan of salvation, whether he is aware of this or not. Every single person is the product of God's beneficent act of creation, which calls into being only what is good and God-pleasing. But every person is also the product of the original sin of man's rebellion against God, and he is subject to God's resultant verdict of damnation on the sinner. However, every single person at the same time stands under God's saving power of grace, which is epitomized in the name Jesus Christ. It is God's will that every person comes face to face with the saving Gospel.[46] The historical confrontation with this promise of grace by Jesus Christ marks man's crisis. In this crisis it will be decided whether he becomes a servant of the Triune God or remains a rebel now doubly rejected. In this crisis it will be decided whether the individual attains participation in the worship of Christ's church, or whether he remains in bondage to the powers hostile to God and thereby is eternally separated from God, is judged and condemned. But if man does achieve participation in the church of Jesus Christ and its worship, we will have to ask how his worship is related to that past, which, to be sure, lies behind him but for all of that is and remains his past, and how, on the other hand, his worship is oriented to his final perfection in the future kingdom of God, and how, finally, through this reference to that past and this orientation to that future, his presence in the church and therewith his present worship is characteristically constituted.

It may now be clear to what an extent a reflection of God's universal plan of salvation is involved here in the existence of the individual. As we take note of this reflection, we will be obliged to define the place of worship by asking: What is the place of worship in the existence of the individual insofar as his existence is related to God's universal plan of salvation and is inescapably encompassed by it? We may term this subdivision of the definition of the place of worship the anthropological one.

But the plan-of-salvation definition of the place of worship discloses yet another, a second, relationship into which we have to fit this worship for an adequate definition. The way which God pursues with man to lead him to the consummation of salvation is something that takes place between God and mankind. But this must not be dissociated from its concrete relationships to the other earthly creatures and to those of the celestial world. In creation God assigned man a very definite position within the circle of earthly creatures. The God-relationship of the prime creature and the God-relationship of the remaining creatures of this earth stand in a peculiar relationship to each other by reason of the special position assigned to man. The

God-relationship of man reveals that also the other creatures of this earth stand in a concrete and real, though not personal, relationship to God, so that we, with Scripture, may speak of a peculiar worship performed by the nonhuman earthly creatures. At no point in the plan-of-salvation phases of worship pertaining to man and performed by him may we overlook how his worship is related to the worship of the nonhuman earthly creatures.

But Scripture also shows us that God's plan of salvation for man is related to the heavenly creatures of God, the angels. We must note that angels even participated as ministering spirits in the preparation of this plan of salvation. But we must note above all that man at the end of the road by which God leads him through the history of salvation is coordinated in a surprisingly positive way with those heavenly beings, while the humanity of the human being is thereby never questioned in the least. That human beings and angels will one day be assembled about God's throne as a diversified, and yet unified, choir, is as surely a part of God's plan of salvation, conceived before the earth's foundation was laid, as the human creature's destiny for a death-free incorruptibility is part of its likeness to God. Thus the worship of the church on earth must be viewed in its orientation to the worship of the angels, just as it must be viewed in its orientation to the worship of the nonhuman earthly creatures.

This attempt to define the place of the church's worship on earth under the aspect of the twofold orientation to the earthly and the heavenly creatures may be termed the cosmological definition. However, we must not lose sight of the fact that also this cosmological definition of place, exactly like the anthropological one, is only a mirror of the comprehensive plan-of-salvation definition of place.

2

THE PLACE OF WORSHIP IN
GOD'S UNIVERSAL PLAN OF SALVATION

14818'72

The focal point of God's plan of salvation is the incarnation of the eternal Son of God in Jesus of Nazareth, His cross, and His resurrection. God's redemptive activity in Jesus is the light in which we behold the totality of these acts of God in the mirror of His Word, from creation on through to the consummation. Therefore the creation of man, his fall, his preservation by God, his pathway in paganism and in Israel become perceptible to us only "in Jesus Christ." That does not mean that the reality of this history of the works of God as an actual activity in time would be subject to doubt through the name of Jesus Christ. It is, rather, a matter of a concretely historical course, run in time and in various forms of revelation, which God pursues with man until the Son of God Himself becomes flesh in Jesus, suffers, and dies; as surely as that course, too, is concretely historical and takes place in time which God pursues with man from the event of the incarnation until the epiphany of the Son of God in glory on the Day of Judgment. But only he who is acquainted with the center of this entire course, the birth, work, suffering, death, and resurrection of Jesus Christ, will know that sector of the way in God's plan of salvation that tends toward this center and the sector that radiates from it.

THE WORSHIP OF THE FOREMOST CREATURE

The last-named principle becomes operative at once as we venture to speak of the worship of the foremost creature.[47] His worship is

35

part of the implementation of his likeness to God. This implementation is manifold, and it embraces his entire existence. But for our deliberations it is important to note that these manifestations of his likeness to God also include such acts as stand out in relief as acts of worship.

As God created man in His image, He created a creature in which His own reality, glory, might, and beauty are reflected within the boundaries implicit in the creatureliness of the foremost creature. The special feature of this mirrored image, by which this creature is distinguished from the reflection of the divine essence in the other earthly creatures, consists in the fact that man became an "I" through God's fatherly address. Therefore the mirroring of God's reality, glory, might, and beauty takes place in man principally through an intellectual act, in which the reality of God, reflected mutely and unconsciously, as it were, in the nonhuman earthly creatures, is perceived, recognized, acknowledged, and returned to the Creator with thanks and adoration. "All the rays of the revealed honor and glory of God diverge and scatter as long as they do not unite in the focus of the created personality which acknowledges them with gratitude and adoration." [48] Man cannot be God's image without the immediate, adoring word of acknowledgment, of gratitude, of glorification addressed to the Creator. Without prayer and laudation, man would not be the mirror of God's glory, he would not be man. [49]

We are led to the same insight when we enter the innermost mystery of man's likeness to God. God wanted man to be the child of His love. God, who possesses the fullness of love's communion in inexpressible perfection in His innertrinitarian life, condescended in His incomprehensible kindness to create a creature which, despite its creatureliness, is His personal associate, the creaturely son of His pleasure, the partner of His love. When God addresses man as His creaturely "thou," He expects the answer to be that of a person bound to Him in love's communion. God does not want man's answer to be like that of the stones, the plants, and the animals, and perhaps also of the stars, all of whom respond to the word of the Creator, lauding, glorifying, and serving God with the changelessness of their natural creaturely laws. Since man is the child of God's love, God expects his answer to be a personal act, consciously and freely performed. Therefore, as God creates man, He simultaneously provides room for the exercise of his creaturely freedom, through which God, in loving condescension, permits Himself to be delimited. This self-delimitation of God over against man consists mainly in this, that He, the immeasurably rich Lord of all things, who even in His loving condescension still is and remains the Lord over against man, makes Himself needy, as it were, over against the child of His love. God waits for His child's answer of love and expects the "Thou, Father," spoken of his own free will by man. The capacity of man's creaturely freedom, prepared by God's love, is therefore simultaneously the capacity in which alone man's turning to God in loving reply becomes a reality. The capacity of creaturely freedom, prepared for man by God's loving condescension, is the basis for all that is called worship.

We do not recognize the immeasurable depth of the freedom conferred on man in creation until we ponder the fact that immediately with creation, man's answer arising from the capacity of this freedom was dropped into the lap of the foremost creature as a gift of God's love. Before his fall, the foremost creature actually said with every breath: "Yes, Father." He did not utter this yes of his love as a choice between yes and no, but in unquestioning, unbroken, spontaneous self-evidence, which knows of no choice and which is nevertheless — yes, by that very fact — the manifestation of the true, pristine freedom of man. Here already we are facing the miracle, which can be nothing but an offense to any outsider but comprises for the believer the blissful fullness of God's love, namely, that man's loving turning to God in prayer, praise, and adoration is both in one: gift of love from above and personal mental act of a creaturely "I."

Although man's likeness to God is stamped on his whole being and activity, as we observed, it nonetheless includes acts which do not manifest themselves in his activity over against the creature and his loving devotion to his neighbor, but which are directed immediately to God. Springing from man's personal communion with God, implicit in his likeness to God, these acts address themselves to the Creator with an unquestioning self-evidence as the emanation and materialization of this communion. The special feature of these acts, and so the special feature of worship rising above the throng of life's activities, is intimated symbolically and mysteriously in the story of creation and of the Garden of Eden by its reference to a specially delimited time, the blessed and hallowed seventh day, and an especially delimited place, the tree of the knowledge of good and evil.

To be sure, the completion of creation by God's resting on the seventh day must be differentiated from the appointment of the

37

Sabbath as a cultic institution,[50] even if the two are connected with each other.[51] But on the other hand, this rest of God which completed creation is also by no means identical with the eternal rest of God in His own, singular essence, through which He is what He is of Himself and through Himself. The repose of His eternal aseity is here changed into a "rest" which is appropriate to creation, is diffused over creation, and thereby first completes creation. Not the work, the act, the labor marks the completion of creation, but the tranquility in which no more work is performed, the solemn celebration in which all work rests because God Himself is resting. Inasmuch as this repose is spread out over creation as its completion, God causes all works of creation to be oriented to an ultimate benefaction which consists in the creature's participation in the divine essentiality, made accessible to the creature and assigned to him.

Man cannot be excluded from this orientation of creation to this ultimate benefaction; for it is chiefly for him that this rest of God and so God's own internal essence are associated with the creature. As all works of God's creation are designed for man and serve him, thus also God's Sabbath rest. In a sense, the saying that the Sabbath was made for the sake of man is applicable here already. Man would not be God's image if he would not already here and now partake of God's Sabbath rest, although only in a preliminary and foreshadowing manner. Admittedly, Gen. 2:1-3 does not report expressly that God placed man into His Sabbath rest. On the other hand, the blessing and the sanctifying of the seventh day was not first carried out at Sinai but here at the completion of creation.[52] This blessing and sanctifying is not done for God but for man. Already in setting aside this day for God, thus sanctifying it, man is to have a preliminary and foreshadowing share in God's rest.

According to the Biblical narrator, the seventh day, blessed and consecrated by God, appears to man in the form of a concrete, earthly day, set apart for God.[53] Man's course on earth begins with this earthly day which is designed for participation in God's rest! This day is the sign under which every workday and the entire work time of man and his history stand. It is God's will that man's relationship to that ultimate benefaction of the rest of God and his preliminary participation in this gift be conveyed and expressed by a concrete sign, by the hallowed seventh day. So long as man with his work is bound to this earth, the workday of man shall be delimited and interrupted — delimited and interrupted from the very beginning by a day on which

38

man rests from his labors and is free for the testimony of the blessed and hallowed seventh day.[54]

This interruption of the workday by the day of the Lord is a positive eschatological sign, but it is a sign that already accords participation in the matter designated. The concretions of those acts of man immediately related to God and implicit in his likeness to God, his acknowledgment of God by way of thanks, prayer, and praise, are of course not confined to this seventh day. But while all work of man rests on this day, the sign of this day must inspire those acts in which man's relationship, as God's image, to his Creator becomes concrete. This day, appointed by God, in which God's Sabbath rest appears to man, is, more so than other days, the concrete time vessel for these acts of man's likeness to God. An essential ingredient would be missing from the concretion of man's likeness to God if God had not completed His creation by providing this work-free time, designed for participation in God's rest. Inasmuch as this concretion may be embedded into the sanctified seventh day, it shares in the eternally enduring rest of God.

Gen. 2:16 f. adds an especially delimited place to this especially delimited time. This delimitation is effected here by a word of God. As Luther says, the whole Bible, Law and Gospel, is included in this word for the prime creature.[55] This word, in many respects, institutes a definite *cultus,* marked by tangible processes. This word already founds the *ekklesia,* and that before matrimony, home, family, and community were established. Just as God's Sabbath rest, appearing to man in the seventh day, precedes man's workday, so the establishment of the *ekklesia* and its *cultus* antedates all other institutions of God. Wherever God's Word is given to man as a saving promise and as an admonishing warning, there the church is founded, not only in the sense that man's relationship to God is now always determined by his faith in this Word but also in the sense that now very concrete acts and signs become necessary for the engendering of faith and also for the manifestation of faith in perceptible acts. With the gift of God's Word, the task to proclaim and to propagate this Word is assigned to hearing and believing man. Adam becomes the first preacher of the Word to Eve and, virtually, to all his descendants. The primary element in the worship of the church is the live transmission of God's Word.

This Word of God produces, simultaneously with its proclamation in the earthly situation, a concrete situation of its own, over against which man's obedience of faith becomes visibly manifest. In the story of the Garden of Eden this situation, which was created by God's Word and which shed light on man's faith, inhered in the tree of the knowledge of good and evil and in the bounds drawn around this tree by God's Word. The respect for this boundary was the concrete perceptible expression of man's obedience of faith. At this barrier the *cultus* of man originated as a physical act. The perceptible physicality is necessarily connected with the perceptible physicality of his whole existence. Luther described very graphically that God's Word drew this boundary about the tree "so that man would have a certain external sign also for his sentient physicality *(animalitas)* for honoring God and rendering Him obedience in an external work." [56] According to Luther's picturesque description, this tree of knowledge was planted there to serve as man's house of God, his altar, his pulpit, around which he should on the Sabbath gather with his descendants, proclaim God's Word, praise God, thank Him for His gifts, ponder that barrier, and as it were visualize it with an outward act *(ritus)*.[57] Self-evidently, the details of this portrayal cannot be pursued further here. The decisive element in this is that God presented man a visible mark with that tree by means of which man would visibly and tangibly demonstrate and exemplify his obedience of faith as he respected the bounds placed for him. The worship also of the foremost creature did not consist only in his heart's inward, invisible turning to God, it did not consist only in the words of prayer and of proclamation, but it also consisted in outward, physical action which related to a definite external situation and included definite external acts.

In the worship of the foremost creature there was no allusion whatsoever to an atonement. There was, for example, no trace of a bloody sacrifice. For, after all, there was peace between God and man. In the worship of the foremost creature, furthermore, every legalistic element, every element of constraint and of penalty, were absent. His worship flowed with spontaneous necessity from the extravagant fullness of his divine image.[58] These distinctive marks are especially significant for the church's worship on earth. To be sure, our worship is determined very decisively by sin, by its deletion through the power of God's grace; our worship displays the trace of the bloody sacrifice by which we sinners are reconciled to God. But inasmuch as the members of the church are fashioned in the image of the Son of God, the foremost creature's likeness to God again shines forth in his likeness to Jesus Christ (Col. 3:10; Eph. 4:24). Therefore the worship of the foremost creature is again revived in a new form in the church of Jesus Christ. The worship of Christians must be a manifestation of their restored likeness to God. Therefore the church's worship will not only be defined and identified by the mark of sin expunged; rather, with and in such a mark a part of Eden's original brightness, which hovered over the worship of the foremost creature, will beam forth again. That glorification of God which directs heart and words to Him and which flows spontaneously and immediately from a personal and loving communion between God and man will be part of the essence of the church's worship, even if this glorification of God can be carried out only fragmentarily and imperfectly "in the weakness of our body" (Luther), until it will one day shine forth in full radiance in the perfection of the world of resurrection when the workday forever lies behind us and God's Sabbath is no longer interrupted by earth's days but has received us into its enduring fullness. The very fact that the worship of the foremost creature again begins to be revived in the church of Jesus Christ imparts to this worship an eschatological orientation by which it, as it were, leaves itself behind and reaches out for a consummation that transcends the confines of time.

But the worship of the foremost creature is furthermore related to ours by the fact that in neither instance the eschatological transformation of our corporeality has as yet occurred. As long as we sojourn in this body our worship will assume a form that is perceptible to our senses and conformable to our corporeality. Like the worship of the foremost creature, it will still partake of the contrast between workday and holy day. It will occupy its own delimited time and therefore also require its own hours and days. Like the worship of the foremost creature, it will require a concrete, outward, visible mark, established by God Himself through His word of institution, so that our worship may, by this divinely instituted mark, find its own physical, tangible expression, until, in the transformation of all things, also the earthly-sensuous ties of our worship cease together with our corporeality and our worship merges into the form of the angels' celestial worship.

Man's Fall and the Beginning of Jesus Christ's Sacrificial Life

The dark mystery of the Fall cannot be discussed here in detail. However, for all the following remarks it must be noted that the Fall consists essentially in the fact that man destroyed the worship given

41

him with his creation and perverted it into the appalling opposite. The bonds of love between God and man were cut asunder by man. The pneumatic reality of being in the image of God, which let man share in God's own life and being, was lost. The bounds which God's Word had drawn for man were wantonly broken. But thereby also the physical, sensuously perceptible adoration of God, its outward act and its outward sign, were flagrantly destroyed by man. In place of the unquestioning, spontaneous, and childlike devotion to the Creator, we now find the slavish surrender to the antigodly, tyrannical spirit-powers of sin, of death, and of the devil. Worship was replaced by slavery to sin, slavery to death, slavery to the devil. No creature on earth and no angel in heaven is able to loosen the bonds which the Fall wove about man through his own fault.

But this apostate man, the bondsman of the antigodly powers, nonetheless remained related to God. God remains the lord also over the sinner, who has fallen prey to the tyranny of the antigodly powers. God's rule over the sinner embraces two items: judgment and grace, execution and revival. This duality of judgment and grace, of execution and revival, in the one rule of God, this duality in this unity and this unity in this duality, comprises, in the final analysis, the mystery of God's plan of salvation.

God pronounces His judgment of death on fallen man. "In the day that you eat of it you shall die." God abides by His word. He abode by His word when man fell into sin. Man, plunged into the realm of the antigodly demonic powers, is under God's wrath, rejected by God, cut off from God's life, and therefore dead before God. And whoever is dead before God is consigned to eternal death. Eternal death is not a biological process, but repudiation, punishment, execution. However, eternal death also reaches into the biological processes. Whoever is consigned to eternal death by God dies a judicial death also in his own body. God's judgment, rejection, and execution are a bloody death.

Adam does not die this bloody death — and yet he dies it, as surely as God abides by His word. Adam will die. All who bear Adam's image will die. But this Adamitic death is not the bloody judicial death of God's rejection itself; it is only a sign, a reference, a comparison which as sign, as reference, as comparison even includes the hope that the bloody judicial sentence of death may not be executed after all. But God does not break His word. Man actually dies this bloody judicial death of God's rejection — in Jesus Christ. That is the inexpressible miracle of divine compassion. God Himself assumes Adam's image and Adam's essence and Adam's guilt and Adam's death in the person of God the Son. This happened in time under Emperor Augustus and under Pontius Pilate, when Jesus was born of the Virgin Mary and was crucified on Golgotha by Jews and Gentiles.

What happened there in time happened to the Man who is the eternal Son of God, consubstantial with the Father. What took place there in time to the God-man is not limited to geographical space or to the time we measure with our calendar. In God's sight, the Golgotha judgment is issued on the Adam-Jesus on the day of Adam's fall and since the day of his fall. The fact that Adam and all who bear his image die only that allusive, symbolical death, which is, all appearances notwithstanding, a gift of God's forbearance, that Adam and his descendants are granted time before their death to beget and rear children, to generate the human race, and to produce a history, countries, cultures, scientific systems, and religions — is founded on the fact that the bloody judicial death of the Adam-Jesus is, already before its execution on Golgotha, actively present before God's throne with its redemptive power. With the fall of man, the sacrificial way of the Son of man is fixed before the throne of God, not as a thought, as an intention, as an idea, but as an accomplished fact. This mysterious presence before God and in God of Jesus' temporally future death on the cross is the fountainhead of God's forbearance and patience, in which all men live and in which all men die from the day of the Fall to the day of Jesus Christ's crucifixion and resurrection.

God Himself interposes His own Son for apostate man, forfeit to the judgment of God, and God's own Son delivers Himself up for the sinner to God's bloody judgment on him. That is the heavenly basis and the eternally valid essence of the one true sacrifice. The mystery of the bloody, sacrificial death of Jesus Christ, which is judgment and grace, death and resurrection, begins before God and in God with the fall of man — judgment and death for us as we behold the certain fate of us sinners in the one Adam-Jesus, grace and resurrection for us as we behold our judgment and our death in Him, in Him who even in the bloody judgment of the cross is and remains God's eternally beloved Son, and who, therefore, rises again from death as this bloodily executed Man and will live in eternity. But just because this bloody, sacrificial death of Jesus Christ involves the salvation for the whole world, He will again return in the end exclusively in judgment on all who by their unbelief dissolve their God-willed in-being in the one

Adam-Jesus and are, therefore — unprotected by His bloody, sacrificial death — consigned eternally to God's sentence of death.

The worship of the foremost creature was destroyed by the Fall. But that is where the worship of Him who is the firstborn from the dead immediately sets in. The one God-pleasing worship of man has now disappeared from the earth, but it will return to the earth in the new Man, Jesus, who is God's eternal Son. Until then the one God-pleasing worship of man is preserved in heaven with Him who is about to enter into our flesh.[59] This one God-pleasing worship of man can now, in consequence of the Fall, be the only sacrifice, the one, God-pleasing, unblemished sacrifice of the Man who is God Himself, of the God-man. With the Fall Jesus Christ began to walk the sacrificial way, with the Fall His sacrificial service, which is now the one true worship, began in the highest heaven. Since the Fall the Son of God, as the coming second and last Adam, performed this worship for us as He took the way into the flesh and walked the way to the cross.

THE IDOLATRY OF THE HEATHEN

In the center section of his fundamental work, *Phänomenologie der Religion,* Gerhardus van der Leeuw offers us a view of what comes to the attention of the intelligent observer as external and internal worship in the world of religions. The reader discovers that phenomena which we recognize as elements of Christian worship again and again show a peculiar phenomenological similarity and relationship to non-Christian rites, sacramentalia, words, and cultic forms. Bearing this in mind, we will have to ask ourselves how to explain this in the light of the Gospel. To be sure, this will necessitate a basically different analysis of the non-Christian religions from that demanded within the framework of a phenomenology of religions. The latter describes and interprets intelligibly what manifests itself in its subject, that which discloses itself to the observer as a basic trait of the phenomenon. However, what manifests itself issues from a base that is hidden. What discloses itself is rooted in a depth which is detectable and penetrable not even to the very essence that manifests itself, much less to the describing observer. What is the *hidden* depth of the non-Christian cultus, which, in spite of its nature to *appear* in this phenomenon, is not perceptible?

Can there be any answer at all to this question? Only God, whose eye penetrates every hidden depth, can behold the hidden depth of the non-Christian cultus. He will reveal these hidden depths in His judgment. There He will turn the innermost thoughts of man to the light of day, to the light of His day (Rom. 2:16; 1 Cor. 4:5). But this judgment on us has already begun with the execution of the Adam-Jesus. With the Word of the Cross a flash of lightning of the Day of Judgment pierces into the hidden, dark depths of human existence. The witness of the Crucified-Exalted stands in the rays of this revealing radiance of God. It is this very confrontation with the Gospel that reveals the heart's recesses, which are hidden to the own "I" and more so to another person. Therefore a hidden depth of the non-Christian cultus is disclosed to the witness of the Crucified-Exalted, and this is manifestly revealed where the heathen, struck by the light of the Gospel, is moved into the brightness of the day of Jesus Christ, in the *ekklesia* is placed before the living presence of God, and "falling on his face worships God" (1 Cor. 14:25), the one true, Triune God. In Rom. 1:18 ff., Paul as an apostolic witness speaks of the unfathomable hidden depth of the pagan cultus that will be revealed in the meeting between paganism and the Gospel in the light of the Day of Jesus Christ. Here the apostle states what the pagan cultus is in its hidden essence, perceptible to God alone. What is the real nature of the non-Christian cultus as it is seen in the history that God enacts with mankind to lead it to salvation? What is disclosed as the existential basis of this cultus when it is moved into the eschatological light of the Day of Judgment? Let us try to clarify the existential analysis of the pagan cultus.

Pagan cultus is the result of an original decision made by fallen man over against a gift of God's revelation. God "did not leave Himself without witness" also to fallen man (Acts 14:17; 17:26 ff.). In this witness He sought him out too. The goodness of the Creator and Preserver, borne by the effectual power of Christ's future sacrifice, holds a door open for fallen man, through which the rays of the divine essence actually reach him. "For what can be known of God is plain to them, because God has shown it to them" (Rom. 1:19). Whatever of God is knowable to all men is something invisible, thus something basically hidden; but something that is revealed and disclosed to them by an act of God. This invisible element, made manifest to man by God, is God's might, which is never exhausted but is eternal.

Thereby the element is revealed to man which distinguishes God from all creation and makes Him God over against creation. God placed a recognizable and perceptible proof of His being God before man.

Man was given to perceive that he and the world together with him do not comprise the sum total of all reality, but that world and man are creatures, invisibly confronted by One who is not creature but who is God in His eternal power of creation. The medium of this revelation is God's work of creation. This is the open door through which God shows and certifies Himself to man as God. God has made His works of creation translucent, as it were, and He has left them translucent also for fallen man, so that man, viewing them with his mental eye, can and must perceive something of the Creator's outline (Rom. 1:20). God provided all the presuppositions to enable also fallen man to arrive at a knowledge of God in keeping with his estate and at a veneration of God commensurate with it.

But the apostle carries his existential analysis of paganism a step further; for we have not yet come face to face with the root and ground of the pagan cultus. The apostle's decisive words read: "For although they knew God, they did not honor Him as God or give thanks to Him" (Rom. 1:21). These words contain an uncanny riddle. They reveal the hidden, mysterious decision of man in which his cultus is rooted as pagan idolatry. Man is actually reached by the ray of light which God causes to shine from His world and from His essence by means of the works of creation. Man arrives at a knowledge of God. But to know God, does that not imply to acknowledge God, to acknowledge Him as my God, as my Creator and Lord, as I drop to my knees and with words and works of adoration, praise, glorification, and thanks return to Him the glory reflected in His works? Is this worship which God expects of fallen man and which He, on His part, also enables man to perform, and the presuppositions of which even become subjective reality with man — is this worship, this factual acknowledgment of Him, not most natural and self-evident?

Indeed, the fact that man does not do this is perfectly unnatural and antinatural. Although man has been struck by the ray of the knowledge of God, he fails to drop to his knees in adoration, but instead refuses God, the revealed and known God, factual acknowledgment. Man stifles the knowledge of God imparted to him. He himself extinguishes the light that illumined him. He violently tramples underfoot the reality of God, which was divulged to him and which touched him directly. By this wickedness man willfully suppresses the truth (Rom. 1:18). Here truth is nothing other than the reality of God Himself, which is disclosed to him and which flashes through him like a ray of light as he beholds the works of creation. Man forcibly sup-

46

presses the disclosure of God's reality by the practical answer which he gives to God's self-revelation. The door leading to a genuine, legitimate worship of God and communion with God was open also for fallen man — even in his own heart. But man slams the door shut because he will not acknowledge that there is someone above him before whom he must fall down and to whom he is "indebted" for everything. Man proves himself a true son of Adam. Here he, too, shows himself the rebel who rejects the hand extended to him in compassion by God.

This self-willed rejection on the part of man over against the reality of God's revelation, disclosed to him in the works of creation, is the very foundation of his existence as a heathen. An attempt to gain an insight into the historical event in which this self-willed rejection took place might be futile within the history of religion open to view. Even if this were possible, it would hardly reveal the event which the apostle had in mind. For this event as such will not come to view in the history of religion. This act of man's self-willed rejection over against God's revealed reality reposes in that hidden depth from which that which history displays first emerges. Thus this self-willed rejection, despite its awful reality, despite its concrete existentiality, cannot be assigned to single demonstrable events as such, since it is the hidden basis of all demonstrable events. Rather, the entire historical existence of the man outside God's elect people must be understood as a result of a hidden original decision in which fallen man repeats the Fall, as it were, as he again refuses the hand God extends to him.

With this self-willed rejection man has entered an inclined plane with an eerie precipice. For him who has actually come into contact with God's reality but has willfully shut himself out from it, this contact will release the wrath of God as a formative power for man's existence. And within the compass of God's wrath man now fashions his cultus on the background of that self-willed rejection. Arrogantly man has again rejected the living God, who sought him out. As a result he is forfeit to the idol. The fact that man has actually been touched by the knowledge of God cannot be undone. It continues to operate, but now it operates as a judgment, which manifests itself in the practical conduct of man. The inevitable consequence of man's rejection of God's revealed reality will be that henceforth utter unreality will replace reality and be regarded as real and that absolute falsehood will replace truth and be regarded as valid. When the reality of God is denied by man's unnatural negation, man must fall prey to the empty irreality of the idol, which now, as a pseudo-reality, replaces the reality of God and exercises, weirdly logically, an uncanny, godlike, demonic power over man.

That is the essence of the pagan cultus, revealed by Paul in Rom. 1:21b-26 as resulting from that self-willed rejection on the part of man: men become "futile in their thinking." In his heart, in which the light of the knowledge of God was willfully extinguished, a darkness is produced. A perversion which one is tempted to call tragicomical now develops: while man boastfully esteems himself as wise, he is made a fool. Note the passive voice! The known but rejected God acts in it. That self-willed rejection on the part of man over against God releases an eerie, practical, and logical sequence of events. The abandonment to the futile, the obscuration of the mind, and the befogging of the insight by folly lead to an absurd exchange. The glory of the everlasting God, which beamed upon man from the works of creation, is exchanged, is traded for, the image of an idol. Man robs God of the glory which is due Him. Instead of letting the ray of that glory of God which shone upon him beam back upon God in adoration and worship, man holds fast to this ray as a spoil and arbitrarily transfers to the creature what belongs to God. That begets the idol, and with this it begets the pagan cultus. Now man owns the idol, in place of God, as his lord. In place of the revealed, all-encompassing reality, he now has an image fashioned by himself, an empty nothing, an embodied lie, a chimera, to which he is now subservient as a quasi-divine power.

Whoever forcibly displaces the truth, which is God's self-revelation, inevitably falls prey to the lie. Man has exchanged God's truth for a lie, as he has exchanged God's glory for the image of an idol. The pagan cultus reflects man's perverted relationship to God. Man's self-willed rejection over against God, who revealed Himself in His works of creation, results in a perversion of the center of man's spiritual essence, namely, at the point where he is inescapably related to God. Therefore the pagan cultus is not one of several phenomena of truth, it is not a dimmed half-truth, it is not a preliminary stage to truth, but it is a perverted truth, consequently a lie. A lie, however, arises only from the reality of truth. A lie is the murdered reality of truth. Therefore pagan cultus is possible only by reason of the fact that the ray of the true God's glory has actually beamed on man. This fact is the basis of reality of pagan cultus, but in a manner that in it God's truth is perverted into lie from beginning to end and in every particular.

The fact that these deliberations do not deal with an abstract religious-philosophical theory but with the exposition of the very basis of man's existence is shown as the apostle continues his analysis (Rom. 1:24-32), to which we can only allude here. If man is perverse in the core of his immediate relationship to God, then this perversion displays itself in his entire conduct. The antinature of that self-willed rejection over against the revealed God forces the entire practical conduct of man into an antinature, which results in the deadly dissolution of his being. Perversion of the cultus results in the perversion of the moral behavior. The immediate worship of God proves to be the controlling center of man's existence. His whole existence is determined by this center. If man serves God in this center in practical acknowledgment, in adoration, praise, and thanksgiving, then he will also serve God in his whole conduct in accord with God's will. But if this center is perverted, then the perversion of this worship will spread and permeate man's entire behavior and place him in opposition to God's will in all of life's manifestations.

The church of Jesus Christ embraces people who were Jews and people who were heathen. Until the apocalyptic dawn of the last things heathen-Christianity will typify the church of Jesus Christ. Israel was elected from the midst of heathendom. The heathen-Christians came into the church of Jesus Christ directly from heathendom. Membership in the people of God always implies a rupture with the heathen past and the heathen cultus. The relationship between heathen cultus and the church's worship can never be defined as a transition from a preliminary stage to a crowning maturity. There is an unbridgeable gulf fixed at all levels between the heathen cultus and the church's worship. There is nothing whatsoever to join them. They are as different as God and devil (2 Cor. 6:14-18). Therefore the conversion from heathenism to the church rightfully involves a renunciation of the devil, which as such is simultaneously a renunciation of the pagan cultus.[60]

But this very recognition of the radical line of demarcation that separates the heathen cultus and the church's worship will at the same time indicate the nature of the relationship of the two to each other, namely, that of the lie to the truth, of the murdered to the living, of the perverted to the original and natural. Through its absolute rejection of the pagan cultus, the church's worship brings delivery from its demonic bondage to the former, reversion of the lie into truth, restoration of life to the murdered, transformation of the perverted into the God-willed original. Therefore the worship of the church will include and absorb that worship which was to become reality at the point where fallen man was struck in his heart by the bright ray of God's glory.

To be sure, the worship of the church will not lead the heathen back to that point, it will lead him beyond that, as surely as God's revelation has in the meantime immeasurably transcended the manifestation of His Godhead through His works of creation. However, the church's worship will not extinguish that worship which was rejected and misapplied by the heathen. As surely as the worship of the church will extinguish the heathen cultus, it will adopt God's truth perverted in that cultus. In the worship of the church it will come to pass that the creature accepts the Creator's glory beamed on it, but that it does not cling to it as a spoil but beams it back upon the Creator in adoration, praise, and thanksgiving.

Worship in the Old Covenant

We do not propose even to sketch the Old Testament cultus with regard to its origin, its history, its form, and its function.[61] Also in this section we shall attempt to indicate the plan-of-salvation foundation on which the Old Testament cultus rests; we shall show which hidden realities appear in it when moved into the light of Jesus Christ's day, as this is done in the New Testament, for instance, in the letter to the Hebrews. As we do that, it will also become necessary to cast our glance beyond, to the worship of Jesus Christ and to that of the New Testament church. We will find the relationships and associations materially closer here than they appear at first glance. Israel, Jesus Christ, the *ekklesia* of God, this triple stage in God's plan of salvation, present an interrelated and connected whole, in which each member is present in the other in a mysterious manner, but without affecting the individuality of any one of them.

"Now the Lord had said unto Abram: 'Get thee out of thy country . . .'" (Gen. 12:1). These words introduce an entirely new intervention of God in the history of mankind. They initiate the segregation and the election of Israel.[62] They initiate the history of God in which He works the eternal salvation from the Fall and from its terrible consequences. The pathway of Jesus' sacrifice, which already began in heaven, now descends and continues here simultaneously with Abraham's calling and Israel's election, appearing in the Old Testament worship in a preliminary, foreshadowing, and pledging form.

The all-important presupposition for the possibility that the sacrificial life of Jesus Christ can appear in earthly worship is rooted in the fact that the one true and living God Himself becomes present here on earth. From beginning to end, the personal presence of God on earth is the center and core of that worship which involves the preparation, the acquisition, and the distribution of eternal salvation.[63] God's great judgments in the world's early history, the deluge and the destruction of the Tower of Babel, were followed by the withdrawal of God's presence from humankind. He ascended into heaven, and from there He descends only in judgment at the building of the Tower of Babel. From now on the nations of the world are really far removed from God. Surely, God is operative as Creator and Preserver also in the heathen world; but that particular gracious presence which permits and materializes a personal association of God with man and of man with God is withheld from the pagan world until it is incorporated through Gospel and Baptism into the elect people of God, into the church of Jesus Christ.

With God's call to Abraham, His personal and gracious presence among men begins anew. God gives His Word to men in Israel, in which He is actively present. Now God may no longer and must no longer be served in disregard of, or in opposition to, His Word. Also what we are wont to call the Old Testament cultus is bound to God's instituting Word. This does not preclude that the divine institution of the Old Testament cultus appears to us in a process of religious history in the course of which an abundance of extra-Christian elements are implanted into the Israelitic cultus. But this very implantation is carried out through a revelatory activity of God.

God's presence in His Word belongs to the mysteries of worship by reason of the fact that God's own utterance enters into the creature word of man and still remains God's Word. A creatural factor, human speech, is chosen by God for His own communication and action. A changing, never fixed character identifies the Old Testament Word-presence of God. This Word bursts forth with ever new thrusts. It is not bound to any fixed institution. With perfect freedom it selects its own charismatic bearers. At times this Old Testament Word-presence of God may appear abundantly, and then again scantily, it may cease, set in again, and finally become extinct. It eventuates wherever this Word, stemming from God, is actually spoken by man. The preservation of this once-spoken Word, its conservation in tradition and in Scripture must be sharply distinguished from this. When God does not actually speak His Word, then His real presence in the Word has been removed from the people, even though they reverently preserve and remember the once-spoken Word and its content. Therefore the Word spoken by God in the Old Covenant is multiform and divided into many words. God did not speak once for all in the Old Covenant.

When God bestows His Word, He often couples this event with His own appearance. In Israel God appeared to man in His theophanic form. This self-manifestation of God in His theophanies gave rise, as a rule, to a certain worship and adoration in the place of this manifestation. There were undoubtedly outstanding places of such manifestation, but God's presence was never bound exclusively to these, nor was it confined to a certain theophanic form. God's manifestations in His theophanic forms were always transitory. And they were multiform, scattered, often lasting but a moment, under certain circumstances enduring a bit longer, but never permanent.

The days of the patriarchs, which marked the beginning of the Word-presence of God, were also distinguished by a large number of theophanic manifestations of God, among which the "Angel" of the Lord was especially significant. He was no created angel but the most person-like form of the theophanic presence of God. In the earliest history of the nation, in the time spent in the wilderness, we witness an intensification of God's manifestations, both with regard to their number and with regard to their extent and their duration. Almost all the important Old Testament manifestations of God are concentrated here: the angel of God, the countenance of God, the splendor of God, the pillar of clouds and the pillar of fire, the ark of the covenant. God did not appear to individuals in these theophanic forms and manifestations, as He did in the days of the patriarchs, but to all the people. After the occupation of the country, only the manifestation through the ark of the covenant remained; and after the construction of the temple this developed into a temple manifestation. This was, of course, intended for the entire nation, but it was hidden from the eyes of the people. It was a presence that was mediated by the priests. In addition to this presence, we find the Word-presence of God mediated by individual charismatics. Thus the people as a whole were now dependent on a priest- or prophet-mediated presence of God.

However, God's presence was not bound to the temple. It was

presumptuous and complacent to rely on the temple as on "an iron-clad guarantee of God's presence" (Eichrodt) (Micah 3:11 f.; Jer. 7:4, 12 ff.; 26:9). The temple-presence of God could cease, and it did actually cease. Ezekiel witnessed its departure (Ezek. 10:18 ff.; 11:22 ff.). And there remained only the prophet-mediated Word-presence, which appeared in particularly rich development especially in connection with the judgment on people and temple. To be sure, the temple was rebuilt; but the new temple was without the ark of the covenant. It was no longer the same dwelling place of God among men as the old one had been. Rabbinical theology of Jewry must contend with the question whether God's glory was still present at all in the temple.[64]

Moreover, the prophet-mediated Word-presence of God also terminated. The tide of Israel's history seemed to ebb into a virtual forsakenness by God. "We see not our signs; there is no more any prophet," laments Ps. 74:9. The Scribes' construction of God's presence in the written law and in its study was already beginning to supplant God's living and saving presence in the charismatic Word and in theophanic self-manifestation.[65]

Then God appeared in the flesh. The eternal Word itself became flesh. But Israel rejected this self-manifestation of God proffered in the last hour. It crucified its Anointed. And again a judicial withdrawal of the bodily presence of God ensued. Since Christ's ascent into heaven, Israel is deprived, according to the flesh, of the Messianic presence of God. Its Messiah is seated on the right hand of God the Father and is actually and really present solely in the temple of the Holy Spirit, in the *ekklesia* of Jesus Christ, until His return ushers in the fulfillment of all self-manifestations of God in the New Jerusalem and the great voice announces from the throne: "Behold, the dwelling of God is with men." (Rev. 21:3)

The Old Testament worship, which was made possible by the real presence of God, was basically and intrinsically of a sacrificial nature. Without the light of the Gospel, the Old Testament cultus of sacrifice appears as a special form of a cultic element which was spread over the whole world and was also found in related pattern in Israel's environs. "It is almost always possible for the history of religion to fit all things, institutions, rules, and events of the Old Testament cultus into their ethnological connection and to make it intelligible from that angle." [66]

And yet this Israelitic cultus of sacrifice was, in its essence, in its pneumatic reality before God, vastly different from the pagan cultus of sacrifice — despite the abundance of formal correspondence between the two. This fundamental difference of the Israelitic cultus of sacrifice, this singular particularity of its spiritual essence and reality, is disclosed to us solely in Jesus Christ and in the testimony of His witnesses. Since Jesus Christ, God's Son, is the Messiah of Israel, who fulfilled every sacrifice of Israel in His own sacrifice, we are certain that the sacrificial worship of Israel was instituted by God Himself, and was for that reason not pagan wantonness, not pious arrogance of pious man, not a waste-pit, but that it involved an actual part of the way of salvation until the coming of Christ. For the sake of the one sacrifice of Jesus Christ and by virtue of it, atonement, reconciliation, appeasement of God's wrath have a place in Israel, more particularly, in its sacrificial worship, even though only in an incipient, preliminary, and vaguely promising manner. Ludwig Köhler described the central idea on which Old Testament sacrifice is founded thus: "God's wrath is live. It must be allayed. The sacrifice composes God's wrath . . . The odor of appeasement has become the common denominator of the sacrifice's purpose." [67]

It is incomprehensible that God's anger can be placated. The official arrangement of sacrificial worship as a continuous, uninterrupted institution indicates that God is angry not only with this or that misdeed of man, but that there is somehing inherent in man as such that must be covered or removed, lest God's wrath erupt with consuming vehemence. There is something that must be set right between God and man; amends must be made for something that man committed against God. The appeasement of God's wrath takes place when a gift is offered to Him. In many instances blood plays a particular role in this gift. It is especially the blood of the sacrificial animal that is endued with an atoning quality.

To be sure, the idea of vicarious satisfaction is not developed in the Old Testament. The death of the sacrificial animal is not viewed as a substitution for the death of the animal's sacrificer. However, there is a close and a mysterious relationship between the sacrificed animal and the sacrificer. One may even speak of "a correspondence between their lives. This idea may be very old despite its late attestation." [68] On the great Day of Atonement (Lev. 16), the sins of the people may be laid on a scapegoat, which is then led out into the wilderness and in that way bears the transgressions of the people away with it.

54

What is actually taking place here? Is man himself venturing, by means of widely spread and prime cultus elements, to undertake an *actio* over against God, with which he would influence God and safeguard himself from His menacing wrath? This interpretation would misjudge the very essence of the Old Testament sacrificial worship. In Israel the living God took those prime elements of pagan piety into His hands and converted them from a self-chosen way of man to God into a way of God to man. In Israel the sacrifice was a way opened by God's mercy to man for erasing sin, for allaying God's wrath, and for preserving the communion of the covenant. The sacrificial worship of Israel was a gracious permission and an institution of God's mercy, not a work undertaken presumptuously and arrogantly by man.[69] Already in the Old Testament God Himself supplied the sacrifices intended for the appeasement of His anger. The cultus activity, which atoned for sin and eliminated it, did not emanate from man, but from God; however, it was carried out through the agency of man. The atoning act, instituted by God, had to be performed by man here on earth. Just as the Word sought and required the prophet as its bearer, so the sacrifice required the priest for its execution.

The priesthood in the Old Testament was a closely circumscribed institution. Not everyone was a priest. In the sacrificial worship of the temple, the individual required the services of the priest. Sacrifice, atonement, expiation — that marked an act performed in a particularly delimited area, which not everyone was privileged to occupy, in which really no one could stand unless he was authorized by God. Whoever stepped before God with the sacrifice, thereby entered, so to say, a danger zone, which only he might enter who was vested with special authorization. Therefore the priest, as it were, took the sacrifice from the hand of the individual and brought it to God. In that way the priest became the mediator in the sacrificial worship. The individual could deal with God in this sacrificial worship only through the mediation of the priest.

The priestly institution showed furthermore that the working of reconciliation was not dependent on the initiative of the individual. The presentation of the sacrifice became an event which was far detached from the worshiping congregation.[70] The appeasement of God's wrath was effected *for* the worshiping congregation. The people of God did not effect the reconciliation but lived from the reconciliation. Basically, effecting the reconciliation preceded the real wor-

ship of the people of God. The concentration of the sacrificial worship in the priestly institution and the consequent distinct separation
of this worship from the worship of the congregation signified that the
appeasement of God's wrath was actually brought about solely by an
institution of God, by an act initiated by Him *for* the people and not *by*
the people. By its divinely instituted execution, the sacrificial worship
of the priests created, objectively, a new situation for the position of
the congregation and of the individual before God, and this came to
the congregation and to the individual as a gift procured for them.
As far as reconciliation is concerned, the congregation and the individual could only let it happen to them and accept as a gift the
blessing vouchsafed to them in this phenomenon.

Finally, the linkage of the sacrifice to the priestly institution
demonstrated that the sacrifice had to be presented continually. The
atoning act dared not be interrupted. Every moment of the day the
people stood in need of the appeasement of God's anger. A single
sacrifice could not accomplish that. A never ending chain of sacrifices was necessary. Manifestly, the gracious presence of God among
the people depended on the uninterrupted presence of the sacrifice
before God. The ties of the sacrifice to the priestly institution pointed
to that goal. But this institution could obviously no longer reach that
goal. Instead of the everlasting presence of the one sacrifice before
God, the priestly presentation of sacrifices in the Old Testament after
all affected only a chain of single, separate, detached sacrificial acts.
The conclusion of each of these acts pressed for repetition and thereby
admitted its preliminary character, its symbolical character, which
only represented the real object, the really necessary object, and
thereby also conceded its own innermost impotence.

In 1 Cor. 10:18 Paul called attention to an effect of the Old Testament sacrificial worship of which we have not yet made mention
— the *communio*. It might well be a distinguishing mark for the Old
Testament situation that this effect of sacrificial worship was distinct
from the sacrifice rendered for reconciliation, the sacrifice of gifts,
and that this was concentrated in the communion sacrifice.[71] Whereas
the gift sacrifice was intended solely for God, the communion sacrifice,
which was always a slaughtered sacrifice, was intended for God only in
small part, but was essentially designed as a meal for the sacrifice communion. The partakers of this meal were mysteriously united through
this sacrificial meal into a sacral communion and simultaneously entered into a corresponding sacral communion with God, who Himself

partook of the sacrificial meal as a tablemate. Here the "covenant" was actualized. God and man entered into a most effectual communion, which at the same time became the center of a circle uniting the partakers of the meal equally effectually and obligingly with one another. Thus the governing motive for the communion sacrifice was the achievement of the *communio,* the *communio* with God and with the brethren in one.

This entire sacrificial worship of Israel must be conceived as a gift of God to man, the proper acceptance of which first enabled man to serve God truly. In this connection it is of secondary importance that men took an active part in this sacrificial worship. The real protagonist in this worship was God Himself. Therefore there was hardly a stronger sign of Israel's inner violation of the covenant than its supposition that God was the one dealt with by man in the sacrificial worship, that God through His presence in the temple had unmistakably given Himself into the power of man, that man now enjoyed free disposition over himself, since he had God at his disposal in the cultus. We know that above all the prophets exposed this perversion of Israel's worship and contended against it. This shows clearly that the gift of salvation effected by the cultic institution did not yet save through the mere performance of the cultus as such. The act of acceptance of the gift of salvation and the act of obedience to the God of the covenant, implicit in the former, were decisive.

Just because the people of Israel were chosen, because God dwelled in their midst, because reconciliation was granted them in the promising sign, they were also judged when they denied God the worship which He enabled them to render through election and self-manifestation and sacrificial service, the worship which He expected of them and concretely demanded in His Word. That this worship was never achieved and performed by Israel as a whole but only by a "remnant," that Israel in consequence stood forth as a people condemned of God long before Christ's birth, must also be regarded as a factor which reflects the preliminary and shadow-like character, the not-coming-to-the-goal nature of the Old Covenant. God's provisions for salvation in the Old Covenant show a delimitation with regard to the proffer and the appropriation of salvation, in which, in the final analysis, the pre-Christian judgments on Israel are rooted: despite the sacrificial worship in the Old Covenant, the actual death of the sinner and the actual renewal of the dead from the life of God did not take place. The Old Testament is ignorant of the New Testament rebirth in Christ's death and resurrection; it is ignorant of the eschatological transformation of the heart through the power which resurrected Christ from the dead; it is ignorant of the outpouring of the Holy Spirit; it does not offer the gift of salvation in its final eschatological form. The Old Covenant really broke up on its preliminary character, which directed to and promised, to be sure, but which did not dispense the reality of salvation itself. But perhaps it was this very inadequacy, this breaking up, which pervaded and shaped its whole history, that made it the most forceful and palpable reference to the coming fulfillment.

Thus the worship of the Old Testament was shrouded in a peculiar, hardly penetrable twilight. It was something valid from God and valid before God, and it was, simultaneously, the revelation of the great plan-of-salvation "not yet." By way of conclusion, we shall try to clarify this dual character of Old Testament worship in a few sentences.

1. In the worship of the Old Covenant man dealt with the one true and living God. God instituted the worship, and God received this worship instituted by Him and performed by man. The worship of the Old Covenant was based on God's revelation in His Word.

2. The removal of the burden of sin, which oppressed man as a real power and which provoked God's wrath, was the center of this worship. God Himself established the provisions by means of which His anger was to be appeased and the sins removed. He instituted the sacrificial worship and the priesthood, He granted forgiveness and communion.

3. To be sure, sin was recognized as reality opposed to God, which has to be removed in a realistic manner; but it was still widely conceived as a cultus-ritual impurity and its removal as the restoration of a cultus-ritual purity. To be sure, that recognized the objective and real character of reconciliation, the transference of the sinner from the antigodly to a God-pleasing status; however, the worship in the Old Testament could not do adequate justice to the personal relationship between God and man, to the personal guilt character of sin, and thus also not to the personal experience in reconciliation.

4. To be sure, it was recognized that the sacrificer, the sacrifice, and the priestly presentation of the sacrifice belonged together; however, in the performance of the sacrifice the three were separated. The unity, necessary for reconciliation, between the person to be

reconciled and the sacrificial offering and the reconciling priest broke asunder.

5. To be sure, a mysterious association between the giver and the gift existed in the sacrifice. To be sure, in many instances the shed blood of the sacrifice was of special significance for its atoning effect. But the atoning judicial death of man himself did not take place. The atoning sacrifice itself was not consummated.

6. To be sure, the necessity for salvation of the enduring presence of the atoning sacrifice before God was vaguely perceived, but it was not materialized. The Old Testament sacrifice was consumed in its consummation. Its impotence hid in its constant repetition.

7. To be sure, the two sides of the sacrifice's effect were recognized, the appeasement of God's wrath and the attainment of the holy *communio*. But in the performance of the sacrifice they divided into gift sacrifice and communion sacrifice.

8. To be sure, the necessity of the priestly service was recognized, namely, the bringing of the sacrifice into the immediate presence of God. However, there was no priest who was able to place the sacrifice before God without first requiring a sacrifice for himself. Therefore no truly atoning sacrifice could be made, since the Old Testament priest used and consumed the power of the sacrifice for himself.

9. To be sure, it was recognized that the worship which issued from man's grateful obedience, which pervaded his whole life, and which consisted in the fulfillment of the commandment incorporated in the covenant, was part of the divinely instituted worship and a response to God's gift of salvation. However, the Old Covenant did not convey to the people of the covenant the eschatological transformation and rebirth of the heart, which truly enabled and effected such fulfillment.

10. To be sure, the worship instituted by God in the Old Testament accorded salvation. However, it did not place the redemptive gift as such in the midst of the people, but only the sign which pointed to the gift, the symbolizing and promising sign, so that only the faith which followed this sign and looked to the future materialization of the gift received salvation in such faith.

11. To be sure, it was recognized that the central mystery of worship was found in the revealed and saving real presence of God. For sacrifice, altar, and God, who was really present by virtue of His

manifestation, belonged together. However, God's self-manifestations and Israel's worship were separated. God's self-manifestation at the place of sacrifice became problematical. Israel's history ended in an abyss of real forsakenness by God.

12. To be sure, Israel was chosen in behalf of the nations of the world. Its worship was performed vicariously for humankind, as it were. However, its worship still remained bound to a very definite place here on earth, to very definite earthly seasons, to very definite people, to very definite rites, to absolutely binding and minutely detailed rites. This ritual legality marked it as a part of this passing eon. Therefore Israel's worship itself would pass away when the new eon of the final time would dawn and release worship from its carnal-legal bonds and free it from its cultic attachment to the world and place it into the universal pneumatic liberty of the one *ekklesia,* which embraces Jews and Gentiles.

GOD'S SERVICE IN JESUS CHRIST AND JESUS CHRIST'S SERVICE BEFORE GOD

The worship of the Old Testament is not immediately joined and followed by the worship of the church of Jesus Christ. These are separated by the event which is summarized and comprehended in the one name "Jesus." We know that this event is the light that has guided us hitherto on our way and that alone also casts its truth-revealing rays over all that follows, consequently, specifically also on the worship of the church of Christ. We now face the task of peering into this source of light itself and of envisioning in how far not only the precursory, promising, foreshadowing reality of salvation of the Old Testament worship was based on what happened to Jesus, but mainly in how far also the pneumatic reality of the church's worship on the threshold of pneumatic fulfillment is based on this; for the pneumatic reality of the church's worship is no independent reality, it is derived from the pneumatic power of what took place in and through Jesus.

In the Second Article of his Catechism, Luther expounded for children and the home what was done to Jesus on the part of God for our salvation. As we follow and take up Luther's exposition, we shall on our part attempt to express the mystery of Jesus Christ. This can be done only by indicating the conceptual contour of this mystery, recognizable through the Spirit in the mirror of the Word. The mystery of the Jesus-event is the salvation-event coming to pass in Him. All pneumatic reality which belongs to the worship of the church derives solely from this salvation-event which has become reality in Jesus. Thus our conclusions regarding the essence of the church's worship are basically dependent on our knowledge of this salvation-event in Jesus. A study of worship does not exempt us from the task of a dogmatic interpretation of the content of the Second Article; no, it thrusts this task upon us. To be sure, this subject can be dealt with adequately only in connection with a study of dogmatics; it transcends the framework of our present deliberations. And it will be necessary to impose a strong formal, if not a material, limitation on our efforts. We shall endeavor to delineate briefly the constitutive basic elements of the salvation-event, from which worship derives its pneumatic reality.

The response to the question what happened in Jesus for our salvation will be the response of faith. But the fact that this response is supplied by faith does not rule out that a real, physical event is involved here, which eventuated as surely here on earth and in the course of definite years, months, and days, as it did not originate nor end on this earth. The response of faith is not a gnostic myth but the weak and imperfect relaying of the apostolic words of witness, a response constantly in need of revision, deepening, and interpretation of these words, in which alone all that happened in and through Jesus for salvation is truly revealed to us.

In that man Jesus, whom a Jewish maiden, the Virgin Mary, bore during the reign of Emperor Augustus, God caused that method by which He wanted to redeem us children of Adam once for all from our lost condition to become a concrete, historical event. Everything that God in His ineffable goodness had appointed in Christ before the foundation of the world for the salvation of us creatures, that He had begun to materialize with the creation of man, that He had placed before His Godhead in the unity of His holiness and His love to repair the loss of our fall, in order to let it emerge from Him in the fullness of time and place it in the midst of us men here on earth — all that became concrete, historical reality in that man Jesus. This man Jesus, placed by God into the space and time of this earth, is the instrument for our salvation from the eternal death merited by us. In that man Jesus, God placed an event from heaven into our earthly history which effected for all men, simultaneously with the delivery from eternal death, the final goal of His salvation, which

He had borne in mind and had designated for us and all creatures from the very beginning, namely, the realization of His kingdom among the creatures. Therefore what happened in that man Jesus is, despite His true creatureliness, humanity, and historicalness, an event in which God Himself acted.

To be sure, God Himself also acted in the creation of all things, in the abandoning of the heathen nations to their darkness, in the election of Israel, in the institution of the Old Covenant at Sinai, in the calling of His prophets, in the execution of His judgments on His chosen people, in the sending of John the Baptist; but in Jesus, God was active in a unique manner. In Jesus, God was active by being in Him Himself. Consequently, what took place in Jesus and through Jesus worked and achieved salvation because this man Jesus is God Himself. This man Jesus is a historical personality in this earth's history only because His humanity from the first moment of His reality in the womb and in every moment of His concrete and real being to all eternity was effected, sustained, and given existence by His being God. Being man, which is common to us all, becomes real among us men only inasmuch as it is ever mine, ever yours. Only by reason of the fact that an "I" is bearer of being, does this concrete person appear, which is I, which is you. As being man is indissolubly united with my "I" and possesses this unique, concrete existence only through this unity which is I, thus the entire being man of Jesus, inclusive of His human "I," is united from the beginning with His being God, in a manner that this being God is the basic bearer, which lends Jesus' being man, also His intellectual "I," its concrete, unique existence.

Thus Jesus is God sent into the flesh. The historical existence of the man Jesus presupposes a sending act of God, through which God *(deus)* sent God *(deum)* into the flesh. God the Father sent the Son, consubstantial with Him, into our flesh. However He, as the Son, is not the Father and not the Spirit but the Son, who was born of the Father and from whom, together with the Father, the Spirit proceeded. God the Son took upon Himself what we are, our humanity. He adopted our humanity, not as an idea, as a general concept, but *realiter* as humanity of flesh and blood. In the act of this adoption and through the act of this adoption the being man of the Son is in all eternity this concrete, individual being man of the one Jesus of Nazareth.

Thus God acted in a twofold way in Jesus. God acted in Jesus as the Father, who sent the Son into the flesh for our salvation; but in Jesus God also acted as the Son, who is sent into the flesh and who is of one essence with the Father. What happened in Jesus is, therefore, already in its supermundane presupposition, but above all in its earthly, historical temporality and into its never ending eternity, an event between the Father and the Son and consequently an event in God Himself. Therefore, what happened in Jesus was directed to God the Father from the very beginning and in all eternity. But what happened in Jesus was at the same time in itself a divine-human happening. God the Son completely and in every moment pervaded all that Jesus did. For our salvation everything, yes, everything depends on the fact that the lowly, poor, humbled, and broken humanity of Jesus, His suffering and death, was joined in the indissoluble, mysterious, personal unity with His true deity and was for that reason profoundly and completely permeated by His true deity.

And what happened in Jesus through this twofold act of God happened for us; it affected us; it was an act of God on us. Only by way of the mystery of the God-man does God's redemptive activity relate effectively to us. Only by reason of the true deity and the true humanity in the one Christ Jesus does salvation become a reality for us. Thus the union of Jesus' humanity and His deity, and His activity, suffering, and death in this essence are God's one all-embracing means of grace. The being and the work of Jesus face us in unimpaired creatureliness, humanity, and historicalness, and yet they are simultaneously tool, vessel, place, and manifestation of the being and activity of God; this by reason of the fact that the humanity of Jesus on its part is existent only because it is borne entirely by the deity of the Son. Thus this man Jesus is, precisely with this divine-human being and this divine-human activity, our materialized ultimate salvation of God. In His being and in His activity, this man Jesus is already the materialized kingdom of God. The kingdom of God and, together with it, the end of all things will come; but in Him, in His work, in His person, it has already dawned in a wonderful, hidden present. The man Jesus is the end of the ways of God. Jesus' humanity from His birth to His death on earth already embraces the eschatological transformation of all things.

Thus the humanity of Jesus is none other than the original eschatological mystery. A factor of this world of ours, the man Jesus, is bearer and conveyor of the one true, living God. With our eyes we behold only this creatural, historical factor, the man Jesus. But in this man the complete fullness of the divine essence is incarnate. Whoever touches this man, touches God in every instance, whether he is aware of it or not. Whoever sees or hears this man, sees and hears God Himself. Whoever receives this man in his home, shelters God under his roof. Whoever eats and drinks with this man, eats and drinks with God; in a hidden way he already sups with God in His kingdom. Whoever gave birth to this man, gave birth to God. Whoever nailed this man to the cross, murdered God.

We cannot enlarge on the fact here that the earthly activity of Jesus already demonstrated in a hidden manner that He was actually the eschatological Finisher. We can only intimate here that many signs during His earthly sojourn attested that the preliminary provisions and agents of salvation of the Old Testament were invalidated and that a new order was taking effect, because Jesus was the materialized ultimate salvation of God in person. We may cite several utterances of Jesus which seem to imply a conservative attitude over against the Jewish cultus: Matt. 5:23 ff.; 23:16-22, 34-36; John 2:16 ("My Father's house"). In Matt. 23:21 Jesus seems to accept God's dwelling in the temple and, with this, also the sacrifices as a valid reality of salvation. Manifestly, not priests and temple, but Scribes and Pharisees were the most significant front against which He had to fight, consequently, that form of worship which, as study and work of the Torah, was already beginning to detach itself from the temple cultus.

Actually, the veil of the temple first tore at Jesus' death, symbolizing the termination of the Old Testament offering of sacrifices as an institution of salvation valid before God. To be sure, we do not hear that Jesus ever participated in the sacrifices in the temple, not even at the time of the Passover, although He functioned as the head of a household and consequently should have slain the Passover lamb in the temple.[72] However, the events in the temple evidently still enjoyed a relative right until the death of Jesus, but, to be sure, only a relative one, actually an already defunct right, a peculiar, dialectic combination of tolerant affirmation and negation in principle, which was clearly and pregnantly expressed in the pericope dealing with the temple tax. (Matt. 17:24-27)

During Jesus' sojourn on earth it already became evident that the mediation of salvation was no longer bound to the cultus institutions of the Old Covenant, but to Him. Wherever Jesus, the Holy One of God, was found, there the antigodly, impure, demonic powers gave way, and not wherever the high priest functioned, who was also called the holy one of God, but no longer was that (Mark 1:23-26).[73] The offering of the prescribed sacrifice by the man healed of the palsy (Mark 1:44) was by no means meant to confirm the temple cultus, but it was intended to witness to the bearers of the temple cultus that He had appeared who was with full authority doing the deeds of the eschatological Savior, with the result that all cultus of sacrifice had arrived at its goal and conclusion. The story of the paralytic (Mark 2:1-12) contains a latent but strong attack on the cultus of sacrifice. According to the Old Covenant order of salvation, the sacrifice instituted by God and offered by the priest was the decisive means for the bestowal of forgiveness. But now "the Son of man" had come who was vested with the power to remit sins, explicitly here and now, just as though the definitive judgment of God were being pronounced here and now. In Jesus the new, definitive, and ultimate provision of God for salvation had come, which dissolved the former provisions and immeasurably transcended these. "The authority manifested by Jesus' words of forgiveness and addressed to the sick cannot be placed alongside the cultus provisions, but it must replace these. The seeming juxtaposition becomes a deadly contraposition: not by priest and sacrifice, but exclusively by the Son of man are sins forgiven. . . . The time has come when the sins of the people are conclusively blotted out; the Son of man has come, who remits them — in the face of the reality of this eschatological event, which is just as manifest as it is hidden, also the former institutions of this cultus lose their significance. Even though they were once upon a time instituted and hallowed by God, now they become the work of man and pass away, in the measure in which that fullness becomes reality." [74]

The life of Jesus and of His disciples illustrated that the cultus-ritual legality was already abrogated among them. For Jesus and His associates the eschatological consummation, begun in Him, broke through the boundaries of this cultus-ritual legality. The controversy that arose over the plucking of the ears of grain on the Sabbath (Matt. 12:1-8) shows very clearly that the entire temple cultus was virtually annulled. Even David laid claim for himself and his companions to that which was reserved for the priests, the bread of the Presence. Priests perform work in the temple on the Sabbath which profanes that day, but they do this without committing sin. "I tell you, something greater than the temple is here." Here stood one whose authority regarding the means of salvation far surpassed the ritual act in the temple. Consequently, His exemption far exceeded that of David and the priests in the temple. Jesus laid claim for Himself, for the sphere of Him in whom the kingdom of God had come, "to the prerogative which the Law assigned to the temple." [75]

The real presence of God and His kingdom in the person of the eschatological Finisher of salvation supplanted the gracious presence of God in the temple. With Jesus and His disciples a new eschatological temple sphere actually made its appearance, in which "mercy" replaced the Old Testament sacrifice. Did not Jesus quote Hos. 6:6 here as a Messianic prophecy now fulfilled? Now the words that God uttered there through the mouth of the prophet had come to pass. Now God no longer delighted in the sacrifices offered in the temple; now He desired "mercy." The eon of sacrifice was now terminated, and the eon of end-time mercy had dawned. When the Son of man appeared, in whom God was well pleased, Israel's offering of sacrifices was actually invalidated, as well as all that was connected with it; the entire cultus-ritual legality died through the Messiah.

This pericope already conveys that Jesus' work was oriented to a new, a different temple. This fact becomes most apparent in the story about the "cleansing of the temple" (Mark 11:15-18; John 2:13-17). As Jesus cleansed the outer temple, the forecourt designated for the Gentiles, He intimated that the eschatological temple of the church of the nations was about to be erected. "The place that God had designated as an abode of prayer for the nations was being prepared for them." [76] Jesus was no longer at all interested in the Jews' temple of sacrifice. It had actually grown "old" already. Also the obscure words pertaining to the "destroying" and "raising up" of a temple must be fitted into this context (John 2:10-22; Mark 14:58; 15:29; Matt. 16:61; 27:40; Acts 6:14). [77] The words originally spoken by Jesus may well have read thus: "I shall raze this temple and build it [a different one] in three days." Indubitably, these words had a multifold and yet a basically unified meaning in the apostolic tradition. The fact that the eschatological Finisher of all of God's ways of salvation had appeared, implied the actual end of the already vanishing self-manifestation of God in the temple and of the sacrificial worship connected with this. The conclusive, eschatologically new self-manifestation of God was already present in Jesus, in His person, in His real humanity. God's glory no longer dwelled in the temple, but in the Incarnate Word. Thus the end of the temple had come because Jesus had come.[78] This termination of the temple was sealed with Jesus' death. The sacrifice on Golgotha terminated all sacrifices offered on the altar of the temple. The "dissolution" of Jesus' body in His bloody death actually involved the dissolution of the sacrifices and of the temple. As the Jews nailed the body of Jesus on the cross, they actually also destroyed the temple in Jerusalem.

But this antithesis to the Jewish temple cannot exhaust the meaning of Jesus' words spoken here. His statement on the destruction of the temple must contain a second fact, a positive fact. The duality of His statement is not only an element of form; rather, this element of form bears a central, substantial, theological significance, it is of Messianic significance. That antithesis to the Jewish temple stems from a hidden, eschatologically new temple reality, which is already in the process of materialization. The indestructible reality of the kingdom is already present, though hiddenly, in the eschatological Finisher and in the environs of His sphere. Therefore the bloody death of Jesus, through which the temple died, could not and will not be the death of the already hiddenly materialized eschatologically new temple, which is Jesus and which will include those who share in His gracious presence. It is precisely through His death and from His broken body that this eschatologically new temple will appear. The eschatological self-manifestation of God in the human form of Jesus did not cease with His death. And for that reason, too, the human form of Jesus does not cease to exist with His death. On the contrary, in the resurrection it became, in an inexplicable manner, the vessel for the real presence of God.

But also the manifestation of the eschatological Messiah congregation is rooted in the resurrection.[79] Therefore, this eschatological Messiah congregation, which lives by reason of the death and the resurrection of the Messiah and which has its existence in this death and resurrection, forms the new temple, the other temple, which is "greater" than the old temple, and which for that reason also encompasses the old temple, namely, by way of fulfilling, transcending, and abolishing it, as surely as the one sacrifice on Golgotha has absorbed and fulfilled and, in that way, replaced and displaced the innumerable sacrifices in the temple. — Thus Jesus' words on the temple, in the apostolic tradition, "have surely been interpreted variously and applied to the eschatological temple, to the Christian congregation, and to the body of Jesus." [80] But these three are one!

Now we have approached the very core of the service which God renders us in Jesus Christ and which Jesus Christ renders God for us, namely, the cross on Golgotha. The work of Jesus Christ, as related in the Gospels, already tends toward this core and moves in its light. What is the pneumatic reality of this *leiturgia* of God, which is carried out there on Golgotha in the very profane forms of an execution, of a judicial murder?

There God served us sinners. There the love of God the Father was consummated, as He surrendered His own Son into sinful mankind in order to save it from the wrath of His justice. There God ordained the new, eternally valid order of salvation, which brought about the participation of all men in the consummation of God's salvation. There God established the means of atonement through which He reconciled the world to Himself (2 Cor. 5:18 f.; Rom. 3:25). There He procured for the world the only sacrifice which penetrated the iron wall of sin between God and men and wiped out the debt of sin truly and for all times.

The man Jesus, mysteriously united with God the Son, served us sinners on Golgotha as the Lamb that bore the sins of the world. From His birth the man Jesus is the new man of God; from His birth He is, by virtue of what He is and does, the Son of the uninterrupted pleasure of God; He is and remains without sin despite His complete, true, and real humanity. But He did not "grasp" and hold the pleasure of God as a spoil (Phil. 2:6). In obedience to the love of God which sent Him forth, He placed His sinless humanity at man's disposal, so that all sins of all of mankind are now placed upon Him. In His suffering and death, Jesus was not just a certain individual, a mere number in the countless host of human beings. As the incarnate Son of God, this man Jesus was, also in His suffering and death, an "Adam," the second and last Adam. Here already He was the determinant Head of a new, God-pleasing humankind. But the fundamental deed through which Jesus actualized this His headship was that He, the Sinless, in a manner inconceivable to us and yet real, took the sins of all human beings into His physical existence, assigned them to His body, and bore them into God's judgment of wrath as His sins in His own body. Thus the incarnate Son of God took us with our sins into His humanity in order to redeem us in Himself, in His suffering and death, from our sins and their terrible consequences, and in order to hallow and re-create us for God in Himself, in His bloody, broken, and dying body.

This hidden, mysterious in-being of the redeemed and hallowed sinners in the historical, physical existence of the dying man Jesus will reveal itself to us as the foundation of the church's worship-event. The members of the church, the communion of those redeemed from sin, death, and devil, together with their sins and their accursed estate, are already in the bloody body of Jesus Christ as people who are to be redeemed, in order to receive also on their part, through what happened to this body, the execution and the judicial separation from God — there on Golgotha, in God's judgment, to which the Son submitted voluntarily.[81]

The surrender of Christ's pure and immaculate body, however, a body laden with the sins of the world, to the accursed death under God's wrath was instituted by God's love and fulfilled by Christ's obedience. Such a surrender is a surrender to God, is an offering before God, is sacrifice. The only just person became sin and curse for us in the freedom of His loving obedience. The sacrificial character of this surrender was rooted in its freedom. What Christ did for us on the cross He did simultaneously for God. In order that God's love, which sent the Son, may now become free for each of us and may encompass every one of us, Christ, the God-pleasing Son, offered Himself with His curse-laden body to God's judgment — in our stead and in our behalf. He is the Priest, who Himself presented His broken body, condemned by God's judgment, to God as the atoning sacrifice. This sacrificial blood of Jesus' body is the expiation which truly appeases God's wrath and draws the light of God's love on us, so that we, who are cocondemned in the bloody body of Christ and covered with the bloody body of Christ, are now also covered in the same bloody body of Christ with God's pleasure.

This Golgotha sacrifice is the true and eternally effective atonement. Why? It issued from the heart of God. It was instituted and ordained by God Himself. It was without blemish itself. It was the pure humanity of Jesus. It was the God-pleasing, eternal Son Himself. It was not the blood of animals. Nor was it ordinary human blood. It was the blood of Him who was man in personal union with God the Son. In this sacrificial body "the whole fullness of deity dwells bodily" (Col. 2:9). This sacrificial body contained the shattering and victorious power of the Creator. This sacrifice burst the palace of death's might asunder. It shattered the satanic fetters. It also forced an entrance for us, through the hitherto closed doors, to the holy of holies in the highest heaven. This sacrifice gained access to the heart of the Father. This sacrifice was as perfect an act, as perfect a priestly deed, as it was perfect in its essence; for essence and act, sacrifice and sacrificing priest are, of course, one! The act of sacrifice was nothing else than the obedience fulfilled in Jesus, the eternal Son, who had the Father send Him into our flesh. This obedience of the eternal Son was identical with the obedience of Jesus in His suffering and death. The sacrificial act of the man Jesus was the one human act of obedience which fulfilled all of God's commandments in one and which endures eternally before God.

In Jesus' death on the cross all was fulfilled. In this bloody and broken body of Jesus God had reached His goal. In this crucified body the earth's history had virtually come to its close. The all-shattering power of this death on the cross reached down to the deepest foundations of our earth's history and up to the highest peaks of the supermundane powers and principalities. Its power opened all of history for the admission of the Last Day. Therefore, this death on the cross was an apocalyptic sign. Apocalyptic darkness veiled it. The earth quaked. Graves were opened. The dead arose. The veil in the temple was torn. That was the dawn of the end. The earth on which this death on the cross transpired was no longer the same as before. What happened there in the bleeding and dying physical body of Jesus, what happened there in this body with us and for us, induced the end of time, it was the beginning of the end of time, it bore within it the hidden fulfillment of the end of time. The content of the end of time, now dawning and fulfilling itself, was nothing else than the manifestation of what happened in the bloody body of Jesus on Golgotha, a manifestation which will take place forthwith in heaven in the heavenly *ekklesia*, and in time on the earth through the earthly *ekklesia*, until the content of this Golgotha event has become perfectly manifest in heaven and on earth. Whatever takes place in heaven and on earth is now in its innermost essence the result of what happened in the body of Jesus on Golgotha. On the Last Day, when history terminates, nothing else will come to light and be revealed than what already happened in Jesus' body on Golgotha, the last judgment and the last redemption, the last hell and the last heaven, the last unending death of damnation and the last unending life of blessedness. Thus the Last Day was already mysteriously present in the hour of Jesus' death. The cross of Jesus already looms at the end of all things as surely as it has a place in the Jewish calendar of feasts. In Jesus' birth, in His life and work, the beginning of the eschatological epoch was ushered in; in the death of Jesus it came to pass. In the death of Jesus the eschatological eon of the last things unfolded. In the dead body of Jesus the day of God's new world dawned for all eternity.

The fact of this breakthrough and the Last Day embraced by it were revealed to the supermundane principalities and to the heavenly powers in the resurrection of Jesus' body that died and was buried but was eschatologically transformed and revived through the Spirit and life of God. This breakthrough was also disclosed to the disciples in the appearances of the risen Christ between Easter and the Day of Ascension. But to the creatural, nonhuman powers, to the spirit powers, this breakthrough was immediately manifest in the resurrected Christ. The risen Christ, that is, the eschatologically transformed humanity of Christ, His crucified and glorified body, and the eschatological redemption-event concluded in Him now fill heaven and earth and already encompass everything except the demonic powers of the eternally antigodly, satanic kingdom. Therefore, since Christ's resurrection from the dead His sacrificed and glorified body now stands before God's throne, surrounded by the celestial hosts. His sacrificial act is not confined to the measurable season of His suffering and death here on earth. His resurrection, His ascension, His sitting at the right hand of the Father belong to this sacrificial act. With His glorified body the crucified and exalted Christ places for all times the redemption-event, which took place in this same body on Golgotha in gory, historical reality, in identical but in eschatologically transformed actuality into the heavenly realm of God. The crucified and exalted Christ remains the Presenter of His self-sacrifice, He remains the presented Sacrifice, He remains the Priest who places the self-sacrifice in heavenly, real presence immediately before God as the fulfilled expiation of all sin and as the completed new creation. By virtue of Jesus' cross, His resurrection and ascension mark the beginning of the never ending, world-redeeming, and world-renewing celestial *leiturgia*, consummated by the Lamb that was slain and is now seated before God's throne amid the heavenly hosts.

This then, is the worship of the New Covenant: the Father's sending the Son into the flesh; the obedience of the Son, who became man, born of the Virgin Mary; the assumption of Jesus' humanity into a personal union with the deity of the Son; the permeation of Jesus' humanity with the fullness of the real presence of the divine essence; the obedient submission of this humanity to the curse of the Law and the burden of sin and the wrath of God which rested on us;

71

the submersion of this spotless body, in which God's full essence was hidden, into our lost existence; the incorporation of our sinful being into His sinless body; the vicarious but real surrender of this body, together with the sinful beings incorporated into Him, to the judicial death demanded by God's wrath; the presentation of this body as expiating sacrifice before God; the appeasement of God's wrath; the removal of the separating wall; the purging and the hallowing and the re-creating of the sinful beings incorporated into His body; the breakthrough of God's love for the Person rejected and condemned to the cross and yet loved with a perfect love on that very cross; the breakthrough of God's love for all who are reconciled and hallowed in the sacrificed body of Jesus; the bursting asunder of the ancient cords of demonic bondage and tyranny through the divine power of this sacrifice; the apocalyptic opening of the world's history for the Last Day; the dawn of the eon of the last things; the raising and the eschatological transformation of Jesus' sacrificed body and, with this, also the eschatological re-creation of the human beings incorporated in Him; the filling of the universe by the sacrificed, glorified, re-created body of Jesus; the eternal presentation of the Golgotha sacrifice in the heavenly liturgy of the High Priest; the manifestation of the people, Jews and Gentiles, embraced and redeemed by this sacrificed body as the *ekklesia;* and in all of this the never ending glorification of the Triune God by the redeemed creatures — that is the worship of the New Covenant. This worship of the New Covenant is the historical place of redemption in which the worship of the church of Jesus Christ stands here on earth.

Worship in God's Universal Plan of Salvation

Why are Jesus' death and resurrection not actually and empirically the death and resurrection of all men? Why is the Last Day only hiddenly present in Good Friday and Easter? Why are cross and resurrection of Jesus not the factual, empirical end of all things, since the end of all things has already begun in Jesus' cross and resurrection? Did God's way of salvation that He designed for us not actually come to an end in Christ's cross and resurrection? Are we not incorporated into His body on the cross by God's institution and by Jesus' obedience, and are we not also for that reason in His body which fills the universe and which is enthroned at the right hand of God? If the victorious words of the dying Savior: "It is finished!"

(John 19:30) are really true, why has His kingdom not actually come with His death?[82]

First of all, we must emphasize the significance of the fact that, with the exaltation of the crucified Lord, the church in Christ is an entity already present in heaven before God's throne. Therefore also that unique worship, which belongs to the end time and brings salvation to full materialization, now takes place where, in Christ's glorified body, His crucified body is placed before God and affirmed as the one atoning sacrifice in an eternal, priestly act of the crucified and exalted Christ. Immediately with Jesus' resurrection and ascension, this salvation-effectuating worship has been removed from the earth and ushered into God's heaven.

And the earth? Does it sink into oblivion? Are the events on earth as nothing when measured by the events in heaven? By no means. The appearances of the resurrected Christ between Easter and the Day of Ascension were the signs which revealed that the church is to participate in the events in heaven. The church here on earth and its worship here on earth are founded on these appearances. There is a very particular correspondence between what takes place in heaven since Jesus' resurrection and ascension and what takes place in the church here on earth. The church of God, which stands before God's throne in the crucified and glorified body of Christ, has a future even here before God's throne, which is fulfilled by what takes place on earth in and through the earthly church. Before the throne of God this future of the church is already revealed, that is, the church is already manifest before God's throne with regard to its future. But also before God's throne this future is fulfilled in the present only in association with what happens through the church and in the church on earth.[83] This future of the body of Jesus is carried out on earth bit by bit, as it were, through all that God works in and through the earthly church. As the future of the body of Christ is fulfilled step by step on earth through these events, something new, something real is also happening in the body of Jesus before God's throne.

In what does this fulfilling of the future of Jesus' body consist? What is effected in the body of Jesus before God's throne through the activities in the church on earth? Through the activities in the earthly church the indwelling of sinful and hallowed human beings in the crucified and glorified body of Jesus is actualized on historically concrete individuals and in that sense is now first validly realized. We have seen how the incarnate Son of God as the second, new, and last

Adam, together with the sins of all men which He assigned to His own body, also bore in Himself all sinful human beings for the purpose of hallowing and re-creating them in the bloody death of His body. Even now we should not and dare not question and weaken the reality of this indwelling. And yet, there is to be further development. This indwelling has not yet attained its ultimate form in the death and the resurrection of Christ's body. This indwelling will and must also be realized concretely and historically in the body of each individual. The historical fact of my being derived from my physical birth is not annulled by the eschatological redemptive event of Jesus' cross. God takes this historical fact of my personal existence at face value. In materializing my salvation, God does not bypass the historical fact of my existence. He deals with every individual personally and person-like, with the intent of actualizing and converting the virtual indwelling of the human existence in the body of Jesus into an ontic-real indwelling in the historical setting of the individual human existence. Here we confront a fact analogous to the one we already encountered in the worship of the foremost creature. In order that man's worship be and remain a service within the real freedom of love, God left a path of history open for the foremost creature, during the course of which He wished to lead man to a definitive exclusion of sin and death and thus to the definitive eschatological *transitus*. Also on the path to the eschatological *transitus*, opened through Christ's cross and resurrection, God, for the sake of the real freedom of love, does not want to arrive at the final goal of salvation without dealing with the individual personally and person-like in a concrete, earthly-temporal history.

Thus we have recognized the plan-of-salvation meaning of the earthly church and of its worship activity: The virtual indwelling of all human beings in Jesus' crucified body shall, within the concrete historical existence of each individual, be converted into an ontic-real, personally apprehended indwelling, be actualized and led to its definitive form. Through this conversion and actualization the future of the body of Jesus is fulfilled before God's throne. As the ontic-real indwelling in the body of Jesus is realized, personally apprehended, held fast, and deepened here on earth in the individual through the worship activity of the earthly church, the body of Jesus grows in heaven and on earth, and the reality of its fullness with which it fills the universe increases. Through the worship activity of the earthly church the integration of the body of Jesus on the earth, in the universe, and before God's throne is fulfilled. Thus the epiphany of Jesus'

74

body is carried out in the earthly church through its worship activity. When the ontic reality of Jesus' body has been filled, then the future of Jesus' body is fulfilled before God's throne; but then also all earthly events are fulfilled, then the body of Jesus will appear in its fullness as the end of earthly history, then Jesus Himself will appear in the fullness of His glory, and God will be all in all.

We have recognized the earthly church and its worship activity as the agency through which God builds the body of Jesus and thus realizes His kingdom in the universe, as He already realized it earlier in the earthly body of Jesus in Galilee and in Jerusalem and on the cross. The central question, how the church of Jesus Christ originated here on earth after His death and resurrection, how it appeared in the very beginning to become an instrument for the building of Christ's body, still goes unanswered. Attention has rightly been called to the fact that the church of Jesus Christ did not come into being during His earthly activity.[84] To be sure, Jesus called men into His discipleship. Moreover, this discipleship was unmistakably related to the kingdom of God, which had approached, which was already present in Jesus' person, and which manifested itself in His activity, but which, after all, still lay in the future. However, in this group of disciples — aside from the person of Jesus — neither the kingdom nor the eschatological congregation of salvation was realized. From the number of His disciples Jesus appointed twelve apostles. Obviously these twelve were related in some way to the people of God in the Old Covenant. As apostles they were also oriented to participation in the coming kingdom. Nor was their being called during Jesus' lifetime without anticipatory significance for their subsequent call by the resurrected Christ. However, they were not the *ekklesia* of the New Covenant during Jesus' lifetime. All of life's experiences which they shared with Jesus, especially the common meals, were replete with a hidden eschatological presence of salvation; but they were not the church of Jesus Christ. We are constrained to say that, aside from Jesus Himself, the church could not as yet be present during His earthly sojourn. If the church is the epiphany of the body of Jesus, then the reality of the church during His earthly life was confined to the bounds of His earthly body. These bounds had first to be broken down if His body was to appear so as to include also people in their personal reality. The church could first be after Easter.

This does not exclude, but it includes, that Jesus knew about the church also during His life on earth, that He willed its future appearance, and that He also worked with a view to its realization. The Messiah-King and the Messiah-people belong together. As the concept of the Messiah included, implicitly, the Messiah-congregation, thus the Messiah-Jesus, who had now appeared, also already embraced, hiddenly, His people within Himself. He would build His *ekklesia!* He would create His people! The words of institution of Holy Communion prove without a doubt that the coming church, which, as our study of Holy Communion will clarify, was the epiphany of the crucified body of Jesus, was not identical with the epiphany of the kingdom of God in the consummation of all things. Before His death, Jesus beheld the interval which stretched out between His last earthly meal and the new meal in the kingdom of God beyond the Day of Judgment (Mark 14:25). It is precisely into this interval that He placed His Communion Meal, in which He presented His crucified, sacrificial body to His disciples, by means of the blessed food, and thus incorporated them into His crucified, sacrificial body. Thus Jesus' Last Meal may be termed a proleptic epiphany of Christ's church on earth.

We may also call the appearances of the resurrected Christ during the 40 days between Easter and the Day of Ascension a proleptic epiphany of the church, in a certain sense even a proleptic epiphany of the kingdom of God itself. These 40 days were, at all events, the time in which Jesus laid the foundation of the church and revealed the pneumatic reality of its future worship. The appearances of the risen Christ established the Gospel, as He made His disciples eyewitnesses of the risen Christ, and through His delegating words made apostles of eyewitnesses, on whom He built His church. The appearances of the risen Christ revealed the new, eschatologically transformed corporeity of Jesus. They revealed the complete disengagement of the one crucified body of Jesus from all bounds of our earthly corporeity, which He, too, had borne. But the appearances of the risen Christ also revealed that Jesus, despite the divine boundlessness of His eschatologically transformed corporeity, despite its boundless, divine fullness, presented Himself to the disciples as an entirely concrete, bodily presence, made miraculously perceptible to them. The type of corporeity in which the risen Lord became audible, visible, and perceptible to the disciples was of course not the same type of corporeity with which He simultaneously fills the universe bodily and simultaneously is present before God's throne bodily — and yet it is the same corporeity. The risen Lord had the power to concretize His divinely derestricted corporeity in a special manner for His disciples, to make it perceptible to them, and thus to make it a medium of communication and of communion. Without prejudice to the divine derestriction of His eternally enduring, true, and real humanity, but, rather, in the divine power of such derestriction, the risen Lord in His Easter epiphanies granted the disciples His wonderfully corporeal sight, His wonderfully corporeal Word, and His wonderfully corporeal table fellowship. These epiphanies were so to say the prime form of the church's worship, inasmuch as they prototypically showed forth the enduring, salvation-giving, real, corporeal presence of Jesus among His followers.[85]

But this association of the risen Lord with His disciples during the 40 days was still preparation; to be sure, it was the last preparation for the epiphany of the church on earth. The final epiphany took place in the outpouring of the Holy Spirit on the Day of Pentecost. Now we have reached the point where the eschatological transition, which includes the sacrifice on Golgotha's cross, begins to operate on earth in visible events. What happened on the Day of Pentecost was something novel. There had been no such Pentecostal outpouring in the Old Covenant, nor in Jesus' earthly activity, nor in the epiphanies of the Lord during the 40 days.[86] With the outpouring of the Holy Spirit on the Day of Pentecost Jesus appeared — although He remained physically invisible — to His followers and entered into them as Pneuma. His epiphany in the Pneuma was the fruit of His cross and of His exaltation and, with this, the fruit of God's entire, past plan of salvation. With the outpouring of the Spirit, the fruit of the suffering and death of Jesus was poured out. Here the concrete, ontic-real incorporation of the individual into the crucified body of Jesus, now filling the universe and present before God in glory, took place. The outpouring of the Spirit gave the body of Jesus the final, the pneumatic derestriction, the pneumatic presence, through which He reaches out to the individual and integrates him into Himself in a pneumatic and yet concretely historical event. The ontic-real corporeity and inwardness of this integration and incorporation was the eschatologically new gift of Pentecost. They whom the Spirit touched at Pentecost really died in the body of Christ with Christ and were really awakened with Him in His body to the life of God. Thus the outpouring of the Pneuma effected that all that had happened on Christ's body by death and resurrection was concretely realized and actualized on him who was apprehended by the Pneuma. Therefore this Pentecost event was the epiphany of the crucified, risen, universe-filling, present-before-God's-throne body of Jesus on this earth. Thus Pentecost marked the epiphany of the church on earth.

When we attempted to point out the significance of the outpouring of the Spirit on the Day of Pentecost, we simultaneously described the essence of Baptism. That was not a mere coincidence. The Baptism-event is the means instituted by God for the propagation of the Pentecost-event. To be sure, the Spirit was poured out only once in the manner in which this happened on the Day of Pentecost. But the event itself did not happen once for all on that day. What happened in the outpouring of the Spirit at Pentecost shall happen ever anew, although in a different form. The fundamental epiphany of the church through the one-time event on the First Day of Pentecost was, at the same time, the authorization to the newly created church henceforth to employ the means ordained by God for the actual perpetuation of the Pentecost-event. And Baptism is the decisive instrument for this perpetuation. The Baptism-event is ever a renewal of the Pentecost-event. Therefore Baptism came into immediate use on the First Day of Pentecost. The baptisms administered on that day constituted the goal of the Pentecost story (Acts 2:41); for the epiphany of the church, instituted by the wonderful outpouring of the Spirit, was perpetuated in these baptisms.

But Baptism cannot be applied without the preceding apostolic testimony of eyewitnesses. With the epiphany of the church, the apostolic service of witnessing, which leads to Baptism, appeared on the scene; but this witnessing also renders a service beyond Baptism to the church, which has come into being through it. As we step across the boundary drawn by Baptism, we immediately find ourselves in the worship of the *ekklesia* on earth. Indeed, the first sentence following this reference to Baptism in the Pentecost story describes the worship of the church on earth: "And they devoted themselves to the apostles' teaching and fellowship, to the breaking of bread and the prayers" (Acts 2:42). Our next chapter will call attention to the hidden pneumatic activity of this worship. Here we wish merely to outline, retrospectively, the plan-of-salvation place of this worship, insofar as this place determines the hidden, pneumatic activity of this worship.

1. The worship of the church stands at the end of the road which God has taken with humankind for the realization of salvation. This end appeared in Jesus' cross and resurrection.

2. Like the church itself, worship is an eschatological phenomenon.

78

In the act of worship the Messianic congregation of the last days, set off from the world and already integrated into Christ's body, is gathered as it awaits the return of its Lord. But in the interval between the Lord's ascension and His return, the church, through the mediation of the apostolic Word, has Jesus Himself, His very body, really present in its midst in the Pneuma, in the Baptism-event, and in Holy Communion, so that this body of Jesus becomes manifest in the church itself and is again and again actualized and integrated through its worship activity by virtue of the instituted means.

3. The worship of the church has its place in the heavenly sanctuary, which was opened by Jesus' self-sacrifice; it has its place in the opened access to the Father. The worship of the church is freed for the performance of the celestial liturgy before God's throne. The worship of the church takes place in the Pneuma, that is, it takes place in the body of Christ appearing in the church on earth. Because the worship of the church takes place in the Pneuma, it takes place in Christ. Consequently, the worship of the church is a participation in the one world-redeeming, never ending worship of the crucified and exalted Christ before God's throne.

4. The worship of the church has its place in the precincts of humankind which are marked off by Baptism and dedicated to God. In passing through this boundary, the believer's indwelling in Christ receives its basic, ontic reality. What happened in Jesus' body on Good Friday and on Easter Sunday is now carried out in the individual in a sacramentally hidden but sacramentally real manner. In crossing the threshold of Baptism, man dies with Christ and is again raised up with Christ. Thus he is integrated as an individual in his historical existence into the one crucified body of Jesus.[87]

5. What happened to the individual in crossing the threshold of Baptism imparts its essential content to the earthly worship of the entire body. Through the apostolic Gospel the access to the Father's heart, opened by Jesus' sacrifice, is kept open in the worship of the church, the Spirit is imparted, the effected implantation into Jesus' body is strengthened and rooted, the once-effected dying with Jesus is made ever operative, and the once-effected living with Jesus is ever nourished anew. Especially in Holy Communion is the once-effected establishment of the members as the body of Christ ever and again renewed through the reception of Christ's sacrificial body. By virtue of the Pentecostal epiphany of Jesus' body to the individual at his

79

baptism, the epiphany of Jesus' body, enduring to the Last Day, takes place in Holy Communion for the congregation partaking of the Meal.

6. Thus the worship of the church has its place where the world is already in the process of passing away and the new world of God is already dawning. In the worship of the church, the dawn of the new world of God, which came to pass in Christ's cross and resurrection, continues, as surely as Christ's cross and resurrection are the living, dynamically operating presence in the epiphany of His sacrificed and glorified body.

7. In worship, the church awaits the last epiphany of its Lord and His body on the Last Day. The real presence of Jesus, vouchsafed ever anew by the Word-bound Pneuma and by Holy Communion, stimulates the expectation of that real presence of Jesus' body, which is already materialized before God's throne. The church awaits the hour when the already operative power over death and life of the cross of Christ manifestly and factually kills everything in the church that is judged and manifestly and factually quickens everything that is awakened. It awaits the time when its indwelling in Christ's cross and resurrection appears in a final, definitive form, in which the hidden, sacramental reality of this indwelling, passing through the eschatological end-transformation, emerges in perfected manifestation. In the worship, the church awaits the hour when it beholds the Lord face to face. Thus the place of worship is the interim in which the church yearns for the eschatological *transitus*. Sustained by the Word-bound Pneuma and the Word-bound sacrament, the church hastens toward this last epiphany of the Lord and His body. This hastening-toward is carried out principally in its worship.

8. Thus the worship of the church encompasses the entire past of God's plan of salvation. The worship which God implanted in man in creation begins to shine forth again in the worship of the church. The perversion of the worship by paganism is cast off. In the worship of the church, the pagan lie is liberated for the truth of God. For the truth of God, stifled by the pagan lie, the revealed reality of the divine essence itself again becomes really present in the Pneuma in a new, an eschatologically new, manner. The worship of the Old Covenant is "dissolved" in the sacrificial event on Golgotha and in the celestial liturgy of Jesus before God's throne. The worship of the Old Covenant is linked to that of the church solely by this sacrificial event on Golgotha and before God's throne. Therefore the worship of the Old Covenant — its purpose of effecting reconciliation, its never fulfilled, symbolic, promis-

ing nature, its legal-ritual dependence on places, times, and persons, in general, its thoroughly legal-ritual form, and in conjunction with this, the provisional and foreshadowing character of its entire plan of salvation — has been surmounted once for all in the worship of the church. The fact that God appeared on earth in the body of Jesus Christ in the time between the worship of the Old Covenant and that of the church constitutes the fundamental difference in the plan of salvation between the worship of Israel and the worship of the church. In the body of Jesus all members are prophets, priests, and kings. In the body of Jesus every worship partakes of freedom from legalistic ritualism. In the body of Jesus every worship partakes of the once-for-all-times completed eschatological salvation-event on Golgotha. But thereby also the reality of salvation, which was promised in the worship of the Old Covenant and appeared there in a preliminary form, was absorbed into the worship of the church, the pneumatic reality of which derives solely from Christ's sacrificial service on Golgotha and in heaven. In the worship of the church, the salvation-event, which took place once for all in the body of Jesus on Golgotha and is now eternally valid before God's throne, is really present. For in the worship of the church the pneumatic epiphany of Jesus' one body is carried out through the Word-bound Pneuma and the Word-bound sacrament.

9. But the worship of the church also encompasses, in a peculiar, preliminary way, the future of God's plan of salvation. The Pneuma epiphany of Jesus' body is already the actual beginning of the kingdom of God in this world. In the worship of the church the coming kingdom of God is manifested in advance through the Pneuma and its gifts. Especially in the Lord's Supper do we find an advance manifestation of the eschatological table fellowship of Jesus with His followers in the kingdom of God. In all of this, the worship of the church on earth already reflects something of its ultimate form in heaven. For the worship on earth already contains a certain participation in the heavenly acclamation and proclamation of the Kyrios Jesus, which is performed in the realm of the cosmic spirit powers in its manifest ultimate form ever since Christ's exaltation. (Phil. 2:10) [88]

10. But withal the plan-of-salvation's "not yet," implicit in the church's worship on earth, still remains. The reality of the future of the kingdom of God and of its worship, which is still to come, is not extinguished. This "not yet" of the plan of salvation is shown in the church's worship in the following features:

a) Despite the uniqueness of the Baptism-event, worship includes a constant return to Baptism. It is a constant repentance, a constant new reception of the forgiveness of sin. For the worship of the church still takes place in this old eon, and for that reason in the zone of attack of the antigodly powers, and therefore also in the realm of temptations and the factual sinfulness of its earthly bearers. Consequently, repentance and the reception of the forgiveness of sin remain a basic characteristic of worship here on earth.

b) The mediation of the blessings of salvation remains bound to the words spoken by man and to the sacraments with their creatural elements, consecrated by the Word. Therefore the reception of the blessings of salvation remains bound to faith, which does not behold but which adheres to the invisible as though it beheld it.

c) The epiphany of Jesus' body in the Word-bound Pneuma and in the sacraments is not yet the definitive epiphany of Jesus and of His body in glory. Therefore, in this life the participation in the salvation-event, realized in the body of Jesus, is still confined to a pneumatic, sacramental form of participation. In this pneumatic, sacramental participation, the eschatologically new life is, as such, still "hidden with Christ in God."

d) Therefore the critical question regarding the proper *usus*, regarding the correct pneumatic application of the present gift of salvation, hovers over every single worship of the church on earth. Every worship presents a crisis to the assembled congregation. It arraigns the flesh which is still powerful in it and which still contends against the pneuma. It remains an open question whether or not this court of justice attains its goal and the pneuma prevails over the flesh. The gift of salvation, present in the pneuma, may be received for one's judgment, that is, it is possible to reject it, and not to receive it, as a gift of salvation.

e) But even with the proper *usus*, the church's worship on earth remains but a fragmentary beginning, a weak imperfection and preliminariness, more a sign of what it shall be than a manifestation of what it could be. Therefore, in this world the pneumatic reality of worship is always in the process of becoming, not in the state of being. The worship of the church may even degenerate, it may be corrupted, it may deteriorate. Then the church itself is degenerate, corrupted, deteriorated, and it and its worship stand in need of a reformation.

11. The plan-of-salvation character of the present, in which the

church's worship is placed, is constituted by its relationship to the past and to the future of God's plan of salvation. Christologically formulated, this present is described in the Second Article of the Apostles' Creed as "sitting on the right hand of God the Father Almighty." Pneumatologically formulated, this present is described as the eon of the Spirit pentecostally poured out. Therefore this present may be defined "theologically" as the dawn of the eschatological transition, in which God, the Creator of heaven and earth, already placed this heaven and earth, through the Pneuma-presence of His Son's body on earth, under the sign of that end which ushers in the new heaven and the new earth.

3

THE ANTHROPOLOGICAL PLACE
OF WORSHIP

Now we pose the question: Where does worship find its place within the history in which God deals with the individual from the time of his birth to his death in order to lead him to his redemption and perfection? This history of God with the individual can be but a reflection of God's universal plan of salvation itself. The fact that the individual is integrated into this universal plan of salvation and borne along with it constitutes man's salvation. Where is worship placed in this salvation-event? The answer to this question is rendered difficult by the fact that we first have to translate, as it were, our situation marked by the practice of infant baptism into conditions in which the church exists as a missionary institution amid heathen environment. This does not mean to imply that the practice of infant baptism is a distortion of the "real" situation of the church, provided that this practice really conforms to the prescription of the Gospel. As far as the objective problems and realities are concerned in which we are interested in this chapter, there is, as a rule, no difference between the missionary church with its predominance of adult baptisms and the home church with its infant baptisms.

In man's birth,[89] creation by God, enslavement by sin, death, and devil, and heathen defection are all present in a mysterious simultaneousness. In his birth, man is created by God as His creature through the agency of his parents. With his birth, man is therefore appointed to that worship which is rooted in his likeness to God and which must be conceived as a function of this likeness. Man can never withdraw from this creatural, and therefore essential, appointment to worship. From his very origin his being is appointed for this worship.

However, in contradistinction to the foremost creature, this appointment is not realized through our birth; indeed, it cannot at all be realized in the condition inherent in our birth. We must be born anew. As surely as man from his birth is appointed to worship and to revere God, so surely is man from his birth factually "incapable of worship." Through his birth he shares in the fall of man and its consequences.[90] That applies also to children of Christian parents. Ability to worship cannot be transmitted and inherited. Rather, with the essence "man," every person born of father and mother necessarily falls heir to the defection from God, which since the Fall belongs to the core of this essence, and to the surrender to the antigodly powers implicit in it; in fact, every such person basically and essentially collaborates in this defection and forfeiture. Therefore the newborn child is by nature and by reason of its essence a child of the wrath of God (Eph. 2:3) and is as such incapable of worship. Also the possibility, which God opened to mankind through His "prime revelation," His works of creation, is forever lost through man's basic pagan decision. From man's birth as such nothing can issue but a perversion of the worship of God into a worship of idols, a self-destruction of human existence under the wrath of God, and finally death and rejection.

Consequently there is but one real avenue to participation in God-pleasing worship — penitent faith wrought by the Gospel of Jesus Christ and Baptism.[91] It is very significant for the doctrine of worship that we have to paraphrase this gateway to it with two terms: penitential faith and Baptism. The avenue to worship is therefore a way that covers a certain distance and at the same time a threshold that is crossed with a single step. The way from the first encounter with the Word of Christ up to the crossing of the threshold may in special cases be compressed into a few hours (Acts 2:41; 8:35—38; 16:19-34); however, as a rule this course leading to the threshold will require a rather long time. This way is filled with the missionary proclamation of the Gospel to unbelievers and with the eventually resultant catechetical instruction of such as desire to be received into the *ekklesia* by way of Baptism.

We may query whether such proclamation and instruction are to be called worship (*Gottesdienst*) and whether the crossing of the threshold itself, Baptism, may be called that. Assuredly, the missionary proclamation of the apostolic Gospel is worship in a similar sense in which the apostle himself called his own service worship (*Gottesdienst*). However, we observed that this service to God does not really signify the worship of the *ekklesia*. Let us take, for example, the apostle Paul's meeting with the Athenians on the Areopagus (Acts 17:22-33). To be sure, Paul is here preaching in the name of Jesus. To be sure, such preaching is serving God. To be sure, God is actively present in such a sermon. But this gathering on the Areopagus is in itself not a gathering in the name of Jesus. Therefore this meeting of Paul and the Athenians is no *ekklesia* meeting. We miss the distinguishing mark which would justify our terming it worship — the gathering of the assembly in the name of Jesus. It is already becoming evident that the worship of the church must, in its essence, be more than a missionary proclamation of the Gospel.

The catechumens who receive the church's baptismal instruction are already addressed as servants of God by the church. The acceptance into the catechumenate of the church already draws the catechumens into the circle of the church's worship. Therefore the worship of the church will present structural elements that are materialized by the missionary proclamation of the Gospel and by a resultant instructional exposition of it. The worship of the church will always bear in mind that missionary proclamation and catechetical instruction are its presuppositions. The presuppositions will be so effective in their execution that they mold its essence and its form. Acts of worship especially designed for catechumens will also be necessary. In these the apostolic words will be given voice; prayers will be spoken; in the early church, acts were also performed on the catechumens, for example, in exorcisms. But is the catechumen in such instances really the sponsor of worship? He receives and accepts God's Word by way of instruction; he experiences acts of worship performed on himself; he participates in the worship of the church, which is accessible also to catechumens when it includes the elements of a missionary sermon. But the heart of worship, the celebration of the Lord's Supper, is still closed to him. Only the baptized may enter this precinct, only the baptized is qualified to worship and is a fully authorized sponsor of worship.

This is closely related to the fact that it is Baptism which first procures man's ontic-real implantation into the body of Jesus. To be sure, this implantation may under certain circumstances take place through the physical death of one who already believes in the Gospel, who is on the way to Baptism, and who, while on the way, is unexpectedly called away by God, perhaps even by way of martyrdom. However, Baptism is the regular way by which man in this life is incorporated into the body of Jesus. Without a doubt, a penitential faith in the Gospel, preceding Baptism, yields the believer a personal bond to Christ; but this faith does not yet transform a man, with regard to his being, into a member in the body of Christ. The new birth, in which man is judicially crucified with Christ and is made alive through God's life with Christ in the power of the resurrection, is first effected in the rite of Baptism.[92] The individual reaches the place of the earthly church's worship in God's universal plan of salvation only by crossing the threshold of Baptism.

Do these considerations also apply to the circumstances attending infant baptism? In answering that question, we have to note two factors: the necessary association of Baptism with the missionary proclamation and the catechetical instruction of the church, the association of Baptism with a charism-evoking blessing spoken over the infant, accompanied by the laying on of hands (Acts 8:17; 19:6; Heb. 6:2). With these two factors in mind, we will have to answer our question thus: Christ's act on man is identical in infant baptism and in adult baptism. The church knows of only one Baptism. Therefore the baptized child no longer stands before the threshold, but is in the house, in the body of Jesus; it is reborn a member in the body of Jesus. But the church, which administers infant baptism, must provide that the way which leads to the threshold is, in a manner of speaking, subsequently made up by the baptized child. This is done as often as the child is brought into contact with the Gospel of Jesus Christ. It must properly also include instruction by such servants of the church as are delegated to perform this office. And it devolves on the church above all to ascertain publicly that the child's "subsequent pursuit of the way" has actually taken place.

This cannot be an external bureaucratic process, but it must include an act which corresponds to that act in which the catechumen confesses his faith in the Gospel before his baptism and expresses his desire to be baptized. The ascertainment that the instruction demanded by infant baptism has been satisfactorily concluded also includes the baptized person's profession of his baptism and thus also his profession of the church's doctrine of Baptism. Only after this profession are the spiritual rights conferred on the baptized, which he may now exercise in the communion of the *ekklesia* by virtue of his baptism. Therefore the baptized first becomes an authorized bearer of the worship of the *ekklesia* after his profession of faith in his baptism. Not until now is he admitted to the Lord's Table, and not until now is he authorized to carry out the church's worship at the place where the church is entirely secluded and separated from the world "by locked doors." [93]

Also the second point, the association of Baptism with the consecration which produces charismatic gifts, must be considered here. Baptism is certainly complete in itself, even in the absence of such a consecration in immediate connection with it. But to be a Christian requires more than that fundamental, once-administered, ontic-real integration into Christ's body. From this pneumatic rebirth must spring a pneuma life with many different facets. The Pentecost-event, which perpetuates itself by means of Baptism, is, as we see from the original report in the Book of Acts, already connected with the charismatic Spirit. Every member of the body of Jesus receives a share of these gifts. Also the administration of worship by the people of God is effect and display of the charismatic Spirit. Only by it can the acclamation of the Lord be carried out here on earth (1 Cor. 12:3). The cooperation of the people of God in the proclamation of worship through psalm and song, the prayer-confirming and -sealing amen-acclamation, in general, the pneumatic coadministration of worship in the proper *usus*, include the charismatic Spirit, which is exemplified in gifts and services from which no baptized person is to be excluded.

The aforementioned consecration of the baptized, accompanied by the laying on of hands, serves to awaken the charismatic Spirit. To be sure, the awakening of this Spirit is not bound to this act. But it would betray indifference were we to neglect this apostolic custom in the moment when the baptized crosses the threshold which makes him a spiritual sponsor of worship, a co-prophet and co-priest and co-king of Jesus Christ. This consecration is a call, a commission, and a preparation for service in the *ekklesia*. Therefore only the adult may receive this consecration. Thus it is objectively proper to separate the consecration from the rite in the instance of infant baptism and postpone it to a more mature age. But at the point where the pneumatic service of the Christian in the *ekklesia* begins, where the Christian is authorized to coadminister worship, there consecration is in place, there it must not be omitted. In adult baptism, therefore, it is to be combined with the baptism immediately; but in infant baptism it is to be postponed until the public conclusion of the catechetical instruction.

Therewith we have indicated what the rite of confirmation is, and how it, on the one hand, is related to Baptism and, on the other, to worship with Holy Communion. Confirmation, as a rite distinct from Baptism, presupposes infant baptism. In this event, confirmation contains the following elements:

1. Public conclusion of the subsequent but necessary instruction in the Gospel of Jesus Christ.
2. Profession of faith in the Baptism received as an infant and thus a repetition of the baptismal vow.
3. Admission to the Lord's Table and, included in this, the authorization to participate in the administration of worship as a qualified member of the people of God.
4. Consecration and appointment to those charismatic services in the *ekklesia* in which every member shares by virtue of Baptism.

In conformity with this, we must lay down the following principle: Only the baptized and confirmed Christian is authorized and equipped for the administration of worship in the *ekklesia*.

Now let us concentrate on the Christian who has crossed the threshold leading to worship. He has died with Christ — and he still lives in the life of this eon. He has risen with Christ — and day by day he approaches his physical death and the decomposition of his body. He is a new creature, born of water and the Spirit — and yet the old Adam with its lusts and works still bestirs itself within him. He is in the Spirit — and yet he is exposed to the lusts of the flesh. Covered with the crucified, sacrificial body of Christ, he is righteous and holy before God — and yet, because of daily sin and guilt, he is a sinner before God.

It is one of the mysteries of history, in which God deals with the individual for the achievement of his salvation, that Baptism-death and Baptism-quickening really take place in the sacrament but are not yet the factually manifest death and the factually manifest quickening. The factually manifest death and the factually manifest quickening will one day emerge from the Baptism-death and the Baptism-quickening. Baptism-death and Baptism-quickening lead to the factually manifest death and the factually manifest quickening, the power of which they already bear within. It is one of the mysteries of God's history of salvation, which He enacts with every individual, that the Christian is in the Spirit from the time of his baptism to his physical death but that he, for all of that, does not always walk in the Spirit. To be sure, through Baptism the Christian is freed, in the very core of his being, from the tyrannical power of sin; but God does not exempt him from combat against this power. And this combat is not exclusively victory, but also records daily defeats, as we clearly confess in the Lord's Prayer. Although God has, through the Word-bound Pneuma and Baptism, thoroughly extricated man from the realm of the antigodly powers and transplanted him into Christ's sphere of power, it is still possible for man to break the baptismal seal of salvation, to relapse into the power of darkness, to lose the pneumatic life of a member in Jesus' body, and again to become like one outside the body of Jesus, although he can never undo and delete the fact of his baptism. Wherever this occurs, man also forfeits his authority and his qualifications for conducting worship and, with this, the sacred right to receive the Lord's Supper. But in such an event the possibility of return and conversion is also present. The forfeited membership in the body of Jesus may be restored through contrition and faith, through confession and absolution, and thus the power of Baptism once received may again assert itself. On the other hand, a final defection of the baptized, justified, and reborn Christian may also take place. (Heb. 6:4-8)

Earlier we posed the question why Jesus' death on the cross did not mark the factual end of the world and its history, why Easter was not the Parousia of Jesus. As touching the individual, this question is now formulated thus: Why is the Baptism-death not also the factual physical death of a Christian? Why is his Baptism-quickening not also his factual physical quickening from the dead? The answer which we gave at that time with regard to humankind and the *ekklesia* and its universal history now reappears in its application to the individual: God desires man's service to be the free answer of a beloved child. God does not lead me to perfection with a stroke of magic, because I am a man, because I was created in His image, because He wants me in His service only as a person. God also leads the individual to perfection only through a special history, which He initiates with him in Baptism and carries out as genuine history between thou and thou until the factual end of life of the individual. As extremes, this history includes, on the one hand, the death of the martyr, which may be granted him by God already on his way to Baptism, and on the other, the final apostasy of one who had already savored the powers of the future world.

90

In the midst of this genuine, eventful history with its possibilities that are to be realized anew daily, worship is conducted by the individual in the assembled *ekklesia.* This worship, too, is characterized by an interim: It takes place between Baptism-death and factual physical death, between Baptism-quickening and factual physical quickening. The salvation-history situation of the individual Christian, characterized by this interim, must simultaneously put its imprint on his worship in the assembled *ekklesia.* The worship of the *ekklesia* must absorb this salvation-history situation of the individual Christian into its essence.

Therefore the pneumatic reality of this worship, the salvation-event consummated in it, will be of a dual nature as long as this worship is conducted on earth. What happens in worship will include a constant achieving of the Baptism-event, which is also twofold in itself. Worship will, therefore, offer the means of salvation ever anew to him who is saved in Baptism. But the means of salvation are comprehended in the one factor: the distribution of the remission of sins for the sinner. The forgiveness-dispensing Gospel, the forgiveness implicit in the FOR YOU of the Lord's Supper, is the one component in the pneumatic reality of worship.

But forgiveness cannot be received unless the new creation eventuates simultaneously in man. As the Baptism-death purposes to produce a daily and ever increasing mortification of the old Adam in the concrete existence of man, and as it actually does effect this where Baptism is received and preserved in faith, so the Baptism-quickening daily and in ever increasing measure engenders and manifests, through the power of the Pneuma in the concrete existence of the believer, something of the new man who is born of God. And whatever is manifested here also enters into the worship of the *ekklesia* and forms there the second component of its pneumatic reality. This second side of worship's reality is already turned toward the future world of God, it is the beginning of that worship activity which will endure in eternity and which is already reality among the angelic hosts and the blessed in heaven. Here the Christian, a donee with regard to forgiveness and re-creation, may become a donor and let the ray of God's love beam back in gratitude, adoration, praise, and glorification. The presentation of the gift of salvation by the donor, God, and the glorification of God by the donee, man, are the two sides of reality in the essence of worship.

Later we shall have to enlarge on these two sides. For the time being it is important that we recognize how both sides correspond exactly to the Christian's plan-of-salvation situation for the time intervening between his baptism and his physical death. Because we sin much daily until we die, because we are daily grievously assailed by our flesh, the world, and the devil, because we obviously walk ever more on the brink of the deadly precipice of temptation, God presents to us ever anew in worship the forgiveness-bestowing apostolic Gospel as a means of saving us from sin, death, and devil. Therefore God grants us ever anew the epiphany of the crucified body of Jesus in the Lord's Supper to receive us ever anew into the saving power of the cross of Christ. Because God, through the Gospel and the Lord's Supper, grants to him who died and is still dying with Christ also the life springing from Christ's resurrection, the Christian may, in the vitality of the Pneuma, glorify God even before his physical death as the angels and the blessed in heaven glorify Him, although only in this preliminary and earthbound form. However, the heavenly worship is already present in this preliminary and earthbound form, the worship willed by God before the earth's foundations were laid, the worship which, after the passing of this world, will appear in fullness as the enduring, ultimate goal of everything.

Bestowal of forgiveness of sins through Gospel and Holy Communion is the side of the reality of worship that is closest to us. For us this bestowal is the most urgent — it is necessary for our salvation, it is the foundation on which alone that other side of reality can be constructed. But this fundamental, nearest-to-us worship activity relates only to the Christian who is still on his earthly pilgrimage. It is the pilgrim side of our worship. This passes away. Proclamation of the Gospel to the sinner, confession, absolution, Holy Communion will cease. But that second side of reality of the worship activity never ends. Seen from the viewpoint of the end, the glorification of God, which begins here on earth with the worship of the Christian in the *ekklesia,* is the decisive activity, the activity which is God's ultimate aim, the enduring activity, the activity already distinguished by eschatological validity, in which the enduring, immovable, eternal kingdom of God dawns upon this passing world. In this second reality-component of worship our heavenly citizenship manifests itself. Therefore the church's worship is worship of imperiled, faltering pilgrims and, simultaneously, worship of heavenly citizens, who, in the Pneuma, are already on the verge of the goal, the heavenly Jerusalem, and whose worship will one day be swallowed up in the worship of the citizens of heaven.

Hence, the anthropological place of worship may be summarized thus:

1. Worship is placed between Baptism-death and physical death, between Baptism-quickening and heavenly perfection.

2. Worship is placed into a pneumatic activity, in which the old Adam is daily given into death and the new man is quickened.

3. Worship is placed where the sinner is justified, receiving remission of sins ever anew, and where the justified person, endued with the power of sins forgiven, glorifies God in the newness of a pneumatic life, together with the angels and the blessed. Worship is placed where God's gift of salvation comes to us and where we, in return, may glorify God with our gratitude.

4. Worship is placed where our status as pilgrims and as heaven's citizens finds expression in one activity. Worship is placed where also in the Christian's existence this world is in the process of passing away and the kingdom of God is in the process of appearing.

5. Worship, therefore, is placed in the eschatological *transitus* from death to life.

4

THE COSMOLOGICAL PLACE OF WORSHIP

So far we have spoken exclusively of the history which God enacts with humankind in general and with each individual in particular to realize their salvation. Now we must focus our attention on the fact that this history of God with us has a twofold border in which it is enclosed. The lower border of this history is formed by the nonhuman, earthly creatures, the upper one by God's creatures in His heavenly kingdom, the angels. God's history of salvation does not glide through these two borders unrelatedly, as a river does between the banks of its bed; no, these borders themselves participate in the salvation-event. They are related to it from the very beginning. They are also apprehended by it, carried along with it, and in the end of all things, at the point where the stream of God's history of salvation empties into the final consummation, united with this stream into a wonderful unity. Perhaps at no other place does the relationship between God's history of salvation and its twofold border come to light so clearly and significantly as in worship. The church's worship on earth tends toward the point where it may unite in an eternal unison with the worship of the celestial hosts and also with that of the nonhuman, earthly creatures. Therefore, to define the essence of the church's worship on earth, it is necessary to ponder how dynamically it is related now already to the worship of the heavenly hosts and to that of the nonhuman, earthly creatures.

THE WORSHIP OF THE ANGELS

Angels are creatures. But they are creatures that are immediately face to face with the mystery of the Triune God. They are not subject to the space and time conditions of our world. From the very beginning they are part of God's heavenly world. Therefore the angels are those creatures on whom God's glory lights immediately and who reflect this glory of God immediately. Because the angels are part of God's heavenly world, they are the first and immediate witnesses of the divine plan of salvation; for God's plan of salvation has its origin in heaven and descends from His heaven to the earth. God's history, which runs its course on earth, has its origin in heaven and is directly known to the angels before it is indirectly revealed to us men. In its execution God's history on earth has a side that is turned to the heavenly world, which the angels perceive, but which is disclosed to us only through their ministry (Luke 2:10 ff.; Mark 16:6). From the beginning (Job 38:7) the angels are the immediate and truest witnesses of God's deeds, as they are from the beginning the immediate and truest mirrors of the divine might and glory. As such living mirrors and witnesses of God, the angels are, above all other creatures, the agents for God's glorification. They are the exemplary bearers of the praise of God. The offering of God's praise by the angels constitutes the heavenly worship.

This heavenly worship also has its own history as surely as the performance of God's great deeds on earth leave their impression in God's heaven. A comparison between the vision of Isaiah (Is. 6) and the visions of the seer John (Rev. 4; 5; 7; 19) will reveal a bit of this impression on the heavenly worship. The angel who remained angel and did not become demon with the devil attained perfection once for all. Indeed, the angel who did not become demon but is witness to the demonic apostasy will never apostatize. Consequently the worship of the angel is the already perfected worship of the creature. In his perfected praise of God, the angel is himself perfected. The praise of God has become the inviolable nature of the angel. He finds his being exclusively and definitively in the praise of God. Although the angel is an "I" and does not lose his freedom also in his perfection, but perfects it there, in his worship he is nonetheless nothing other than "an echoing wall," which echoes God's being and God's deeds in words of praise and witness. The freedom of the "I" and the compulsion of the essence have become one here.

Therefore the praise of the heavenly beings suffers no interruption (Rev. 4:8). Since this act of praising is the angel's nature and existence in one, his praise of God is nothing other than the reality of his being. But since the angel simultaneously is and remains an "I,"

95

his praise of God is no mechanical reflex but an intellectual act, an intellectual act that has become his nature. Therefore the angel's praise is a song rendered in uninterrupted, perfect spontaneity. The praise of the angel is the hymn in which the creature melts away in praises before God.[94]

We have already called attention to the fact that the execution of the plan of salvation on earth leaves its mark in God's heavenly world, whence it comes, and thus also forms the content of the laudation of the angels. That is already evident from the fact that the heavenly beings offer God not only honor and glory with their Sanctus but also thanks, thanks for the merciful act of salvation on the earth below (Rev. 4:9).[95] Moreover, the visions of the seer John bear witness that the crucified and exalted Christ is the core of the angelic worship ever since His exaltation (Rev. 5:6-12). In the center of the heavenly Jerusalem, in the center of the many thousands of angels stands Jesus, "the Mediator of a New Covenant, and the Sprinkled Blood." (Heb. 12: 22-24)

Therefore the worship of the angels revolves about the same center as that of the church on earth, even though the real presence of Jesus and of His blood in heaven is of a different type and form than His real presence in the worship in the church on earth. But He who is present is the same: Jesus with His shed blood. Therefore inasmuch as the worship of the angels is entirely oriented to God, it is simultaneously oriented to the worship of the church on earth. To be sure, the worship of the earthly church is, with regard to intensity, purity, and fullness, only a dim and fragmentary reflection of what is done in heaven. To be sure, the worship of the angels excels the worship of the church on earth in every respect. But the worship of the angels and the worship of the church are not separated by an iron curtain. Because they have the same center, the Lamb that was slain, they stand in real communication with each other. The church on earth may already join in the praises of the angels and pray God to grant that its voice on earth may unite with the Sanctus of the angels in heaven.[96] Where the church assembles in worship around the crucified Christ, present in the Pneuma and in the Lord's Supper, the worship of the church is opened to and oriented to the worship of the angels, just as, conversely, the worship of the angels is oriented to the worship of the church, surrounds it, envelops it, and supports it. (1 Cor. 11:10; Rev. 8:3 f.; 1 Tim. 5:21) [97]

One day these two will merge. The church's worship on earth will blend into the worship of the angelic hosts. They who were privileged to make their way through the contending and suffering church on earth to the Church Triumphant are already participating in the administration of the heavenly worship. Despite all the differences in the type and form of being, the worship of the church on earth and that of the angels in heaven is an inseparable activity. The worship of the church on earth is in immediate touch with the worship in the heavenly Jerusalem and takes place in real association with it. (Rev. 7:9-12; Heb. 12:22-24)

THE WORSHIP OF THE NONHUMAN, EARTHLY CREATURES

In the moment in which the crucified and exalted Christ takes the sealed book of history from God's hand to remove the seal and to execute its content, "a new song" resounds in the heavenly throne-room. A song of praise of the celestial hosts, in relays of choirs, is intoned to glorify the Lamb. All the remaining creatures immediately join in this laudation, "every creature in heaven and on earth and under the earth and in the sea, and all therein," crying, "To Him who sits upon the throne and to the Lamb be blessing and glory and honor and might for ever and ever!" The four creatures before the throne confirm and seal this acclamation with an "Amen," and the 24 elders carry out the προσκύνησις (Rev. 5:8-14). This laudation of the creatures in verse 13 reveals that something decisive has happened in the apocalyptic history of God. The entire domain of the earthly creatures — "exclusive of man's" [98] — has been joined to the heavenly worship. Also the lower border of God's history of salvation empties into the interminable sea of the eternal adoration of God and the God-man.

This inclusion of the earthly, nonhuman creatures into the eschatological jubilation, which will burst forth at the end of God's history, is already seen in Deutero-Isaiah and in the psalms and is, as a rule, in the form of a hymnic appeal:

> Rejoice, ye heavens, for Jehovah has done it;
> Shout, ye depths of the earth;
> Break forth, mountains, into jubilation;
> Forests and every tree in them;
> For Jehovah has redeemed Jacob,
> And He is glorified in Israel.[99]

Also at the return from exile, which the prophet views as an event of the impending end time, heaven and earth, mountain and hills

97

will break forth in the eschatological song of jubilation (Is. 49:13; 55:12). We find the same thought expressed in the psalms which envisage the eschatological breakthrough of the kingdom of God. When the kingdom of God is proclaimed among the nations of the world and in that way is realized, when the judgment of God is executed on the nations of the world, then the path is open to the jubilation of the end time for all earthly creatures.

> Let the heaven be glad and let the earth rejoice;
> Let the sea roar and all that fills it;
> Let the field exult and everything in it;
> Also the trees of the forest shall jubilate
> Before Jehovah's countenance, for He comes,
> For He comes to judge the earth.
> He judges the world with righteousness
> And the peoples with His truth.[100]

But this eschatological jubilus of nature at the epiphany of God, the King of the end time, already finds its preliminary form in the present time.[101] The worship of the people of God on earth unites not only with the worship of the heavenly creatures but also with the praise of God by the nonhuman, earthly creatures. All the works of God "in all places of His dominion" praise the Lord together with the angels and with my soul (Ps. 103:20-22). Among God's works of creation, the starry heaven above me is mentioned especially as an instrument of the creatural praise of God. God's name is glorious in all the world, for God's glory manifests itself in the heavens (Ps. 8:2). "The heavens declare the glory of God."

> The heavens are telling the glory of God,
> The firmament proclaims His handiwork.
> Day to day pours forth words,
> Night to night declares knowledge.[102]

Whereas otherwise invitations are frequently issued to the creatures in the form of a hymnic introduction to join in the praise of God, we here find the fact of such a service of praise and witnessing expressed. In a mysterious way, the tidings of God's might demonstrated in the works of creation resound through the cosmos. The psalmist speaks of a universal proclamation and manifestation of God's glory by the heavens, by the firmament, by the day, and by the night. He seems to intimate something akin to an uninterrupted cosmic "tradition" through which God's glory is made known under all the heavens. The cosmos, so to say, apprises itself in ecstatic rapture (v. 3a) of the glory of God with which it is arrayed since the time of creation and thus, as it were, perpetuates and conveys this manifestation of God's glory into every zone and into every time.[103]

The phenomena of nature that operate in conjunction with the theophanies of God are of special importance. In God's theophanies, elements of nature such as thunder and lightning, fire and smoke, comprise the extreme seam of His theophanous form (cf., e. g., God's appearance on Sinai, Ex. 19:16). He makes the wind His messengers, fire and flame His ministers (Ps. 104:4). With regard to their function, wind and fire are here likened to the angels of God. Indeed, as 1 Kings 19:11-13 shows, they may precede the theophanous form of God as His messengers who announce His coming. The strongest testimony for this inclusion of nature in the praise of the angels and of mankind is offered in Ps. 148, after which the benediction of the three men in the fiery furnace is patterned.

1. Praise Jehovah from the heavens,
   Praise Him in the heights!
2. Praise Him, all His angels;
   Praise Him, all His host!
3. Praise Him, sun and moon;
   Praise Him, all shining stars!
4. Praise Him, heaven of heavens,
   And the waters above the heaven!
5. They shall praise Jehovah's name;
   For He commanded, and they were created.
6. He established them forever and ever;
   He gave a law which they do not transgress.
7. Praise Jehovah from the earth,
   You dragons and all deeps,
8. Fire and hail, snow and fog,
   Stormy wind fulfilling His word;
9. Mountains and all hills,
   Fruit trees and all cedars;
10. Wild animals and all tame animals,
    Creeping things and winged birds;
11. Kings of the earth and all peoples,
    Princes and all judges of the earth;
12. Young men and also the maidens,
    Old men together with the boys!

13. They shall praise Jehovah's name,
      For His name alone is exalted.
14. His glory is above earth and heaven,
      And He raised up a horn for His people.[104]

In the form of a dual hymnic introduction consisting, first, of a descending line (vv. 1–4), and then of an ascending line, which begins with the lowest class of creatures and rises to the highest, man (vv. 7–12), all the creatures in the heavenly world of God and in the cosmic heaven and then all creatures on earth are invited by God's people, assembled in worship, to glorify the name of the Lord. The name of the Lord is manifest, is known among the people of God, in their worship, inasmuch as this worship manifests God Himself in His redemptive might. But this manifestation of God among His people radiates through the universe, so that all that is in heaven and on earth must join in the laudation of God and in the glorification of His name.

How are we to understand these Biblical testimonies? Do we do justice to these texts if we declare: "Nature reflects the mood of the poet"? [105] Surely not! "Such an appeal to the creatures to praise God was not simply a figure of speech in Israel." Or does this merely involve "the original animation of nature," which was "still in the blood of the people of that time" [106] as a primitive mythical remnant? Of course, also the Biblical witnesses can speak of the worship of the nonhuman creatures only in human terms, and thus only in anthropomorphic terms. However, that which is expressed by these terms is undoubtedly to be affirmed as an objective fact, the reality of which is not dependent on man's saying it. What is involved in the praise of God with which the nonhuman, earthly creature glorifies God?

The decisive answer to this might be contained in the Sanctus recorded in Is. 6:3: "The whole earth is full of His glory." This cannot be conceived as applying to the future. We recall that God's works of creation are from their inception translucent, as it were, for the splendor which is inseparable from God's being and essence. Everything that exists bears, by reason of God's creative words, an imprint of the hand of the Creator in its essence. The words through which creatures are called into being from nonexistence imprint the law of their essence into them. They are what they are by the words of the Creator. In their being, the nonhuman, earthly creatures correspond directly to the words that created them. Their creatural being is the constant, never ceasing response to the words of God addressed to them. "The creature may exist so, that in its existence . . . it duly responds to His (God's) existence, to His word, and His work. In existing, it will express itself so, it will itself be an expression that corresponds to Him as its Creator and Lord. . . . The creature may praise God. It cannot do this of its own free will but only in answer to His command, only in obedience to Him." [107] This praise of God may and must be expressed also by the nonhuman creature. "To conceive also of the being of all other creatures as thanks to God is not only necessary but also salutary, because it constrains us to perceive our human being together with all other creatures as creatural being. As man thanks God and is man by reason of this act, he does no more and no less than all other creatures also do with their being: he does no less than the sun and than Jupiter, but he also does no more than the sparrow on the street or than the commonest mayfly." [108]

The manner in which the nonhuman, earthly creature praises God, the manner in which it exemplifies its relationship to God, the language in which it lauds God, is hidden to us.

> Look how the floor of heaven
> Is thick inlaid with patines of bright gold:
> There's not the smallest orb which thou behold'st,
> But in his motion like an angel sings,
> Still quiring to the young-eyed cherubims;
> Such harmony is in immortal souls;
> But whilst this muddy vesture of decay
> Doth grossly close it in, we cannot hear it.[109]

Even if we cannot hear the nonhuman creatures' hymn of thanksgiving, we do have intimations of its content. We revert to Ps. 148. Here sun, moon, stars, the heavens, and the waters of heaven are exhorted to praise God. Why are these creatures under obligation to do this? Because they are created by God's words of command. "He established them forever and ever; He fixed their bounds which cannot be passed" (v. 6). Perhaps the same basic idea is expressed in Ps. 19:5. A guideline, a canon, has been impressed into the heavens and the firmament which these creatures obey in their being as an inviolable law and which they in that way proclaim to all the world. The implanted word-relatedness of the creatures' being, the logos-nature of the law of their creatural essence, which we perceive only dimly — if not even in a distorted image — in a mathematical, physical, and chemical formula, which approaches us a bit more closely in the inner

101

beauty of its form, but which, in the final analysis, remains hidden to us — it is the means by which these creatures reflect God's glory as they beam this glory forth.

It is evident here that this worship of the nonhuman, earthly creatures is closely related, in one respect, to the worship of the angels. Similar to the angels, these creatures are an "echoing wall." The praise of God issues from them with the inviolability of the law of their essence, which they, in contradistinction to man, do not transgress by their own decision. Therein we find the sublimity, but also the limitation, of this praise. The limitation prevents these creatures from performing an act of love born of personal freedom of choice. It is perhaps, after all, not a mere coincidence that the nonhuman creatures, even the angels, are exhorted by God's people on earth to join in the praise of the congregation. No matter how poor, how imperfect, how dimmed this praise of the congregation may be here on earth, it is nonetheless unique in this respect, that it is in every moment a matter of free choice and results from such a free choice. We noted that also the praise of the angels involves a free choice; however, this is a choice which was made once for all times and, therefore, is really no longer free. There is no personal decision whatsoever involved in the praise of God by the nonhuman, earthly creatures. Therefore their praise obviously first resounds fully when it is joined to man's praise and is thus, in a sense, also released. First in this union will the sounds of the echoing wall develop into the hymnic song. As the worship of the angels is, so to say, open downwards, in order to absorb the worship of the *ekklesia* in the ultimate consummation of all things and to lend to it the mysteriously definitive unity of personal freedom and essential compulsion, the worship of the *ekklesia*, on its part, is open toward the worship of the nonhuman, earthly creatures, in order to absorb it and to carry it to its consummation, as it transmits participation in the eschatological jubilus to it.[110]

Indeed, also the worship of the nonhuman, earthly creatures has, in a certain sense, its history, determined by God's plan of salvation. Through man's likeness to God a mysterious connection was established between man and the nonhuman, earthly creature. In accord with the story of creation, man is the crowning glory, the reigning head, and the sustaining center of the creatural world. What happens to him also affects every other earthly creature. The fracture of the foremost creature's worship by the Fall also casts its shadow into the realm of the remaining creatures. Who has ears to hear, hears not only the uninterrupted praise of God by the creatures, but he also hears some of their "groaning in travail" (Rom. 8:19-23).[111] The world was cursed because of man (Gen. 3:17). Because of man, God placed all of nonhuman, earthly creation under "the bondage to decay" with man. Thus also the praise of God by these earthly creatures is subdued and hidden under sighing and pining, not by reason of their own guilt, but by reason of their relative association of fate with guilty man.

However, also their hope is rooted in this association with man's fate. God's service in Jesus and Jesus' service before God does not only change man's fate, but in doing that it also creates for the nonhuman creature an opening into a new world with a new heaven and a new earth. Thus the incarnation of God also casts its rays into the realm of the mute creatures. Not only the angels but also the beasts assemble about the Son of man (Mark 1:13). The divine power of Christ's sacrifice not only bursts open the doors of the debtors' jail of humankind, but in doing that it also throws off the shackles with which the nonhuman, earthly creature is held in the bonds of futility and decay. With Jesus' resurrection from the dead, the eschatological turning point came also for these creatures, through which the new heaven and the new earth will be materialized in them. When the members of Jesus' body are transformed for the ultimate freedom of their glory, the yoke of bondage will be removed also from the nonhuman, earthly creatures. Then their praise of God will not only be delivered from their pining and sighing but become a new revelation of God's glory. Then these creatures will receive that voice with which they can join in the liturgy of the celestial beings. Then their sounds will become a clear doxology. (Rev. 5:13)

It is obvious here that the hidden center of nature's praise of God is not only God the Creator but also the Redeemer. Not only the eternal Word of the Father arouses the word-nature of the mute creatures to resounding song of praise, but this song of praise will relate especially to the Incarnate Word, the crucified and exalted Christ. The heavenly liturgy of Jesus before God's throne occupies the center of the eschatological jubilus of all creatures, also of the planets, of the beasts, of the plants, of the mountains, of the valleys, and of the seas. For, as the eternally valid sacrifice of Jesus on the cross opens history's sealed future and carries it to its consummation, it also bursts nature's prison and calls forth even from its deepest depths the acclamation of worship, which is directed simultaneously to the Enthroned and to the Lamb.

THE WORSHIP OF THE CHURCH BETWEEN THE LAUDATION OF THE ANGELS AND THE LAUDATION OF NATURE

Also the cosmological place of worship is to be defined as an "in between." On the one side the church's worship on earth is bordered by the worship of the angels, on the other by the worship of those creatures which are still mute to us. The worship of the angels and the worship of the mute creatures form the two extremes. They are so widely separated because, at the one extremity, the greatest sublimity of a personal, ministering devotion to God finds expression in an uninterrupted outpouring of hymns, while at the other extremity, where a devotion springing from a freedom of decision is excluded, the praise is, for the time being, confined to mere sounds, sounds born of the creature's inborn essence. But both extremes meet, inasmuch as both angels and nature serve God as "echoing walls" with the inviolability of their essential laws: the angels with an inviolability springing from a past free decision, the nonhuman earthly creatures with an inviolability materialized by God's Word immediately in their being.

The present worship of the *ekklesia* occupies a position between these two poles. It is distinguished from its two neighbors by the fact that it takes place in a struggle and always springs anew from a decision. It is also distinguished by the fact that it is always interrupted by time, above all, however, by the fact that it is always corrupted by the carnal nature of its representatives. The worship of the church is related to the worship of the angels: It is conducted in a personal freedom and devotion. It is an act, an act vouchsafed by God, but an act executed personally by the members of the church. It is not carried out with the sounds and tones that issue from an inherent law, but, as among the angels, with a speech that approximates the hymn of praise, the loftiest expression of personal devotion. But the worship of the church is also kindred to the worship of the nonhuman, earthly creatures: It is conducted in the same earthly corporeality and in the same transitory place. These two practitioners of worship, man and nature, share an indissoluble communion of fate. Both attain their goal only through the freeing power of Jesus' sacrifice.

And here the worship of the nonhuman creatures is engaged in a movement toward the worship of the *ekklesia*. With its worship the *ekklesia* sets the example for the worship of the earthly creature; with its worship it beckons the earthly creature to join in lauding the mercy of the Lord. Through God's electing act, the earthly creature is deemed worthy in Baptism and Holy Communion to be bearer and conveyor of Jesus' redeeming work in the power of the Word, in Holy Communion to be also bearer and conveyor of His own body and blood. This happens exclusively in these two sacraments, in each in its own way. We are strictly forbidden to deduce from this a general symbolic quality of the creature for Jesus' redemptive work and His grace. But this distinction of the earthly creature in the sacrament nonetheless is poised like a token of promise over all of earthly creation. The hidden, incomprehensible, intracreatural omnipresence of Jesus' sacrificed body, which is materialized since His exaltation at the right hand of God by virtue of the intracreatural omnipresence of God, erects a bridge between the worship of the earthly creature and the worship of the church, in which the sacrificed body of Jesus is also present, namely, in special accretions, in the Word-bound Pneuma and in the Word-bound, Pneuma-borne sacrament. Thus the worship of the *ekklesia* is not inimical to the earthly creature, but stands ready to absorb it with its worship when the Day of the Lord comes.

Would it not also be pertinent here to raise the question regarding the relationship between the church's worship and art? Does not also the nonhuman creature serve in the church's worship, which is, of necessity, conducted in the forms of earthly corporeality? Is this fact not, in the final analysis, the basic reason for all art? May art not be thought of as an act which imprints on the nonhuman creature the sign of its future release for a new mode of being, in which it is fraternally associated with man? Where else could this sign be erected more appropriately than in the worship of the church? Is it not true that all the arts encounter a crisis and fall into decay when they digress from their center of worship? Should not the worship of the *ekklesia* be the place where perhaps also the arts might come to the parting of the ways and find their way back to the particularity of their essence and of their function? May the space which art in every instance will occupy in worship not be understood as the place in which the nonhuman creature is symbolically drawn into the praise of God by the *ekklesia*? May art in worship not be conceived as the sign for the fact that the worship of the church is eschatologically

105

opened for the worship of the nonhuman, earthly creatures, thus also as a sign for the communion of fate between the children of God and the creature in this matter?

Many questions may remain unanswered here. However, it may be stated definitely that the worship of the angels, the church, and the earthly creature has the same focal point, namely, the One seated on the throne and the crucified and exalted Jesus at His right hand. This focal point is present to each, to the angels, the church, and the earthly creatures, but in a different way: in heaven above, the immediate presence on the throne within immediate view; here among us men, the Word-bound Pneuma-presence and the Word-bound, Pneuma-borne sacramental presence, viewed only by faith, down below, in the creatural depths, the general intracreatural omnipresence. But in all three realms it is the Triune God and the one sacrificed and crucified Body that awakens and receives this service offered to God. Therefore this triple worship shows a dynamic movement which tends toward an ultimate organic unity at the end of all things.

Thus the worship of the church finds itself in a threefold "in-between": between the ascension and the return of Jesus; between Baptism-death and the physical death of man; between the supermundane, heavenly creatures and the nonhuman, earthly creatures. The worship of the church finds itself at a point where God's coming world bursts into this world through Pneuma and sacrament, where the new man, resurrected with Jesus, takes form through faith and love and hope in the death of the old man, where the praise of God by the nonhuman creature tends toward the praise of the *ekklesia,* and the praise of the *ekklesia* joins in the praise of the angels. The worship of the church takes place in a threefold, dawning eschatological *transitus:* in the *transitus* of this world to the kingdom of God; in the *transitus* of this mortal, temptable body to its resurrection from the dead; in the *transitus* which liberates nature for the freedom of the children of God and transforms the children of God into angelic being. Essence and form of worship are bounded by its place in this threefold *transitus.*

PART II

THE SALVATION-EVENT IN WORSHIP

5

THE SPIRITUAL NEED FOR WORSHIP

Now that we have recognized the place of the church's worship, we shall attempt to describe what happens in this worship. A description of those outward events in worship that are open to any observer's view does not adequately express what actually takes place there. To be sure, all that happens in worship from beginning to end presents itself to the eye as the activity of man. These human words, gestures, and acts are the physically perceptible body of what takes place in worship. However, what takes place cannot itself be seen, observed, and determined. It cannot be recognized by a "neutral" observer. It is perceived solely by faith. Our task is to express what faith perceives to be taking place when those human words are spoken or sung in worship and when those human gestures and acts are carried out. Therefore what happens in worship is a hidden mystery. We intimate this mystery when we speak of the salvation-event in worship. God is the exclusive subject of this event. The fact that God Himself works on man in acts executed by man makes worship a mystery.

The Christian has accepted the saving Gospel in faith. He has received Baptism and affirmed it in faith. Does he really require another special act in which God does something to him for his salvation? Has not worship as a salvation-event become superfluous for the believer? Does not the Christian's worship consist exclusively in the presentation of his whole life as an offering to God in the love for his neighbor? Can the true love for God be expressed otherwise than in the love for their neighbor? It is granted that a missionary proclamation of the Gospel which calls to faith is necessary. It is granted that Baptism must be administered where the Gospel has been accepted. But is there any call for "worship services" (*Gottesdienste*) as temporally delimited acts beyond the bounds of Baptism and in addition to that one worship which encompasses a person's whole life? And if there should be such other modes of worship, can these be anything but an indication that the Gospel and the salvation vouchsafed in Baptism were not as yet truly accepted? Thus can special modes of worship be anything but a continuation of that missionary proclamation which calls to faith? Are those modes of worship not intended for the imperfect, immature semi-Christian, who did not as yet truly apprehend salvation in his baptism or his confirmation, who must, therefore, really be regarded as a catechumen and thus requires special forms of worship to lead him on to faith? Can these forms of worship be anything other than a training toward the Gospel, than regular missionary arrangements for the people at large? Are these forms of worship not superfluous for the true believer?

The situation in our congregations, a widespread practice in our church, and last but not least a conception of worship which directs many pastors, consciously or unconsciously, in their preparation and administration of worship tend to answer this question affirmatively. Who would deny that the conditions in our congregations render nothing more urgent than the missionary appeal for a true acceptance of the Gospel, which, despite Baptism, instruction, and confirmation in innumerable instances hardly touches the thoughts and the desires of the heart today and therefore does not affect the outward conduct. We shall see that worship dare not withdraw from this missionary task. However, he who would trace the inner need of worship to the obligation of educating the immature and imperfect semi-Christians into whole Christians would thereby destroy its true essence. Whoever beholds in worship only an agency for the completion of an incompletely executed missionary undertaking is undermining worship instead of establishing it. The reasons adduced for the need of worship must prove their validity by the very fact that this need also exists when the missionary task may be regarded as basically solved. It must be shown why worship is an inner, spiritual necessity especially for the true believers, for those who earnestly desire to be Christians. Only when the function of worship for the true believers is recognized and this is made the standard of its essence and its realization, only then may this same worship, without any change in its essence, also assume

110

missionary interests, even though these interests at present undoubtedly demand special programs of the church for the indifferent, the estranged, and near-apostates, programs which do not coincide with the worship of the congregation or cannot be absorbed into it.

In a sense it is true that the worship which takes place beyond the boundary of Baptism adds nothing to the salvation received by the believer when he crossed this boundary. However, this salvation must be preserved until the time of the believer's physical death. That this is done is far from self-evident. Salvation may be lost, frittered away, forfeited. Therefore its preservation involves an act wrought in the power of the Holy Spirit. This act, too, can hardly be designated as anything else than faith. This faith is of course not a constantly repeated step from unbelief to belief. A relapse into the dominion of the antigodly, demonic powers may also occur, which entails the lost condition of unbelief. In that event, indeed, a renewed step from unbelief to belief is necessary, analogous to the first crossing of the boundary to Baptism. This new step will never consist in a repetition of Baptism. It will properly be taken through confession, absolution, and stated reacceptance into the congregation.

But the preservation of salvation through the act of faith does not presuppose the loss of salvation, but it excludes this loss before it occurs. To be sure, the salvation-preserving faith is acquainted with temptation, with trials, with struggles, with affliction. For that reason it is aware that we can never stand before God by virtue of the empirical quality of our conduct and of our heart, but solely by virtue of the faith which apprehends and clings to the saving mercy of God in Jesus Christ. The believer is fully convinced that he sins more daily than his self-observation will ever disclose to him. In this life he remains dependent on his acceptance of sins remitted. Therefore he remains dependent on the Word, through which forgiveness is proffered, distributed, and mediated. For that reason, every spiritual event within Christendom, also worship, is oriented to the forgiveness of sin.[112] Salvation can be preserved only by remaining in the Word, through which the saving act of Jesus Christ embraces and envelops us. In the preservation of salvation all depends on our remaining in the crucified and exalted Christ, into whom we were received in Baptism. To preserve our salvation means nothing less than to preserve the in-being in Jesus Christ that has become fact with us. But to remain in Him means to remain in the Word, in which He is close to us with His saving deed.

111

But to remain in the saving Word involves more than the private reading of the Bible. The saving Word must be addressed to me. The saving Word is vibrant in what takes place between persons. There must be a person who addresses this Word to me in the name of God. This address may and must also take place in a conversation between brother and brother, or in confession by means of absolution. Since my baptism I no longer occupy an isolated position. Since my baptism I am integrated into the people of God of the end time, into the *ekklesia,* which is, in a hidden manner, an epiphany of the body of Jesus Christ on earth. They who have been joined together as members of the body of Jesus cannot do otherwise than retain and preserve this being in Christ especially by means of this togetherness. They assemble as *ekklesia* to the end that the saving Word may become vital in this assembly and the believers may be preserved in the faith. The worship of the *ekklesia* is necessary because we are unable to preserve the obtained salvation in this earthly life otherwise than by resorting ever anew to the living Word, in which Jesus Christ Himself is present with His acts and fruits of salvation and with which He works on us. If someone were to declare that he no longer stood in need of this Word, vital in the *ekklesia,* or that he could speak the Word to himself, he would misjudge his own situation before God in which he finds himself between his baptism and his physical death, he would misunderstand the vitality and the historicalness of the saving Word and the Word-bound Spirit-presence of Jesus Christ, he would deny his membership in the body of Jesus.

But did our deliberations thus far not after all reduce worship to a type of continuation of the missionary proclamation of the Gospel? We will still have to fix our attention on the association of the Word which is vital in the *ekklesia* and which edifies the *ekklesia* with the fundamental missionary Word designed for those outside the *ekklesia.* At the same time we will have to envisage the difference existing between these two forms of the Word. To elaborate this association and this difference probably poses one of the most difficult homiletical tasks. If one takes note of the particularity of the edifying Word, it will become clear that what takes place in worship cannot be construed as a mere continuation of missionary activity even if we bear only the proclamation of the Gospel in worship in mind. This proclamation bears a specific character and has its specific forms, by which it is differentiated, even with the same substance and content, from the purely missionary proclamation. It will be a mistake if the sermon in

112

worship fails to take cognizance of this difference and fails to do justice to the specific character of that Word which is vital in the *ekklesia*.

This misconception of worship as a continuation of the church's missionary activity will arise with a certain logical force so long as we conceive of this saving Word in isolation from Holy Communion. All attempts to demonstrate the inner, spiritual need for worship will remain not only incomplete but also problematical and exposed to misunderstanding so long as they ignore the words "This do in remembrance of Me." In the early church, the newly baptized went to the Eucharist directly from their baptism.[113] A confirmation which is not immediately followed by the confirmands' reception of Holy Communion — practical considerations may occasionally necessitate a short interval — is fragmentary; it has basically repealed itself. As little as there can be an affirmation of the Gospel which does not lead to Baptism, so little can there be an affirmation of Baptism which does not lead to the Lord's Table. Jesus' particular gift to the baptized is this very Lord's Supper.

No one can say exactly what reason moved Jesus to give His disciples His Supper. But the Lord's Supper instituted in the *ekklesia* indubitably preserved it from becoming a "school" with a "doctrine" after the manner of an ancient school of philosophy, or a Jewish sect, or a modern society for the fosterage of a religious *Weltanschauung*. The Lord's Supper proves itself the power which assembles the believers and the baptized again and again as *ekklesia* and which organizes them as such. The celebration of this Meal is the sustaining foundation of the *ekklesia* assembly. There a brother is able to impart the words of forgiveness to me. The basic form for confession and absolution is that of individual confession. As spoken words, the Gospel may be vital also in the family circle. But Holy Communion exists only where the congregation is assembled as *ekklesia*. Nowhere else is the need to assemble for worship seen so singularly cogent as where the command "This do in remembrance of Me" is heard and is obeyed as a blessed prerogative.

The Lord's Supper was instituted by Christ particularly for those who are already members of His body, for the mediation and preservation of salvation. Holy Communion is the specific means of grace of the already formed congregation of disciples. If the preservation of the in-being in Jesus Christ, actualized through Baptism, is the preservation of salvation, then this in-being in the crucified and exalted Christ is executed ever anew through the celebration of the Lord's

Supper and the believing reception of the Eucharistic food. Later on we will have to expand on what takes place in Holy Communion. Here we have to affirm first of all that the desire for Christ's body and blood, given and shed for us, is indelibly imprinted on the believers who were accepted into the body of the crucified Christ and received as members of this body by Baptism. Wherever the Baptism-event is received and preserved in faith, there will also be a desire, reflecting an inner, spiritual need, for the Holy Communion-event. There is no repetition of Baptism; but there is a kind of continuation and renewal of the Baptism-event in the Holy Communion-event. Baptism is the open door leading to the Lord's Table. One cannot pass through this door in faith without being directed to the Lord's Table with the inner compulsion of the Spirit. This urging can never be explained rationally and logically; it will never be intelligible and lucid to me. But it is effectual by the power of the Spirit. One cannot be grafted as a member into this one body of Jesus without an ever new desire for a union with this body and thus for the hidden epiphany of this body. The effect of Baptism, in conjunction with Jesus' institution of His Supper, substantiates the need for the believers' assembling together as *ekklesia* for worship in which the Lord's Supper is celebrated.

We shall see that assemblies for worship are possible without the celebration of the Lord's Supper. Sermon services and prayer services, especially horary prayers, fall into this category. However, such services in which the celebration of Holy Communion is not planned must be conceived, basically, as an isolation of worship elements rooted in the worship service in which Holy Communion is celebrated. Such services tend toward Holy Communion worship services, and this is true particularly of sermon services. They also derive from the Holy Communion worship service, as one might observe especially in the horary prayer. Thus the Holy Communion worship service is the hidden, vibrant center of all worship services. If these detach themselves from this center, if the Holy Communion worship service is no longer preserved as the center supporting the entire worship life, then these detached services will necessarily become stunted and dwarfed. The old horary worship services of the Lutheran Church, which developed largely into a catechetical drill of Biblical texts or even into a vehicle for learning the Latin language, had to vanish.[114] The independent preaching services, which lose their hidden relationship to the Holy Communion service, can hardly be protected from a rationalization of their content and form. Above all,

114

however, the inner, necessary connection of these worship services with the believer's existence remains problematical so long as their need is conceived without its ties to the Holy Communion service. This shows that basically there can also be no theological justification for the worship of the church that is not centrally based on the command "This do in remembrance of Me."

We can, to be sure, establish that Baptism, apprehended in faith, necessarily and logically leads to a desire to partake of Holy Communion. We can also understand the inner association between the gift of Holy Communion and the gift of Baptism. But we are, in the final analysis, at a loss for an intelligent answer to the question why we should also receive the gift of salvation by means of the Lord's Supper after this has already been presented to us through Gospel and Baptism and is kept alive and presented to us ever anew in the proclaimed apostolic Word. The salvation mediated by Word and Baptism does not want for saving power. The forgiveness of sin dispensed by the spoken Gospel and by Baptism is the same as the forgiveness dispensed by Holy Communion. But the mode of presentation is different in Holy Communion from that of the spoken Gospel or Baptism. We do not know why we must receive salvation also in the manner in which Holy Communion conveys it. To be sure, in Holy Communion the gift of salvation itself is concretized in a singular way. The specific manner of the impartation of salvation in Holy Communion also becomes a specific gift of salvation here. In Holy Communion I am not only assured of the remission of my sin by the testamentary words of institution, but this forgiveness is also conveyed to me by a physical reception of the truly present body and the truly present blood of the crucified and exalted Christ, creating here, in the proper *usus*, that wonderful unity of a spiritual and a physical reception. As isolated substances, Jesus' body and blood are, of course, no special gift of salvation. On the contrary! The unbelieving, "unworthy" reception of Holy Communion transmits only the body and blood of Jesus, devoid of the inherent gift of salvation; and in that way body and blood are received only to one's damnation. Thus it is unbelief which rejects the gift of salvation present in Holy Communion; it is this unbelief that causes Jesus' body and blood, in isolation from the inherent gift of salvation, to be received to damnation.

But that does not exclude that the sacrificial, salvation-bestowing body of Jesus is "very profitable," and not "unprofitable," where the wonderful unity of a spiritual and a physical reception takes place, that is, that it itself is taken into the gift of salvation and itself belongs to the gift of salvation. When received in faith, forgiveness of sin and Jesus' sacrificed body form, also with regard to the gift of salvation, an indissoluble union.

But any attempt to ascribe the necessity for the reception of salvation in the special manner of Holy Communion to any other reason than its institution by Christ will miscarry. Also every attempt to explain the necessity of the bodily reception of Jesus' body and blood as an essential reality of the gift of salvation by any reason other than that of Jesus' institution will miscarry. I do not know why I stand in need of precisely this gift of Holy Communion. Jesus Christ alone knows that. I know of my need for this gift only from the fact of His institution; but from that fact I know it with absolute certainty. Therefore the Spirit of Jesus leads, with His peculiar prompting, to the reception of this gift, so that the compliance with the command "This do!" is no legal obedience but an act of the Spirit's spontaneity. However, the imperative form of Christ's institution will result in damnation wherever His institution is disdained in disobedience.

But the spiritual need for worship does not inhere solely in the fact that the believer requires personally and for himself the spoken Gospel and Holy Communion for the preservation and ever new appropriation of the received salvation. Since every member of the *ekklesia* is equally in need of this, it must be a commandment of brotherly love, yes, its foremost commandment, that one brother witness the Gospel to the other and that one serve the other at the Lord's Table. The Holy Spirit cannot be received unless He opens the believers' lips for testimony.

Inasmuch as the proclamation of the Gospel has been entrusted to the church as a whole, this service, too, is entrusted to the entire congregation assembled for worship and in that way also to its individual members, and not only to the ordained and called servants of the Word. It is particularly the Spirit-borne, intracongregational proclamation of the Word, the chief form of which is prophecy, that is not confined to the individual charismatic bearers of this special gift; but also the congregation assembled for worship takes part as such in all of its members in the administration of this gift, as it proclaims, in a manifold way, in the Spirit-filled and Spirit-giving Word the great deeds of God (Acts 2:17 f.; 1 Peter 2:9; 1 Cor. 14:24; Col. 3:16; Eph. 5:18). The Lord will not withhold the prophetic service from those whom He has made prophets and kings. With the inner compulsion of the Spirit, the *ekklesia* assembly will thus become the place in which this service is rendered by individuals especially qualified for this, but simultaneously also by the entirety through each individual member. No member of the congregation may be excluded from the charismatic-prophetic cooperation in the service of the proclamation of the Word, which is administered by the assembled congregation in its entirety. The gifts received in Baptism and in Holy Communion constrain every Christian persevering in the faith not only to witness personally to the world by words and conduct, but they also constrain him to engage in the charismatic-prophetic service in the *ekklesia*, in which the one addresses the Spirit-filled and Spirit-giving Word to the other, and all address it to all.

This participation in the prophetic service of the *ekklesia* already includes also the cooperation of every member of the congregation in the commemoration of Jesus Christ as this is done in Holy Communion. For the establishment of this commemoration is itself proclamation of the Lord's death (1 Cor. 11:26). But this cooperation reaches beyond that. It is indispensable for the proper administration of the Lord's Supper that this Supper is actually celebrated. In default of this, the gift of salvation of Holy Communion does not appear. When I participate in the Lord's Supper as recipient, I am, at the same time, related to my brother at my side; indeed, I am participating in the distribution. My participation in the Meal is not only a proclaiming witness to my brother, but in the realization of the Lord's Supper it is also a cooperating factor in the presentation of the gift of salvation. The commandment "Do this!" contained in the institution does not only place every member of the *ekklesia* on the side of recipients, but it also places him under the spiritual obligation to cooperate actively toward the fulfillment of this command, lest this dispensation of salvation be slighted. But the decisive and fundamental form of cooperation consists in the individual member's coadministration of the Meal itself, which, in a sense, also includes a codistribution of the gift of salvation.

However, the spiritual need for the believers' assembling for worship is not based solely on their need for the preservation and the appropriation of salvation. What takes place in the worship of the church goes beyond that. The God-willed goal is not only our salvation but in our salvation also His glorification through the vital communion with saved sinners.

117

Where the saving gift of salvation is dispensed, the Triune God Himself is present in the dispensing means. Surely, the presence of the Triune God dare not be confined to His presence mediated by the spoken Gospel and Holy Communion and to the event of this mediation; for even the glorified humanity of Jesus shares in the divine intracreatural omnipresence. Also the presence of the Pneuma in the believer dare not be confined to what takes place in worship. The indwelling Pneuma will not forsake the believer as long as he retains the faith, no matter where he may abide. Amid the anxieties of this world, amid trials and temptations, in the quiet chamber, in the cell of a prison, even when the indwelling Spirit is grieved by our conduct (Eph. 4:30), the believer may be assured of the real Spirit-presence of the Lord. Therefore there is no situation in which the Christian does not have immediate access to the Father through Jesus Christ in the Holy Spirit.

At the same time, the distinctiveness of the actual presence of the Triune God through the spoken Gospel and Holy Communion dare not be overlooked. This presence of God in the assembled congregation conveyed by Word and sacrament derives from the presence of God in the flesh of Jesus; indeed, in a new manner it is this presence itself. Between the time of Jesus' ascension and His return, the Word- and sacrament-bound Pneuma-presence of God is the only possible manner for God's presence, incarnated there and then in Jesus' earthly humanity. Today we encounter the humanity of Jesus as the vessel of the saving presence of God actually only in the proclaimed Gospel and in Holy Communion. God's presence through the incarnation of the Son will have to be claimed as the effectual basis for all other modes of God's presence. Therefore every other presence of the Triune God with which the believer may comfort himself is rooted in this presence of the incarnate Jesus, who lived in Palestine, who was exalted to the throne of God, and who fills the universe, for this presence is given us and made apprehensible to us now through Word and sacrament. Thus the particular character of this presence of God granted us through the proclamation of the Word and the celebration of Holy Communion consists in this that God presents Himself to us here in the actually and really present humanity of Jesus, in which Jesus as our human brother in a mysterious union with the eternal Son suffered, died, and rose again for us. That presence of God, which was, is, and ever will be in the flesh of Jesus, is apprehensible to us prior to Jesus' return only in the *ekklesia* assembled about the

118

Word and sacrament, for that flesh of the Eternal Word becomes present for us only in the Word-bound Pneuma and in the Pneuma-borne sacrament.

All praying and professing and praising of the believer is based on this particular, actual presence of God in the God-man, which is indissoluble from Word and sacrament. The cry "Abba, Father!" arises only where God Himself is present in the humanity of Jesus, rendered pneumatically present through Word and sacrament. We can address God with "Thou, Father!" only because God fills, by means of the spoken Gospel and of Holy Communion, the congregation assembled for worship with His presence incarnated in Jesus' humanity. This incarnation-presence of God in the *ekklesia* calls forth the cry "Abba, dear Father!" with the spontaneous urgency of the Spirit. He who loses this presence of God, loses prayer and confession and praise.

To be sure, prayer, confession, and praise pervade the entire life of the believer; but in the everyday life of the Christian these must be nourished again and again from their fountainhead. But this fountainhead is the praying and confessing and praising that wells immediately from the particular, actual presence of God in the God-man, that is, from the presence of God in His *ekklesia* assembled about Word and sacrament. In this praying, confessing, and praising of the assembled *ekklesia* that saving communion between God and man is realized which God had willed from the beginning, which was made possible again through His redemptive act in Jesus, and which one day will be brought to perfection. The fact that this communion is actually carried out and perfected, that God and His people are united in the eternal covenant of love — that is the chief content of the one immutable will of God, into which all other contents are incorporated.

Therefore, we are subject not only to the command to proclaim God's name to all the world, but also to the command to call upon God's name, to pray, to confess, and to praise. But this command is fulfilled only in the Spirit, who is the Word- and sacrament-bound epiphany of Jesus' humanity in the *ekklesia*. What was said of the commandment "This do in remembrance of Me!" might also be said of the commandment "Pray, confess, and praise the name of the Lord!" Its fulfillment springs from the spontaneous urge of the Spirit. Where the particular presence of God in the God-man eventuates and is apprehended in faith, it follows inevitably that the believers pray, confess, and praise with one accord and in the unanimity of the Spirit, and thus beam back on the Giver of all good gifts the light of the eternal glory that burst upon them in the Incarnate Word.[115]

When the glorification of the Triune God by the *ekklesia* through prayer, confession, and praise is recognized as the "ultimate" meaning of worship and as the very core of the eternal will of God, then the question arises in a radically new aspect: What is the relationship between this particular worship of the congregation assembled in the name of Jesus and the service the believers render God in their daily life? The opinion that in this world the only possible orientation of the Christian existence to God is its orientation to ministering love toward the neighbor must be ruled out as a fallacy. To be sure, as Luther explicitly shows in his explanation of the Second Table, it is correct to say that the believer is oriented to God and serves Him especially where he loves and serves his neighbor in emulation of Jesus' example. But that does not abolish the fact that a First Table precedes the Second Table and is preeminent to it; and the obedience to this First Table yields Spirit-wrought manifestations of the fear and love of God, which are oriented directly to God.

Already in this transitory world God demands of the believer and gives to the believer an activity in prayer, in confessing invocation, and in lauding glorification, which is oriented directly to Him. It is correct to say that this Spirit-wrought activity may become a testimony and proclamation to the neighbor and in that way prove of help to him. However, this is not the immediate intention and the real aim of this activity, but it is, in God's pleasure, an additive; however, it will not be that if it is thus planned and intended. It is correct to say that the discipleship of Jesus which serves the neighbor in love flows from the Word- and sacrament-mediated particular presence of God in the God-man; but it is not true that this particular worship of the terrestrial church fulfills its purpose exclusively by making possible that worship which consists in love for the neighbor. It is implicit in God's plan of salvation that the church here on earth serve Him in two related, yet distinct, manners: in the particular worship of the assembled congregation and in a life of obedience. These two cannot unite into one act as long as the physical resurrection from the dead has not taken place.

Nor may the earthly worship consisting of prayer, lauding confession, and glorification be designated as a questionable emergency in view of the final worship goal reached in the resurrection of the flesh. For in this particular worship of the *ekklesia* the imperishable

120

element is already present, which will one day swallow up and absorb the second manner of worship, the believers' everyday life of obedience. It is precisely this particular worship of the congregation assembled in the name of Jesus that already reaches out beyond the preliminary and the perishable into the eternal, the enduring. In this worship a part of the ultimate and enduring worship already appears, while the Christians' "worship by life" is bound to the conditions of this world and will pass away with them. The believers' longing for the return of the Lord and for the heavenly Jerusalem, where there will no longer be a temple, includes this very longing that their entire physical being, in eschatological transformation, be engrossed in something which they in this flesh can perform only fragmentarily, distortedly, and feebly, namely, to magnify God with all angels and creatures in unending praise, thanksgiving, and adoration.

This eschatological expectation and longing completes the basis for the spiritual need of worship in the congregation of believers assembled as the *ekklesia*. The Spirit, who heralds the coming eon of the physical resurrection, cannot but, already in the *ekklesia* on earth, let that glorification of God begin which will itself be perfected in the final consummation and remain in perfection in all eternity.

6

DUALITY IN THE PNEUMATIC EVENT OF WORSHIP

In the Apology of the Augsburg Confession, Art. XXIV, *De missa,*
Melanchthon devoted a rather lengthy study to the question: "What
is sacrifice and what are the species of sacrifice?" (16—65), which is
basic for the doctrine of worship. He introduces his study with a
differentiation between sacrament and sacrifice. He uses the word
"ceremony," or "holy work," as a general term embracing both sacrament and sacrifice. With this he refers to the visible acts performed
by man by way of worship. Such a ceremony, or holy work, may
be either sacrament or sacrifice.

A sacrament is that external act of worship "in which God presents to us that which the promise annexed to the ceremony offers."[116]
Baptism is mentioned as an example for such a sacrament. When
using the term "sacrifice," we must distinguish two types: the propitiatory sacrifice (*sacrificium propitiatorium*) and the thank offering
and praise offering (*sacrificium* εὐχαριστικόν). The former renders
satisfaction for guilt and sin, placates God's wrath, effects reconciliation, and procures forgiveness of sin; the latter, on the other hand,
does not propitiate, but it is offered by those already reconciled to
express their gratitude to God for His gift of mercy. Christ's death
is the only propitiatory sacrifice, the various symbolical prefigurements
of His sacrifice in the sacrifices of the Old Covenant notwithstanding.
Thank offering and praise offering are "the preaching of the Gospel,
faith, prayer, thanksgiving, confession, the afflictions of the saints, in
general, all the good works of the saints." [117] Also the "ceremony of

the mass" may be termed a praise offering.[118] Consequently, there are also acts of worship which are sacrifice. "Sacrifice is a ceremony or work which we render God in order to afford Him honor." [119] A sacrifice comprising an act of worship can never be a propitiatory sacrifice presented to God by us; it is a thank offering and praise offering. *Sacramentum* and *sacrificium*, God's gift of salvation to us and our devotion to God in thanks and praise, are therefore, according to Melanchthon's Apology, the two pillars of all that takes place in worship.

Melanchthon's exposition shows that Holy Communion, for example, may be viewed under a double aspect. For undoubtedly the aforementioned definition of a sacrament also applies to Holy Communion: in it God bestows His salvation on us. However, it may also be conceived as thank offering and praise offering. The preaching of the Gospel, cited by Melanchthon as an example for praise offering, also fulfills all the conditions here laid down for the concept of a sacrament. It is an act of worship to which God in His Word attached great promises. The content of these promises, namely, forgiveness of sin, life, and eternal bliss, is offered and conveyed through the Gospel sermon. We will have to agree that the function of conveying salvation expresses the essence of the Gospel sermon more immediately than its function as praise offering. Also the Gospel sermon is, in Melanchthon's thinking, simultaneously sacrament and sacrifice.

Melanchthon's differentiation between sacrament and sacrifice within the compass of ceremonies reveals the peculiar dual structure of what takes place in a hidden, namely, pneumatic, manner: during the external, perceptible acts of worship: God transmits His gifts of salvation to us *(Deus nobis exhibet)*, and we present thank offerings to God in prayer, confession, and praise *(nos Deo reddimus)*. In adaptation to Melanchthon's terminology, these two sides of worship have been called the sacramental and the sacrificial.[120] This differentiation coincides essentially with Luther's well-known concept of worship, as he expressed it, for example, in a sermon delivered on the Seventeenth Sunday After Trinity, on the occasion of the dedication of the castle church in Torgau. The ultimate mission of the new church consists in this "that nothing else be done in it than that our dear Lord Himself talk to us through His holy Word and that we, in turn, talk to Him in prayer and song of praise." [121] In more recent discussions on the essence of worship attention is repeatedly called to this twofold activity in worship.[122] Melanchthon's elaborations have also shown us that one dare not divorce these two sides of worship activity and mechanically assign them to individual parts of worship.[123] Rather, the two sides pervade each other in the individual acts of worship, as the examples of sermon and Holy Communion illustrated.[124]

The reason for this pervasion will be seen in the following facts. In worship, the Lord becomes present to His congregation only by man's proclamation of the Gospel and the administration of Holy Communion in obedience to the command of institution. Proclamation of the Gospel and celebration of Holy Communion vouchsafe the congregation the presence of the Lord and of His gift of salvation, because they are carried out in conformity with Christ's divine mandate of institution. Therefore the people who proclaim the Gospel and administer Holy Communion must place their human acts into the institution context implicit in Christ's mandate. And in a large measure this is done also by the invocation of the mighty name of Jesus. The human actions which fill the worship service from beginning to end are entirely dependent on the Triune God's filling them with His action. In view of His promise we are certain that the Lord will proclaim His own Word through the apostolic words uttered by human lips, and that He, in the "ceremony" of Holy Communion, will cause the bread and the wine to be His body and blood given and shed for us. But that certainty includes the very conviction that an activity "in the Spirit," a pneumatic activity, is involved here, which, on man's part, is entirely bracketed and borne by prayer. The Gospel can be proclaimed and heard only by way of prayer, the Lord's Supper can be prepared, administered, and received only by way of prayer. Therefore prayer is "a total dimension of worship"[125] which also pervades its sacramental side.

On the other hand, the congregation's Spirit-effected response to the gift of salvation, conveyed in Word and sacrament, is itself word. Also where this response involves a physical gesture, this gesture is not mute, but vital through the words accompanying it.[126] This responding, confessing, thanking, and glorifying word of the congregation will always recall the great and saving deeds of God's might; it will acknowledge, laud, and glorify them prayerfully, and in this manner also proclaim and present them to others. It is precisely the priestly service of the congregation that thus becomes a proclamation of the wonderful deeds of God (1 Peter 2:9). Above all, however, the "Eucharist" will become a grateful proclamation of the Lord's death, especially in the consecration of the bread and the wine (1 Cor. 11:26;

10:16). It is particularly in the Lord's Supper that we find God's gift and the congregation's devotion united into an indissoluble union. — This mutual pervasion of the two sides of the worship activity does not eliminate the right to differentiate between the acts whose principal function it is to convey God's gift of salvation and such as pertain principally to the congregation's devotion. It may have become clear now why the sacramental side of worship never appears without the sacrificial side, and, conversely, how the sacrificial side may always include the sacramental function.

The side of spiritual activity in worship immediately directed to God is based exclusively on that activity through which God addresses Himself to man and offers him and conveys to him His gift of salvation. The Word evokes the response, the gift of God evokes man's devotion to God. Admittedly, no rigid law for the organization of worship can be deduced from this. The congregation assembling for worship is always derived, as a congregation of baptized believers, from the Word received and the gift received. Every worship is response from the very beginning, response to the gifts received in Baptism and in confirmation and in every preceding worship service. And yet also the form of worship will reflect a bit of the fact that prayer, confession, thanksgiving, and praise arise in response to the newly granted presence of God. Therefore we, too, are obliged to bear in mind first of all God's granting and giving as we attempt to describe what happens in worship in a spiritual way.

7

WORSHIP AS A SERVICE OF GOD
TO THE CONGREGATION

THE FUNDAMENTAL AND EDIFYING WORD

We may speak of the fundamental Word in a double sense. There is a Word which is fundamental for the church's proclamation in all situations until the end of time. That is the Word spoken by the witnesses of Christ's resurrection, who were commissioned with this proclamation by the risen Lord. This original testimony of Jesus' resurrection is peculiarly related to the prophetic Word of the Old Testament. The content of the original apostolic testimony of Jesus' resurrection, combined with the Word of the Old Testament, is the church's rule and guide for all times and for every proclamation. Since the death of the last commissioned witness of Jesus' resurrection every proclamation of the church can be only a transmission of this Word which founds the church itself.[127] In that sense, every proclamation of the church since the death of the apostles is a word founded on the fundamental Word.

But we may speak of the fundamental Word also in another sense. The Word by which a congregation is called into being from Jew and Gentile, the Word through which the individual is added to the congregation, may also be designated as the fundamental Word. To be sure, historically the apostolic Word was, also in the aforementioned sense, chiefly a fundamental Word, a Word that founded individual congregations and converted individual people. The first historical presentation of the Word necessarily had to be such a Word, a Word that invited to the *ekklesia*. But this Word that engenders congregations and the Christian estate and is fundamental in this sense cannot be confined to the historical Word of the apostles. In every age the church must proclaim to the world the Word that is fundamental in the sense indicated here.

The apostles did not only lead Jews and Gentiles to conversion, to faith, to Baptism, to the *ekklesia,* but they also proclaimed their Word in the *ekklesia* and for this *ekklesia* that was called into being by them. In this sense the Word of the apostles was not only fundamental but also edifying, it was not only a planting but also a watering Word. In fact, in the New Testament we have the apostolic Word, which remains fundamental for the church's proclamation, only in the form of edification for the congregations. This is seen especially in the epistles of the New Testament but also in the gospels. The form and the function of the apostles' Word which calls the unbelievers to faith must first be disclosed by us from the New Testament writings, but the form and the function of the apostles' Word which addresses itself to the already believing congregations is witnessed to us in the New Testament directly. It becomes evident here that a distinction must be made between the Word which calls the unbelievers to faith and the Word addressed to those who already believe, but also that the Word that edifies the congregations ever reverts to the Word that engenders the congregations and thus is nothing other than a repetition, a recollection, a development, a deepening, and an application of that same Word which once called the congregations into being.[128] The Word that edifies, nurses, nourishes, leads, and preserves the congregations always contains, in substance, the Word which founds the congregations, even though the expression, the form, the thought-pattern, and the function of the Word may change. And therefore the edifying Word shares fully in the promises that inhere in the Word which calls the church as a whole and each individual congregation into being, provided that the edifying Word is identical in content and substance with the Word of the commissioned eyewitness of the resurrected Christ.

The Forms of the Proclamation of the Word in Worship

The missionary Word, which calls the unbelievers to faith, has basically but one form: It is the heraldic cry of the commissioned witness, who confronts those whom his testimony calls as the one bearer of the one message. The edifying Word, on the other hand, has a multiplicity of forms and bearers. In the New Testament there is "a fairly confusing wealth of pneumatic speech characteristic" of this edifying Word.[129] To be sure, this wealth does not manifest itself in the same manner at all times and at all places. The diversity of the intracongregational Word is dependent on the diversity of the spiritual gifts, which cannot be produced by force but are gifts in the strictest sense of the word. But no congregation of baptized and confirmed Christians that gather about Word and sacrament is devoid of gifts of the Spirit. Therefore also the proclamation of the Word in such a congregation must not have only one bearer and consist in only one form, but must be attended to, depending upon the measure of gifts and services, by several bearers and, above all, also by the congregation as a whole. The apostolic Word of the New Testament is an urgent appeal to every era to blazon forth the intracongregational Word in the multiplicity of its forms. The basic forms of this proclamation of the Word which have maintained themselves in the church's worship through the years, but which by no means exhaust the wealth of the forms possible, will be shown here in their framework and in their occasional specific meaning.

The Reading of Scripture

The reading of Holy Scripture is the most important form of proclamation of the Word, especially the reading of the New Testament. Not every reading of Scripture need be expounded by a sermon. The congregation is entitled to come face to face with the prophetic and the apostolic Word of Scripture also directly and without an accompanying exposition. The apostolic witness whose indissoluble connection with the prophetic witness of the Old Covenant we constantly bear in mind has a right to address the congregation directly without the interposition of expounding comment. Of course, every gospel and every epistle of the New Testament is dictated and modified by a certain situation. But the concretion which the apostolic witness received at the time by its respective situation does not in any way contravene the enduring apostolic authority of the concrete Word. Precisely in the concretion which it received there and then in the decades after Christ's death and resurrection, it must be for all times not only the exclusive authority for the church's proclamation but also the foremost, the most inviolable, and the noblest instrument for the revelation of what happened in Jesus for our salvation.

In the reading of the apostolic Word, the apostle of Jesus Christ here and now steps into the midst of the congregation with his church-founding testimony in order to nourish it with this Word. For we have no other access to the salvation-event than this testimony deposited in Holy Writ. The apostle is part of God's plan of salvation because, in the absence of his Word, the saving act of God in Christ and thus every act of salvation from the beginning of the world would be mute. First through the apostolic Word is God's saving activity disclosed to us as an activity now and here and as conveying our salvation now and here.[130] This Word is "the perceptible medium of God's uninterrupted, gracious presence in His congregation on earth."[131] The Spirit-presence of Jesus cannot be granted us without the presence of the testimony issuing from the lips of the apostles. The historical form of the church-founding Word must, as such, also become immediately the present, edifying Word. And this is accomplished by reading the Scriptures independently of the sermon. This act of reading liberates the essentially oral and living Word of the apostles from its necessarily written form and again imparts to it its character as oral testimony with Messianic, proclamatory, executive authority. This is especially true of the gospels and of the chief content of every gospel, the Passion and Easter story. The proclamation of these stories through the reading of Scripture in the worship service bears within it the apostolic power of a pneumatic manifestation of the Jesus-event.

The Sermon

Here we construe the sermon as a specific type of proclamation of the Word. An individual arises in the assembled congregation and expounds Scripture in the form of testimony. No worship may be without the proclamation of the Word. No worship may be without the reading of Holy Scripture. One may pertinently ask the question whether gatherings for worship may be conducted without the delivery of a sermon, as for instance, the daily prayer worship. If what we said about the reading of the Passion and Easter story is true, then the sermon may, under certain circumstances, be omitted also from a worship service in which these stories are read. However, in the church's life the sermon must necessarily occupy its place at the side of the Scripture reading as the second basic type of the proclamation of the Word. Excluding very unusual exceptions, it dare especially not be absent from the worship which gathers the ekklesia about Word and sacrament.

129

With this statement we stand firm against the sermon problem *(Predigtnot)* of the Evangelical church. This problem will not be surmounted by having the delivery of the sermon recede into the background in favor of other acts in the church's worship life. In view of the plenitude of pneumatic speech in the New Testament congregations, especially the Eastern Orthodox Church and the Roman Catholic Church of the West, to whom the sermon problem of the Evangelical church seems unknown, must be asked whether their worship services have not to an alarming degree lost the apostolic Word in the form of a free, witnessing, pneumatic speech, so that, in the place of our sermon problem, they suffer from a far more incisive worship problem, which is all the graver when it is not recognized as such. There can be no renewal of the church's worship life when the spiritual necessity of the sermon is overlooked and its indispensable function in the proclamation of the Word is questioned. Neither can the sermon problem of our church be overcome so long as the sermon is viewed in isolation and its articulate function in the totality of worship is ignored. The preacher will not be able to serve the congregation properly through the sermon so long as he, as the congregation's mouthpiece, cannot pray properly with the congregation. To overcome the sermon problem decisively, the church, its ministers, and its members will have to become sensitive to the fullness of the act of worship and translate this into a proper pneumatic execution. If that which is not "sermon" in the worship service becomes vital and vibrant in such pneumatic execution, then we may assume that the healing and quickening Spirit will not have passed the sermon by either.

The sermon serves the apostolic Word. This is not a timeless Word. It is a concretely historical Word. It must become a concretely historical Word also today. Just as it was adapted to the situation of its day in the original concretion, so it will also address itself to our situation today and in its present concretion permit itself to be molded by our situation. To that end it requires the expositor, the minister of the apostolic Word and as such also its witness. For it is all-important that the same apostolic Word which was proclaimed there and then as the church-founding testimony of Christ be spoken identically in substance now and here. The church contends for the preservation of this substantial identity of the apostolic Word in its arduous dogmatic controversies, which result in the formulation of its dogma. The content of the dogma, which preserves the substantial identity of the apostolic Word in the church's manifold proclamations, must therefore also determine the content of the sermon. That does not imply that the sermon must repeat dogmatic formulas, just as little as a sermon is comprised of a conglomerate of Bible passages. But this does mean that the sermon, as it reconcretizes the apostolic Word and thus performs its main function, dare not contain statements which conflict with the aforementioned dogma. Whoever assumes that he can preserve the substantial identity of the apostolic Word and the real substance of the dogma in a new concretization of the Word, as he pronounces statements, for example, with regard to Jesus' return or to His incarnation which contravene the explicit statements of Scripture or the Scriptural confessional writings, is laboring under a delusion. The message which indeed requires a new concretion from time to time by exposition and testimony is incarnated in a very concrete word form (1 Cor. 15:2), which is by no means confined to the one name Jesus Christ but also consists in word-bound unfolding of all that this name involves.

This dependence of the sermon content on Holy Scripture and the Confessions in no way militates against the historical, free, concrete, pneumatic character of the sermon. The Pneuma, which enables the sermon to become pneumatic speech, is the Pneuma of Jesus, which was poured out over the apostles at Pentecost, which is poured out over the baptized in the rite of Baptism, and which is granted the minister of the Word in his ordination as a gift for his ministry (1 Tim. 4:14; 2 Tim. 1:6). Without detracting from its vitality, its newness, its power, which apprehends and pervades the present moment, this Pneuma draws from no other source than the Word in its original apostolic form. The Pneuma is poured out only in association with this concrete, historical apostolic Word and only by means of this Word. Therefore the free pneumatic speech of the sermon, which issues from this Pneuma, never contradicts the apostolic Word of the Gospel.

With this point clarified, we may and must now emphasize the pneumatic freedom of the sermon. A true exposition of Holy Scripture is out of the question if the Word of Scripture is not reborn by the Holy Spirit in the preacher. The words of the sermon reveal that the apostolic Word possesses the power for its own reproduction in the words of the witness. A sermon is an exposition of the apostolic Word in the form of testimony. The testimonial character of the sermon consists in this that the Word of the apostles is attested by man as a

Word apprehended, believed, and experienced in its saving power. In the sermon the apostolic Word meets the congregation through the preacher's testimony as a dynamically operative word. The sermon already derives from the event toward which the Scripture reading tends. The reading of Scripture purposes, in the power of the Spirit, to communicate the salvation-event, witnessed in the apostolic Word, as a present event to the *ekklesia* and through the *ekklesia* to the world. No one is able to preach aright unless this present revelation of the salvation-event through Word and Spirit has been imparted to him. It is true that "faith comes from what is heard" (Rom. 10:17); but it is likewise true that the sermon of the church constantly flows from faith. Thus the sermon serves the apostolic Word in this way that by it (not by the preacher's "confessions") the power of the apostolic Word is attested, and by this power the past salvation-event is revealed and presented as present salvation. The sermon is a ministering instrument for this inherent power of the Word, placing the salvation-event carried out in Jesus' flesh into the present time and dispensing here and now the salvation effected in that event. As expounding testimony and as testifying exposition, the sermon, as an activity in the Pneuma, builds a bridge between the there and then of the salvation-event in Jesus and the now and here of God's presently saving activity in us.[132]

By virtue of the substantial identity of the sermon's content with the concretely historical Word of the apostles and by virtue of the new Word concretion, born of the working of the Spirit, the sermon becomes the medium by which the Triune God Himself offers, conveys, and dispenses the salvation in Jesus to the hearers. Therefore the sermon is related in substance to the Absolution. To be sure — and this becomes especially clear from the New Testament epistles — words of admonition and of guidance for the present-day, practical problems of life will not be lacking in the sermon. However, in its core the sermon will convey, in the form of expository testimony, the comfort of Jesus' gift of salvation, it will dispense the forgiveness of sin gained for us by Jesus.[133]

This dispensation is the hidden center of the sermon; surely not so, that this hidden center appears in each and every sermon in like manner; surely not so, that a formal pronouncement of the forgiveness of sin will be made in the sermon — although it is not entirely out of the question that, in certain circumstances, this hidden center may come to the fore directly and in a concrete verbal form. At all events, the promise of the forgiveness of sin will always be the hidden center of the sermon in a manner that all that is said in it is spoken as in the presence of Jesus' cross and resurrection and is therefore illumined by this cross and resurrection. Even where the sermon admonishes and exhorts the congregation to conform its life to Christ's life, yes, especially there, will the sermon not be distracted from what happened in Jesus' cross and resurrection, but from the vantage point of this event and with a view to the time when this event will culminate in Jesus' return will the sermon chart the course for the congregation's life.

The Absolution

In the Absolution the hidden center of the sermon emerges as a special act. There the spoken Word of the Gospel is presented in a very concentrated form. Absolution is a condensation of the Gospel as Word, comparable only to the condensation of the Gospel in the reception of the body and blood of Jesus Christ. A concentration in the personal transmission of the gift corresponds to the concentration of the gift itself: absolution is pronounced to the individual who confesses his sins. It is the most individual form of the Gospel proclamation; in this respect it is entirely comparable to Baptism. Therefore individual or private confession and individual or private absolution are the basic forms of this act. This does not preclude that confession and absolution may be arranged for a number of people and made a common action, representing a specific worship service. And more than that. Also in other worship services, especially in the so-called main service (Hauptgottesdienst), an opportunity should be afforded the entire congregation, even if only occasionally and not regularly, to confess its sins publicly and to receive the comfort of forgiveness. This may be done at the beginning of worship or, occasionally, also after the sermon. No matter what detailed order may be adopted here, under no circumstances should the confession of sins by the entire congregation and the resultant comforting promise of forgiveness be omitted. Of course, the wording of the formula of absolution in private confession and the wording for the pronouncement of forgiveness in the case of public sin may and perhaps should be different. It is entirely appropriate that this concentrated proclamation of the Gospel should take various forms, changing with the diversity of the act.

However, this does not preclude that a pronouncement of forgiveness digressing from the wording of the formula of absolution in the case of a public sin shares in the promises of absolution without restriction. This pronouncement of forgiveness does not merely indicate that forgiveness of sins is to be found, let us say, at the cross of Jesus. In fact, according to Luther's bold statement against Karlstadt, forgiveness of sins is not to be found for us at the cross. The cross gained forgiveness of sins for us, but does not dispense forgiveness. Forgiveness is dispensed in the Word.[134] The words of absolution or the pronouncement of forgiveness following a public sin actually grant God's remission of sin for Jesus' sake. These words bring God's forgiveness immediately to the people who hear them, so close that they can apprehend it. The gift itself is present in these words, to be received and accepted in faith. The fact that the oral proclamation of the Gospel is the vessel that conveys Jesus' gift of salvation is seen nowhere else so clearly as in the words of absolution. Therefore, in addition to the pneumatically free words of Gospel proclamation in the sermon, each worship service should contain a few concise and comprehensive words of promise of the gifts of the Gospel. Under no circumstances may this form of proclamation of the Word be dispensed with in confession itself.

The Salutation and Benediction

The worship service is interspersed with a number of formulas which are, similar to the Absolution and the pronouncement of forgiveness of sins, a concentrated proclamation of the Word. Salutation, Pax, Pulpit Salutation, Pulpit Benediction, and the Blessing spoken at the dismissal of the congregation fall into this category. The function of these formulas of salutation and of benediction is closely related to the function of the words of absolution. Luther rightfully called the *Pax Domini* in Holy Communion a public absolution for the communicants.[135] Salutation and Benediction merge into one another.[136] The Salutation includes a benediction, which is carried out, significantly, at the beginning of an action. The Salutation joins the participants in the action through the gift transmitted in it. This joining function of the Salutation becomes especially apparent in the mutual salutation.

In a specific sense, the Benediction stands at the end of an action, at the end of the sermon, at the end of the entire worship service. This benediction is always a "final" word, comprehending all other words spoken thus far. It is spoken, as it were, on the threshold of a farewell. It dismisses the person blessed into a new situation, into a new task. The Benediction pronounced over confirmands and over called officials is likewise such a final word spoken on a threshold, which

134

simultaneously introduces a new reality, a new gift, and a new task. The Benediction spoken over a couple entering the state of Christian matrimony also fits into this framework. Even the burial formula, which ventures to address the deceased and announces his future resurrection from the dead to him on this threshold, manifestly partakes of the internal structure of the words of benediction.

This structure of the words of salutation and of benediction resemble the words of absolution inasmuch as they also possess an exhibitive character. These words have a meaning far different from anything that the words "to wish" convey. To be sure, they include an imploring, petitioning address to the Lord; but the words of benediction are, at the same time, spoken with the certainty of being heard. With the conviction of fulfillment, the Benediction places the gift petitioned for upon those who are being blessed. It is spoken "in the Spirit," consequently, in Christ and in His power. To be sure, Christ did not issue to His church any explicit mandate to pronounce blessings; but He Himself blessed (Mark 10:16). When departing from this earth, He pronounced a blessing on His disciples (Luke 24:50). The entire work of Jesus is summarized in His mission to bless, because Abraham's blessing was fulfilled in Him (Acts 3:25 f.). He let His disciples share in His power to bless (John 14:12). The disciples' salutation of peace is not an empty formula, but filled with pneumatic reality (Luke 10:5 f.; Matt. 10:12 f.). And the resurrected Christ does not withdraw the power and authority which He here bestowed on His disciples. The words of the departing Christ: "I am with you always, to the close of the age" (Matt. 28:20) richly confer this power on them.

A church which would only ask for a blessing in the form of prayer but would no longer venture to bless in direct address would be of little faith and disobedient to the obligation implicit in the transmitted authorization to bless. The Lord, who is present with His power to bless in the words of the Salutation and the Benediction, makes these words the vessel of His gift of blessing. Jesus does not grant peace through His disciples as the world gives peace (John 14:27), for the world can merely wish itself "peace." "The salutation with which the disciples enter a house is not a wish, but a gift, which is either accepted or declined; it is so real that in the instance of declination the εἰρήνη ("peace") returns to the disciples." [137]

As in the Absolution, the sacramental character of the words is clearly seen in the Benediction. In the power of the promise of Christ, in the power of His Word-bound Pneuma-presence, the words of the Benediction convey the gift which they express. In his exposition of Gen. 27:28 f., Luther recognized and expressed this exhibitive character of the Benediction with unexcelled clarity. The words of the Benediction are by no means "only an empty rigmarole," they are not *exoptatio* ("wish"), but *donatio* ("gift"), they are "real blessings." They are not to be conceived as optative but as indicative. "They actually send and convey what the words express." This is true not only of the patriarchs' blessing in the Old Covenant; no, "through Christ's priestly office we, too, have blessings of this type in the New Covenant." Luther illustrates this with the Absolution, proving that the inward structure and the function of the words of the Benediction resemble the words of the Absolution.[138]

With this exhibitive conception of the words of the Benediction we are by no means promoting a "word-magic"; for the Triune God Himself is operating in the Benediction through the agency of words and by reason of His promises. In Num. 6:27 we find the promise attached to the Aaronic Blessing that the Lord Himself will bless His people if His "name is put upon" the congregation.[139] The Lord alone is the Giver of the blessing. The actual receipt of this gift by man by no means coincides with its mere presence. Similar to the gift of absolution and the gift of the sacraments, this gift is received only by faith. Faith does not effect the exhibitive power of the words of the Benediction, but it receives the gift, offered as a present benefit by virtue of the exhibitive power of the words of the Benediction. For that reason the Benediction also involves an act of judgment when the proffered gift is rejected. Just because of its exhibitive power, the Benediction becomes identical with a curse for unbelief.[140]

The Salutation and the Benediction are so often viewed as incidental formulary matters, both by him who pronounces them and by them who are addressed in them. But as a matter of fact, they number among the most important parts of the service. Since the special confessional service is the legitimate place for the words of absolution, it is very important that the remaining services contain analogous exhibitive words of power in the Salutation and Benediction as a fixed component of the service. For a revival of a proper and objective understanding of what goes on in worship, it is decisive that all participants regain the true pneumatic use of the Salutation and the Benediction.

The Biblical Psalm and the Psalmody of the Ekklesia

The Psalter of the Bible plus the Old and New Testament canticles are the church's prayer book and its hymnbook in one. When these Biblical psalms are prayed and sung in worship, the words of Holy Scripture are directly proclaimed. In verbal content, the singing of psalms is closely related to the reading of Scripture. The element of witnessing proclamation is not lacking either; this is already intimated in the manner of presentation. When the church takes the psalms on its lips, as for instance in the prayer psalms, it testifies that it has taken these words into its heart and now professes them as its own. Especially the antiphon and the Gradual psalmody present the Word of Scripture in such a manner that the hearers and certainly also the singers may, so to say, steep themselves in them. This type of presentation of the Word may effect a meditative appropriation, a spiritual "eating" of the Word such as is achieved in hardly any other form of proclamation in worship.

Significant importance must also be assigned to the psalm singing inasmuch as the Scriptural words are here presented not by an individual, not by pastor or preacher, but by the choir and choir director. The congregation already participates in this concentrated form of presentation of the Word in the mutual salutation. In the singing of the psalms, authorized members of the congregation face the remaining members as preacher and lector do. Thus the singing of psalms represents a prime type of participation in the charismatic-prophetic service of proclamation by nonordained members of the congregation. The segment of the congregation not immediately participating in the singing must also lend ear here as it does to the sermon and the reading of Scripture. The true hearer is by no means condemned to passivity. Whoever listens properly, will also join in prayer and praise. The reception of the Word involves real activity on the part of the believing recipients, however, in a manner that they, in this activity, rest from all "works" because God grants them His rest.

In the *ekklesia's* psalm hymn the entire congregation participates in the proclamation of the Word. The word "hymn" applies not only to the psalm songs found in the Evangelical hymnal, which reconstruct the Biblical psalms to hymns for the congregation, but also to that type of songs to which 1 Cor. 14:26; Col. 3:16; Eph. 5:18 manifestly allude, the content of which may be inferred from the New Testament canticles, from the hymn of the celestial church of the Revelation of St. John, and from the fragments which found their way into New Testament epistles (1 Tim. 1:16; Phil. 2:6 ff., etc.), and which live on, especially, among the hymns of the Reformation era.

In these hymns the great deeds of God, as they are apprehended by the congregation's faith from the apostolic sermon and as they live in the congregation's faith, are affirmed and glorified in hymn form. Thus these hymns approximate a confession of faith, as also a prayer of thanksgiving. In the framework of the multiple forms of proclamation they are related to the sermon, inasmuch as, in contradistinction to the reading of Scripture, the message is here affirmed in a new version which is already appropriated and accepted in faith. In the terminology of Melanchthon and of the Erlangen liturgiologists, the sacramental element predominates over the sacrificial in these songs. The genuine congregational hymn always embraces also the sacramental element. "In it the congregation not only carries petition, praise, and thanks before God, but it also preaches to itself, it proclaims and testifies, it reproves, admonishes, and comforts itself mutually." [141] Those hymns of the church in which this preaching, proclaiming, and witnessing are preeminent we here call the psalm hymn of the *ekklesia*. In the Reformation, Christendom was favored with a revival of the spiritual gift of New Testament psalmody. The majority of the hymns of the Reformation adopted by the Evangelical hymnal may claim to be such "psalms"; they are proclamation of the Word in the fullest sense of the word.[142] As the church sings these songs with its lips and its heart, it itself becomes the Preacher Zion on the mountaintop. Here the Pentecostal prophecy of Joel, quoted in Acts 2:17 f., is fulfilled. This proclamation of God's great deeds in hymns at times approaches the New Testament charismatic-prophetic service even more closely than the sermon of the pastor. According to Eph. 5:18, the psalm hymn of the *ekklesia* as Spirit-wrought Word is simultaneously Spirit-imparting Word. And as 1 Cor. 14:26 declares, its words edify the congregation no less than doctrine and prophecy do. Issuing from the Word-bound, pneumatic presence of God's deeds of salvation, the "past" becomes "today" in these hymns. This becomes very evident, for instance, in Luther's hymn "Dear Christians, One and All, Rejoice" *(Nun freut euch, lieben Christen gmein).* Thus the psalm hymn of the *ekklesia* is an instrument through which God serves the congregation by the transmission of His salvation. In its employment for worship, these hymns are the vessel bearing the Pneuma-presence of Jesus.

138

Indirect Forms of the Proclamation of the Word in Worship

The *ekklesia's* psalm hymn forms the transition to the indirect types of the proclamation of the Word. Strictly speaking, there are no exclusively direct types of proclamation since Christ's ascent into heaven. All types of the church's proclamation, also the missionary sermon of the apostles, and to a greater extent types of worship such as Scripture reading, the sermon, the words of the Absolution and of the Benediction, involve a petitioning and a glorifying address to God. Thus Paul himself termed his missionary proclamation a "priestly service" (Rom. 15:16). But after all, the chief aim of the reading of Scripture, of the sermon, of the Absolution, and of the Benediction is the presentation of the Word, whereas there are other acts of worship whose express purpose is petition, thanksgiving, and praise. Also the verbal form of these acts differs from the form of the proclamation which addresses man directly. But in the execution of these acts, also the words addressed to God become, indirectly, a proclamation of the Gospel. Here the indirectness of the process is decisively important. When a hymn of praise or a confession or a glorification in worship performs the function of the proclamation of the Word accidentally a "sermon" may not specifically be contemplated or intended.

All genuine hymns partake more or less of this indirect form of proclamation. Such a proclamation is carried out most distinctly in the Credo. In it the content of the apostolic proclamation is concentrated and envisaged as in the focus of a lens. Although its words express devotion to God and praise of God, although this sacrificial side, perhaps, even contains its original and essential function, it is nonetheless also a proclaiming word, in which the congregation affirms the great deeds of God to itself and to all the world.

The hymn of praise is, also with regard to this double function, closely related to the profession of faith in worship. Luther displays a very fine understanding of the original association between *confessio* and *hymnus* when he proposed to admit the Te Deum to the early church's confessions.[143] In his brief characterization of this text he emphasizes that confession of faith and praise of God here merge into one.[144] The hymn of praise is a mirror that has captured the great deeds of God and lets this self-manifestation of the divine glory beam back on its origin. But precisely in that way, the hymn of praise becomes the proclamation of God's deeds, the demonstration of God's glory, which manifests itself in them. Miriam's song of victory is a very simple illustration of the basic structure of the hymn of praise by which it becomes the indirect form of the Word's proclamation:

Sing to the Lord, for He has triumphed gloriously;
the horse and the rider He has thrown into the sea (Ex. 15:21).

These hymnic "for"-sentences may also be replaced by a relative clause or by the hymnic participle, which is especially common in the Psalter. Thus the words of the Agnus Dei "that takest away the sin of the world" are a hymnic relative clause.[145] In these "sentences of glory" (Gunkel), which may also appear as independent declarative clauses, as for instance in the Te Deum, the proclaiming function of the hymn of praise becomes easily apparent. The ray of divine glory ascending to God in the hymn of praise illumes the church and through it the entire world in this verbal agent.

From the hymn of praise to prayer marks but a short step. It is significant, for instance, that the great prayer of the church in the first epistle of Clement is introduced by a hymnlike section, in which the charisma of the apostolic congregations to create psalms, similar to the Magnificat, is still vital.[146] What we find developed in abundance here, is still often found in the short collects, where the characteristic relative clause is appended to the words of address: "O God, who dost gladden us with the yearly anticipation of our redemption, . . . who hast made this most holy night to shine with the brightness of the true Light, . . . who hast let Thy Word become flesh, and who dost suffuse us therein with the new light of Thy grace, . . . who by the death of Thy Son hast overcome sin and death, and by His resurrection hast restored innocence and eternal life . . ." [147] This also applies to the Prefaces, which, with the exception of the "Common Preface," contain either the hymnic "for"-clause or the hymnic relative clause or the simple declarative sentence in their corpus.[147a] Read these hymnic elements of the collects and the prefaces consecutively, and you will be impressed how richly God's redemptive acts are affirmed and thus also indirectly proclaimed in these short glorifying anamneses.

Evidently these hymnic elements of prayer experienced the greatest condensation already in the prayers of the apostolic congregations that were spoken in the celebration of Holy Communion at the consecration of bread and wine. Those hymnlike passages of the New Testament epistles, such as Phil. 2:6 ff.; Col. 1:12 ff.; 1 Tim. 3:16; 1 Peter 1:18 ff.; 2:22 ff.; 3:18 ff., might well convey an intimation of the prayers spoken in the apostolic congregations in the celebration of

Holy Communion. These sections, whether based on "psalms" or "prayers," are anamneses of Christ. But the point of crystallization for these is the celebration of the Lord's Supper and, in particular, the consecration of the Eucharistic bread and wine.[148] The fact that these anamneses of Christ are the background of the texts of the New Testament epistles and that these were, at least in part, adopted almost word for word, is tangible evidence of the close relationship between the liturgical anamnesis and the intracongregational, edifying word of proclamation. The liturgical anamnesis itself, whether carried out in the hymn of praise or in the prayer of thanksgiving, possesses proclamatory character. For Paul, this proclamatory element of the Eucharistic prayer is even preeminent. For the proclamation of the Lord's death, as recorded in 1 Cor. 11:26, is executed not only through the act of the Lord's Supper as such, but chiefly through the thanksgiving pronounced over bread and wine.[149]

Finally, also various doxological acclamations, such as the Gloria in excelsis, the Sanctus with the Benedictus, also the Maranatha-cry, the words of which, moreover, were taken directly from Holy Scripture, belong to the indirect type of proclamation related to the hymn of praise. Whereas the congregation's prayer is spoken by the lips of an individual and is then adopted, confirmed, and sealed by the congregation's Amen as its own (1 Cor. 14:16), the congregation as a whole is again bearer of this indirect proclamation, performed by doxological acclamation. As we shall see, the doxological acclamation originated under an especially strong impulse of the Holy Spirit. And by reason of this origin, it also possesses an especial immediacy and spontaneity of the Spirit. Although the doxological acclamation finds its place in a fixed formula today, it may still be viewed as that word in worship which, by reason of its origin, embodies the charismatic-pneumatic essence of the Word most purely. The indirect proclamation of the Word, which results involuntarily in these types, might therefore also indicate impressively how the congregation as a whole speaks prophetically in the Holy Spirit.

THE SALVATION-EVENT IN THE PROCLAMATION OF THE WORD

The proclamation of the Word in worship is not different in its spiritual essence, in its authority, and in its central, objective content, from the proclamation of the Gospel to all the world. The proclamation of the Word in worship is a proclamation of the Gospel also when

141

it "recalls," when it unfolds, and when it applies this Gospel.[150] The intracongregational proclamation of the Gospel is the continuation of the Gospel's proclamation to the world. Therefore this proclamation of the Word also partakes of the promises of power and authority vouchsafed in the proclamation of the Gospel.

The Authority of the Proclamation of the Word

The authority of the proclamation of the Word derives from the commission issued by the risen Lord (Matt. 28:18-20; Mark 16:15; Luke 24:46-49; John 20:21-23; Rom. 10:14-17). The Word, emerging directly from this mandate and resulting from the outpouring of the Holy Spirit, is the church-founding Word of the apostles. But from this commission and from this outpouring of the Spirit in the church also stems the transmission of the Word of the apostles to all generations. From the calling and the commissioning of the apostles springs — despite the special, unique authority of the apostles — also "the office of the ministry" (*ministerium ecclesiasticum*, Aug. Conf., V), thus also the intracongregational proclamation of the Word, which, moreover, never loses sight of the "outsiders." (1 Cor. 14:23-25) [151]

Thus the commissioning order of Jesus Christ generates, through the obedient servants of the Gospel, the living Word of God in the form in which it is to materialize God's plan of salvation between Christ's ascension and His return. The two, God and His Word, belong together. From eternity to eternity God is Word in Himself. The Word spoken from eternity to eternity by God in God is God the Son. Through His eternal, intratrinitarian Word, God speaks His Word also to the outside and thereby creates all creatures from the void. Through this almighty Word God sustains and preserves everything that has creatural being. But from the beginning God also speaks in a special manner to man made in His image. Through His Word God creates history, through which He purposes to make man the perfect mirror of His glory and lead him to a complete participation in His life. Therefore God spoke through His Word in the prophetic witnesses of the Old Covenant. Furthermore, God's eternal Word became flesh in Jesus. Until the final Word of God resounds on the Last Day from the lips of the Lord returning in judgment, every word of God available for us men on earth stems from the incarnate, eternal Word of the Father. Without the miracle of the Incarnation, no word of man would be the Word of God. Man's authorization to proclaim, in Jesus' stead and until His return, the Word of God, the Gospel of salvation, which now extends to the whole world, issues from the lips of the incarnate, eternal Word, which was verily glorified in His flesh by the resurrection and ordained to almighty sovereignty.

It is the authority of the glorified God-man from which the apostles' proclamation and the proclamation of the apostolic church is derived. Jesus' victory on the cross marks the origin in which the institution of the apostolic proclamation of the Word is rooted. The authority of this victory, the authority of this Victor is the authority of the saving Word instituted by Him. And the Spirit poured out in the church actualizes this authority of victory. Where the apostolic Word is proclaimed in obedience to Jesus' instituting command by the Spirit-wrought testimony as the message of salvation for all the world, there God's own Word is present in the word of man, there the almighty sovereignty of Jesus Christ in the world is already executed, there the kingdom of the Anointed already has its beginning, hidden under the cross but yet in Messianic power, there the Triune God already calls from death into His life, as He remits sin and creates the new creature, until Jesus Himself will again speak in the judicial power of the Father, calling all people, the quick and the dead, before His judgment seat, where He will pronounce His final word.

The Intracongregational Word as the Anamnesis of Christ

The congregation assembled for worship is called and gathered by the proclamation of the apostolic Gospel of Jesus Christ. Its members spring from their acceptance of the kingly call of Jesus addressed to the nations of the world. They spring from their baptism, which made them members of the one body of the crucified and exalted Lord. Now it is all-important that they remain in Christ. And that implies, first of all, that they remain in that Word which saved and recreated them. Therefore the intracongregational proclamation of the Word is first and foremost the continuing call to the one Gospel which transformed everything in their life. This intracongregational call is, consequently, the ever-continuing call to their baptism. This proclamation of the Word, which calls back to Gospel and Baptism, always puts the congregation in mind of its origin, which sustains it and molds its life to the end. The congregation really "knows" all that is necessary for its salvation. That is shown again and again especially by the New Testament epistles. But the congregation must be "reminded" of what it knows. The Word once transmitted to it must not sink into oblivion and into the past; it must remain present for the congregation (cf., e. g., 1 Cor. 4:17; 15:1; 2 Tim. 2:14). The entire Epistle to the Romans purposes to be nothing other than such a "reminder" which enlivens and keeps alive that which was once given the congregation (Rom. 15:15). In the New Testament epistles we see very vividly how such reminding is carried out.

To be sure, this can be done only by a renewed witnessing to the congregation of the founding Word, which had originally called and gathered it. When the congregation recalls the Word that founded it and the sacrament that engendered it, it is not to be reminded of the events experienced by individuals when they came to faith and were baptized. One does not call the Gospel and Baptism to mind as one recalls a biographical event or a historical date which has escaped the memory and which one tries to recollect. The congregation's remembering Gospel and sacrament is not a neutral process, which takes place in the psychological realm of what we call "remembering" today. This remembering, rather, implies that man's understanding and thinking and willing and doing are shaped and molded by it in essence, kind, and content. Therefore this remembering is a power decisively determinant for one's existence. It is oriented to the object, to the content of Gospel and Baptism; it is a renewed apprehension, a renewed appropriation, a renewed acceptance of the salvation proffered in the Gospel and in Baptism.

Therefore the reminding Word can have no other content than this object, this event, this person of Jesus Christ, His Word and His work. As an anamnesis of the Gospel and Baptism, the intracongregational word is necessarily an anamnesis of Christ. The congregation assembled for worship in the name of Jesus marks the place where the word that executes the anamnesis of Christ is vital. The gospels, too, sprang from this word of the anamnesis of Christ in worship. New Testament research is establishing the worship character of the gospels ever more clearly. For example, the distinctiveness of the Gospel of St. John may surely be thought of as lying in the distinctiveness of the anamnesis of Christ on which it is based, as is indicated in such passages as John 14:26; 16:13-15.

Because this anamnesis of Christ is carried out in worship, it is carried out in the effectual, vital Spirit-presence of Him of whom the congregation is being "reminded." Of course, every anamnesis of Christ, also that which, for instance, is concentrated on Jesus' cross and resurrection, refers to a past historical event. Therefore the anam-

144

nesis of Christ can never be divorced from a report on something that took place in a given time and place. But since this anamnesis happens in the Pneuma-presence of Him who comprises its content, the One of whom the anamnesis reports past words and deeds is as present with His words and deeds as only He can be present to His congregation. It is precisely by this anamnesis in worship that the Lord manifests Himself as present to His congregation together with all that happened to Him and through Him in a given time and place. This present self-manifestation of the Lord and the salvation-event comprehended and concluded in Him in a given time and place are the all-embracing gift which is vouchsafed the congregation in the anamnesis of Christ by the Triune God through the intracongregational proclamation of the Word.

The Anamnesis of Christ as the Spirit-Wrought Presence of the One and Only Salvation-Event

What takes place in the anamnesis of Christ in the church's worship is the eschatologically fulfilled form of what already took place in the worship of Israel. The investigations of Mowinkel, Pedersen, Weiser, von Rad, and others have proved at least that the reports of the sacred story of Israel's genesis were founded on certain cultic festivals. We cannot, for instance, understand the origin of the Pentateuch if we fail to recognize that the literary "sources" which merged in these books are based on an original oral report on Israel's sacred history, which was given voice at these cultic festivals. These cultic festivals were the place where the great deeds of God were proclaimed and where His miracles were commemorated.

It is important to recognize that the story of God's revelation and salvation, which is Israel's origin, foundation, and reality of life in one, becomes a present reality, a "today" for the worshiping congregation through this sacred Word, which effects the "recollection" in worship. This is done in a peculiar and almost incomprehensible way. Gerhard von Rad has shown very strikingly how this "today," stemming from the cultic manifestation, has molded the entire proclamation of Deuteronomy, so that this book "still breathes that passionate actualization of the redemptive events, as only worship . . . can effect it." [152] In this connection he points, for example, to Deut. 5:2-4:

> The Lord our God made a covenant with us in Horeb. Not with our fathers did the Lord make this covenant, but with us, who

145

are all of us here alive this day. The Lord spoke with you face
to face at the mountain, out of the midst of the fire.

Von Rad comments: "The revelation of God at Sinai is not a past event,
not a historical matter for the living generation, for the generation addressed, but it has a reality which is determinant precisely for the life
of this generation. This inversion of time would be meaningless in
a literary sketch. . . . But in the worship experience, where past, present, and future activities of God fuse into one unprecedented actuality
for faith, there this statement is indeed possible, in fact, it is necessary."
The traditional sacred history of Israel presented at the cultic festivals
signified "not only a recollection of past life and events, but also ever
present life and events." [153]

To be sure, at a later day the original power of such a manifestation in the present diminished, but it did not vanish entirely. For
example, even in Jesus' day the Passover festival was still far more
than a modern commemorative festival. Those who celebrated the
Passover were themselves present at the exodus from Egypt. Their
celebration of the festival again placed them into the situation surrounding the exodus. The celebration was entirely oriented to the
present. This is demonstrated clearly by the provision in the Mishnah
tract on the Passover festival which reads: "Every generation is obligated to regard itself as having itself journeyed forth from Egypt." [154]

An inquiry into the reasons that enable the holy words in worship
to present Israel's sacred history as present to the congregation will
have to take cognizance of two factors: the revelatory character of
those historical events and the revelatory character of the words referring to those events. In this revelatory character, those events in
history and these words which move them into the present in worship
meet. And that means that they meet in God, in God's activity. In this
particular activity of God, directly oriented to the realization of the
eschatological salvation, from which the salvation-event in history
and the words which move this event into the present proceed, the
historical event and the words regarding this event are indissolubly
united.

The revelation-event in history already has a "word-nature." It
is created by the Word of might spoken by God. After the completion
of a historical event, the word-reality of that event does not drop into
the abyss of the historical past. In the word-reality of the event, the
event itself remains related to every present time and projects itself

into every present time in which the word-reality itself is expressed. God sees to it that this word-reality of the salvation-event which entered history is actually expressed. God gives His servants His Word, which discloses His saving action contained in the historical event, reveals it as such a saving, revealing action of God, and by such a revelation places the salvation-event in its revealing and saving power ever into the present time, where the Word is pronounced, published, and proclaimed in the execution of the "recollection."

It is all-important here to recognize that God's re-creating power and might is operative in His deeds which aim at the realization of His eschatological salvation. This actually creative presence of God in the historical events of salvation is a power and a might which cannot be confined by the time and space limits of those events; nor are their effects dependent only on the association of spatial-temporal continuity, as other historical events are. By reason of the fact that God granted us a Word regarding these deeds and instituted a "remembrance" of these deeds, this dynamic of God, operative in the historical events of salvation, breaks down all barriers of space and time that ordinarily hem in every historical event. Therefore, in the anamnesis of the Word in worship the people of God directly encounter the saving event of a time and place in the past as a present work of God; indeed, God's still unperformed and future activity of salvation already projects itself into this worship-present. "By this recollecting, an event or a person becomes really present to the subject. The activity of the object here marks a skipping-across, executed in the categories both of space and time. The ingress of the past into the present is the normal feature, but also the inclusion of the future into the present can be demonstrated." [155]

When God carries out His acts of salvation within the framework of history for the realization of His eschatological salvation, the power of the last things announces itself in these acts. The Lord of all might, of all time, and of all space already let His end-time power of salvation become operative in the historical event of salvation. In the power of the Re-creator, this end-time redemptive might of God is sovereign and superior to the space and time limitations of the order of preservation. With the historical deeds of salvation and with the Word creating and announcing these, this end-time, re-creating redemptive might of God occupies a sovereign position in the historical existence of the people of God and in worship draws them into the sphere of the last things.

147

All that takes place in the church's worship in the administration of the anamnesis of Christ as the proclamation of the Gospel, whether this be in the reading of the basic apostolic anamnesis of Christ, or in the exposition of this apostolic Word through the sermon, or in the words proclaimed in psalm and song by the congregation, all must be viewed from this background of the Old Testament. All that already pertains to the sacred Word in the worship of the Old Covenant reaches its fulfillment in the worship of the church of Jesus Christ. For the eschatological salvation of God is realized in Jesus. In Jesus, history tending toward the realization of this salvation has attained its consummation and its end. But through the redemptive action of God in Jesus the end of history itself has dawned.[156]

This end of history is effected by the entire Messianic history of Jesus on earth, but in a special manner by His cross and His resurrection. In the death of the Messiah, in the death of the Man who is God's eternal Son, in the act of God by which He leads this dead Man through death and grave into the glory of His life, all worlds and all powers are shaken in their very foundations. In this event the end of the world is present. By means of Good Friday and Easter, by means of the pathway God walked from Good Friday to Easter, God opens a door for His people, through which His world, His kingdom, His reign already dawn in the dynamis liberated and released through Jesus Christ over the new humanity of believers — and this despite the still existing, old, and vanishing world.

The history of Jesus Christ, which in its time took place there in Palestine under the governors of Rome's Caesars, unlocks the door through which this history — its historical uniqueness notwithstanding — enters into the new world of the dawning kingdom of God. Whatever old history of this earth may still exist is no longer endowed with the power to incorporate and contain the history of Jesus after this end-time breakthrough. Pontius Pilate and Rome's Caesar remain contained in this old and still existing history of the earth and operate only with the deadweight of all merely "historical" events in the plane of spatial-temporal continuity, which is part of the preservation order of the earthly world of man. But the fact that God's eternal Son came into the flesh, that He died on the cross, that He arose from the grave — these events penetrated, in the sovereign and eschatological power of God, the power of the eons, they broke through the barriers of time and space, which God set for the old history of the earth; these events stand in the end-time reign of God, and therefore in the royal eschatological freedom of the kingdom which endures into the eternities of the eons.

However, a second factor must immediately be added. God's redemptive act in Jesus is completed in His institution of the means through Jesus by which this history of what happened in Jesus, by virtue of its breakthrough to its eschatological liberty, already becomes prehensible, tangible, acceptable, and effectual for us men on this earth in time and space and translates all who participate in it by faith into the eschatological *transitus*. We know that these means are the Gospel, Baptism, and Holy Communion. We are here speaking of the proclamation of the Gospel as a member in this series of means. In the explanation of the Third Article of the Large Catechism, Luther clearly stated how this God-ordained means of the Word belongs to the completion of God's redemptive act in Christ.[157] The cross, devoid of the apostolic Word of salvation, is not salvation; reconciliation in Christ, devoid of the Word and the ministry of reconciliation, is not reconciliation (2 Cor. 5:18-20). "In order to be effective, the cross of Christ needs the Word of the cross; reconciliation demands the Word of reconciliation in order to reach man. . . . Faith adheres to the resurrection of Jesus; however, this does not take place without its proclamation, but by means of it. . . . What happened must be told; it cries out for proclamation. In Paul the oral character of the founding Word is directly connected with this indissoluble interrelation of the subject and its being told." [158] There is, indeed, an "indissoluble interrelation" of the redemptive event and the apostolic proclamation of this event. In the Word of the cross, the cross-event itself reaches out to man in the power of its eschatological freedom and presence. In the Word of reconciliation, the reconciliation takes place by virtue of the power of what took place on the cross.

This recognition implies that the cross-event is disclosed as a redemption-event only in the Word of the cross. Only in this God-ordained proclamation of the message of salvation is the salvation-event present as such. "The salvation-event is an eschatological event by the very fact that it does not become a fact of the past, but constantly takes place anew in the present. . . . Thus the salvation-event is present in the Word." [159] Through the kerygmatic proclamation, through the anamnesis of worship, the words and the deeds of Jesus, His cross and His resurrection, stand in the midst of the congregation in eschatological, sovereign freedom, and yet are as prehensibly, tangibly, and concretely present in the Word as food and drink are on a table.

This presence of the one and only historical redemptive event, which Christ presents to His congregation through Word and Spirit, is His own pneumatic, Word-bound manifestation in the present time. The living and exalted Lord is actually present in His Word which relates His words and His works, really present as Jesus, really present in His historical and now glorified humanity. Therefore, in this His Word-bound Pneuma-presence all is likewise present that took place in Him and through Him for our salvation. The Word of Jesus, the Spirit poured out by Him, and His earthly and now glorified physical humanity — these three are one in the anamnesis of worship by virtue of the divine institution of Jesus Christ. Because the present-time manifestation of the humanity of Jesus, united in the *unio hypostatica* with the eternal Son, eventuates for our salvation in the proclamation of the Gospel, God's end-time redemptive act, performed in Jesus' humanity here on earth, also becomes concretely present.

The Proclamation of the Word as a Conveyance of Salvation and of the New, Eternal Life

"Neither you nor I could ever know anything of Christ, or believe on Him, and obtain Him for our Lord, unless it were offered to us and granted to our hearts by the Holy Ghost through the preaching of the Gospel. The work is done and accomplished; for Christ has acquired and gained the treasure for us by His suffering, death, resurrection, etc. But if the work remained concealed so that no one knew of it, then it would be in vain and lost. That this treasure, therefore, might not lie buried, but be appropriated and enjoyed, God has caused the Word to go forth and be proclaimed, in which He gives the Holy Ghost to bring this treasure home and appropriate it to us." [160] Here Luther clearly recognized and affirmed the exhibitive power of the proclamation of the Gospel. The apostolic Gospel, instituted by Christ and wrought by the Holy Ghost, is a bestowing Word. It contains God's gifts of salvation and dispenses them. Because Jesus Christ Himself renders His redemptive deeds, which have penetrated into the plane of eschatological freedom, present in His congregation through this Word, this Word simultaneously contains the treasure of these redemptive deeds within it in order to distribute it by way of proclamation. The real presence of the one and only redemptive event also lends this Word the fullness of salvation itself

150

as a treasure disclosed to us and proffered us for our appropriation. Therefore this is not an empty Word. As God's Word of revelation it is a creatively active Word of power. It effects what it says. By virtue of its institution by its Lord, it bears within it that Messianic power of execution to which we referred earlier. "The Gospel contains . . . the entire reality of salvation of Him whom it proclaims, and it transmits this as it proclaims." [161]

The opinion that the Word of proclamation merely points to the salvation in Christ's work which the hearer must follow to gain contact with the work of Christ, which is separated from us by time and space, and that he must find this contact beyond this Word and in an imperceptible sphere of the Spirit, is foreign to the testimony of the New Testament and to the Bible's message. The studies of Schmitz, Schniewind, Asting, and others clearly demonstrate that. Word and Spirit, Word and salvation, Word and forgiveness, Word and eternal life are one, provided the proclamation is carried out in obedience to Jesus' institution and, consequently, in real conformity with its apostolic content. By disobedience man may cause his words to be but human words and not the Word of God, despite his claim that they are proclamation. But where the apostolic Word is read from the Scriptures in the congregation assembled for worship and the name of Jesus is invoked, where forgiveness of sin is announced to the penitent congregation, where the anamnesis of Christ is carried out through the voice of the congregation in psalm and song, there the Word of God is also present, even though it might be obscured by the pastor's sermon. If the proclamation conforms to the institution of Jesus Christ, if it is accompanied by prayer in the name of Jesus Christ, and if it retains the mark of apostolicity through its content, then such proclamation is, by virtue of the unswerving faithfulness of Jesus Christ, His saving, life-giving Word.

There is no room here for dialectic doubt; absolute certainty prevails here! The eschatological freedom of grace is shown by the very fact that it is present in this Word with absolute certainty. To be sure, whoever does not recognize and trust the authority and power of the resurrected Christ's institution, whoever doubts the gracious condescension of the Triune God in the means of salvation ordained by Him, whoever questions the concrete presence of Jesus' humanity in Word and sacrament, whoever presumes to be "more spiritual" than the incarnate God, whoever would withdraw from the approaching embodiment of God's revelation — nothing remains for him but the uncertainty of the open question whether or not the proclaimed word is really God's Word. Whoever would question the words of absolution pronounced by the minister in confession, uncertain whether this word is really in every instance God's own Word of forgiveness, or whether the fulfillment of this Word, together with the gift of forgiveness and of life, is not, rather, dependent on the working of the Holy Spirit in a manner that at one time it is a word fulfilled, at another it is but an empty word, and whoever would, finally, even make the fulfillment of the words of absolution dependent on their acceptance in faith, whoever, consequently, would construe the acceptance in faith as evidence that in this event, and only in this event, God Himself pronounced His Word, that person did not hear the Bible's message aright, and did not recognize the salvation-event in the proclaimed Word correctly.

The Proclamation of the Word as an End-Time Mystery

What happens in the proclamation of the Word in worship? With the eye we behold only a human activity. One or many or all open their lips to speak or to sing. Any outsider or any disinterested party observing these proceedings cannot but shake his head in bewilderment as he compares this with what we attempted to describe as the content of this activity. Nothing of what happens, according to our conviction, in, with, and under the proclamation of the Word is empirically demonstrable. The statements regarding all that takes place in worship as the work of God are statements of faith, which clings to what it cannot see and what it cannot apprehend with the hands as though it really beheld it. This is the same faith which recognizes the incarnate and eternal Son of God in Jesus of Nazareth. Whoever looks upon Jesus without that saving faith can behold only a human being in Him. He may eulogize Him with ever so lofty attributes, Jesus nevertheless remains a mere human being for him. Faith acknowledges that this Man is truly and substantially God, without detracting from His inviolable humanity. Therefore faith speaks of the two "natures" of Jesus Christ, of His true deity and of His true humanity, which are united in the mystery of the *unio hypostatica.*

Analogous to this mystery of the person of Jesus Christ, faith must also profess two realities regarding the proclamation of the Word in worship, which are united with one another and which pervade one another. Faith may profess the duality and the unity of human and of divine action in the Word of the Gospel. It would be folly to dispute that human beings are here acting in a human manner. We cannot conduct a worship service without resolving to read or to expound this or that section of Holy Scripture, without singing this or that song, without employing this or that order of service. Our human activity, our willing and thinking, our speaking, our hearing, our heeding are included in every part of worship. God wants us to engage in all of this in order to make it possible to conduct worship. And in particular does God want us to perform all that is necessary for the proclamation of the Word. Our entire activity, if properly carried out, reflects nothing other than our obedience to the words of Christ's institution.

But here we face the mystery which pervades all of worship and which first becomes evident to us here in the proclamation of the Word: The Triune God places, invisibly and yet actually, His own doing into our human doing, performed in obedience to Christ's institution. It is the work of God which is performed in the human work of proclamation. But as God places His doing into this human doing, He places Himself, His redemptive presence, revealed for us in Jesus Christ, into the Gospel proclaimed by man. God's incarnation-presence, materialized in the incarnation of the Word, effectually works and yields the saving presence of God in the proclaimed Word. The Incarnate One is really present as such in the outpoured Pneuma under the human words of proclamation. The human words of proclamation are the agency by which God in the incarnate Son becomes present, prehensible, and palpable to us men through the Pneuma. Therefore, the treasure of all of Christ's gifts of salvation is deposited in the human words of proclamation, available and ready to be apprehended, to be taken and to be received by us.

This poor and wretched word of proclamation is, thanks to God's gracious condescension, pervaded and permeated with God's saving presence, which is materialized in His Son Jesus for all eternity. The outpoured Holy Spirit unites, *realiter,* with this human word as the epiphany of God's incarnation-presence in Jesus. In this Pneuma-pervaded Word, the One who is the Bread of Life can Himself be received and eaten (John 6), so that, in the reception of this Word, Christ's righteousness becomes our righteousness, Christ's divine life becomes our life, Christ's union with the Father becomes our union with the Father, until in the resurrection from the dead also the medium of the Word will be eliminated, and we shall see Him face to face and be with Him in immediate communion.

153

This indissoluble and incomprehensible interrelation of human word and God's saving Jesus-presence in the Spirit, this *unio spiritualis* of the historical, human word with the resurrected Lord and His gifts makes the proclamation of the Gospel the *sacramentum* of the end time, which vouchsafes us God's incarnation-presence in the Pneuma of Jesus (2 Cor. 6:16) in the time from God's incarnation-presence during Jesus' sojourn on earth (John 1:14) to God's incarnation-presence in the new world of the resurrection from the dead. (Rev. 21:3) [162]

The Proclamation of the Word as an End-Time Crisis

The proclamation of the Word as an anamnesis of Christ, the proclamation of the Word as the Spirit-wrought presence of the one and only, historical salvation-event, the proclamation of the Word as an exhibitively bestowing word of authoritative power, the proclamation of the Word as an eschatological mystery — all of this aims at making the sinner righteous, of saving him, sanctifying him, re-creating him, and making him obedient to God through the Word. All that we have elaborated thus far would not only be incomplete but also misleading if we were to omit the culminating point of the proclamation of the Word, which it itself projects: saving faith. God does not prepare the mystery of the proclamation of the Word because of the mystery, but because of the saving, justifying, re-creating faith.

God, and not our faith, creates the eschatological mystery from the apostolic proclamation of the Word. Whether you believe or not, in either event you encounter the end-time mystery, replete with the powers and gifts of God's future world, in the Scripture reading in worship, in the testimony of the apostolic Gospel, in the words of absolution. Everyone who met the Lord Jesus during His earthly sojourn met the Messiah, the Son of God; not only Peter and the other apostles and those who believed in Him, but also the Pharisees and the scribes and the high priest and the governor of Caesar. Everyone who comes into contact with the apostolic Gospel thereby comes into contact with the same Jesus, the same Son of the living God, the same God, the same Salvation, with whom the disciples and the Jews and those Romans came into contact in their time and place. From God's viewpoint, the apostolic Gospel, eventuating in its proclamation, is this salvation-filled, end-time mystery — independently of our belief or disbelief — just as Jesus is the incarnate, eternal Word of the Father and by that very fact the end-time mystery of the God-man — whether people believe in Him or are offended by Him and crucify Him.

Jesus came to save and not to judge. He sent His Word as the powerful means of salvation and not of judgment. But it is precisely this encounter with the saving Gospel that places a person before the end-time decision, which involves eternal life and eternal death, since belief and unbelief are involved here. The pneumatic content of the Word, which we have endeavored to identify, lends the Word the power to place the person encountering it before the final decision. This pneumatic content of the Word is invitation and enticement to eat and to absorb what is tendered and proffered here. And over and above this, this pneumatic content of the Word possesses the power of victory, the ability to penetrate into the core of our human existence, to open our hearts, and to make way in them for God and His gifts. Because the Word partakes of the victorious power of Him who burst the bars of death and the grave asunder, this Word is also able to burst the lock to the door of our heart asunder. Now the truly critical question confronting us reads: Will we let this be done to us or will we resist it? Now that God has already actually penetrated into the center of our life, the crisis arises which decides whether the salvation-event in the proclamation of the Word attains its end, that is, whether it is accepted in faith, whether it redounds to my salvation and to my life, or whether this event is rejected with inexplicable obduracy and with resultant eternal death.

God bestows faith; but as He does this, He respects our personal entities. God bestows faith in a manner that this faith is nonetheless my faith. God does not create His salvation in me without making me, as His beloved thou, a partner in this in the power of His Spirit. But right here we find the enigmatic possibility that man may not let himself be loved by God and drawn into partnership with Him. The puzzling possibility remains that man may repudiate this affirmation of faith which God, through the Holy Spirit, is about to place into his heart and on his lips, before heart and lips repeat this affirmation after God. And there exists also the puzzling possibility that an already spoken affirmation of faith may be disavowed and, at times, disavowed conclusively.

Therefore God's salvation is not present for us otherwise than that it places us on the spot of final decision, a decision which will be manifested on the Day of Judgment. There is the closest association between today's encounter with God's pneumatic incarnation-presence implicit in the Word and the future, face-to-face encounter with the returning Lord. Whether a verdict of acquittal or of condemnation will be my lot in the Last Judgment is decided now and here in the living Word of the Gospel. Whoever does not accept God's justifying sentence of acquittal in the Word of the cross and of the resurrection now, and, in spite of sinning much daily, does not accept it again and again and cleave to it until the end, will, if he has really encountered the acquitting Word of God and rejected it impenitently, be constrained to give ear in the Last Judgment to the Lord's words of eternal rejection.

Thus the intracongregational proclamation of the Word in worship is, no less than the missionary proclamation of the Gospel to the world's nations, actually "a two-edged sword" (Heb. 4:12), "a fragrance from death to death" or "from life to life" (2 Cor. 2:16). The congregation assembled about the apostolic voice of the Gospel is the place where eternal life and eternal death are at stake; for this proclamation is end-time salvation-event. Therefore it is the end-time crisis for all who encounter it.

The Salvation-Event of the Proclamation of the Word as a Glorification of the Triune God

Man's hardening of the heart in unbelief poses an uncanny riddle. The affirmation of faith is a blessed miracle. As surely as God's Son did not die in vain on the cross, so surely the blessed miracle of faith is also performed — despite that eerie brim that surrounds the miracle of belief as the riddle of unbelief. God's victory remains His own secret. But God's victory is certain. It cannot be called into question by unbelief and impenitence. God's new race of men with Jesus Christ as its Head becomes reality. The Gospel actually bursts the bonds of sin and guilt asunder. Lost sinners are rescued for eternity through the Word. People as dead as corpses before God are resurrected to a new life by the Word. The disobedient become obedient to the will of God. Faith, hope, and love are engendered, nurtured, and matured. In this Gospel-bound redemptive event God is glorified, as man is saved and re-created. Man's salvation is God's victory over sin, death, and devil. God's kingdom, God's power, God's glory are enhanced precisely by this fact that His will of redemption is fulfilled in us. Where sins are forgiven and new, God-given life is created, shouts of joy arise that ring through all the heavens (Luke 15:10).

Not only the proclamation of God's great deeds in the anamnesis of Christ is a laudation of the Triune God and of His great faithfulness, but also this invisible, pneumatic salvation-event, through which the WORD is received and appropriated in the Word, the rescue of the lost — that constitutes God's glory and praise. God's glory, Christ's dominion, the Spirit's creative power shine nowhere more resplendently than in that unpretentious, deeply hidden salvation-event, which is effected through the proclamation of the Word; for in this event God's kingdom comes to us now, until it dawns on the Day of Judgment in fully revealed glory.

The Salvation-Event in Holy Communion

In Holy Communion the members of Jesus' congregation are among themselves. Here the doors to the world, which remained open on principle in the proclamation of the Word, are closed. Therefore our statements on Holy Communion express the most characteristic features of worship. Holy Communion is the heart of the worship of the congregation assembled in the name of Jesus.

Necessary Preliminary Questions

Our task consists in stating what happens in the congregation's celebration of Holy Communion. Thus the subject of our statements is the present-day Holy Communion of the church. Our task is not primarily to expound a text but to interpret an action that takes place in our midst.

Our interpretation of what takes place in the present-day Holy Communion is doctrine, it is dogma. For the knowledge of what happens in the present Holy Communion of the church is knowledge of doctrine. We derive the latter from the words of the apostles, which the church proclaims down to the present day and every day. Whatever happens in the celebration of Holy Communion can be nothing other than what the apostolic Word proclaims to us as content of this event. If it were otherwise, Holy Communion could not be Holy Communion but a cultic rite invented by us or by others. As we state what happens in the church's present-day celebration of Holy Communion, we necessarily and simultaneously state the content of the apostolic Word on Holy Communion as it is found in the Holy Scripture.

The content of this Word is manifold. For instance, what Paul

157

says in 1 Cor. 10 and 11 on Holy Communion is something particular and is not identical with Luke's statement in Acts 2:42-47. In 1 Cor. 11:22, 33 f. we observe clearly that Paul makes a far-reaching change in the form of Holy Communion as this was originally celebrated by the congregations and as it is reported in Acts 2. He represses the idea of satisfying the appetite in the celebration of the Lord's Supper and crystalizes its sacramental character. Furthermore, the different reports on the institution of Holy Communion (1 Cor. 11:23-25; Luke 22:14-30 with the omission of vv. 19b and 20 in Manuscript D and in the Old Latin translation; Mark 14:17-26; Matt. 26:20-30), especially the divergent forms of Jesus' words about the bread and the cup, vary in accent. In addition, we have the mysterious treatment of the Eucharistic Meal in the Gospel of St. John, particularly in John 6 and John 13–17, and the doctrine on Holy Communion partly adopted and partly formulated by Paul, as found in 1 Cor. 10:14-22, and 11: 26-32. All of this presents conceptions of what takes place in Holy Communion which we must distinguish, and it shows us outlines of a history which the conception of the sacrament experienced within the apostolic era. An attempt to clarify this history will necessarily involve also a study of the history of the words of institution with the aid of the method of tradition history. We will not be able to ignore the questions which words were actually spoken by Jesus in the night in which He was betrayed and what meaning He associated with these. For the result of this investigation will assist us in arriving at a better understanding of the passages before us and of what takes place in Holy Communion as it is disclosed in these.

Therewith we have pointed to the rights of the historical-critical, tradition-historical analysis, but also to the limitations of its dogmatic validity. There was a time — and it seems that it has not passed entirely — when the historical-critical method of investigation of New Testament texts on Holy Communion was backed by the conviction that only what Jesus Himself, according to our historical-critical knowledge, said and thought when instituting Holy Communion could be binding for the proclamation and for the belief of Christians. What was said and thought at a later date about the Holy Communion-event by "the congregation" or even by Paul and by the Gospel of John was to be declined as addendum, as a later development deviating from the original, or as a distortion. Various reasons prompt us to oppose this view.

This conception overlooks, first of all, the working of Jesus Christ in the apostolate ordained by Him. If St. Paul is an apostle of Jesus Christ, if the office of grace and the gift of grace of the apostolate are bestowed on him, then he, as an authorized messenger vested with apostolic power, can also declare what Holy Communion really is. The same applies to the apostolic anamnesis of Christ transmitted to us by the Gospels. As surely as the institution and the ministry of the apostolate belong to the Messianic salvation-event, so surely the apostolic proclamation on Holy Communion expresses, in conformity with the will of Jesus Christ, the pertinent facts regarding Holy Communion. In the Word of the apostles, made audible to the church in the New Testament writings, we meet the Word which Jesus Christ Himself spoke and which is binding for the church to the end of time. Therefore the probably original form of Jesus' words of institution, ascertained with the aid of the historical-critical investigation, and the meaning of what takes place in Holy Communion, probably contained in these reconstructed words, cannot be the dogmatic canon for the church's doctrine of Holy Communion. Nor can any single phase in the development of the conception of Holy Communion, delineated one way or another by historical-critical science, be this dogmatic canon. The dogmatic canon is exclusively what the New Testament writings themselves actually declare about Holy Communion. But in order to gain a proper conception of what the New Testament writings actually tell us about Holy Communion, we must attempt again and again — which, to be sure, must remain a self-critical attempt — to trace that history of the words and of the understanding of Holy Communion.

Our opposition to a dogmatizing history is rooted, in the second place, in an immediately intelligible knowledge, in a knowledge made irrefutable by facts, that the historical-critical analysis of the texts on Holy Communion and the retracing of the history of the Holy Communion conception in the apostolic (and postapostolic) era, based on this analysis, cannot arrive at any absolute and unanimous certainty about the historical process. The self-critical investigator is aware, especially as a historian, of the greater or lesser measure of probability of his theses and hypotheses. He will be convinced, especially in view of the "sources" extant in New Testament tradition, that, for example, neither the question regarding the exact words spoken by Jesus in that night at table, nor the question regarding the meaning of these reconstructed words can be established by historical-critical analysis with that certainty which may otherwise be demanded in historical research. What would have become of the church's doctrine of Holy Communion if the church in the course of the last century had adopted as the basis for its doctrine the views advanced from time to time by this or that group as assured "conclusions" of historical investigation? Certainty and unanimity can be achieved in the church as we view the factors that are decisive for the apostolic proclamation of Holy Communion, as expressed by the New Testament texts before us. As matters stand, a glance at the history behind these texts will never yield any certainty based on cogent reasons.

The church's doctrine on Holy Communion would indeed find itself in a precarious position if it could be shown that there is not only a difference but also a mutually exclusive contradiction between the "original meaning" of Holy Communion as ascertained by historical-critical analysis, and a "later" conception found in the New Testament. The church's doctrine would be in equal jeopardy if mutually exclusive views could be shown to exist within the historically traced development of New Testament conceptions of Holy Communion. If compelling proof could be advanced for that, then the apostolicity of the New Testament would indeed be called into question. Then the anamnetic power of the Pneuma, of which John 14:26; 15:26; 16:13-15 speak, would be called into question. Then the Pneuma would indeed no longer derive from the Incarnate One what It says through the tradition preserved in the New Testament; It would no longer "glorify" the Incarnate One, but It would speak of Itself without having heard anything. Then the guideline for the doctrine of Holy Communion would indeed have to be sought elsewhere, outside the texts given us, whereby the essential compulsion directing the choice of this guideline could not transcend the compulsion of a subjective personal decision. Then a doctrine of Holy Communion of the church would be impossible. Then only a thesis of "a faction of the church," united by the same personal opinion, would be possible. Repeatedly attempts have been made to prove that the New Testament contains mutually exclusive doctrines on the Gospel in general and on Holy Communion in particular, and in our day this is being done with renewed vigor. These attempts have never been able to submit any convincing proof even on the plane of historical-critical investigation, and they will never succeed in this if Jesus Christ is really the Lord, who in the full power of the exalted God-man ordained the apostolate, which upholds the church, and who activated the apostolate by the outpouring of the Holy Spirit.

160

It cannot be our task to undertake a historical-critical, tradition-historical analysis, which is necessary for an exposition of the New Testament passages on Holy Communion. We must also forego expounding these texts themselves in detail here. We must presuppose the adoption of this detailed exegesis and its conclusions. On the basis of this, we attempt to state what the church must teach about what takes place in Holy Communion. This teaching church can be only an obedient church, obedient to the apostolic Word. It cannot be "a faction in the church" which exalts itself arbitrarily above the apostolic Word of the New Testament. Therefore the church must lend ear and bear witness not only to one part but to the entirety of the New Testament proclamation on Holy Communion. It must receive the variety of the New Testament emphases and contents into its concept of Holy Communion and construe these as testimony of the articulate and full meaning of this event. That involves no "unscientific harmonization." It would be unscientific to maintain that every New Testament passage that speaks of or refers to Holy Communion expresses this articulate fullness of meaning. We refrain from asserting that. This process would be unscientific if it could be proved convincingly that the full meaning of the New Testament texts accepted for our doctrine of Holy Communion contained mutually exclusive doctrines. That proof cannot be presented. To be sure, our process is dogmatic and "unscientific" from a certain extratheological viewpoint, insofar as our statements are supported by the belief that every Lord's Supper which the church has celebrated since the first Pentecost and will still celebrate, that wherever the church as church has celebrated this sacrament, it bears within itself the reality of the one Supper of that night in which Jesus was betrayed. This certainty lies beyond the boundary of anything that might be ascertained by means of a scientific, historical cognition. But without this certainty there can be no doctrine of what actually takes place in the Holy Communion that we celebrate.

The Power of the Church's Holy Communion

Does anything at all take place in our celebration of Holy Communion besides what is clearly open to anyone's view and besides what takes place in the consciousness of every participant: his thoughts, views, inner experiences and convictions? We reply: Yes, indeed! Precisely that which takes places additionally in Holy Communion in, with, and under the visible and psychologically determinable is the salvation-event, on which we want to focus our attention. How does it happen that something hidden and nonetheless real eventuates in Holy Communion besides the visible and psychologically determinable? We reply: because Jesus invested this His institution with His power to effect that event which constitutes the salvation-event in Holy Communion.

All New Testament reports on the "institution" of Holy Communion are understood as reports on the institution of the sacrament as it was observed by the congregations. That applies also to the reports of Mark and Matthew, which do not contain the command relative to the repeated celebration of the sacrament. That is the unanimous opinion of New Testament investigation. The Lord's Supper celebrated by the congregations is, in accord with the apostolic teaching of the New Testament, the Lord's Supper only because it derives from the Supper which the Lord celebrated with His disciples in the night of His betrayal. This Supper initiated the long series of all of the church's celebrations of the Lord's Supper. This Supper is an institutive act. It places all celebrations issuing from it into institutional association. Only in this association emanating from Jesus' institutive Supper is there a Lord's Supper in which a salvation-activity eventuates. The certainty of this association, the certainty of the concrete, historical origin of this association in the instituting act of Jesus is immediately implicit in every administration or in every reception of Holy Communion as a certainty of faith vouchsafed through the apostolic Gospel. Here the certainty of faith dependent on proclamation, which must be differentiated from every other assurance and which is superior to every other assurance, is clearly seen. It is especially clear here that this certainty of faith also includes a certainty regarding a concrete, one and only, historical event that is the basis of every celebration of the Lord's Supper.

But Jesus' instituting act must not be viewed in punctual isolation. The salvation-event which this instituting act injects into the church's Holy Communion can be perceived in its fullness only when the instituting act is placed into a history that covers both the preparatory and the operational stages of the institution. We are indebted particularly to Ernst Lohmeyer for recognizing the importance of bracketing the act of institution with the preparatory stage. And we are indebted especially to Oskar Cullmann for pointing out that its connection with the events of the 40 days is also of great significance. The institution of the Lord's Supper has a history that pervades the entire activity of Jesus on earth, His pre- and His post-Easter activity, but it culminates in the Lord's Supper instituted in the night of His betrayal.

The synoptic words of Jesus at meal, the meals He ate in the company of sinners and publicans, the miraculous feeding, and also the meals eaten together with His disciples during His earthly sojourn — all of this already contains within it Holy Communion's salvation-event, released through the institution of the Meal in the narrower sense. For this Meal-event of Jesus during His days on earth is a Kingdom-event. It is already part of the New Covenant. It already bestows participation in the final salvation which appeared with Jesus' person. In this pre-Easter Meal-event — as well as in Jesus' words and miracles — the kingdom of God, the fulfilled reality of which will constitute the real table fellowship with God, already dawns, hiddenly, to be sure, but nonetheless really.

As Jesus' words and deeds possess Messianic executive power, thus also this table fellowship, conforming to the ordinary customs of the Jewish meal, imparts to His tablemates participation in the epoch dawning with Him and already bearing the final salvation of God within it. This anticipation of the salvation-event implicit in Holy Communion, which takes place in the ordinary and yet, in many respects, wonderful table fellowship with Jesus during His earthly life and which is retained in the miraculous feeding as in a type, may be emphasized so strongly that the backward-looking eye of faith beholds, as we see in John 6, the entire Holy Communion-event as already materialized in this table fellowship.

Something similar may be said about the risen Lord's eating and drinking with His disciples. These Eastertide meals with the resurrected Lord are not yet the Lord's Supper which the church celebrates, but they do contain the reality of this Supper in a very special way. Although Jesus died on the cross, the Kingdom-event does not cease. Although Jesus was buried, it is still possible to eat and drink with Him. Although the physically risen Lord no longer appears and is present to the disciples in a sensuous-physical, organic existence of an earthly human body, He is nonetheless really, truly humanly, and personally present to them with His true humanity, and in this real presence eats the meal with them, in which the meal fellowship of His earthly days is continued in a peculiarly altered form. This meal fellowship of the resurrected Lord with His disciples fulfills, in the apostolic testimony, the function of an actual interpretation by Jesus of His earlier meal fellowship and especially of His "last" Meal in that night of betrayal. In the meal Jesus becomes actually present to His disciples with His true humanity and thereby grants them participation in the blessings of His kingdom, until He will one day eat and drink anew with them at the table of God in the splendor of the kingdom of God.

And finally, in accord with John 19:34, we discover in Jesus' death on the cross itself the act which institutes Holy Communion. In fact, the power which effects the salvation-event flows solely from the victorious power of Jesus' cross. As far as the reality of the salvation-event is concerned, Holy Communion, as well as Baptism, wells forth from Jesus' sacrificial body on the cross. But without Jesus' antecedent words of institution, this mighty, ever vital, dynamic association between Jesus' death on the cross and our celebration of Holy Communion would be hidden from us.

The particular and singular meaning of the Meal celebrated in the night of betrayal is to be found in the fact that the mystery of His death on the cross becomes the mystery of His Meal through His deeds and words. No matter how we may conceive of the words and act of His "last" Meal in detail, there can be no doubt that they build a bridge between His death, this Meal, and the tablemates. Regardless of what else might be said about what takes place in Holy Communion, it must at all events be affirmed that Jesus, through word and act in that "last" Meal, in one act of authoritative anticipation, incorporated into this Meal and transmitted to His disciples through this Meal the salvation embodied in His death. The fact that Jesus "vouchsafes participation in the atoning power of His death" [163] by word and deed in that last Meal must be incorporated in every statement on the salvation-event of this Meal. What was yet to happen in Jesus' death on the cross for our redemption He deposited anticipatorily into this last Meal through word and deed as fully valid in the present and transmitted this to the disciples.

For the time being we still refrain from defining more closely the essence of what Jesus placed into this Meal by word and deed. In this connection it is, first of all, decisive for us to know that the presence of this salvation-event in this Meal is effected by Jesus' word and deed. Jesus' deed and word are deed and word of power and authority also in Holy Communion. They create, they generate their content. Also in this Meal, Jesus acts with Messianic executive power as the Incarnate Word of God in whose person, word, and deed the kingdom of God truly appeared. The authoritative power of Holy Communion is the authoritative power of its Founder. The authoritative power of Holy Communion is the authoritative power of the Messianic executive power, which inheres in Jesus' deed and word. The authoritative power of Holy Communion is the authoritative power of the deed and word of Him who in death was the Lord of all lords and is very God in eternity.

But this also implies that this last Meal exerts its effectual power beyond this nocturnal hour and beyond this group of disciples in a chain of similar celebrations of the Meal reaching down to Jesus' return. Also the passages in Matthew and Mark, which do not contain the command to repeat the Meal, state that the Holy Communion of the church was instituted and called into being through the institution of the Meal celebrated in the night of betrayal. These passages express this not only by their regarding themselves as the foundation of the Meal now celebrated in the congregation. Nor do they express this only by the fact that they place this Meal at the boundary line of the "dark interval" which originated when the previous meal fellowship of Jesus with His disciples was terminated and the "new" meal fellowship in the kingdom of God still lay in the future.[164] They express this above all by the words "for many" (Mark 14:24; Matt. 26: 28; also cf. Mark 10:45 and parallel passages, and Is. 52:14 f.; 53:10-12). "All" are meant; all the nations of the earth are meant for whom the Messianic salvation prepared by Jesus' atoning death is intended.[165] The universality of the words FOR YOU, in conjunction with the exhibitive character of the instituting Meal, demand cogently that the transmission of the atoning and redeeming power of this death and of the end-time salvation implicit in it is not confined to the group of disciples on that evening but that it reaches out into the future, in which also "the many" are added to the people of the New Covenant.

Furthermore, we must consider that Jesus' deed and Jesus' words at that last Meal present the reconstruction of a ritual meal, and that the ritual character within the framework of this meal partakes, above all, of a "commemorative" nature familiar to Jewry down to the present day. The question whether or not Jesus' institution of the Meal was carried out in conjunction with a paschal meal is quite independent of the fact that Jesus' new deed and new words certainly are connected with a meal which itself bore ritual character.[166] As surely as the framework of the Meal in which the institution took place demanded repetition by reason of its ritual character, so surely the new

165

institution is already a rite in the moment of its institution, a reconstructed rite, but nonetheless a rite, which as such, although instituted
on the threshold to the day of death, nevertheless — enigmatically
enough — points to a mysterious future already in the moment of its
first administration, to that future which the risen Lord will inaugurate
with His appearances and His new meal fellowship.

Finally it must be affirmed that the apostolic tradition, becoming
apparent in Paul's words (1 Cor. 11:24 f. and Luke 22:19b), bases the
anamnesis command implying a repetition in the worship service on
the instituting Meal itself. We may regard it as probable that the
oldest version of the words of institution, just because of its liturgical
character, did not contain the command touching repetition. "But by
no means may we deduce from that that it is unhistorical, for the
repetition directive is not absolutely part of the liturgical formula,
since the celebration itself represented its execution." [167] In view of
the anamnetic character of the Israelitic-Jewish cultus and the Jewish
meals, it is improbable that the repetition injunction was first formulated under the influence of Hellenistic commemorative festivals.[168]
We have already seen that the real content of the word anamnesis can
be understood only from the Israelitic-Jewish, worship-ritual tradition,
because this anamnesis-event is possible only where the realization of
a redemptive event, emanating from God and tending toward the
end, is involved. Even when remaining on the plane of historical
argumentation, no cogent reason can be adduced to show that the
apostolic tradition, which connects the repetition command with Jesus'
instituting Meal, is "unhistorical" in the modern sense of the word.
Rather, everything favors the assumption that Jesus' last Meal bore the
anamnesis-character from the very beginning. The anamnesis-character of Holy Communion carries the anamnesis-event of the Old
Testament cultus and especially the anamnesis-character of the Paschal
meal to the consummation fixed in the new institution of the New
Covenant.

Let us summarize. A Holy Communion that is actually Holy
Communion, a Holy Communion in which a salvation-event actually
occurs, exists only by reason of the fact that Jesus Christ, endued with
Messianic executive power, instituted this feast which we now celebrate. This Holy Communion exists only because it emanated from
this institution of Jesus Christ and because it partakes of the Messianic authority and power of that institutive Meal. This Holy Communion exists only because the same Lord, who acted then with His

Messianic authority and power, also acts with the same authority and power in the celebration of every Holy Communion springing from that "first" celebration. Thus Holy Communion is Holy Communion only because, by virtue of its connection with Christ's institution, it bears within it the effectual power of that instituting Meal. The instituting Lord and His unswerving fidelity to His covenant with which He is devoted to His institution for our benefit, the authoritative power of His instituting act and of His instituting word, the presence of this Lord, the presence of His fidelity to His covenant, the presence of His instituting act and of His instituting word in our Holy Communion — that makes our celebration of the Meal the Lord's Supper in which a salvation-event takes place.

Holy Communion as a Proclamation

Without Christ's word, that "last" supper would not be the Lord's Supper. The Lord's Supper is not mute; as the Gospel of St. John shows in an exemplary way, it is filled to the brim with His word. From beginning to end, Holy Communion is bracketed with proclamation of the Word. From its very origin, Holy Communion is the place where the anamnesis of Christ is carried out in a multiformity of words. All that we said about the anamnesis-character of the Gospel's proclamation applies particularly to the words voiced in Holy Communion. The consecrated bread cannot be eaten and the consecrated cup cannot be drunk without proclaiming the Lord's death as the event which effectuates the New Covenant and its salvation (1 Cor. 11:26). This proclamation is surely also carried out through the words spoken in connection with this eating and drinking.[169] It is carried out particularly through the words pronounced as prayer over the bread and the wine.[170] These words of proclamation, glorification, and thanksgiving have an anamnesis-character throughout. In these very words, as in the intracongregational proclamation in general, the anamnesis is executed which moves this one and only event into the present time. All that we said about the salvation-event which takes place in, with, and under the intracongregational proclamation of the Word must also be stated, by reason of the Word-character of Holy Communion, of its celebration.

But over and above this, also the act in Holy Communion which is not word but action linked to the word becomes proclamation. Holy Communion's proclamation is "drastic" because it embraces action as proclamation. The passage referred to (1 Cor. 11:26) can

167

hardly be understood otherwise than that also the eating of the bread and the drinking of the cup, that is, the act itself, the *dromenon* (δϱώμενον — act, procedure), is part of the proclamation. Just as Jesus' instituting word and His instituting act in the first Holy Communion blended into an indissoluble unit, thus also word and act are one in the proclamation which is carried out in Holy Communion. Thus the anamnesis-character is not only joined to the Word in Holy Communion, but it is also extended to the act. Holy Communion is that ritual form of memorial event which is rooted in the Old Covenant and fulfilled in the end time. Holy Communion is that act of worship in which all that takes place in Jesus, especially His redemptive death, is made palpable and prehensible through word and act by virtue of the proclamation, in which it becomes present as food on the table to be eaten by the congregation of the baptized. Already by virtue of the proclamation-character of the Meal instituted by Jesus, the one and only "establishment" of the New Covenant becomes an ever saving presence in this Meal.

Holy Communion as an Effective Repraesentatio

We observed that word and act become one indissoluble unit in Holy Communion. Therefore the celebration of Holy Communion as a whole is an anamnesis. What takes place in the whole of this act of proclamation cannot be expressed in one sentence. The salvation-event in Holy Communion describes a wide arc; it has a distinctive center, a center peculiar exclusively to it; and this center, in turn, has many radiations, which lend to the whole its differentiated fullness. First we want to consider the wide arc, which surrounds the entire salvation-event of Holy Communion like an effectual frame.

We proceed from the sign-character of the rite of Holy Communion. As in Baptism, so also in Holy Communion the visible act partakes of the nature of a sign which points to the event hidden in this act. In Baptism this sign consists of the water bath and the submersion in water or the aspersion with water. In Holy Communion this sign is to be found in the distribution of the bread, in the presenting of the wine, and in the eating and the drinking. The breaking of the bread does not symbolize violent death as the breaking up of a living unit. The breaking of the bread serves the purpose of distribution and is part and parcel of the act of giving. The words "given for you" (Luke 22:19b) are mirrored in the breaking and the giving of the bread. The breaking and the giving of the bread indicate that

168

Jesus' body is a body meant "for you" (1 Cor. 11:24). Also where the words pertaining to the bread speak only of the body and contain no additional reference (Mark and Matthew), the preceding breaking and giving of the bread is a sign pointing to the distribution of Jesus' body. The words "shed for you" (Luke 22:20b; cf. Mark 14:24; Matt. 26:28) are reflected in the presentation of the cup filled with (red) wine. The target of the words FOR YOU is mirrored in the eating and drinking of bread and wine. Whatever signs are contained in the rite of Holy Communion are indicated by the words FOR YOU. That the duality of bread and wine is also a sign of the death as a sacrificial death and in this way again mirrors the FOR YOU in its great gravity and seriousness, will occupy our attention later.

This act of Jesus has very appropriately been compared with the symbolic acts which occasionally accompany the proclamations of the prophets. Such a prophetic, symbolic act, as related in Is. 20:1-6; Jer. 19:1 f., 10 f.; Ezek. 4 and 5; also Acts 21:10 f., is an *oth*. A prophetic *oth* is "a drastic prediction," an effectual sign, which "announces" what is signified, brings it to pass, and lets it, hidden in a sign, already become effectual presence.[171] An *oth* effectively releases the happening indicated in it. When Ezekiel seemingly plays at laying siege to a fortified city, as a child might (Ezek. 4:1 ff.), his "game" is a most serious matter. It is reality. The words (Ezek. 5:5) "This is Jerusalem" are to be taken seriously. What happens in the *oth*, happens in reality. What happens in the *oth* is the realistic anticipation of a coming event. When Jeremiah (19:1 ff.) breaks the earthen flask, God Himself irrevocably breaks "this people and this city" with this blow (v. 11). Jeremiah, too, might say: You are this flask, this flask is Jerusalem! God's future judgment is effectively present in these symbolic acts.

To call attention to the *oth* of the Old Testament is all the more relevant in connection with Holy Communion, since an *oth* not only effectively represents future events in the present sign, but since it is also a "commemorative" sign, which, in the sign, keeps the past vividly present. Thus the sign of the stones, mentioned in Joshua 4:6, is an anamnetic *oth*. The Passover is a living *oth*, carried out through a ritual observance (Ex. 12:13, 16). God's miraculous signs and His miraculous deeds at the time of the exodus, designated by the same word *oth* (Ex. 7:3; Num. 14:11, 22; Deut. 4:34; Joshua 24:17; Jer. 32: 20 f.; Ps. 78:43; 135:9; etc.), become a living presence in the ritual *oth*. Thus the future and the present may mysteriously merge in the *oth*.

The Lord's Supper may be viewed from this background of the Old Testament *oth*. But as surely as Jesus is more than Solomon and Jonah and the other prophets and the temple, it is more than a prophetic *oth*. The Meal instituted by Jesus is the eschatologically fulfilled, Messianic form of the Old Testament prophetic and the Old Testament ritual *oth*. The symbolic act of this Meal of Jesus stands in the open door through which the new world of God enters into this old eon. It stands where the old world is dislodged, where Jesus' redemptive act disrupts the confines of time and space in the eschatological freedom of the kingdom, and thus, in the power of the final, end-time disruption, places itself, in the performance of this act, into the present. In the Holy Communion-event the cultic anamnesis of Israel arrives at its end-time annulment, completion, and derestriction, because God's end-time act of salvation, toward which the salvation-event of the Old Covenant tended, is accomplished "now" as a historical event in time and space and therefore becomes concretely present and palpable in a very special way through the church's commemorative act.[172]

Thus, in the act of Holy Communion, bracketed with its proclamation, the historical salvation-event concentrated in Jesus' cross is indeed present for us with its redemptive gift "through effective representation." [173] By virtue of the anamnesis-character of Holy Communion, Rudolf Otto's statement applies: "With, in, and under the celebration of the Lord's Supper, Golgotha becomes event here and now — not through our imagining, but through Jesus' institution." [174] Jesus' suffering cannot be separated from His cross. Where the event of the cross in its eschatological-pneumatic freedom enters into the congregation through the act of Holy Communion as a salvation-bestowing, present-time event, there the suffering of the obedient Servant of God, Jesus Christ, is also present, there the entire path of obedience of God's Son from His human birth to His death is also present in the cross. Nor can Jesus' resurrection from the dead be separated from His cross. That the crucified Lord is also the risen and exalted Lord is the very fact on which the singularity of His present-day manifestation and of His redemptive work is founded. The divine act of raising Jesus from the dead is the power of the new world of God through which the one and only redemptive act in Jesus enters our present day in the celebration of Holy Communion. There is no celebration of the Lord's Supper over which the radiance of that Eastertide meal fellowship of Jesus with His disciples is not diffused. Holy Communion is the opposite of a festival commemorating a dead man! It is a meal fellowship with Him who lives, and who, by reason of His resurrection victory, is actually present among His followers through the administration of Holy Communion.

Jesus' cross and resurrection verge on His coming return. Where the salvation-event, concluded in the past, becomes effectually and really present through the anamnesis of Holy Communion, there, hidden under the symbolic act, also future things enter redemptively into the present. Already in Israel's cultus the cultic event is inseparable from eschatology.[175] The anamnetic character of the Jewish Passover opens, with an inner cogency, the eschatological perspective simultaneously with the "commemoration."[176] Also in Holy Communion one cannot "remember" Jesus' suffering, death, and resurrection without at the same time "remembering" His return. The remembrance as *repraesentatio* here passes into a remembrance as *anticipatio.* In the anticipation of the redemptive event that still lies in the future, the anamnesis of worship becomes effective in another direction, in the direction of the future. Both directions of the anamnesis, *repraesentatio* and *anticipatio,* belong together. Thus the fulfilled *oth*-character of Holy Communion manifests itself here once more. It is, in analogy to the prophetic *oth,* a drastic, effect-releasing "sign," in which the salvation-event of Jesus' return, His reunion with His followers in the joyous banquet of the kingdom of God, the marriage feast of the Lamb with His bridal congregation, are already immediately "at hand" as an effective and present redemptive power.

The whole Christ, Christ's entire way of salvation, as the anamnesis of Christ of Phil. 2:6-11 magnifies it in hymnic adoration and as the Second Article of the Apostles' Creed adopted it — that is the salvation-event which becomes palpably and tangibly present to the congregation in a redemptively effectual real presentation through the celebration of Holy Communion. But the focal point of Christ's way of salvation, which marks the turning point of all things, is Golgotha. Therefore Golgotha also stands in the center of the Holy Communion-event, surrounded and embraced by the entire event that is embodied in the name "Jesus Christ."

The Food in Holy Communion and the Real Presence

We have spoken of the real presence of the Messianic, end-time salvation-event which is concentrated in Jesus' cross. But we have not yet spoken of the real presence peculiar to Holy Communion. Our remarks thus far did not carry beyond the salvation-event effected by the proclamation-character of Holy Communion. So far our discussion regarding the characteristic feature of Holy Communion related exclusively to the fact that Holy Communion, in contradistinction to the proclamation of the Word in the reading of Scripture, in sermon, and in song, is a proclamation bracketed with a "ritual" act of worship. Until now the characteristic feature was found only in the mode of proclamation, insofar as an act, linked to the spoken word, itself becomes proclamation, becomes anamnesis of Christ. We do not surrender that position. We must retain the far-reaching anamnesis-arc of the administration of Holy Communion. Indeed, act and act, redemptive act of Jesus there and then and act of worship here and now, merge mysteriously in the celebration of Holy Communion by virtue of Jesus' institution.

But whoever stops at this point has not yet recognized the characteristic feature of Holy Communion. In Holy Communion the words that Jesus utters over bread and wine stand out in meaningful relief. These words effect and reveal the core of what takes place in Holy Communion. There should be unanimity in assuming that these words of Jesus do not interpret the symbolical act. Here an important difference from the prophetic *oth* becomes apparent. In Jeremiah the Lord of hosts says by the prophet as he breaks the flask: "So will I break this people and this city" (Jer. 19:11; cf. Is. 20:3 f.: "as . . . so"). It is most significant that Jesus does not say as He breaks and distributes the bread: So I give My life for you. But He says — infinitely transcending the prophetic *oth*: "This is My body." It is impossible to express the content of these words in one sentence, which would correspond in form to those words in Jer. 19:11 or Is. 20:3 f. "Jesus does not interpret the act of breaking the bread and the pouring of the wine; no, He interprets the bread and the wine themselves." [177] Nor is the presentation, the symbolic character of which may be acknowledged, interpreted, but the objects which are presented. Paul's formulation of the words pertaining to the presentation of the cup show this most clearly (1 Cor. 11:25): "This cup is. . . ." The prophetic *oth* is to be interpreted as an effective metaphorical act. What Jesus, the Christ, does in Holy Communion is no longer a metaphor. Also the broken bread and the red wine are no metaphor, including a *tertium comparationis* to impart a meaning to Jesus' interpretative words. The distributing, the giving, and the receiving, the eating and the drinking of the food, and thus also the food itself, are, to be sure, part of the symbol, but Jesus' words do not explain the symbol of the act or the symbolic character of the food, but they assert what the food which belongs to the symbol of the act and therefore has symbolic character really *is*. The relationship which Jesus' words establish between bread and body, between wine and blood is not "an association by analogy, . . . but an association by identity."[178] The broken bread given to the disciples and to be eaten by them *is* the body of Jesus given for them and for many. The wine in the cup presented to the disciples and to be drunk by them *is* the blood of Jesus shed for them and for many. To be sure, the bread which the disciples now eat is bread and the wine which they now drink is wine. But by the power of Jesus' words this bread is His body and this wine is His blood.

It is widely acknowledged today that the apostle Paul construed the words of institution in the sense of this identity association. In view of 1 Cor. 11:27-32 and 1 Cor. 10:16-22, this should never have been questioned. Moreover, we have no reason to assume that any divergent views were held about A. D. 50 regarding the presence of Jesus' body and blood in Holy Communion. In view of Paul's otherwise controverted position, such would very likely have been voiced. Nowhere do we find any support for the assumption that there was at any time any tension between Jerusalem and Paul touching the doctrine of Holy Communion. In no chapter of early Christian history that is reliably transmitted do we find any intimation that Paul or the "Hellenistic" congregation before him had made any alterations in this salient point of Holy Communion. That does not preclude that Paul, especially in 1 Cor. 10:16 f., further evolved a doctrine of Holy Communion transmitted to him, in the sense of his ecclesiological doctrine of Christ's body. This doctrine is also discernible in 1 Cor. 11:27-32. However, this does not controvert, but presupposes, that according to Paul the partakers of the Lord's Supper do not only share in the redemptive death of Jesus by eating and drinking of the Eucharistic food, but they also enter into communion with the body given for us and into communion with the blood shed for us and, on the basis of this participation and communion, also share in the sacrificial death of Jesus.[179]

Nor does the Gospel of St. John contradict Paul and teach a "spiritualized" conception of the real presence. Rather, the realistic conception is here even fortified over against a gnostic-docetic danger.

That is shown by the last part of Christ's words in John 6, which obviously bridges over into statements on Holy Communion in v. 51. In the words "The bread which I shall give for the life of the world is My flesh," a paraphrase, if not even a direct quotation, of the words of institution themselves, is evident. Here the word "flesh" corresponds more closely to the Aramaic word very probably used by Jesus than the word "body," [180] and simultaneously and unmistakably fends off any gnostic-docetic misunderstanding. To be sure, John 6 knows of a spiritual eating, which consists in the belief in Jesus Christ and in the acceptance by faith of the redemptive act proffered also in the proclamation. But that is precisely the particular feature of the Gospel of St. John that the spiritual partaking of the Savior in faith and the physical partaking of His flesh and blood in Holy Communion do not diverge; rather, that the statements on the spiritual partaking (6:29, 35, 47) end in statements which simultaneously also speak of the physical partaking of the Incarnate One, of His flesh and blood given and shed "for the life of the world" (= "for many") in the sufferings and death of the Lamb (51c, 53-58). The New Testament's proclamation of Holy Communion presupposes the believing reception of Holy Communion as the rule. The "unworthy" reception is the strange exception. Therefore the physical partaking of it is also spiritual partaking. But when it is said that the Savior is "eaten" by faith as the bread of life, the physical partaking in Holy Communion is by no means drawn into question. Anyone who would venture to play the one against the other would misunderstand the very particular feature of the Gospel of St. John.

We note that especial importance must be assigned the words pertaining to the bread in the New Testament.[181] Indeed, these must fully contain the essence of Holy Communion. The words pertaining to the cup were first spoken "after supper" (1 Cor. 11:25). Very likely a rather long meal intervened in every instance between the words spoken over the bread and those spoken over the cup. Therefore the words Jesus spoke over the bread enjoy a relative independence. They in themselves express what takes place in Holy Communion. We shall hardly be able to ascertain with absolute certainty which Aramaic word Jesus used for "body." Therefore it is impossible to construct a doctrine of Holy Communion on it. The entire New Testament proclamation relative to the words about the bread and the accompanying sign of distribution must be decisive for the basic meaning of these words. If this principle is observed, then the body received by the disciples is not part of a human body, not part of a dead or of a physically live bodily substance. With reference to the latter, the words apply: "The flesh is of no avail" (John 6:63). Jesus' body is not given the disciples as a mere physical body. This proffered body is, first of all, the true corporeal humanity of Jesus in its FOR-YOU-character. Whoever eats the proffered bread, eats Him who came into the flesh for our salvation, who gave His flesh into death for us (cf. John 6:57: "who eats Me"). Jesus' body which He gives the disciples in the bread is indeed He Himself as the One who is given into death for us in His whole true humanity in union with the Logos.

This surrender is concentrated in the death on the cross, but it embraces the entire course of obedience pursued by the Incarnate One up to His death on the cross. Jesus' entire divine-human work of salvation, His whole Savior essence is concentrated in His body. In the Eucharistic bread we receive the true bodily humanity of Jesus as a vessel that conveys His entire work as Savior. Jesus' Savior-activity, His Savior-suffering, His Savior-victory, His entire life lived for us, His death suffered for us, His victory achieved for us, are in His body and are His body which we receive with the bread. What Gospel and Holy Communion, as proclamation, already posit as present, is here offered the partaker in the bread, through a mystery absolutely without analogy, for his physical and spiritual acceptance. Wherever the Eucharistic bread is, there the Lord is as body in the sense here indicated. Wherever the Eucharistic bread is received, there the body of the Lord, encompassing the entire FOR-YOU-event, is received physically with the mouth and spiritually by faith.

The words pertaining to the bread in themselves fulfill their meaning with respect to Jesus' death. It is a person who is about to die who speaks and acts here. The saving FOR-YOU-event is drawing to a close. The presupposed meal is actually a "last" meal. Never again will Jesus eat the meal with them as He does in this hour. The body which He offers them is a dying one, His body given into death. Here the all-powerful anticipation becomes operative. The body which Jesus gives His disciples is, by the power of this anticipation, His body suspended on the cross, the body in which for them and "for many" the vicarious judicial death, the atoning, redeeming, sacrificial death, the victorious death of the Messiah who vanquishes all antigodly powers is being suffered. This body and this death are one. We have this death in this body. This real oneness of the crucified body with the redemptive death is the gift which Jesus gives His

175

disciples in His Meal through the bread, consecrated, broken, and distributed by Him.

Now the words regarding the cup assume their function, interpreting the words relating to the bread and conclusively determining their content. In the words pertaining to the cup, the salvation-event is unmistakably concentrated on Jesus' sacrificial death. They name the content of the proffered cup: the covenant blood shed by Jesus and, in this, the established "new" covenant with its comprehensive end-time gift of remission of sin.

Here, too, no particle of blood is to be received as a dead substance. Also in the shed covenant blood the Lord Himself, given into death for us and working salvation for us through this death, is truly present for us. HE HIMSELF in His sacrificial activity is the drink which we receive physically with our mouth and spiritually by faith.[182] And HE HIMSELF in His sacrificial activity becomes prehensible to us in His true blood. The establishment of a covenant demands sacrificial blood. In the blood of Jesus, shed on the cross, the "new" end-time redemptive order of His kingdom is established. In Holy Communion the end-time redemptive order of reconciliation established at the cross comes to us through the blood of Jesus offered us in the Eucharistic drink.

Body and blood, the duality of bread and wine, the duality of body and blood, now again become significant. This duality again focuses our attention on the death of Christ. For this duality also signifies that blood, differentiated from the body, and a body, differentiated from the blood, is proffered. This distinctiveness of the body and this distinctiveness of the blood point to the isolation of the blood from the body in the sacrifice.[183] This isolation is essential for every sacrifice in the Old Testament, particularly for "the blood of the covenant" (Ex. 24:6-8), for the blood of the great atonement (Lev. 16:14 f., 18 f., together with 27), but also for the Passover (Ex. 12:7 f.; here we also find the isolation of the blood of the lamb from the blood-drained body). The Letter to the Hebrews speaks explicitly of this isolation of blood and blood-drained body in the sacrifice and applies it to Jesus' death (and in that way, very probably, also to Holy Communion): "We have an altar from which those who serve the tent have no right to eat. For the bodies (τὰ σώματα) of those animals whose blood (τὸ αἷμα) is brought into the sanctuary by the high priest as a sacrifice for sin are burned outside the camp. So Jesus also suffered outside the gate in order to sanctify the people through His own blood" (Heb. 13:10-12 and Lev. 16, especially v. 27). When Jesus, in instituting Holy Communion, speaks of His body and blood, His body is the sacrificial flesh and His blood the sacrificial blood. The duality of bread and wine, of body and blood, points to the fact that the sacrificed body and the atoning and covenant-effecting sacrificial blood and, with this, Jesus' sacrifice on the cross, are present to us under the Eucharistic food and presented to us with the bread and the wine.

Here we must be reminded that Jesus' sacrifice on the cross is not inanimate, as all sacrifices on the great day of atonement and all slaughtered Passover lambs are. He who makes the sacrifice, He in whom it consists, is God's eternal Son. Jesus' true humanity is effectually united with the true substantial deity of the eternal Son. His body and blood are begotten by the Spirit and pervaded by the power of divine life even in the days of His earthly sojourn and even in the hour of His sacrifice. His flesh is not flesh such as that of the Old Testament sacrificial animals and as that of the Old Testament Passover lamb. The flesh of the incarnate WORD is not divorced from God the Spirit who quickens. Mere flesh would, indeed, not avail. But this sacrificial flesh and this sacrificial blood are, as flesh, also Pneuma; there is divine life also in the voluntary sacrificial surrender to death. Therefore this flesh will not be devoured by death, but, on the contrary, it itself devours death and lives in absolute sovereignty over death in all eternity.

Thus Jesus' death on the cross, together with His resurrection and ascent into heaven, has penetrated all heavens and all eons and made its way to the throne of God, and now stands eternally alive, eternally effectual, eternally atoning in the High Priest before the face of God. As Jesus "through the eternal Spirit offered Himself to God" (Heb. 9:14), so this sacrifice stands, also in the power of the quickening Spirit, as a living sacrifice before the throne of God in a nonearthly, nonsensuous, pneumatic reality, but in a reality physically identical with His bloody sacrifice on Golgotha. In its eschatological pneumatic freedom, this sacrificial body, this physical sacrificial blood, this one and only sacrifice offered on the cross at that time becomes contemporary in the Eucharistic bread and in the Eucharistic drink. Through the real presence of Jesus' body and blood the *repraesentatio* carried out in Holy Communion receives its real and present concretion. The real presence and the *repraesentatio* are not mutually exclusive. The *repraesentatio* executed by Gospel and by Holy Communion as proclamation is, as it were, the pneumatic-dynamic field of operation of the end-time mystery, in the realm of which the real presence related to bread and wine eventuates. But this real presence concretizes the end-time mystery of the anamnetic salvation-presentation in a manner very specific and absolutely without analogy, effected only through the food in the Lord's Supper. It should not be disputed that, according to apostolic doctrine, the suffering and death of Jesus Christ, His physical sacrifice on the cross with its eschatological dynamic bursting asunder all confines of time and space, becomes really and objectively present for us in a mysterious way by means of what happens to bread and wine in Holy Communion, to take us into themselves and to be received by us. "The New Testament clearly teaches that Holy Communion makes the sacrifice of Jesus Christ contemporary and really bestows what was achieved by this sacrifice." [184]

Consecration

We have spoken about the Meal which Jesus instituted as a new meal and celebrated with His disciples in the hour when He supped with them for the last time. And we simultaneously spoke about the Holy Communion which we now celebrate. Our Holy Communion is derived from that Meal of institution, but not in a manner in which a custom or a rite grows from a certain historical occasion and is then perpetuated. Our Holy Communion is far more closely connected with the Meal of institution; nothing in custom and in rite corresponds to it. For our Holy Communion has the instituting Meal with it and in it. To be sure, it is not a copy of the instituting Meal. The external form and the persons are different. But the Lord and His act are present in our Holy Communion with the power effecting the gift of the Meal, as they were in that instituting Meal. Without the presence of the divine authoritative power of Jesus Christ, without the presence of the almighty words from His lips, there would be no real presence of His body and blood either in that instituting Meal or in our Holy Communion. That Jesus Christ Himself is present with His Meal-instituting, powerful, and authoritative act and with His words creating the gift of the Meal is premise to the fact that the bread is His body and the wine is His blood also in our Holy Communion. The Meal-instituting presence of the Lord is premise to the fact that the real presence of His body and blood eventuates.

This poses two questions for us, which must be viewed both in their differentiation from each other and in their dependence upon each other: (1) How is the Meal-instituting presence of the Lord effected? (2) How is the real presence of His body and blood in this Meal-instituting presence of the Lord effected? Perhaps it is clear already that the Meal-instituting presence of the Lord is the bracket which encompasses the real presence of His body and blood. The Meal-instituting presence of the Lord is the comprehensive factor that pervades the entire act. The real presence of His body and blood is appointed as something particular in this comprehensive factor, and is then again dissolved.

The Meal-instituting presence of the Lord is dependent on the assembling together of two or of three or of a hundred — or of any number — in His name as the *ekklesia* already constituted through Gospel and Baptism for the purpose of doing what Christ's followers are enjoined to do in remembrance of Him. The Meal-instituting presence of Jesus Christ is certified for us only in an act of worship in which the name of the Lord is invoked and His Word is proclaimed. The celebration of the Lord's Supper, too, is prayer worship from beginning to end. However, a particular feature, not found in every act of worship, is added here: the concrete obedience to Jesus' one and only institution in the night of His betrayal. The congregation assembled in His name must be assembled with the intent of doing what the Lord did at that time for His disciples. To celebrate this entire, newly instituted Meal, that is what Jesus' disciples are to do in remembrance of Him. Where people do not wish to do what Jesus wants to have done in remembrance of Him, there He does not grant His Meal-instituting presence.[185] Consequently, there must be bread; there must be wine in a cup. Bread and wine must be "consecrated." This is not to be an ordinary meal with bread and wine. Bread and wine are to be lifted out of the purpose which they ordinarily serve in a meal and assigned to this special service of rendering Christ's body and blood present. This Jesus did as He took bread into His hand, spoke a prayer of thanksgiving over it, broke it, and distributed it, and then proceeded to do something similar with the cup. And then this bread must be received to be eaten and this wine to be drunk.

But the "remembrance" of the Lord must also be carried out in a manner in which the congregation fits its Meal concretely and unmistakably into the context of Jesus' institution. The celebration of the Meal must show a "liturgical" order, which clearly reflects a compliance with Jesus' command to do this in "remembrance" of

Him. The anamnesis of Christ must be executed as anamnesis of His instituting Meal. Then Christ vouchsafes His active presence, by which He has His Meal eventuate among us anew. As the *repraesentatio* of the salvation-event, effected by the real presence, is imbedded in and bracketed by the Lord's self-manifestation and His saving act, effected by the proclamation-character of the celebration, so the real presence of Jesus' body and blood is imbedded in and borne by the comprehensive, Meal-creating presence of the Lord. The Augsburg Confession (Art. X) clearly expresses the purport of our words when it stresses the fact that body and blood of Christ are truly present "in Holy Communion" under the bread and the wine.[186]

Since the real presence is dependent on the Meal-creating presence of the Lord, every act by which this Meal-creating presence of the Lord is given us is also important for the bestowal of the real presence of His body and blood. However, that does not preclude, but rather demands, that we view that specific presence of Christ's body and blood, which we designate as the real presence, as an event which took place and was concluded at a definite time in the action. A glance at Jesus' act of institution compels that view. Jesus' words pertaining to the broken bread and to the proffered cup indubitably are of special significance for effecting the real presence —, to be sure, in association with the entire Meal-event. When Jesus says: "This is My body, this is My blood of the covenant," the event which effects the real presence has come to pass with these words. By virtue of the Meal-creating presence of the Lord, He Himself pronounces these miraculous words even today with Messianic executive power through the mouth of His minister. After these words have been pronounced over the consecrated and broken bread and over the consecrated and proffered cup, I may be assured that I am receiving the Lord's body and blood as I receive this bread and this wine.

That clearly affirms that it is not the act of accepting the bread and the cup, not the eating and the drinking, nor the distribution of bread and wine as such that effect the real presence, as surely as distributing, accepting, eating, and drinking are part of that which, as component of the anamnesis, accords us the Meal of the Lord. But the utterance of those words of Christ which declare what this bread and this wine now are constitute the consummation of the event which bestows the real presence of body and blood and, simultaneously, announces the real presence as a consummated event. After these words have been spoken, bread and wine are as surely

Christ's body and blood also before I receive and eat and drink them as they are when I receive and eat and drink them.[187]

This reflection might also remove the misgiving and uncertainty which is widely felt with regard to the question of a reconsecration. A reconsecration is demanded when the bread or the wine over which Christ's IS-words have been spoken has been consumed and therefore has to be replenished for those who are yet to commune. In such an event it will surely not be necessary to repeat the entire rite. But a special act should indicate clearly that the newly added bread or wine is now accepted into the service of the anamnesis enjoined by Christ and is placed under His words of institution. This is done very distinctly if the pastor takes the newly added bread and pronounces Christ's words of institution over it before he continues with the distribution. He proceeds similarly with the cup. To be sure, where the words of institution relating to bread and wine are also used "referringly" as the formula of distribution, the special consecration of the supplemented bread or wine may under certain conditions be omitted, since the formula of distribution here simultaneously assumes the function of consecration. However, when bread and wine have to be distributed several times, the administration of Holy Communion should differentiate also liturgically between the words of consecration and the formula of distribution.

The following guidelines for the treatment of the consecrated elements that remain at the conclusion of the sacrament issue from our doctrine of consecration. With the conclusion of the distribution and the dismissal of all Communion guests from the altar, the act conforming to the institution, the *actio* as *sacramentum* and thus the *usus* of the sacrament, is consummated and ended. Therefore also the presence of Christ's body and blood peculiar to Holy Communion has ended. The claim that the sacramental *unio* of Christ's body and blood and the elements continues after the conclusion of the sacrament contradicts Christ's institution. Since the real presence is bound to the institutional act and its duration, Christ's body and blood cannot be preserved beyond the conclusion of this act to be carried about in a procession or, much less, to be exhibited for adoration.

On the other hand, there can be no doubt that the consecrated food remaining after the conclusion of the sacrament was actually the bearer of Christ's body and blood. This has a bearing on the treatment of this food. Luther entertained serious misgivings about placing consecrated wafers together with unconsecrated ones after

181

the conclusion of the sacrament, or mixing consecrated wine with unconsecrated wine and preserving these for the next celebration of the sacrament.[188] To do that was not in keeping with his doctrine of Holy Communion; it seemed too profane. His scruples were not evoked by any consideration for members weak in the faith. They were obviously rooted in the fact that the creature which had been taken into the sacramental *unio* by Christ merits reverent treatment, to be distinguished from the regard we owe every piece of bread as a gift of God. In Luther's view, the best solution to all such problems was to make provision that no consecrated bread or wine remained. In Luther's day and in the periphery of the Reformation the rule evidently prevailed that all the consecrated elements be consumed before the conclusion of the sacrament. Luther made the officiating clergyman — in contradistinction to the assisting deacons — responsible for the consumption of the consecrated food at the conclusion of the sacramental act: the last communing guests or the co-communing clergymen or the officiating clergyman are to eat or drink the consecrated elements before the conclusion of the distribution. Wherever the Lutheran doctrine of the real presence is really accepted, the propriety of this procedure cannot be questioned.

On the other hand, this procedure cannot be made a law. When at the discussions of the Concord of Wittenberg, 1536, the question was raised by the Lutherans regarding the treatment of the remaining consecrated elements, Butzer replied that it was customary among them to place these back in the container, adding that this was done "with proper reverence." [189] Luther was evidently satisfied with this reply. Indeed, where proper reverence is shown, no basic misgivings can assert themselves against this position, which was also espoused by the later dogmaticians of Lutheran Orthodoxy. However, in regard to the cup used in the distribution, the procedure recommended by Luther will have to be viewed as the best. If wine has remained in the cup and this cannot be kept for the next celebration of Holy Communion, no objection may be raised against its use as a beverage, provided that the proper respect is observed in every way.

The Gift of Holy Communion

Holy Communion is a proclamation of the Gospel in the unity of Word and act. Therefore all that was stated before regarding the proclamation of the Word as means of transmitting salvation and the re-creating Spirit also applies to Holy Communion. Therefore it is possible to receive the bread of life and to "eat" the Lord in Holy Communion (John 6) even when the participant does not receive the bread and the wine. However, in the reception of the Eucharistic food the redemptive gift is presented us in a manner in which this special manner itself becomes gift.

The first item to be named as the special characteristic of this gift is contained in the words of the apostle Paul (1 Cor. 10:16): κοινωνία τοῦ αἵματος τοῦ χριστοῦ, κοινωνία τοῦ σώματος τοῦ χριστοῦ ("communion of the blood and of the body of Jesus Christ"). This *koinonia* is still different from the communion with Christ conveyed by the verbal form of the Gospel. The particular feature is, first of all, the concreteness of this communion with the *Christus pro nobis* vouchsafed in Holy Communion. The selfsame true humanity of Jesus which He received from His mother Mary becomes present to us under the Eucharistic food. Here Jesus Christ steps into our midst not only in the omnipresence of His deity, not only in the Word-bound Pneuma-presence of His divinely derestricted humanity; no, He actually gives this His bodily humanity, in substantial identity with His earthly body, to everyone who receives the bread and the wine in Holy Communion. The Eucharistic real presence vouchsafes the congregation of disciples the "continuation" of the physical presence of Jesus' true humanity in a new, transformed, end-time manner. In the Eucharistic real presence the congregation of disciples has in its midst even now, in a manner in which it may apprehend Him also bodily, the same Jesus who lay in the manger, who traversed Galilee, who suffered in Jerusalem, and who died on Golgotha. But in the Eucharistic real presence it has also, and even now, in its midst in His transformed, derestricted, glorified humanity, deeply hidden, to be sure, and yet prehensible and palpable, the exalted Christ who is seated at the right hand of God and who will one day return visibly to all. Consequently, the gift of Holy Communion is the presence — given us to be apprehended and received and objectively approaching us in the Eucharistic food and thus indubitably present physically — of the One who is the Savior of His followers from His incarnation until His return for judgment.

However, this *koinonia* of Christ's body and blood embraces more than that. It accords the disciples a communion with the dying and departing Lord which could never be theirs before His departure and which they can first receive now as Jesus gives them His Meal anticipatorily, as though death had already separated them from Him.

His departure from us, His going to the Father is indeed "to our advantage" (John 16:7). For precisely this withdrawal of His presence and of His communion through the cross grants the disciples an entirely new communion with the Lord through the resurrection and the outpouring of the Spirit, a communion which touches and pervades and incorporates them in an entirely different way from within. The miracle of Holy Communion consists in this that this incorporating communion, as carried out first and basically in Baptism, is vouchsafed through the reception of the Eucharistic food in an actuality and a reality which is transcended only by the physical resurrection from the dead.

The fact that the one body of Jesus is received physically and spiritually by the believers' lips and soul and that the recipients thereby partake anew of the incorporating communion with Jesus — that is indeed an end-time mystery. Luke offers us a companion picture of this in the Easter report, in which the risen Lord takes of the broiled fish and consumes this earthly food before the eyes of the disciples in order to convince them of the physicalness of His being (Luke 24:42 f.). Two worlds meet in this scene: the physical pneuma-world of the resurrection from the dead in the risen Lord and this earthly world in the morsel of earthly food. The risen Lord still holds sway over earthly things without any detraction from His eschatologically transformed physicalness. If the Lord here takes earthly food into His heavenly body, then He is certainly able to give us earthly-physical beings His body both physically and spiritually, the body which was given into death and raised from death for us all. For Him, the Victor, the boundary between the physical Pneuma-world of the resurrection and our earthly world of the body, forfeit to death, no longer exists. He already breaks this boundary asunder as He effects the Eucharistic real presence and makes the unaltered elements the bearers of His body and blood. But He also disrupts this boundary in every act of Communion as He conveys, both physically and spiritually, to us earthly-physical creatures His body, which is bound by no earthly barriers. It should now be evident that this transcendence of boundaries by Jesus Christ in Holy Communion, as in Baptism, involves the hidden dawn of the resurrection from the dead.

If Jesus places His body of death into us in Holy Communion, then He thereby also places us into this body of the cross, which fills the universe since Easter, and of which we have already become members through Baptism. The reception of the communion of Jesus Christ's body and blood is an event in Christ, in the body of Christ. This event confirms, fortifies, renews, and engenders ever anew this in-being in Jesus' body of the cross. As those who gather in His name and believe in His name receive the Eucharistic food, the many are united in this celebration into the body of Jesus, embracing and including the entire church. The Christ-event in Holy Communion is, as such, simultaneously an ecclesiological event, an event that actually constitutes the *ekklesia*. Through the reception of Jesus Christ's one sacrificial body the many are truly joined together into this body.

As our communion with Jesus Christ's body and blood places us into His sacrificial body, comprehending and encompassing the whole church, it also accords us the communion of the saints, the *communio sanctorum*. We noted that our celebration of Holy Communion shares in the Meal of the night of betrayal. We participate in the celebration of the Meal which was given to the disciples in that night. Our Lord's Supper, which the Lord prepares for us through His Meal-creating presence, is in its substance none other than that which He prepared at that time for His disciples. This participation of the church's Holy Communion in the instituting Meal, this hidden presence of the instituting Meal in every celebration of Holy Communion by the church, joins all celebrations of the sacrament of the past, of the present, and of the future in the context of Jesus' institution, and all participants in these celebrations, beginning with the disciples and the apostles down to us, transcending all times and all geographical boundaries, even all denominational boundaries, into one great Holy Communion, compressed into one wonderful Communion of "today," under the one Lord in His one sacrificial body. The one relation to the institution and the one sacrificial body together create, in the administration of Holy Communion, the communion of saints in the one holy church.

But thus far we have not yet mentioned the most particular item involved in the gift of the Meal. Amid all the plenitude of meaning and content which we endeavored to recognize and to sustain we reverted again and again to this theme: Jesus' atoning sacrificial death. The FOR-YOU, which pervades and molds the entire Christ-event, has Jesus' death as its center, or rather its telos, from which the entire FOR-YOU-event, from Christmas on, derives its power. In Jesus' cross the new end-time order of salvation is established, in which the kingdom of God, the resurrection from the dead, and the transformation of all things dawns. Golgotha is the only entry into this end-time order of salvation. The kingdom of God makes its way into this world only through Christ's sacrificial body; for reconciliation is effected only through His blood. Therefore, Holy Communion's comprehensive gift of salvation is Jesus' atoning sacrificial death, which directly apprehends us in its really present sacrificial body and in its really present sacrificial blood and receives us into God's reconciling act. Reconciliation through the remission of sins in the body and blood of Jesus Christ, that is the end-time gift of Holy Communion, which was made available to us by Jesus' suffering and death, and which opens and brings the kingdom of God to us. This forgiveness of sins, realized through Jesus' sacrificial body, bursts all bonds of sin and of guilt, of death and of the devil, asunder. Therefore this forgiveness, enclosed in Jesus' sacrificial death, is really the end-time gift of God's kingdom. Indeed, where this gift is, there the Spirit is which is poured forth, there the new life is which conquers death, there salvation is which extricates us from judgment and perdition and corruption of death. Where there is forgiveness of sins, there eternal life begins.

Forgiveness of sin, eternal life and blessedness are in particular and in a special way the gift of Holy Communion. Holy Communion bestows this gift enclosed in this really present and true sacrificial body of Christ itself. The treasure house, the sacrificial body, and the treasure, forgiveness, are one here. Nothing intervenes between the tree of the cross and the gift of forgiveness. The source of the gift and the gift are actually one here. Only here, where Jesus offers us His true body and His true blood in the form of bread and wine for our physical and spiritual reception, He gives us the actual oneness of His sacrificial fruit with His sacrificial body.

With this gift the fetters and the bonds of this world are rent asunder. Endowed with this gift, we ourselves are placed into the open door which Jesus' death on the cross forced ajar for us and which leads into the kingdom of God, into the world of the new creation. Therefore Holy Communion itself is — by the power of Jesus' sacrificial body present in it and by the power of the end-time forgiveness — the opening of the door, through which God's consummation of all things begins to enter into this world.

The Lord's Supper as a Festive Meal in Anticipatory Preview of the Lamb's Wedding Feast in Glory

When Jesus instituted the Lord's Supper, He Himself looked forward to His future royal feast in the glory of the kingdom of God: "Truly, I say to you, I shall not drink again of the fruit of the vine until that day when I drink it new in the kingdom of God" (Mark 14:25; cf. Matt. 26:29; Luke 22:18). Even the Old Testament views the fullness of salvation of God's coming kingdom as a festive meal (Is. 25:6-9). Jesus awaits this blessed meal at the table of God together with the kingdom of God. And those who belong to Jesus will also partake of this meal (Matt. 8:11; Luke 13:28 ff.; 14:15-24). This meal will be His royal marriage feast which He celebrates with His kingdom congregation, with His bridal congregation. (Matt. 22: 2-14; 25:10; 2 Cor. 11:2; Rev. 19:7; 21:2, 9; 22:17)

However, for those who are His, this nuptial joy of God's kingdom has already begun with Jesus' coming and His sojourn on earth. With His person, with His Word and work the kingdom is indeed already present in Him. Where He is present in person, His followers cannot fast and mourn, but, as wedding guests, celebrate the feast with the Lord with the joy of fulfillment (Mark 2:19, and parallels; Matt. 11:18 f.; John 3:29). This meal fellowship of the earthly Lord with His disciples, marked by poverty and lowliness and yet also illumined by the light of the coming meals in glory, are now discontinued with the institution of the Lord's Supper. Through Jesus' surrender to death they are discontinued by Himself. But this is done only for the purpose of making a breach through which the way leads to the "new" meal in the eschatologically transformed world of glory. Here "old" and "new" do not only contrast with one another. This "old" meal fellowship of Jesus is not merely a figurative reference to that which is to come. That which is to come in the glory of the kingdom is a continuation and consummation of what is happening now. What is happening now already contains, in a hidden manner, something of what is to come. "This verse (Mark 14:25) does not only point to an eschatological event, but it also interprets an eschatological event already in progress; the introductory and concluding clauses are pervaded by it in every expression. What will one day come to pass, the perfected communion of the meal, is already being realized now; the present hour and its event thus belong to the eschatological reality of the kingdom of God." [190]

When the Lord's Supper originates in this hour, it becomes, as the interim between the now discontinuing old and the coming new meal communion with Jesus, the mirror which captures and retains the redemptive reality of the old table fellowship together with the fullness of salvation of the future meal in the kingdom of God. In anticipatory "remembrance," the Lord's Supper becomes a symbolic pregift of Jesus' nuptial meal with His bridal congregation. If the prophetic *oth* makes already present future eschatological events, how much more will this meal token of the Messiah become a vessel in which that which is to come is already very much present!

But it is not only prophetic *oth* that is being fulfilled here, but also and above all a function of Old Testament worship which goes back to the oldest times and pervades the entire cultic life of Israel and of Jewry, through which it, especially in the meals associated with it, lets the great festive meal of the end time and its salvation become a "today" even now.[191] That applies particularly to Israel's anniversary celebrations, which are basically covenant-renewal festivals and are characterized by the anticipatory view of this covenant's fulfillment in the end time. Therefore "festive joy" prevails at these feasts (Deut. 16:11, 14; 14:26; 26:11; 2 Chron. 30:23, 25 f.; Ezra 6:22; Neh. 8:10; in the Apocrypha cf. Book of Jubilees 49:2, 6, 22). Eschatological certainty of salvation of the people of the covenant, festive meal, and "liturgical" joy (Bo Reicke) form a solid unit. In the cultic festive meal a trace of the Paradisiacal supermundane richness of God's new world is already apparent.[192] The cultic proximity of the eschatological boon of salvation is the root of the cultic-liturgical joy.

We must not forget that this Israelitic-Jewish festive joy registers a breakthrough through external distress. Originally it is a rejoicing over a deliverance. A deliverance from the land of death and into the life of liberty vouchsafed by God cannot be celebrated commemoratively unless the final deliverance of God, the final breakthrough to the ultimate freedom, is already comprehended in this deliverance. In the cultic anamnesis the exodus from Egypt and the entry into the Promised Land become the eschatological *transitus*. Death's agony and salvation's joy, remembrance of distress and expectation of the time of salvation, are not opposed to each other but are juxtaposed. The liturgical joy of the Israelitic-Jewish festivals is rooted in this movement from the agony of death to the joy of deliverance, from the memory of misery to the expectation of the time of salvation. This breakthrough from the distress of death to the Messianic joy of the day of the Lord is mirrored in many psalms which are closely related to Israel's tradition of worship, as, for example, the psalms that deal with Christ's Passion (Ps. 22; cf. especially vv. 25-27) and the psalms that were sung at the end of the Passover meal (Psalms 116–118; cf. especially Ps. 116:8-13; 118:13-18).

These deliberations are of great significance for an understanding of Jesus' Meal, of the Holy Communion of the early congregations, and of our own Holy Communion. Jesus' Holy Communion is the end-time fulfillment of the Old Testament sacrificial covenant meal. Thus the Lord's Supper is also the end-time fulfillment of the Old Testament festive joy. The "remembrance" of His death and the rejoicing over their salvation with which the early congregations celebrated this Meal in their worship services do not exclude each other, as we see from Acts 2:46, but they belong together.[193]

Precisely because these two points are bound together in a rationally incomprehensible manner, this rejoicing of the Christians in their worship services is devoid of any secondary motive, of any self-seeking and egotism, devoid of fanaticism and zealotism, but is allied with sincere, upright, and loving devotion of the heart (ἁπλότης). The rejoicing over salvation becomes egotistically, factiously, fanatically, zealotically distorted when it detaches itself from the remembrance of Jesus' sacrificial death. And because this was happening in Corinth, Paul again moves the anamnesis of Christ's cross into the center of Holy Communion, not in order to suppress the congregation's rejoicing over its salvation, but to link it to the sacrifice of God's love and to make it amenable to the sacred pneumatic propriety and sobriety befitting those who await the Lord with this very Meal and for that reason can never forget the boundary of the interim during which they reflect on the coming joy.[194]

This joy which is no longer of this world springs from the recollection of Jesus' death, from the reception of His sacrificial body, from the communion of His body and blood. As we are received into Christ's sacrificial body, we transcend death's boundary and obtain a share in the life which was achieved through Christ's victory on the cross and came to light in His resurrection. His *ekklesia*-body is constituted precisely through the communion of His body and blood; and this *ekklesia*-body yearns for its visible reunion with its Head in glory. Only in the communion of His body is the church the "pure bride" (2 Cor. 11:2) who goes out to meet and eagerly awaits the returning Messiah, and who in such waiting may already be united with Him precisely through Holy Communion.

189

What will happen when the cry resounds in the heavens: "The marriage of the Lamb has come!" (Rev. 19:7) is foreshadowed in the celebration of Holy Communion: the bride goes out to meet the Bridegroom. When Holy Communion is celebrated, there is no room for fasting and mourning. When Holy Communion is celebrated, the wedding feast (Hoch-Zeit) again becomes present in a new form; and amid the sorrows of this earth, Jesus' fellowship with His disciples lends this wedding feast that radiant joy which hovers over the dawn of end-time fulfillment. "Your sorrow will turn into joy" (John 16:20). This ancient cultic transitus of the Old Covenant attains its final, end-time, fulfilled form in the sacrificial meal of the New Covenant, until it finds its consummation in the apocalyptic epiphany of the bridal congregation and of the Bridegroom for all eternity and all eons, when the crucified and exalted Christ will drink anew with us (Matt. 26:29) in the splendor of the kingdom of God.

This royal marriage feast of the Lamb is heralded in Holy Communion. That meal is "close" in this Meal. That meal is immediately before the door in this Meal (Rev. 3:20). In this Meal that meal becomes hidden presence, veiled in the earthly forms of a meal. In this Meal the bridal congregation already hears the Bridegroom's voice: "Behold, I am coming soon!" (Rev. 22:7). And the Spirit, poised over the congregation and dwelling in the congregation, as well as the congregation itself in its pneumatic bridal form, reply: "Come. And let him who hears say: Come! And let him who is thirsty come, let him who desires take the water of life without price. . . . Amen. Come, Lord Jesus!" (Rev. 22:17, 20). Where bride and Bridegroom approach each other, in this dialog, across the last threshold and await each other for the enjoyment of perfect bliss, there the Holy Communion of the church of Jesus Christ is found. Therefore, in the anamnesis of Jesus' death and victory on the cross this Meal is an eschatological festive meal of joy; it bestows the joy which is no longer of this earth.

Holy Communion as an End-Time Mystery

The end-time mystery of the proclamation of the Word is similarly compressed in Holy Communion as the commemorative character and the means-of-grace character of the proclamation of the Word are. Also in Holy Communion everything remains human. Everything remains earthly. Even the bread remains bread and the wine remains wine. The eschatological transformation of the creature is still in abeyance. Everything remains symbol. But this symbol is filled to the brim with the latent reality of the kingdom of God and His world. Transcending by far the mystery of the proclamation of the human word in worship, the bread and the wine themselves become mystery in Holy Communion in an unparalleled, absolutely incomprehensible manner. The *unio spiritualis,* of which we had occasion to speak in connection with the proclamation of the Word, here becomes an *unio sacramentalis* in the bread and the wine. In the union of the bread and of Christ's body and in the union of the wine and of Christ's blood the sovereign freedom and the divine omnipotence of the true creatural humanity of our risen and exalted Lord manifests itself.

This bread, His body; this cup, His blood, this mystery verges on that other mystery, in which it, in the final analysis, is rooted and which bears all the mysteries of the church — this true body, the body of the Eternal Word; this shed blood, the blood of Him who is true God from true God. As Jesus Christ offers Himself to us physically in this Eucharistic food in His true humanity united with His deity, He actually delivers Himself into the hands of sinners. He does not disdain to be touched and held by us, who can live only by the forgiveness of His sacrifice. In this event the eternal Son again verifies that He is the Incarnate Word. In this event the Lord "appears" anew, as He makes bread and wine in Holy Communion the epiphanic form of His suffering and death and coming until He returns in the epiphany of His glory. The consecrated broken bread and the consecrated given cup as the epiphany of the slain Lamb in His *ekklesia* — that is what makes Holy Communion the mystery of the end time in the interim between the resurrection of the crucified Christ and His return.

In the power of this Eucharistic mystery, Holy Communion becomes the mystery of the church. We behold only these frail and fallible individuals gathered about the Lord's table. At this table we acknowledge that we are sinners who stand in need of forgiveness. However, as forgiveness is vouchsafed us in the reception of Jesus' sacrificial body, an invisible miracle takes place: the many become one body. In the power of the received sacrificial body the many become this one body itself. As the Lord grants and gives us His sacrificial body in Holy Communion, He forms and preserves it among us, and in it He unites us beyond the confines of time and of space with all who are "in Him"; and thus He creates His body anew and perfects it in His church. No one can see that. And yet it takes

191

place. In fact, the miracle happens with such reality that it comes to us as judgment if we conduct ourselves "in an unworthy manner" (1 Cor. 11:27) over against it, that is, if we conduct ourselves contra-body, contra-*ekklesia*, contra-agape.

The end-time mystery of Holy Communion reaches even further. We declared that the prophetic *oth*, when stated with the authoritative power of God's messenger, is endued with an effectual power. It effects the event designated in it. Holy Communion, too, has not only an effectual power with regard to rendering the past redemptive event present, but also with regard to future events. It is not indifferent for world- and kingdom-events whether or not the recollection of Jesus' death is carried out on earth. Paul intimated that when he declared that the anamnesis of Christ be carried out "until He comes" (1 Cor. 11:26). This "until" is not merely a formal stipulation of time. The meaning of the words "so that" also pulsate in it.[195] As anamnestic proclamation of Jesus' death on the cross, which ushers in the end time, the celebration of Holy Communion is simultaneously a comprehensive Maranatha: "Come, Lord Jesus!" In its administration and in its words Holy Communion is the church's prayer for the final breakthrough of the kingdom of God. The fact that the church celebrates the remembrance of Christ by prayer, proclamation, and act thus becomes an event which elicits the remembrance of the Lord Himself. But when God remembers, something happens. God's remembrance bids His promises, His fidelity to the covenant, become effective and create something new (Gen. 9:15 f.; Ex. 32:13; Deut. 9:27; Ps. 105:8).[196] "God's remembering is an effective and creative event." [197]

But this remembering of God is released not only by the prayer of the individual (Judges 16:28; 2 Kings 20:3; Ps. 74:2; 89:51; 106:4; 132:1; etc.), but also by cultic celebrations (cf., e.g., Num. 10:10). If the prayers and alms of Cornelius "ascended as a memorial before God" (Acts 10:4), this may be said with even greater reason of Holy Communion as celebrated in obedience to Christ's institution. In the victorious power of Jesus' sacrificial death on the cross the New Testament covenant memorial ascends to God's throne and evokes His active, end-effecting remembering. Holy Communion, too, is not a passive, static "mystery" given us for "contemplation," but it is a dynamic event. In its earthly administration it releases a heavenly event, a kingdom-of-God movement in the heavens, yes, even in the heart of God. In this deeply hidden event, which penetrates all the heavens and actualizes Christ's victory on the cross over all antigodly powers, the end-time mystery of Holy Communion is completed.[198]

Holy Communion as an End-Time Crisis

He who partakes of Holy Communion has been baptized. In his life an end-time decision has already been made. As a member of Jesus' body the baptized person receives the sacrificial body of Jesus in Holy Communion in order to be confirmed, preserved, strengthened, and perfected in this membership. Whereas the question whether or not the hearer will be brought to faith by the missionary proclamation of the Gospel to the world is decided by the very event of this proclamation, in Holy Communion it may be assumed that the communicant approaches the Lord's Table in true faith. But this fact notwithstanding, partaking of Holy Communion also places him anew into an end-time crisis who, in a way, already has made an end-time decision by his acceptance of the Word and his reception of Baptism. For it is this very decision from which the Christian is not dismissed as he partakes of Holy Communion. Holy Communion must not inevitably redound to his blessing, it may redound to his condemnation.

This dare not be construed to mean that my faith first makes Holy Communion what it is in itself by its administration and by virtue of Christ's institution. The presence of the body and blood of Jesus Christ, the presence of the gifts contained in these, depends solely on the sacrament's administration in conformity with Christ's institution. Neither the pastor's attitude nor the disposition of the congregation or of an individual member of the congregation can jeopardize the mystery of Holy Communion, can adversely affect the event of this mystery effected by its administration. But precisely because our partaking of Holy Communion and our reception of the Eucharistic food includes, in every instance, a real concrete encounter with Jesus Christ and the incarnation-presence of God, which is granted us in the sacrament, independently of our disposition and decision, every celebration of Holy Communion becomes a crisis for the congregation and the individual communicant which operates and reaches directly into the Last Judgment.

In conformity with the Holy Communion liturgy of his church,[199] Ignace of Antioch in his letter to the Ephesians (20, 2) terms the gift of Holy Communion "remedy of immortality, antidote against death, to live forever in Jesus Christ." This statement is not erroneous. Also

Paul and John "would adjudge the expression correct" which Ignace uses here.[200] But in contradistinction to the Hellenistic mysteries and their "curative gifts," the gift of Holy Communion does not work mechanically or "magically," but positively "critically." It does not present us with a material medicine. The curative means of the Eucharist is the historical redemptive act of God in Jesus Christ, which is incorporated in the sacrificial body of Jesus and is presented to us as His sacrificial body in the Eucharistic food. He who receives this saving remedy thereby stands in the presence of the Crucified Himself. Therefore our partaking of Holy Communion and our reception of the Eucharistic food always involves the decision anew which we make with every confrontation with Christ. The actualization of faith in Him and the exemplification of love for Him are also included in Holy Communion: "He who loves the Lord, come! May he who does not love the Lord be cast out! Maranatha!" (cf. 1 Cor. 16:22, in conjunction with *Didache*, 10, 6). These words were inscribed above the entrance to the celebration of Holy Communion by the apostolic congregations, and they emphatically point to the "critical" character of the sacrament.[201] Because Holy Communion is celebrated on the threshold of Christ's return for judgment, its eschatological joy will not degenerate into a selfish and complacent possession of redemption, but it will reflect the seriousness of death and judgment and of the return of Christ. In that very way this joy will prove itself a gift which is no longer of this world.

The critical character of Holy Communion is intensified by the sacrament's working of the body. The sacrificial body of Christ, which we receive in the Eucharistic food, makes the recipients the *ekklesia*-body of Christ, which is and remains His sacrificial body. Through Holy Communion the Christian is in every instance received into the one sacrificial body of Christ, just as a person is in every instance molded into a member of Christ's body by Baptism.[202]

The recipients of Holy Communion may overlook this becoming His body which is taking place. They may overlook the specific sacrificial character of the body of Christ. They may overlook the fact that the one *ekklesia*, which "the many" become through Holy Communion, lives only from the power of the sacrificial body of Jesus, consequently, in the power of His love. He who overlooks that "does not discern the body" (1 Cor. 11:29).[203] He does not know the power of the real presence of Christ's body and blood, which lays claim to any service with the might of Christ's sacrificial love. Consequently, not to discern the body also means: to reject with our deeds the love of Christ which approaches us concretely in Holy Communion. Thus, to discern the body also means, last but not least: actually to accept Christ's love, mediated to us in Christ's sacrificial body, and, in consequence, to be united in fraternal responsibility in the love of the *ekklesia*-body.

Where the body of Christ is overlooked and rejected in this power which determines our practical conduct, there the bread and the cup of the Lord, though received physically, are received "in an unworthy manner." Who violates the agape of the *ekklesia*-body of Christ by his daily conduct offends against the Lord's body and blood themselves. Then the judgment comes to pass of which Paul writes in 1 Cor. 11:27-32. And to him who is not chastened by this judgment of the Lord and does not repent, it will become the final judgment by which the world is condemned. With the help of the Old Testament "prototypes" of Baptism and Holy Communion, Paul made it impressively clear in 1 Cor. 10:1-12 that the physical reception of the sacraments as such is by no means a protection against the judgment of God. Also the Sacrament of the Altar saves only when received in the faith which includes love and exercises it.

Holy Communion as the Glorification of the Triune God

It would be wrong if Christians who are aware of the critical character of Holy Communion would on that account be deterred from doing what they are obliged to do in memory of Christ in accord with His institution. In no way can the Christian escape the end-time crisis implicit in the presence of the end-time salvation. He who thinks he jeopardizes himself less by exposing himself only to the end-time crisis inherent in the proclamation of the Word, deludes himself. Thereby he denies the Lord the service of remembrance which Jesus demands of His followers. This disobedience and this dearth of love will surely accuse him. By itself, the end-time crisis which arises from the presence of end-time salvation will not become a menace to us. The danger does not issue from the presence of salvation, but from the malice of the human heart. That end-time crisis does not purpose to be the turning point to judgment, but to salvation. It results in judgment for the impenitent heart, involuntarily as it were, only because it is replete with deliverance and salvation.

But if we humbly accept what the Lord does for us in Holy Communion, if we do not oppose His gracious activity by inward and outward act, but permit His will to be done on us, then we receive forgiveness in Jesus' blood of the covenant, then we enter through the New Covenant into the end-time order of salvation, then the body of Christ is built through the quickening Spirit, then the body grows into its full stature, then the Kingdom comes. By our acceptance of the gift of salvation, our poor and imperfect commemoration of Jesus Christ enhances the manifestation of God's glory. By the administration of the salvation-event in Holy Communion, our celebration becomes a mirror which reflects our God's power and glory of love as it appeared in Jesus. Assuredly, God's power and glory are not diminished by His giving Himself to us. But God expects to see His power and glory shine forth also on this earth and increase also in us and through us. That is done wherever the power and glory of His love is beamed forth on the *ekklesia* as the sacrificial body of His Son and floods us in this sacrificial body with the light of heavenly radiance. God's glory appears in the Incarnate One. Today and in this world it does not appear otherwise than in the embodiment of His sacrificial love. Every celebration of Holy Communion is — hidden under the veil of the end-time mystery — an epiphany of God's sacrificial love in the sacrificial body of His Son, which is also the pneumatic body of His *ekklesia*. Therefore every obedient administration of the anamnesis of Christ in Holy Communion materializes the glory of the Triune God here on earth and on us men, the glory of the Father, who sent the Son into our flesh for our reconciliation, the glory of the Incarnate One, whose sacrificial death is His glorification, the glory of the Eternal Spirit, who, as agape, enlivens the sacrifice of the Son in His *ekklesia*-body and preserves it live to all eternity.

8

WORSHIP AS THE CONGREGATION'S SERVICE BEFORE GOD

We have observed what God does for us in worship. Now we turn our attention to what we as members of the congregation assembled in Jesus' name do in worship insofar as our actions are directed to God. We are unable to speak of the latter with the same certitude as we may with regard to the former. Whether or not our action in worship is actually a service to God is a critical question which must be posed at the beginning of our deliberations.

The congregation's service before God becomes real by reason of the fact that God Himself presents the congregation with the act of service as His gift. If God does not arouse us to His service through the Holy Spirit, all that we do in worship remains dead. That does not preclude that God's Word and the Lord's Supper are and remain God's Word and the Lord's Supper even when the minister is a hypocrite and when there are unbelievers and disobedient among the hearers and the communicants. What God presents to us in Word and Sacrament is not rendered questionable by our qualifications. However, our action addressed to God is questionable from the very beginning. All participants in worship are constrained to concede that their worship is constantly endangered by their old carnal essence. The struggle between flesh and spirit, which pervades the entire obedience of the Christian, is perhaps nowhere so brisk, so incisive, so inexorable as it is here where we are gathered as members of a congregation in service to God and before God. It is absolutely decisive for the proper spiritual conduct of worship that we approach it as people who live in Baptism. Also in the congregation's worship, service before God can be properly rendered only insofar as we die with Christ and, as dying, live with Him. And this shows that worship becomes possible only as an act of the new obedience imparted by the Holy Spirit.

WORSHIP AS PNEUMATIC OBEDIENCE

God's forgiveness is perfect. It justifies the whole man. It justifies and saves the person. Our obedience is imperfect and constantly requires forgiveness. But we make a beginning with our obedience; it grows; and it will one day, after the resurrection of our body, be perfected in service before the throne of God. For God's Word and Sacrament are not ineffectual. As surely as the end-time crisis, which the proclamation of the Gospel, Baptism, and the Lord's Supper bring to man, by God's mercy leads to faith and not to impenitence, so surely also a new obedience of the believers, born of the Spirit, is wrought. The area in which we may serve God above all else with the incipient obedience of our faith is, according to His holy will, the worship of the congregation.

This worship is the content of God's commandment. It is God's will that His Word be proclaimed and the memorial feast of the Lord be celebrated. It is God's will that we call upon His name, that we pray, praise, and thank. There are other demands God makes, but He insists that this, too, be done under all circumstances. If we are disobedient in this respect and refuse Him this service, we cannot serve Him properly in any other phase of our life either. That which is decisive for us and for the whole world comes to pass precisely through the salvation-event in the proclamation of the Word and in Holy Communion. If this salient element of service is no longer rendered, no God-pleasing service can be rendered by us in any other area of our life either. If this decisive element is stunted, all other services of the Christian in the world will also be dwarfed, will be amiss, will be fruitless.

The obedience to God's commandment is a new obedience. It is the fruit of what God has already performed on us through Word and Sacrament. Therefore the congregation does not assemble for worship from legal coercion, not from slothful habit, but in the spontaneity of the Spirit. Therefore its service before God does not mark a spasmodic exertion, but a happy privilege. It is true especially of this service designed to praise God that it rests on the gift and the strength which God Himself bestows (1 Peter 4:10 f.). To be sure, all those theories err which construe worship as a celebration in which the piety of the congregation displays itself with an inner cogency, finding expression in certain forms. However, these false teachings on worship register a truth which has to be accepted by the correct doctrine on worship. It is true that nothing in our worship activity serves God unless it has first been given us by God. All that we do in worship is God-pleasing service only insofar as it issues from the Spirit poured out over us.

That, of course, does not exclude our willing, our deliberating, our thinking, our endeavors in behalf of words, signs, and acts. On the contrary! Precisely because we are here assembled as a congregation and our doing is to serve the edification of the whole congregation, every act of worship must be judiciously considered, intelligibly expressed, and executed in an order understandable to all. As 1 Cor. 14 indicates, worship does indeed have a rational side. This rational side is engaged in the service of the communion-character of worship. The word character, which stamps the entire worship, is an expression of this rational side. For "word" involves thinking, even where we approach the ultimate of the expressible, as in the hymnic word. But this our conscious, rational, willed doing, which encompasses the entire worship from beginning to end, must not emanate from our old being, but from the re-creating Spirit. It is wrong to picture this working of the Spirit as something confused, disordered, obscure, or even as something excessively emotional. The Spirit is lucid. The Spirit creates "order." The Spirit illumines reason. The Spirit speaks in intelligible words. The fact that the abstract word in the congregation's worship is distended to its utmost limits in the hymnic word and does not break but withstands this rupture test, and that it, moreover, remains the comprehensible, intelligible, clear Word of God in this ultimate and most elevated form with which man serves God — that is the Spirit's miraculous work performed on the language of man.

This orderly, rational clarity of worship activity is a mystery. It is the mystery which is materialized in every act of the new obedience. The mystery consists in the fact that our willing, thinking, speaking, and doing no longer derive from ourselves, but are given us, are "inspired," and yet are our willing, thinking, speaking, and doing. Our activity in worship is legitimate only by reason of this passivity, and yet it remains our activity. Thus worship does not become an act performed by us, but a gift placed into our lap, which we may take into our hands and use as our doing. Therefore the obedience with which we serve God in worship partakes of a child-like, imperturbable joy. This obedience is, in fact, related to the self-forgetting, unconcerned play of children. We recall that wisdom stands before God dallying like a child and playfully pursues its work on God's earth (Prov. 8:30 f.). The worship of the church participates in this wondrous play when it is administered in the Spirit, in Christ. Therefore the hymn is cogently a part of worship. The obedience of this service is not attended by grumbling, but is joyfully rendered with song.

But nonetheless this Spirit-wrought, childlike, happy, and playful obedience remains under the clear commandment of God. It does not follow its own course. It does not trust its own notions. As Spirit-wrought obedience it holds to the course of the Word, conveyed to us by God through His prophets and apostles, without lapsing into legalistic rigidity or ritualistic constraint. God's commandment contained in His Word and the Spirit working in the congregation do not oppose each other, but, as it were, embrace each other. What God commands us in His Word respecting our service before Him and what the Spirit, poured out over the congregation and working in us, makes of our willing, speaking, and doing, correspond, and will one day, after the resurrection, completely merge into one.

Worship as Prayer

We have already recognized that worship as a whole falls within the dimension of prayer. But it is imperative that this prayer also appear as a special act of the congregation, that it be performed as a particular act which is clearly differentiated from the remaining events by invitational words such as "Let us pray" or "Let us give thanks."

Prayer presupposes the manifest presence of God. Prayer presupposes that presence of God in which God is present *for us* so that we may speak to Him as He speaks to us. Prayer takes place in the incarnation-presence of God.[204] Prayer takes place in the open door, burst open for us by Christ's cross and resurrection. But this special presence of God confronts us particularly in His proclaimed Word and in the celebration of Holy Communion. Therefore proclamation of the Word and the rite of Holy Communion elicit the prayer of the congregation.

However, also the converse is true: Prayer presupposes that the Word may be proclaimed in obedience to Christ's command and Holy Communion be celebrated in keeping with His institution. As we invoke the name of the Triune God in the proclamation of the Word and in Holy Communion, these are moved into Christ's institution-context. That God approaches us through His Word and in His Meal with His incarnation-presence is not a mechanical, but a pneumatic event. Therefore we implore God for the gift of this particular presence.

It is especially our recognition of the end-time crisis, ushered in for us by the Word and the Lord's Supper, that compels our prayer. To be sure, God grants us His incarnation-presence in the words of the Gospel and in Holy Communion; but we pray that this may become a gracious presence for us too. We pray that we may accept Him and His gifts in faith, and that we do not reject them impenitently. He who recognizes the critical aspect of the salvation-event in the proclamation of the Word and in Holy Communion is aware why he is praying and for what he is praying in this event.

Thus the prayer of the congregation encompasses all that God does for us in worship. The pneumatic character of God's presence, the end-time crisis which it entails, impels the congregation in advance to pray, just as, conversely, God's incarnation-presence in the proclaimed Word and in the Lord's Supper cannot be recognized and accepted unless we, through Christ our Lord, may say to God, who is present and dealing with us, "Thou, our Father!"

In no other phase of worship does its mystery become so immediately present to us as in prayer. We do not know what to pray. Our words of prayer are only the vessel for Another One, who, hidden under our words, represents us with His words, with His inexpressible words, with His inexpressible sighing. All depends on this Other One, the Spirit Himself, that He enter into our words of prayer and plead before God for us with His inexpressible words, in, with, and under our words of prayer.

In no other phase of our worship does our worship problem become so immediately apparent as in prayer. For this is the critical question, whether that Other One, the Spirit, actually enters into our words of prayer and deposits these directly before God, or whether our words of prayer remain mere rote, which causes nothing but an agitation of sound waves. In view of this, the mutual benediction of pastor and congregation, expressed in the salutation, is highly appropriate. And this surely involves a special responsibility for him who pronounces the prayer as the congregation's spokesman. The question whether the pastor prays properly with the congregation is as consequential as the question whether he preaches properly. The decisive breakthrough in our life of worship must be sought at this point. If the congregational prayer, through the work of the Holy Spirit, actually reaches its mark in God's heart, then every worship problem is overcome. However, if we do not pray in the Spirit, but only prate liturgical words, even the best order of worship will not help us.

As surely as a believing reception of the Lord Jesus Christ and of His salvation is achieved through the Gospel, through Baptism, and through Holy Communion, so surely the true pneumatic prayer of His congregation is also attained. This prayer is the greatest prerogative of Christians, which God conferred on them as He placed them, justified by faith, into their filial relationship. Prayer is possible only in God's congregational family. Prayer is exercise of the filial privilege in the family of God. In contradistinction to slaves, sons are members of the family. Sons are heirs. Therefore sons share in the responsibilities of all household affairs. Sons are entitled to speak in the family of the Father. Prayer is the permission which God accords His sons to join their voices in the discussion of His affairs. This permission of prayer is the form in which God lets His sons already participate in the reign of the one Son. That the church is composed of a royal people of God is demonstrated especially by the fact that it is permitted to pray and that it avails itself of this permission. As the church executes its conferred authority and power of sonship in prayer, it may already, as the praying, petitioning, thanking, and praising church, share in the royal authority and power of its Head.

It is entirely consonant with the filial position of the believers assembled as a congregation that their prayer be, above all, petition. The sons are entirely dependent on the gifts and grants of the Father. They are still pilgrims, engaged in the eschatological *transitus*. This situation implies that the congregation participates in God's royal government principally by way of supplicating prayer. In the end-time interim of the *ekklesia*, petition is the central content of prayer. The petitionary character of prayer indicates that we are not yet seated at God's table with the Lord as we will be in the glory of the Father. The plan-of-salvation "not yet," which defines the place of the church in God's universal history of salvation, is also distinctly marked by the fact that the church's prayer consists above all in petitioning and supplicating. The petition also conforms to our situation between our baptismal death and our physical death, to our struggle between flesh and spirit, to our role in the universal fight between darkness and light. Petition and end-time combat, petition and end-time hope, are closely allied. In the petition the church acknowledges the eschatological interim as the place assigned it by God until He Himself terminates all petitions and supplications through the epiphany of His Son in glory.

It is consistent with the filial position of the believers collected in a congregation that their petition be, above all else, a prayer for the kingdom of God. The church prays as the family of the sons of God. It prays as the body of Christ in articulate association with its Head. Therefore its prayer revolves, in the main, about the affairs of God, that His name be hallowed, that His kingdom come, that His will be done. But, simultaneously, in its supplication every need which oppresses the church on its pilgrimage may be voiced. When we pray for daily bread, for nourishment of the body, for blessings on the state of marriage, for the proper training of the youth, for good government, we are not petitioning for anything "unspiritual"; these items of God's order of preservation are involved in the history of His kingdom and are closely associated with it. But also sin and guilt, trial and temptation, tribulation and distress, come into the confines of the coming kingdom and may therefore be revealed before God in the congregation's kingdom-prayer down to their very depths, so that He may pour His power, His forgiveness, His life, His salvation into this wretchedness.

Sons converse with their father with the conviction of having their request fulfilled. And since the church prays with this same conviction, its prayer becomes a prayer of thanksgiving. As it supplicates, it already receives the object of its supplication. As it entreats, its eyes are opened and behold the gifts already granted. In its own existence, the church beholds the gifts of the Creator, of the Redeemer, and of the Re-creator. The church cannot come before God in prayer unmindful of the miracle that the creature may as much as exist, exist before God. Creatural existence is anything but self-evident. It is a miracle of God's goodness; it is an existence which even in its original creaturalness bears the stamp of salvation on its forehead. Therefore the church adopts the creature as creature into its prayer of thanksgiving. For there is no redemptive gift which is not preceded by, and based on, the gift of creatural existence. Where no gratitude is expressed for the creature's creation and preservation, there God will also no longer be properly glorified and praised for the creature's salvation and redemption. To be sure, the fact that the lost creature is saved, that sinners are pardoned, that death and mortality are overcome — that forms the core of the church's thanksgiving. It is this very thanksgiving that acknowledges that the church is placed into a fallen world. Creatural being can stand before God only because God's Son Himself assumed creatural essence and died. Therefore, what God did in Christ occupies the center of the church's thanksgiving. In view of what God in Jesus Christ did for us and for the whole world, the church's prayer becomes the "Eucharistia," the thanking anamnesis of the great, redemptive gifts of God.

This thanksgiving finally culminates in the glorification of the Triune God. The church's prayer reaches its acme in this praise of God. The praise of God remains oriented to God; therefore it remains prayer. But in its praise of God the church may, right here in its pilgrimage, share anticipatorily in the service of the saints before God's throne. In the praise of God, the church's prayer transcends the status of the petition. It also surpasses a prayer of thanksgiving for this or for that gift. In the praise of God, the praying church is privileged to join its voice to the laudation of the heavenly congregation, unceasingly and immediately issuing from the presence of God's glory.

WORSHIP AS CONFESSION

Confession, too, comes within the scope of prayer. However, it has its own being, which warrants our differentiation between it and prayer. Prayer is an immediate address to God; it is immediately and exclusively directed to God. Confession does not really speak of God in the second person, but in the third. To be sure, confession is spoken before God in His special presence. But it is characteristic of confession in all its forms that it is simultaneously spoken in public before men. This public may, as in the confessional service, be very secluded and circumscribed. It may consist exclusively of the confessor and the confessing. Nonetheless, the distinctive feature here too is found in the fact that guilt is openly expressed in the confession of sins. The public scene may also be the forum of a civil court. In worship, this public is the congregation, the people of God, which must be viewed as the end-time people, the end-time congregation, over against the civil congregation, which still belongs to the old world. Whatever is confessed to God in the former is very decidedly in public, even if the confessing number is small, and even if "not many wise according to worldly standards, not many powerful, not many of noble birth" (1 Cor. 1:26) are found in it.

The church's confession in worship is the immediate reflex of the fact that it has actually confronted the living God in His revealing Word. In the confession the church expresses the facts with a simplicity of mind and with the spontaneous urgency of the Spirit. It does not question why this is done and how successfully this is done; the church must do this because it has stood face to face with God's reality. Thus confession is also an integral part of the service of the congregation assembled in the name of Jesus. Because the congregation here stands before God's presence, it must also confess the facts before God and before the world and before itself, without any reason, without any purpose, without any secondary motive, but in simple devotion of the heart.

And what is the true situation? What are the facts? All of us are lost from the very beginning by reason of our great guilt. We have all sinned in thought, word, and deed. We are all deserving of God's wrath and can live only by the grace of forgiveness. Therefore both the individual member and also the congregation will be constrained to utter the confession of sin, at one time in this, at another in that form. The question how that is done requires special elaboration which cannot be entered into here. At this time it is important to recognize that a public, general confession of sin cannot be dispensed with in the worship life of the congregation. Of course, it cannot be prescribed that no worship service may be conducted without a confession of sin. In this matter, too, the congregation does not live under legal constraint, but in the freedom of the Gospel. But this very freedom is joined to the inner urgency of the Spirit to express also as an assembled congregation "that which is." The sin of humanity, the sin of Christendom, the sin of the congregation gathered here, and the sin of its members is a reality which must be expressed by way of confession as the congregation confronts the presence of God. This confession of sin also evidences that the congregation is not a summation of individuals, but a body, a unit, in which all bear one another also in their sin.[205]

A confession of sin will be possible only where there is a vital profession of faith. Every worship service as a whole may lay claim to being a profession of the congregation's faith. The congregation professes its faith by the very fact that it gathers about the Word of God and that it convenes for the purpose of celebrating the Lord's Supper. These acts constitute a public testimony before the world and before the church. It would, admittedly, be wrong to make the worship service and particularly the rite of Holy Communion only a sign "by which the Christians could be identified outwardly." However, that does not preclude that we may view the assembling for worship and participation in Holy Communion also as such a sign of profession. (Augs. Conf., XIII)

But above all, no matter in what form the worship service may be conducted, the profession of faith must be made in a straight-forward, unreasoned, and simple manner by the congregation. The hymn will offer manifold opportunities for this. But the profession of faith as Credo also has a fully legitimate place in worship. The Credo is, in a manner of speaking, an expansive amen of the congregation spoken in response to the prophetic-apostolic Word, just as a profession of faith is contained latently in every amen.

As the church professes its faith in worship, it is reminded that it, as a wayfaring church, is engaged in combat. Where faith is professed, the church is involved, as it were, in a lawsuit in which the Credo is advanced as its closing argument. Beginning with Baptism, the Credo denotes a boundary line between world and church. As this boundary line projects ever anew into worship, the church announces publicly before the world that it is not world but that it has crossed the end-time baptismal boundary. Thus the profession of faith always bears the mark of testimony. It is, similar to the proclamation of the Word, testimony to the world; however, it is more extensive than sermon or message. As testimony, the profession is literally a final possibility of proclamation to the world. No verbal testimony may appear subsequent to this, but only blood testimony. As the church bears this testimony of faith, it stands ready to take all the consequences, down to the last, that may result from this testimony. As the church bears this testimony, it confronts not only the judgment seat of this world, but at the same time also the judgment seat of Christ, who will save the professing church from its distress in a trice.

The confession of faith in worship is undoubtedly closely related to the proclamation of the Word. But it is distinguished from this chiefly by the fact that it expresses that which is unreasoned undirected without secondary motive, but from an immediate pneumatic compulsion. Thereby the profession approaches glorification. Profession is not only confession of sin and testimony of faith, but also an offering of thanks and praise. The same word that signifies "to confess sin" in the Old Testament also, yes mainly, denotes "to thank, praise, and glorify God." [206] In the New Testament,[207] *homologein* (ὁμολογεῖν = to confess) means: to confess sin, to profess faith, and to praise God. Referring to the same Old Testament text (Is. 45:23), the same word "to confess" is used to designate both the rendering of an account before the judgment seat of Christ and also the adoring profession which glorifies Jesus as Lord (Rom. 14:10 ff.; Phil. 2:10 f.). If our profession becomes glorification, it at the same time expresses openly "that which is." God has intervened, God has acted in our behalf. We profess and testify what He has done in us and for us. The profession is the public glorifying acknowledgment of God's act of salvation, of Christ's work, of the Spirit's re-creation. It is, therefore, borne by the joy of the saved; it contains jubilance over deliverance. It approximates the hymn of praise, but in contradistinction to it it remains principally oriented to man, to the congregation, to the world; it remains within the dimension of the glorifying proclamation.

WORSHIP AS THE BEGINNING OF THE ETERNAL GLORIFICATION OF THE TRIUNE GOD

When the congregation in worship professes the dominion of God the Father, of Jesus Christ, and of the Spirit, it does something that reaches far beyond this earthly time. With this profession, the congregation anticipates what all created beings will do either voluntarily or involuntarily at the end of all things (Phil. 2:10). The worship of the congregation opens the door to admit the last things, and already participates, in its infirmity and stammering imperfection, in what will one day take place, and is already taking place, before the throne of God. This is a "final" word that we are here trying to express on worship. The entire way of salvation, which God has traversed with man since creation, reaches its goal here. In the realm of the earthly creature, God again finds a mirror here which catches and reflects His glory.

207

Acclamation

When Jesus entered Jerusalem, the throngs again and again burst out in the loud acclaim: "Hosanna to the Son of David! Blessed be He who comes in the name of the Lord! Hosanna in the highest!" (Matt. 21:9). Acts 19:28 ff. portrays a pagan antitype; here we hear the mobs in Ephesus breaking out in the loud and continuing shout: "Great is Artemis of the Ephesians!" Such cries we term "acclamations." [208] In the heavenly church's worship these are frequently uttered by the heavenly beings, as the seer John testifies in his Book of Revelation; e. g., Rev. 4:8, 11; 5:9, 12 f. It is very significant that also the worship of the church on earth is punctuated with a plenitude of such acclamations. The doxological acclamation of the Gloria Patri is related to the psalmody. Short exclamations such as: Hallelujah! Glory be to Thee, O Lord! Praise be to Thee, O Christ! very clearly demonstrate the nature of an acclamation. Also the exclamation Kyrie eleison! originally falls into the category of acclamations, which is also borne out by the many consecutive repetitions of this exclamation. Sanctus and Benedictus likewise fulfill the function of an acclamation.

What takes place when the *ekklesia* assembled for worship breaks out in acclamation? The people pay homage to their King. The dominion ($\varkappa v\varrho\iota\acute{o}\tau\eta\varsigma$) of the Triune God is dutifully acknowledged. The relationship to the profession of faith is obvious. But the acclamation transcends the profession of faith in a peculiar manner. Although principally spoken in the third person, it is no longer spoken toward man; it is spoken in the presence of the Lord; it is, so to say, spoken into the dominion of God; it manifests the lordship of God. To be sure, also the content of these acclamations — the name of the Lord, the honor, the eternities, the holiness-predicates, etc., are of great significance; but the decisive feature is this, that such words are uttered in the presence of this Lord. The entire stress here falls on the utterance of such words in the presence of the Lord. As the homage paid a king is something far different from the expression of an emotion, of an enthusiasm, so these acclamations in worship are no "lyrical" expression of an inward emotion; they rather resemble — in analogy to the idea of homage — legally binding acts. They bind the congregation to the rule of this Lord. They show forth the dominion of this Lord. They are means of the epiphany of this dominion. To be sure, God's throne is firmly established also without the homage of His people. It is not man who places the Lord on His throne. It is not man who supports and sustains His throne. But the throne-power of the Triune God manifests itself in these acclamations in the church's worship. These acclamations press toward God's throne, spread themselves out before it like a carpet, and place themselves before His feet like a footstool of His might.

As this acknowledgment of God's dominion is rendered in the church's worship in an act of adoring allegiance, the worship of the Church Triumphant already projects into that of the Church Militant. The relationship of the *ekklesia* to the *polis* becomes apparent here. Because of the sacred binding force of its acclamations, this worship also relates to the earthly, political powers. The Lord and King to whom the church pays homage in its worship is Lord of all lords and King of all kings (1 Tim. 6:15; Rev. 17:14). The allegiance pledged the Triune God can be pledged no other lord and king. In particular, no other man can be shown the honor which is shown the Son of the Father, who became man. Jesus Christ is the only person to whom the words apply: "My Lord and My God." Of all men only He is in all eternity entitled to the appellation "God." Therefore, the acclamation with which the church in its worship acknowledges and manifests the divine dominion of Jesus Christ is actively executed *theologia* in the original sense of the word,[209] because here the deity of Christ together with that of the Father and the Spirit is acknowledged, proclaimed by word and deed, and thereby becomes known to the world.

The idolatrous worship of the earthly state and of its officials founders on this acclamation. The acclamation rendered the one Triune God in the church's worship, which was otherwise accorded a Caesar or an Oriental god-king, was not the least factor that contributed to the disruption of the ancient sacral state. What happens here in the worship service will exert its "political" effect until the Last Day. Wherever the incumbents of a civil office presume to aspire to the glory of God, presume to usurp the authority of God, the church's worship service will, without the slightest change in its order but solely by its administration, become, with an inward cogency, a political proclamation of war and a political act of war. Moreover, the incumbent of a civil office who arrogates cultic acclamation to himself will find no worse enemy than the Christian, who refuses him this acclamation because Another One is entitled to it alone. Beyond this struggle between Christ and Antichrist, this acclamation of the earthly and of the heavenly congregation, which already blends harmoniously, becomes a cosmic acclamation at the

209

end of all things, in which all powers, thrones, and principalities will join, as they acknowledge "that Jesus Christ is Lord, to the glory of God the Father." (Phil. 2:11)

The Hymn of Praise

It is one of the wondrous works of the Holy Spirit that the acclamation is not the final word of the church's glorification of the Lord. The acclamation is surpassed by the hymn of praise. The hymn of praise is that word of the church about God which contains nothing but a reflection of God's glory. Profession of faith, acclamation, and hymn of praise are contiguous to each other; no sharp dividing line should be drawn, especially, between acclamation and hymn of praise.[210] The song of the angels in the Gloria in excelsis is, stylistically, an acclamation; but this song may become a hymn of praise not only on the lips of the angels but also on the lips of the congregation. That is evidenced, for example, by the fact that the Laudamus, which shows the transition of the acclamation into the hymn of praise, may be joined by the Gloria in excelsis. The same may be said of the Sanctus and the Benedictus. Also the Te Deum and all related songs of praise may be fit into this context.

If the profession of faith represents a final word of the church in its relationship to the world, the hymn of praise is the final word which the church expresses immediately to God and before God. Whereas in the church's acclamation — as in its profession of faith — the end-time struggle is still clearly perceptible, because the conquering dominion of God is involved here, the hymn of praise stands, as it were, already at the end of all struggle. It is basically a "hymn of victory." [211] As the congregation sings the hymn of praise in worship, it participates in the "new" song of the saints of God. It is particularly the hymn of praise in which the glorifying voice of the church on earth harmonizes "with angels and archangels and with all the company of heaven" (Preface). In this harmony the church itself, through the work of the Holy Spirit, is moved toward that resonant wall which echoes only God's glory and thereby magnifies it. In the hymn of praise, the word of the creature becomes the medium of perfect communion between God and creature. The word no longer purposes to proclaim to the world's nations or principalities. The word no longer purposes to supplicate and entreat. This word does not purpose to profess, to acknowledge, and to proclaim anything. There is no longer anything that it "shall" do and "wants" to do. But for that very reason it becomes the creature's purest vessel of God's glory. The hymn of praise is the last word (λόγος) with which the church speaks about God (θεός). The hymn of praise is the final form of *theologia,* enduring to all eternity.[212] In this final word which the creature may say about God, the creature exists only for God, without design, without purpose, undividedly, fulfilling its own essence by the fact that it is no longer, and needs no longer to be, anything but the perfect mirror of God's glory. Thus the hymn of praise is an end-time sign, indicating that God will one day be all in all.

Proskynesis

In Rev. 5, the seer John affords us an insight into the heavenly adoration of the Lamb. The Lamb is accorded a threefold acclamation by three choruses, which expand in ever growing circles and finally encompass the totality of the creatures. After the four creatures about the throne affirm these acclamations with their amen, the following takes place: The 24 elders prostrate themselves and carry out the *proskynesis* (Rev. 5:14). Here an act of worship comes to the fore with a peculiar emphasis, without which act the heavenly worship is inconceivable. (Cf. Rev. 4:10; 7:11; 11:16; 19:4.)

Adapting to Luther's translation, we are wont to call this act "adoration" (*Anbetung*). But we must bear in mind that here — as well as in Luther's expression — a very definite feature of the act of adoration is meant, namely, the genuflecting, the bending down to the ground, "the falling down before God, carried out with the physical, real being of man."[213] 1 Cor. 14:25 shows that this *proskynesis* was very likely practiced also in the worship of the early Christian church. It will also be relevant here to point to the fact that the disciples paid homage to the Lord by *proskynesis* (Matt. 28:9, 17; Luke 24:52). The Gospels relate that Jesus accepted such *proskynesis* without protest also during His earthly sojourn; for instance, "that of the supplicants who desired God's help through Him, and that of the people who accorded God honor in God's Son or in the Messiah when a token of God's might overwhelmed their hearts and moved them to faith. These *proskyneses* increased in adoration-character up to the *proskynesis* before the risen Lord."[214] A passage such as Matt. 14:33 clearly shows the origin of the *proskynesis* in worship: The disciples experienced Jesus' saving power. They saw Him vested with the omnipotence of God. Overwhelmed by this proof of might, they fell down before Him and carried out the *proskynesis,* exclaiming: "Truly You are the Son of God!" The adoration of the risen Lord has a similar background: Now the Lord stood before the disciples as the manifestly divine Lord. The revelation of the Victor evoked the *proskynesis.*

The association between *proskynesis* and acclamation is of special importance. The acclamations of the heavenly congregation are accompanied by *proskynesis,* and, conversely, *proskynesis* is connected with acclamation. The Bible knows of no "mute adoration." Word and gesture belong together.[215] As little as the gesture is mute, even if it may appear as a special act, as in Rev. 5:14, so little does the word of the acclamation remain without this concrete embodiment of homage in the gesture.

In the proclamation of the Gospel and in the Sacrament of the Altar Jesus Christ approaches us in order to serve us. In worship He remains in our midst as our Servant. Here He does not demand our adoration.[216] Here He wants us to accept His service. But one day He will appear, no longer to serve us, but to receive the *proskynesis* of all creatures. This "one day" already casts its rays into the worship of the church. Not coerced, but voluntarily, the church already pays homage to the Lord and through Him and in Him also to the Father and to the Spirit. Where the doxological acclamation is heard, there the physical part of its execution should not be missing. Where the last word which the church utters about God toward God is voiced in the hymn of praise, *proskynesis* becomes the last sign of the creatures with which they affirm the manifestation of God's dominion. Where God's throne-presence appears even from afar, the creature will prostrate itself in adoration. God's incarnation-presence in Jesus' sacrificial body does not demand *proskynesis* legally, but the throne-presence of God, heralded in this presence, elicits it with the spontaneity of the Spirit. The glory of the risen Lord is present behind the veil of the worship service.

Because the risen Lord is really present, because the last things have their beginning in the worship service, it behooves the congregation to drop to its knees even now before the King of kings and the Lord of lords, as it lauds and glorifies Him in its words. Whoever has witnessed the celebration of the Eucharist in a Greek Orthodox church and beheld how priest and believers prostrated themselves and touched the floor with their foreheads, not only receives an impression of the Bible's meaning of "adoration," but he can also divine the connection between the real presence and *pros-*

kynesis. In *proskynesis* also man's body is drawn into his pneumatic response to the event of revelation.[217]

Where the church's worship embraces acclamation, hymn of praise and *proskynesis* in their internal association, it becomes an eschatological-apocalyptic event, in which the feature *polis* is incipiently delineated in the militant and suffering church. Because these last things have their beginning in worship, it receives unequaled publicity-character, even though this worship may be conducted in the most secluded corner of the world. World empires may be shattered on this glorification of the Triune God, on this "adoration" of the *Kyrios* Jesus. However, the publicity of this worship-event extends far beyond this earthly history. The glorification of the Triune God and the adoration of the *Kyrios* Jesus in the church's worship is the only point in the cosmos in which the voice of man unites even now in the indescribable hymn of praise of the angels and the hidden laudation of the nonhuman creatures. Now the first and the last and the eternal meaning of all creatural existence is materialized: to receive the glory of God, so that it may be radiantly reflected in the mirror of the creature, that it may fill the universe, and that God may be all in all.

PART III

THE FORM OF WORSHIP

9

THE DOGMATIC BASIS OF THE FORM

What form is the worship of the congregation assembled in the name of Jesus to assume? This question has accompanied Christendom from the very beginning of its journey through time. The fight that was waged in the apostolic era over the significance of the Old Testament Law also affects the area of the cultus. That is clearly seen in the letters to the Galatians and the Colossians. The Reformation has demonstrated impressively that far-reaching dogmatic decisions are involved in the manner in which we appraise the form of worship and especially in the concrete form in which we conduct worship.[218] Consequently, there must be a doctrine of the form of worship. The task of such a doctrine is not to fix the order of worship in detail; it is, rather, to establish the critical boundaries within which every concrete form must be contained, lest the purity of the Gospel be impaired. In this section we shall endeavor to elaborate the dogmatic guidelines which the church must observe in the formation of an order of service.

THE INEVITABILITY OF FORM

Since we are speaking of the worship of the congregation assembled in the name of Jesus, the question regarding the form of worship is inevitable. Even an individual's solitary worship of God is carried out within certain concrete acts and forms. So long as we sojourn in this body, our worship bears the features of our earthly, physical existence and thus has a physical form. The importance of this form is seen especially when we are assembled with others. This necessarily involves and stipulates order and form. An absolutely formless and immaterial association is impossible for man. Since our worship is to be conducted, according to God's will, in an assembly of people which is determined by this our corporeality, our worship must of necessity have an orderly and specific form.

The necessity of form in worship is furthermore dictated by the circumstance that this being together is determined by the proclamation of the Word and the celebration of Holy Communion. Worship necessarily includes both speaking and listening. Even if all may speak simultaneously in the recitation of a psalm, in the singing of a hymn, in giving thanks, nonetheless the Gospel as message, as consolation, as admonition, as instruction, as prophecy, demands that also individuals arise to speak, while all the others remain seated and give ear (1 Cor. 14:31). But that immediately suggests the problem of order (1 Cor. 14:31 f., 40). The distribution of Holy Communion stipulates, similarly, a distinction between distributor and recipient. Even if we still leave the specific elements of form required by Christ's institution out of the question, nevertheless, the indispensability of a form and order in worship already results from the fact that Word and Sacrament entail a personal confrontation and, accordingly, demand an order of assembly molded by this confrontation. If for no other reason, the assembly of the congregation in worship may not be amorphous because it proceeds throughout, in Word and Sacrament, in the form of personal confrontation.

A similar thought suggests itself when we consider the words spoken in worship as the congregation's address to God. Like the words of proclamation, these words too may be spoken in common. The hymn as prayer and as praise belong to this category. This united action requires a form in which all may join. Prayer, in the narrower sense of the word, is brought before God in behalf of the congregation by individuals. The entire congregation adopts this prayer by an amen or a doxology and thus affirms and confirms it as its own. That mode of praying already prevailed in the worship of the apostolic era (1 Cor. 14:16). The liturgical conclusion of the Lord's Prayer, presented by later manuscripts in Matt. 6:13, indicates that also the Lord's Prayer was obviously recited by an individual and was then affirmed and concluded with the doxology spoken by the congregation.[219] This distinction between the person who prays aloud as the congregation's spokesman and the others who silently pray along and conclude the prayer with an amen is also a factor that presupposes and demands an orderly form.

218

Even when we call to mind that the last things are beginning to take place in worship and that the Spirit of God, as the end-time gift, is operative in the worship of the congregation, we are still obliged to adopt a concrete form for our worship service. Moreover, we would completely misjudge the work of the Spirit if we assumed that the Spirit has anything in common with arbitrariness, disorder, and confusion. Rather, the end-time gift of the Spirit again asserts the original well-being of the creature and its adaptation to a comprehensive, God-ordained order. Spirit and peace belong together (1 Cor. 14:32 f.). Therefore also Spirit and order go hand in hand (1 Cor. 14:40). Both order and peace are embraced by love and taken into its service. And love is intent on building an articulate structure of the congregation and on promoting its services (1 Cor. 12:31; 14:1).

When the power of the future world breaks into our transitory world, no chaos, no deterioration, no dissolution ensue at this point of breakthrough, but a new birth takes place, a new creation, a new structure, a new embodiment of a new form arises. No lesser gulf is fixed between the end-time gift of the Spirit and the spirit of the spirit-philosophy than that which separates the God of Abraham, Isaac, and Jacob from the god of the philosophers. The foremost work of the Spirit is the eschatological transformation and re-creation of our entire physical existence, such as already came to pass on the man Jesus in His resurrection. The Spirit which raised Jesus from the dead is identical with the Spirit which is at work in the congregation (Rom. 8:11). This Spirit never works an amorphous spirituality, but His re-creation results in a pneumatic corporeality. Wherever the effects of the end-time gifts of the Spirit appear in the life of the congregation — and in keeping with the nature of this Spirit, they must necessarily appear, they bear the stamp of orderliness rooted in God's own essence, which is a pledge of the end-time peace of creation. Where the church's worship is really administered in the Spirit, it will be evident that it can never dispense with a well-ordered, decorous, and edifying form.

THE ESCHATOLOGICAL FREEDOM OF THE FORM

Under no circumstances may we conceive of the form of worship as a legal-ritual regulation. We shall still have to consider how far the church's worship contains elements of form which, by reason of the instituting act of the risen Lord, have to be observed "by virtue of divine right" and the compulsion of a divine commandment. But these elements of form based on divine institution are so slight in extent that they have hardly any bearing on the total form of the church's worship. These Christ-ordained elements of form are embedded in the total form of worship and are borne and supported by this total form, which itself is in no wise legally-ritually bound. Rather, the total form of the church's worship shares in the eschatological freedom of Christ and His kingdom.[220]

"Christ is the end of the Law" (Rom. 10:4). Christ is also the end of the legal-ritual form of worship. In that respect the form of the *ekklesia's* worship differs fundamentally from that of the Old Covenant. It shares completely in the eschatological epoch which Christ ushered into the history of the people of God. Proclamation of the Word and Holy Communion, prayer and praise, belong to this Jesus Christ who arose from the dead. This Jesus is free of all ties of this old eon. And he who is in Him shares in His freedom. Differences of race, of national, political, cultural, and cultic ties are surmounted in Him. Therefore also the worship of the church cannot be bound with legal force to certain situations of this our world, to certain places, to signs, to persons.

The New Covenant's end-time order of salvation may be summarized in the one statement that we sinners are declared righteous for Jesus' sake by faith in the Gospel and thus are justified in Jesus Christ. Therefore the outward framework of worship within which the Gospel is proclaimed and Holy Communion is celebrated can in no wise be made a condition for salvation. Questions regarding the pattern of this worship are thus moved into the freedom of those who by faith in the Gospel are liberated from any legal precept which would bind the conscience before God. In his two-front battle against Rome and against the Enthusiasts, Luther showed how a relapse into legalism, especially in the realm of the church's worship, decidedly jeopardizes the stability of the Gospel within the church. The confessional writings of the Evangelical Lutheran Church adhered to and again and again asserted this truth.[221] The questions regarding the details of the church's outward form of worship have been divorced once for all from the question of salvation. The fact that we recognize this and that we act conformably is imperative for the very sake of salvation.

Therefore, no division dare arise over this question in the church. One of the finest statements ever made in Christendom is undoubtedly the "It is enough" in Article VII of the Augsburg Confession: "And to the true unity of the church it is enough to agree concerning the doctrine of the Gospel and the administration of the sacraments. Nor is it necessary that human traditions, that is, rites or ceremonies, instituted by men, should be everywhere alike." Whoever is confronted with the question regarding the form of worship and ignores even for a moment the end-time freedom from every legal bond, vouchsafed by Christ and rooted in Him, he is incompetent to give a valid answer to this question. If someone presumes to invest with the cloak of compulsion and constraint any act of worship, outside the elements of form instituted by Christ, and accordingly makes legal demands in its behalf, the church is duty-bound to reject this demand, demonstrating its freedom in this matter, even though it were otherwise at liberty to adopt the act in question. But also the reverse is true here! If a ceremony which does not offend against the Gospel and is a matter of Christian liberty is interdicted with the same coercion and constraint, the congregation may feel called upon to give proof of its liberty and, in a given case, retain and practice this ceremony, which it might otherwise also omit.[222]

THE SUBJECTION OF THE FORM TO THE WORD: COMMANDED AND FORBIDDEN ELEMENTS

The eschatological freedom of the form is emphasized by the fact that the church's worship contains elements that stem from Christ's institution and are, therefore, enjoined with the constraint of a divine commandment. In that way all that is not commanded is moved into the area of the believer's liberty. With respect to worship — we may disregard Baptism here — the following elements of form are required with the compulsion of a divine commandment by reason of Christ's institution:

1. The Word of God must be proclaimed. That is to say: the witness of Christ, as contained in the prophetic and apostolic writings of the Bible, must be publicized in the proclaiming word. Nothing is commanded with regard to the specific form in which this is to be done. The risen Lord's commission to go forth into all the world is concerned with the missionary proclamation to the peoples of the world. This, too, assumes many different forms, for which no legal precepts whatsoever are given. The demands of specific conditions will dictate the missionary's particular mode of procedure and the manner of his missionary proclamation. Something similar applies to

the instruction of the baptized and the proclamation of God's Word in worship, which issues immediately from the commission to go forth and teach (Matt. 28:20a). Aside from the necessity to proclaim the Word of God to the congregation assembled in worship, no other necessity, for instance concerning the form in which this is to be done, can be deduced from Christ's institution. We must, of course, concede that the reading of the prophetic and apostolic writings in worship marks a most fitting compliance with the positive command to proclaim the Word. But even this reading of a Scripture passage is not based on a legal-ritual precept of the risen Lord. The customary exposition of a Scriptural passage by the preacher is even less such a precept. All forms of the Word's proclamation are again free to those liberated by the Gospel, as long as the one Word of God is actually proclaimed in them through the words of man.

2. Holy Communion must be celebrated by the congregation in conformity with Christ's institution. What must be done in the administration of Holy Communion under the compulsion of divine command can be summarized thus: With prayer and thanksgiving, the Lord Jesus and His instituting Meal must be commemorated, and bread and wine must be distributed and eaten and drunk. The instituting words of the evangelists and of the apostle Paul direct us to this commemoration of the Lord and to His instituting Meal. But the detailed manner in which this is to be carried out is not legally fixed. We do not even have a legally binding version of the words of Christ's institution. Thus even in the celebration of Holy Communion the factor absolutely enjoined by Christ's institution is confined to the celebration of the Meal with bread and wine, whereby the Scripturally affirmed institution of the Meal must be commemorated by an express reference to Christ's words of institution.

3. Both the intracongregational proclamation of the Word and the celebration of Holy Communion must be carried out in a gathering convening in the name of Jesus (Matt. 18; 20; 1 Cor. 1:2), which is, accordingly, identified as worship by invocation of the Triune God.

We must admit that these three points really constitute a minimum of positively prescribed elements of form of the church's worship.[223] But these elements themselves admit, individually, of manifold possibilities of form. Whether we use leavened or unleavened bread, white wine, red wine, or wine diluted with water, how we use Christ's words of institution, whether as special words of proclamation or of consecration, whether in the context of a prayer, whether in the

literal form of one of the Biblical reports on institution, or in a har-
monized form in accord with Luther's Catechism, whether the Word
of God is proclaimed in the form of exposition of a Scripture passage,
or in other forms — all that comes within the range of the believer's
liberty. Not even the use of the Lord's Prayer may be demanded as
an absolute legal-ritual necessity.

The Word-bound nature of worship does not only indicate what
must necessarily be included in the form of worship, but it also excludes what dare not appear in it. The eschatological freedom to
which we lay claim for the form of the church's worship is, as eschatological liberty, radically different from human arbitrariness. The
eschatological liberty of the church is the liberty of the Holy Spirit
vouchsafed by the Word of God. The manner in which the elements
of form of the church's worship, unconditionally demanded by Christ's
institution, take shape dare not contravene the governing might of
Christ's Gospel and of the Spirit granted by Him. In the Gospel and
in the Spirit, the Lord Jesus Christ Himself rules and forms His body,
the church. And we know that His reign is not exercised with the
tyranny of ritual law. The liberty which He gives His own through the
Spirit of sonship is part of the very essence of His rule. But since He
Himself is Lord in this liberty, the worship of the church dare not
assume a form which would infringe on the gracious, liberating lordship of Jesus Christ. Therefore everything that is inconsistent with the
Gospel of Jesus Christ and of the Holy Spirit effective in it must be
excluded from the form of worship.

We noted earlier that the words uttered by man constitute the
dominant material for the form of worship. Both in the ministrations
of God to the congregation and the ministrations of the congregation
before God, words are the dominant element on which the form of
worship is constructed. These words dare state nothing that contradicts the Gospel of Jesus Christ attested in Holy Writ. This demand
must be made the more insistently, the more clearly we note that also
the congregation's response to the Word proclaimed to it presents an
indirect form of the Word's proclamation.[224] The indissoluble interrelation of the sacramental and the sacrificial acts in worship demands
that every word uttered in the course of worship remain under the
jurisdiction of the prophetic and apostolic testimony of Scripture.

This bond of the words employed in worship to the norm of
Scripture in no way annuls the eschatological freedom in the development of the worship service. This bond is, rather, necessary for the

realization of this liberty. Nor does this bond militate against the efficacy of the Spirit. The Spirit is not in opposition to Jesus' words and commandment. The will of the Spirit, poured out over the congregation, and the will of the incarnate Word, expressed in the testimony of the prophets and apostles, are one.[225]

It would, furthermore, reflect an utter misunderstanding of the Word-bound nature of the form of worship if we were to subject this form to a liturgical Biblicism. Our demand that the words of worship correspond from beginning to end with the testimony of prophets and apostles does not imply that only Biblical words or the linguistic style of the Bible be used in an order of worship. No, the Gospel and the Holy Spirit do not insist on liturgical Biblicism. The eschatological liberty of form resists any legal demand of a formal and a linguistic Biblicism. The verbal form of worship participates in every respect in the eschatological freedom of Christ and of His kingdom. It is necessary only that the content of the verbal form agree with the vital subject matter of these words, that it agree with the content attested in the words of the prophets and apostles. Therefore, no words may be voiced in worship the content of which would question or even erase this conformity.

Words are the chief material for the construction of the form of worship. But words are not the only material. They may be accompanied by signs and gestures. If the words are subject to Christ's controlling power, which He exercises through the testimony of Scripture, then the signs and gestures must also submit to it. In judging a symbolic act, a Christian congregation will have to guard against two dangers in the development of a worship service — against the danger of legalistic purism, which rejects even the sign that fits the word, and against the danger of an anti-Scriptural obfuscation of the word content by a symbolic gesture. The liberty for which Christ has freed us and the controlling power of the prophetic-apostolic testimony, implicit in this liberty — both must simultaneously assert themselves in this extraordinarily sensitive sphere.[226]

The Pneumatic Unity of Freedom and Restraint in the Symbolism of the Form

Our deliberations have shown us that the form of worship is regulated by an absolutely binding "Thou shalt not!" Thou shalt not express anything in the words or in the symbolic acts of worship that contravenes the Scripturally attested Gospel. On the other hand, we have seen what is demanded by reason of Christ's institution with the compulsion of a divine commandment. The peculiar problem in the formation of the worship service is posed by the wide area that remains between the two boundary lines of the absolutely forbidden and the absolutely commanded.

The width of this area is characteristic of the place occupied by the church's worship in the history of salvation. The Old Testament worship, which was regulated down to its last details by law, has vanished. The form of worship of the heavenly Jerusalem has not yet appeared. To be sure, Christ's instituting word gives the church definite points about which the form of the earthly church's worship is constructed; but that is all. In the Holy Spirit the power of the heavenly worship becomes effective already, but without giving us a concrete form of this heavenly worship as a guideline for our worship. The formation of worship in that wide space between the absolutely forbidden and the absolutely commanded remains a matter of the believer's liberty. That is the reason why no divisions in Christendom dare arise over the question of form of worship within this wide area. Schisms are inevitable when people adhere to a form of worship which clearly crosses the line of the absolutely forbidden, or when people do not punctiliously observe the line of the absolutely commanded. However, divergent answers to the question touching the form of worship in the area between these two boundary lines dare never give rise to division.

To be sure, there can be no binding law for this wide area; however, there are surely certain viewpoints which serve to guide the church. We shall try to elaborate such. If the church lives in the Word and in the Spirit, it will not be without guidance, without directives in the formation of that free space.

We proceed from our observation that the part absolutely commanded by Christ's institution consists in the three elements of form mentioned above, which pervade the entire form of worship. Proclamation of the Word and the celebration of the Meal instituted in the night of betrayal, both of these executed with invocation and adoration of the Triune God — that comprises the entire worship of the church beyond the line of Baptism. Thus the part commanded by Christ's institution appears in the form of worship. The eschatological liberty of the church manifests itself in the manner in which this commanded element appears. But it will always be this commanded element that makes its appearance in the form of worship, if a true churchly worship takes place. The form of worship, as the mode of manifestation of the element demanded by Christ's institution, will itself become a sign of this commanded element. The forms in which the Word of God is proclaimed, the forms in which we celebrate Holy Communion, the forms in which we invoke the Triune God, must be signs which point to Christ's instituting Word and which actively expound and explain this instituting Word.

It is all-important here that we clearly perceive the connection between the sign and that which is designated by the sign. This connection cannot be logically deduced. A logical deduction is cogent; but the connection between sign and signified is not cogent. Nor can this connection be a coincidence established by human arbitrariness. Then the sign would cease being sign of the concrete which must come to pass. In the church's worship, the connection between sign and signified precludes the cogency of a logical deduction and the arbitrariness of an incidental choice in like manner. This connection is, rather, a peculiar new relation, an eschatological new relation, which appears, beyond the antitheses of cogency and arbitrariness, where the Spirit operates with His peculiar liberty and restraint. In order to express the peculiar indefiniteness and definiteness, in order to express the rationally not perceptible unity of indefiniteness and definiteness of this connection between sign and signified, we speak of the pneumatic appropriateness of the sign. In other words, appropriateness means correspondence in pneumatic freedom, which is always freedom within pneumatic restraint.

If we apply this idea of appropriateness to our question regarding the form of worship, the following guidelines result: Within that area left free to us the form of worship must be appropriate to the fact that this worship is an assembly of the congregation in the name of Jesus. The form must be appropriate to the fact that the Gospel's proclamation, instituted by Christ, is being heard here. It must be appropriate to the fact that the command "This do in remembrance of Me!" is being obeyed here. In that way the form of worship attains the nature of symbolic testimony. To be sure, no question relating to the structure of that wide area may be assigned the importance of a requirement for salvation. Admittedly, each such question may be answered basically in one way or in another. Nevertheless, no answer which we may give here is entirely indifferent, because all that is done or is not done in worship lays claim to being a sign which freely reflects something of what Christ commands us to do.

When we conceive of the form of worship as a free, Spirit-wrought sign of the commanded element and therefore subject it to the rule of appropriateness, we gain an understanding of the mutability of this form in history. It is part of the essence of the free, Spirit-wrought sign that it does not congeal into an immutable form, as the fluid metal does in the casting of a bell. If the rule of appropriateness applies, then the church is thereby authorized and obligated to inquire and to decide ever anew in what the appropriateness of the sign to the signified really consists. The recognition of appropriateness must have its history. This history is by no means based only on our assumption that the church at a time may have been a poor judge of the appropriateness of the sign. Is it not possible that the appropriateness of a certain sign to a certain matter may actually change with changing times and changing situations?

The peculiar variability of judgment on the appropriateness of the sign, which we encounter in the sphere of the church, is closely connected with the question regarding the testimonial function of the form. Testimony, too, necessarily has its history. Testimony is an embodiment in ever new form of the immutable content of the one and only Word of God. The legitimate historical change of the form of worship takes part in the legitimate historical change of the form of testimony. The legitimate change of form is not a matter of a convenient accommodation to the questionable needs of a certain era. The history of worship in the Evangelical church since the era of Enlightenment demonstrates so clearly how the form disintegrates and its service of testimony is rendered doubtful and impossible by such a wrong adaptation of the form of worship to the pattern of this world (Rom. 12:2). Secularization is assuredly not adapted to the form of worship. Just as the witness of the Gospel faces the world vested in a peculiar and singular strangeness, so also the form of worship dare not surrender — precisely in view of its testimonial service — its singularity and strangeness, which is well-nigh incomprehensible to the world. However, the witness is assigned to the world. He exists for the world. The "for us" of Christ's act is effectual also in the working of the Spirit. Therefore the form of worship, too, must, inasmuch as it comes into being under the working of the Spirit, bear the clear mark which signifies that it is in this world for man.

The appearance of this "for us," of this "for man," cannot be determined from the viewpoint of the world and of man. How deeply hidden is this "for us" in the act of Jesus Christ! So long as the world

227

is not redeemed by faith in Jesus Christ, it will never understand that the form of worship serves as a testimony to the world. Therefore the enigmatic strangeness and peculiarity of the form of worship as a sign of its appropriateness remains. But as the testimony addresses itself, without detracting from the immutability of its content, to a particular, concrete world situation and is determined in its form by this, so also the form of worship will, because of its testimonial character, reflect this relationship to a particular, concrete world situation. It is especially the linguistic form of worship that will be subject to change. One can understand that the Roman Catholic Church, when engaged in missionary work among the Teutons, did not surrender its Latin liturgy to the cumbersome Germanic dialects. But that it failed to concede the European national languages in the 16th century the right to become cultic languages indubitably contravenes the testimonial service of the form of worship and is therefore highly inappropriate to Christ's command, which explicitly directs the church to the nations.

But the rule of appropriateness does not only afford us an understanding for the mutability of the form of worship in history; the same rule also directs our attention to the unchanging element in this change. With regard to its appropriateness, the sign is always determined by the thing it wishes to designate. But this thing is comprehended once for all, contingently, in Christ's concrete command. Until Christ's return there will be no new institution of Christ. No new name will be given to men in which they may assemble as the congregation of saved sinners. No new message of salvation is to be proclaimed, no new celebration may be expected "until He comes." That which is to be designated by the form of worship is certainly no eternal, immutable idea, but the unchangeable historical commission of Jesus Christ, the immutability of which reflects the uniqueness and the contingency of revelation. But the Spirit, who is the formative power in the sign, dare never be conceived as the changing spirit of the times. The Spirit who forms the sign is truly alive. He always speaks to the times. He is the one Holy Spirit poured out over the congregation by the exalted Lord. He is the Spirit in which this one Lord becomes present in His congregation with His unique historical words and deeds. If the Holy Spirit creates the symbolic character of the form of worship, then this form will also evince, amid all its timeliness, historicalness, and mutability, a strong, enduring fidelity.

To be sure, the history of worship displays instances of decay, of heretical malformations, and of flinty incrustations. And yet there is perhaps no creation in the cultural realm which has shown such a puzzling constancy to date as the worship of the Christian church. That is true especially of the celebration of the Lord's Supper. The very manner in which Christ's command has always manifested itself in the history of the Eucharist shows a common fundamental outline, which is clearly distinguishable even today, despite the splintering of Christendom, in the large confessional church bodies. The Holy Spirit is not wont to pronounce a yes today and nullify it tomorrow with a no, thereby contradicting Himself. The decisions made in the construction of that free area between the commanded and the forbidden show a constancy in change, a uniformity in manifoldness, which can be understood and appraised correctly only if one recognizes the wonderful unity of restraint and freedom in the realm of pneumatic operation.

If the form of worship becomes a sign in which the command of Christ's institution appears, then Christ Himself will become present to us in this sign with His work of salvation, performed for us. Then the form is appropriate, since it is chosen and dignified to become the vessel of Christ's epiphany, hidden under Word and sacrament. The appropriateness of the form is the event through which the Holy Spirit Himself enters the words uttered by man and Himself speaks, prays, professes, and praises in these human words. It follows that the form as a sign ever and absolutely retains a serving function. The form is maid and never mistress. It waits to be engaged in service by Jesus Christ and the Spirit poured out by Him. It is appropriate if it gives expression to this expectation and perseveres in this expectation. The form dare never be the arbitrary grasping of man for the thing appearing in it and designated by it. The symbolic character of the form must be taken seriously in every detail. Therefore the symbol as such is appropriate if it remains aware of its own continuing in appropriateness. If the form of worship is understood as a sign, it is implied that it dare never lose its symbolic character until this sign is abrogated at Christ's return. The sign is a genuine sign only in the eschatological expectation of its abrogation. Therefore the form of worship is imbued with a sense of humility, which stems from our knowledge that our speaking, praying, professing, and praising are never carried out in a manner truly appropriate to the Lord and His Spirit. Consequently, the appropriateness of the form is found in its openmindedness for whatever the Triune God wishes to accomplish through it according to His good pleasure.

This knowledge simultaneously enjoins the form of worship not to entrench itself against change. It must stand ready to let the Lord enter and rule and mold it. It must stand ready to let the entering Spirit be effective in it. The form dare not indurate itself selfishly, but must remain clay in the hand of the Creator to the end. Especially where it is chosen to be the vessel for the presence of the Lord who governs it must it be a malleable form, because it does not deny the marks of the Lord's presence but will bear the imprint of these until the Lord breaks this earthly vessel of His presence for all times and appears in the vessel of His glorified body in unveiled glory.[227]

The Concrete Historicalness of the Form

That wonderful unity of freedom and restraint realized in the form of worship must also assert itself in our attitude over against traditional form. Form of worship does not stand in an empty space of historical abstraction. We have already observed why it is a form wrought by history. We noted why this historical development of form must contain guidelines for the future form. The element which endures in the mutation of the historical form must be taken seriously with regard to its appropriateness. It goes without saying that the transmitted form must be unconditionally subjected to the two critical boundary lines of the absolutely commanded and the absolutely forbidden, must be tested by this standard, purified by it, and, under certain circumstances, also be rejected by it. Elements of form cannot become authoritative for us simply by virtue of an ancient tradition. Formal traditionalism must never be accepted as the principle for liturgical forms. However, the tradition of the fathers which has passed the test may reasonably expect our respectful treatment, because it is found in that free area between the two critical boundary lines of the absolutely commanded and the absolutely forbidden.

In this area, also free for us today, decisions have been made which only the Enthusiasts can disregard and ignore, who have no fathers and brothers, but are given to the delusion that the people of God on earth had their inception with them. "What! Did the Word of God originate with you, or are you the only ones it has reached?" (1 Cor. 14:36 RSV). This critical question of the apostle, which the Enthusiasts in Corinth had to hear, obligates the church of all times to approach with due respect and reverence the traditions of Christendom which do not conflict with Christ's institution and the Word of God. Just because we are aware of the eschatological freedom of the form of worship, just because we are liberated by the Gospel and are free and cannot be enslaved by the power of tradition, we are liberated also for the acceptance of critically tried and tested tradition. To stand in fear of tradition is by no means a sign of freedom. On the critical presupposition and premise that we belong to Christ, all of Christendom's traditions in worship are ours.

Here it becomes clear why the form of worship, by reason of its concrete historicalness, strives toward an ecumenical basic form. He who honors the fathers seeks the brethren. He seeks the fathers among the brethren. Because that free area, expressive of the essence of the *ekklesia*, is given us in the formation of worship, because this free area is subject to the rule of the pneumatic appropriateness of this sign, the church is here directed to accept, in its peculiar unity of restraint in freedom and freedom in restraint, the tradition of the fathers in a manner that the ties with the brethren are observed as far as possible. To be sure, the ecumenical character of the form of worship cannot be found by mechanical method, for example, by calculating, as it were, an arithmetical mean from the feasible forms that have been used in Christendom. The affirmation of the ecumenical character of the form of worship can be of promise only under the concrete prompting of the Holy Spirit, working here and now. Only on this presupposition will our obedience to ecumenical obligation in the formation of worship become effective as a means of gathering and not of scattering, as a movement toward unity and not toward the organization of another church body.

Thereby we have already intimated that our regard for tradition must never lead us to copy a form of worship in vogue in the past and in a certain place, let us say in the Wittenberg of the 16th century. To attempt such a repristination would not be treating the critically tested tradition as such seriously, namely, in its peculiar width and elasticity, because this would regard a form used in a certain stage of tradition as an absolute norm. Above all, such an attempt would overlook the decisions which the present day demands of us. It would overlook the testimonial character, which was peculiar to that past historical form in its day, and which must also inhere in the form assigned to us. Neither an arithmetical mean of form, calculated from the past, nor the elevation of a certain sector of tradition to an absolute norm will solve the problem of form for us. Nor will an obdurate insistence on the present form in use do justice to the historical concreteness of the form. The concretely historical form of worship assigned to us will have to emerge as it observes the two critical boundary lines,

1. from the affirmation of the ecumenical obligation, which fixes its gaze on the width of tradition in the past, on the manifoldness of forms in present Christendom, and on the basic form, which remains constant amid all change and which exhorts to unity;

2. from the regard for the special tradition of the confessional church to which we adhere;

3. from the recognition that the next step can be taken only on the basis of the form employed at present;

4. from a willingness not to resist what God's Spirit wishes to fashion here and now on our way to a realization of the end-time form, in which the church as an adorned bride is to meet its Head.

Due attention is paid the concrete historicalness of the form of worship only when these four stipulations pervade each other and when they unfold their formative power in the act of formation.

The Subjection of the Form to Love

Without love, the church's liberty is not the eschatological liberty in the Spirit. Love, which rules all charisms, as the head rules the body, also rules the form of worship in that broad and free area between the forbidden and the commanded. Everything that is not excluded by the critical power of these boundaries is allowable. But not all that is allowed us in the formation of worship "builds up" (1 Cor. 10:23). Only that form of worship that is ruled by love builds the congregation. Love beholds the brother. Love is mindful of its responsibility not to encumber the brother's conscience. The New Testament admonitions regarding the strong and the weak (1 Cor. 14—15; Rom. 14—15) must be heeded and absolutely obeyed in the contemplation of the form of worship. What is permissible per se to us in the liturgical structure of worship in that free area must be omitted if the brother's conscience is thereby offended and his faith is weakened. Even if in our judgment a certain feature of an act of worship would be more appropriate to the symbolic character than the prevailing one, we should have to forgo its introduction if this would jeopardize someone's conviction of faith and of salvation and offend his conscience. The form of worship must further the peace and the welfare of the congregation and not engender strife and division. The form of worship must edify the congregation and not represent the worship of an individual (1 Cor. 14:2 ff.). The form of worship must include also the weak members and also prove helpful to them.

That does not mean to say that the form of worship must conserve spiritual faults. Whoever construes love as an accommodation to existing conditions misunderstands its essence. It would be veritably loveless, if love were to assent to any existing perversion. It cannot be denied, for instance, that the obscurity to which the celebration of Holy Communion is often relegated as an adjunct to worship for individual members of the congregation poses a great spiritual blemish. It would be unmerciful if those who recognize this remain silent and refrain from doing all in their power and from lending a helping hand in eliminating this evil. The demand that the form of worship be subject to love must not, under any circumstances, be construed to mean that the congregation dare not be roused from its false contentment with any perversion in its life of worship. However, to use another illustration, if I recognize that the Gregorian psalmody is excellently suited to the symbolic character of the form of worship, I will not insist on the adoption of this element of form without inquiring whether or not this may occasion confusion, dissension, and other spiritual harm and thus cumber the life of the congregation.

Love is endowed with a long life. Love can afford to wait. Love is paired with wisdom. Love does not force a certain form of worship on the congregation. With patience and wisdom love awakens an insight into the inappropriateness and the appropriateness of a sign. With patience and wisdom love strives to lead from the inappropriate to the appropriate. Love waits until, in the spontaneity of spiritual insight, that which is appropriate in the form of worship is apprehended in liberty and realized in liberty. To be sure, love keeps jealous watch over those two critical boundary lines of the commanded and the forbidden and sees to it that their critical power remains intact. But in the free area of free formation love may — to be sure, not passively, but — calmly wait until all the members who share in the responsibility of the structure of worship are willing to take the step from the less appropriate to the more appropriate sign.

10

THE MATERIALIZATION OF THE FORM

BASIC FORM AND CONCOMITANT FORMS

Our deliberations on the dogmatic foundation of the form have showed us why Christendom must forgo a uniformity of worship. The manifoldness of the order of service is a spiritual and historical necessity in Christendom. However, in the face of this multiplicity we must be guided by a will to gather and not by the spirit that would splinter.[228] Within the free area we must affirm what we recognize as the common basic tendency in tradition; and then we must realize this as far as possible from the perspective of our own special tradition by a genuine spiritual decision. For that reason we affirm the basic liturgical decision of the Wittenberg Reformation. It was the decision for that chief form of service which we in the Occident are wont to call "mass." Literally, its basic lines are recognizable to us already in Justin in the middle of the second century. Its roots in the apostolic congregations can hardly be questioned.[229] Even today it is still clearly recognizable in almost all of the great church bodies of Christendom. If any form of worship may lay claim to ecumenical character, it is the one in which the following basic order is observed: After an introductory invocation, God's Word is presented to the congregation by the reading of Scripture and by the sermon; the congregation submits its petitions to God; it collects the thankofferings; and amid thanksgiving it celebrates the Lord's Supper.

This worship, in which the proclamation of the Word and the celebration of Holy Communion are bound into a unit, attracts all the elements of form, which are, by the power of the Holy Spirit,

234

instruments of the salvation-event vouchsafed in worship. The multiplicity of the forms of proclamation, of the forms of prayer, of the forms of praise with which we have become acquainted — all find a place in this worship. Even the rite of Baptism may be drawn directly into this, as the worship service of the early church in the night of Easter shows.[230]

The form of worship is seen in its fullness in the union of the proclamation of the Word and the celebration of Holy Communion. The correspondence between this fullness of form elements and the fact that this worship service purposes to be the assembly of the entire congregation is, of course, not coincidental. In congregational life there is actually a worship service which is rightly termed its main service *(Hauptgottesdienst)*. The spiritual life of the congregation dare not be limited to this main service; but this main service purposes to assemble the congregation in its entirety. In its first part it even reaches out beyond the congregation to include also those who are not yet baptized. This worship service manifests itself as the center of the church's spiritual life, inasmuch as its course from the presentation of the Word through the reading of Scripture and sermon to the celebration of the Lord's Supper symbolically reflects ever anew the pathway from the world to the church segregated as the body of Christ. A worship service in which the reality of the pneumatic body of Jesus Christ, created through the agency of Baptism, is ever constituted anew in Holy Communion must needs lay claim, by reason of this event, to its being the congregation's "main worship service."

This chief form of worship is so rich that other, more specialized forms may ramify and grow from its fullness. We shall desist from considering acts of the worship service of a casual nature, such as marriage and burial service. Confession, too, may be disregarded here. These are not to be viewed as articulate parts of the main service. They are subject to other formative factors, in which the special casual occasion for these acts comes into play. On the whole, two forms emerge from the fullness of the main form, which surround the center structure like the wings of an altar. One of these concomitant forms features, above all, the element of proclamation by Scripture reading and sermon, from which, as we know, the invocation of the Triune God in prayer dare not be omitted. In this way the worship service with sermon comes into being. The other accompanying form serves, chiefly, the purpose of prayer and praise, from which, as we know, the proclamation of the Word in some form dare not be omitted. This form we encounter in the horary prayer. It is most significant that the celebration of Holy Communion dare not set itself up as a special and separate form. Admittedly, special Communion services are possible, which need not explain the step leading from the worship service of the Word with its door ajar to the world to the Lord's Supper celebrated by the congregation in segregation from the world. But wherever Holy Communion is administered, the proclamation of the Word in one form or another cannot be waived, to say nothing of the fact that prayer, thanksgiving, and praise dare not even recede into the background in it. It is incompatible with the celebration of Holy Communion to repress or restrain the proclamation of the Word and prayer in it; the Lord's Supper tolerates no sacramental act isolated from Word or prayer.[231]

The Manifold Confrontation of Liturgical Persons as a Formative Factor

In the following deliberations we turn our attention to the chief form of the worship service. The viewpoints, which present themselves to us from time to time as directives for the realization of this form must be applied to the concomitant forms with appropriate modifications.

Worship is carried out by the assembled congregation. The assembled congregation is no mob, which first has to be compressed forcibly into an artificial-mechanical mold by military regulation. By reason of the manifoldness of its effective gifts and services, the assembled congregation is an articulate whole. This manifoldness and this articulateness must become apparent in worship. Neither are all to do everything, nor is one to do everything (1 Cor. 12). At one time all will act in concert, at another only one will step forth and act alone; and then again several or many will assume certain functions of worship. This manifoldness of liturgically active persons is rooted in the manifoldness of the gifts and services which determine the organization of the congregation.

The fact that individuals or groups from the congregation play active roles in worship is based, furthermore, on the twofold pneumatic salvation-event of worship. God's Word is brought to the congregation. This Word requires a bearer to proclaim it. God's Word demands hearers who lend ear to the proclaimed Word. Though the congregation as a whole may proclaim God's Word in song, nevertheless, its proclamation as a rule presupposes two classes who confront each other, those who speak and those who listen. In the celebration of Holy Communion a similar confrontation necessarily appears. This confrontation is directly demanded by the prototype of the Meal of institution. Only one person takes bread and wine into his hand and, giving thanks, pronounces the words of institution. The administration of Holy Communion requires such as distribute the consecrated bread and the consecrated cup and such as receive these. The congregation does not always talk to God simultaneously and in the same words, but by virtue of the Spirit working in it, it may also have one or more spokesmen who offer prayer and praise to God in its behalf, while the others adopt and affirm these with an "amen." Thus no worship can be conducted without a confrontation of liturgical persons and without a rotation of office.

Liturgical confrontation will inevitably also involve a confrontation between one person who bears a special responsibility for the entire worship service and all the others. One person must bear the responsibility for the conduct of this concrete worship. If this is to be orderly and really edify the congregation, its course dare not be determined by opposing and clashing wills. All the other wills must cooperate with and merge in the will of one man.[232] The administration of the Sacrament of the Altar in particular demands one man, who is also responsible for the admission to it. Thus every administration of Holy Communion also includes an act of church government. Therefore the chief form of worship cannot be executed properly without a man, who, as shepherd of the congregation, administers the main worship service.

On the other hand, to confine the confrontation of the persons active in the worship service to pastor and congregation militates against the pneumatic character of the congregation. To do that is to atrophy the worship service. This is the very place where the congregation must manifest the manifoldness of its organization, effected by its gifts and services. The proclamation of the Word must not be confined to the shepherd of the congregation in every service. The responsible leader of worship and the preacher may very well be two different persons. In a congregation served simultaneously by several pastors, each of these should in some way participate in the Sunday's worship service, each should carry out some liturgical function of that service. Above all, nonministerial members should also render some service in the presentation of the Word, for instance, as lectors. Or they may be entrusted with the service of preaching by reason of their talents and training, although they are not pastors. The liturgical choir, too, may regard its service as proclamation. It is an essential trait of the congregation of the New Covenant to address one another with the words of Christ reciprocally and responsively.[233] In the instance of the spiritual song, this is also expressed perceptibly through the liturgical alternation. To be sure, Holy Communion demands the ministrations of the responsible shepherd, but that does not preclude the cooperation of trained and authorized assistants in its distribution.

The realization that the liturgical confrontation also in the congregation's service before God dare not be confined to pastor and congregation will be of special significance for the form of worship. To be sure, in the instance of prayer — unless a prayer-hymn is involved, which all sing in common — one person will, as a rule, be the congregation's spokesman. But this one person need not be the pastor. In the deaconal prayer the several invitations to pray are not to issue from the pastor. The alternation between choir and choir, between choir and congregation, between sector of congregation and sector of congregation, is characteristic of the psalmic prayer, of the acclamation, of the profession, and of the laudations.

The legend of the genesis of the Te Deum graphically illustrates the spiritual basis of this alternation. It relates that Ambrose intoned the hymn at Augustine's baptism, and that Augustine, prompted by the Holy Spirit, immediately took up the song of praise, and that the two, stirred with a holy zeal, alternately added bit by bit and thus sang the hymn to its end.[234] This legend shows the real basis of the liturgical alternating song in the profession and in other laudations; one person, as it were, takes the words from the lips of another. Both are apprehended by the same Spirit, both are absorbed in the same professing and glorifying devotion. One bears up the other, one leans on the other, one recognizes his own profession and laudation in the other. The congregation's profession and glorification of God does not attain its most perfect form when the whole congregation simultaneously professes and sings the same words, but first when one section of the congregation takes up the words, alternately, from another section. In this duality of alternation the unity of profession and of laudation finds an unequalled expression. Even the seraphim call the Sanctus to each other alternately (Is. 6:3). Also the apostolic congregations "addressed one another" in song in their worship services (Col. 3:16; Eph. 5:19). First the breaking of the Word in alternation abundantly manifests the communion in profession and laudation. The most cogent reason for the form-law of liturgical alternation is the oneness of the pneumatic apprehension, which, astonishingly, creates this paradoxical form — the liturgical alternation — for its unity. Also here this pneumatic unity proves itself the opposite of a mechanically working uniformity. It is the unity of an organized body.

THE MOVEMENT BETWEEN ELEMENTARY SIMPLICITY AND DEVELOPED RICHNESS AS A FORMATIVE FACTOR

The gifts that operate in a congregation vary. Also the natural mental endowments and talents which participate in the formation of worship are different. Our presuppositions for the formation of worship will differentiate between "urban church" and "rural church." It would be unreasonable to expect every congregation to contain members, in addition to its shepherd, competent to expound the Word of God to the congregation in the form of a sermon. It would be foolish to expect every congregation to have a precentor and a choir, able to sing Introit and Gradual. The variety of the spiritual gifts and also the variety of natural talents and their cultivation entail a difference in the structure of the form. The liturgies of the 16th century displayed their prudence by taking the place of their employment into consideration, whether the form was intended for a city or for a village, for a place which had a choir of pupils of a Latin school at its disposal, or for a place without such a group. This shows that a difference in the cultural background, a difference in the cultivation of natural talents, has a right to be heard also in the formation of the worship service. However, we must also bear in mind that today a small town or village, rather than a large city, occasionally presents these presuppositions for a rich development of the form.

But not only the differences in the spiritual and the natural gifts effect differences in the formation, distinguishing a highly developed form from one reduced to its basic elements and from an abundance of intermediate possibilities. The same variation of forms may be produced by special occasions and by the nature of particular days. The main service on one of the Sundays after Trinity will as a rule and under ordinary circumstances display a simpler form than, let us say, the service on Easter or Christmas. How plain and unembellished were the worship services in prisons, in concentration camps, in persecuted and oppressed congregations! And yet this circumstance did not in the least affect the reality of the salvation-event in worship. We must disabuse our mind of the notion that our main worship service can be conducted in a form firmly fixed once for all times. Special occasions and special times of the church year are entitled to consideration in the development of the details of worship, just as special gifts and special possibilities dependent on local conditions are. Therefore, in the construction of the order of service a certain scope should be reserved for free choice, so that more festive and less festive forms, richer and simpler forms, forms more exacting in their mode of execution, also more exacting artistically, and forms that are feasible under the most difficult and poorest circumstances, may alternate.

However, here, too, the principle of alternation and of multiplicity must be restrained. This is done if the same basic form is presupposed in the main service and also in the horary prayer, in village and in city, on the Sundays after Trinity and on Easter Sunday, in a hospital chapel and in the solemn opening of a church convention. The basic outline of this worship service is always the same, even though its execution may at one time resemble a lowly cottage and at another a richly furnished mansion. We are not obliged either to elevate the simplest, plainest, and least artistic forms to a legal or a standard status, or to demand that the attainment of the richest form be the universal goal. Only this may be required for the sake of love, that the structure of the order of service be the same, amid all variations in execution, so that the congregation assembled either in a lowly chapel or in an opulent cathedral always recognizes the same basic outline.

The principles which facilitate the free movement between elementary simplicity and elaborate richness may be reduced, essentially, to two: (1) abridgment and expansion by several parts; (2) variation in the execution of individual parts. The Gloria in excelsis and the Alleluja acquainted us with the first principle. This principle is also significant for the celebration of Holy Communion, inasmuch as it cannot be denied that other prayers, in addition to the Lord's Prayer, may be used in connection with the words of institution. Also other parts, such as Introit, may be affected by this principle of "abridgment and expansion." The Wittenberg Reformation applied the second principle to the creation of a German mass, as it replaced the Gregorian psalmody in the Introit and Gradual with a hymn, or combined both possibilities of execution. To be sure, these principles must be administered with discretion and with regard for the salient constituents of worship. It is surely wrong to reduce the Scriptural lections to one, as is still frequently done. Quite aside from the fact that the traditional structure of the verbal part of our worship service (Epistle, inserted song, Gospel) is acutely disrupted by such a curtailment, it is highly unbecoming the church of the Reformation to present the words of the Bible in its main service more sparingly than the Roman mass does.

THE MOVEMENT BETWEEN CONSTANT AND CHANGING TEXTS AS A FORMATIVE FACTOR

The fact that our main service must present constant texts cannot be disputed in view of the words of institution of Holy Communion. Likewise, it goes without saying that the Scripture passages which are read in worship change from time to time. Thus the difference between the Ordinary and the Proper is recognized as a factor that molds the form of worship. But how can the boundary line between the constant and the changing be determined? What is appropriate here? The history of worship demonstrates that both extremes (almost complete exclusion of all change in the Eastern Church and almost complete change of all parts in the Gallican form of the mass) and also a well-balanced mean (constant Ordinary with a limited changing Proper in Rome) have appeared on the scene. Rudolf Staehlin has pointed out clearly that basic questions are at stake in the application of these varying principles of formation.[235]

The choice made by Rome was retained by the Wittenberg Reformation, without an awareness at the time of the exact basic principles that were involved. Today we are, perhaps, in a position to appraise this choice and to affirm it anew. We must resist a surrender of the order of worship to the predominance, and much more to the autocracy, of the Proper. The wholeness of the salvation-event, comprehended in the name of Jesus Christ, dare not be splintered and dissolved into individual isolated emphases. Therefore the influence of the Proper must be held to a minimum, especially in Holy Communion. On the other hand, particular phases of the sal-

241

vation-event in Jesus Christ will be emphasized at different times in the proclamation of the Word: Christ's birth, His epiphany, His suffering and death, His resurrection, His ascent into heaven, the outpouring of His Spirit, His return. Thus a change in the texts, that is, the Proper character, will be more marked in the first part of the worship service.

If we were asked where the greater danger lies, in too much emphasis on the constant or on the changing, the history of liturgy would reply — and experience to date confirms this — that the Germanic peoples are especially prone, by their predilection for change and for emphasis of the individual aspects of the salvation-event, to jeopardize an appropriate order of worship. Allied with this, we find the present-day inclination to compress all the texts of every worship service into unified themes. Themes such as "Fruits of Faith," "Trust in God," "Cross and Comfort," "The Home and the Training of the Children," "Vocation, Labor, and Earthly Goods," have monopolized the sermonic part of worship in detail also in official agendas.[236] The unsoundness of this development is widely recognized today. Such rational constructions run counter to the freedom of the Word of God. Whatever God's Word wants to say is stabilized and restricted in advance by such a thematic liturgy. But such constructions also oppose the inner laws of a matured liturgy. They bear the mark of the artificial so distinctly. Moreover, also their attempt at pedagogical effect miscarries. The calculated and not infrequently artificial side of such a construction does not serve the proclamation of the Gospel.

To be sure, this danger of a rational construction of the order of worship may be regarded as surmounted today. However, the attractive force which emanates from a minutely defined church year is still stronger today than is good for a sound order of the life of worship. We should resist the attempt to lend a pronounced Proper character similar to that of the main worship service also to the horary prayer. The horary prayer should be distinguished from the mass form of the main service by a marked recession of the Proper. But the congregation should become so familiar with rather long prayer texts through their regular use also in the main service that the members can join in these without difficulty. In view of the use made of his paraphrase of the Lord's Prayer, Luther energetically emphasized the importance of the congregation's memorization of the exact wording of a prayer; in default of this, he said, the members cannot properly pray along.[237] Both in view of its origin and of its popularity in Christendom, the Lord's Prayer itself is the strongest proof that the repetition of the same prayer form by no means detracts from its spiritual vitality. The converse may, rather, be true. A certain restraint in change and a greater willingness to submit prayer, intercession, and praise to God in fixed forms will aid a congregation in the fulfillment of its function of worship as it matures toward the same.

WORSHIP AND ART

If we wish to ascertain how the form of worship must be realized in our midst, we cannot ignore the question regarding the importance of art in worship. Admittedly, our deliberations here enter a difficult area, and we can proceed only with cautious and experimental steps. The following elaborations must therefore, in a special way, bear the marks of an attempt.

The Difficulty and the Inevitability of the Question

Ever since Schleiermacher, the theme "Worship and Art" is part and parcel of the stock and store of an Evangelical doctrine of worship.[238] The deliberations which aim to clarify this relationship with regard to form and content are all influenced by Schleiermacher's doctrine of art and worship, also with regard to content, not only in the 19th century but also far beyond that. Even a man like Theodosius Harnack, and also Georg Rietschel, could not entirely escape the power which emanated from the aesthetics of idealistic philosophy and especially from Schleiermacher's philosophical doctrine of art and religion.[239] This idealistic background, and especially the idealistic philosophy of religion, closely linked with these aesthetics, can no longer be the basis in our search for a solution of the question regarding the relationship between worship and art. On the other hand, this question cannot be solved unless we learn to know the essence of art. Here we face the first difficulty: A philosophy of art into whose realm we may enter as theologians to pursue our course of cognition is not available to us.[240]

The task of beholding the reality of art and in it the possibility of an artistic work in the light of God's revealed Word involves a similar difficulty. This task might well be undertaken within the framework of theological ethics, and if so, in that area which treats of institutional forms of society such as marriage, business, the state, to which also science and art may be joined. But also for the solution of this problem very few attempts have been made to date which might be of use to us.[241]

Perhaps the greatest difficulty in the way of a satisfactory solution is posed by the cultural position in which we find ourselves. The completion of a task assigned to our comprehension depends, perhaps decisively and especially in our case, on the question whether the reality which must be recognized is effectively vital in man's actual practical existence. For approximately 170 years a dissolution and a disintegration of the old forms is taking place not only in the area of worship but also in that of the arts, whose effect on the future no one can survey.[242] In such a critical time of breakdown also a theological doctrine on the relationship between worship and art cannot be the final word but merely an attempt that points to the future.

Nevertheless, a theological doctrine of worship will unavoidably take up the question regarding the function of the arts in the worship of the church. The necessity of such deliberations was brought to the fore most distinctly in the history of the church by the controversy over images. This far-reaching controversy of the old church, enduring for a century and a half, involved not only the question of power, but also and chiefly dogmatic decisions.[243] The Protestant image controversy of the 16th century likewise dealt with the dogmatic bases of the church's doctrine.[244] The recollection of both iconoclastic crises in the history of the church demonstrates that the question regarding the relationship between worship and art certainly contains a dogmatic component which calls for a decision in the realm of doctrine.

It is not the plastic arts that make a basic and systematic study of our theme so necessary. By reason of the essence of worship, words and melody perhaps present the main areas in which artistic construction becomes our task and problem. Holy Scripture itself shows that both its Old and its New Testament message was clad in verbal forms which can be viewed not only from the perspective of aesthetics, but which also exhibit a pithiness of style that constrains us to speak of artistic form. That applies not only to passages that are poetical in structure, but also to narrative passages, not only in the Old but also in the New Testament.[245] The message of the Gospel is peculiarly and manifestly vested in verbal forms which bear the hallmark of art. And the apostolic exhortation in Col. 3:16 and in Eph. 5:19 indicate that this must also apply to the proclamation of the Word in worship beyond the apostolic era. Now the question arises, why this is so.

A special problem for the form of worship stems, furthermore, from the connection between word and melody, the melody determined by situation, duration, and strength. From its very inception, the words of Scripture were joined to the sung melody. It is obvious that a definite musical arrangement was provided for the psalms, which were designed for Israel's worship.[246] But also the Proverbs of Solomon were "sung" when used for oral instruction.[247] The Hebrew accents "are intended first of all to regulate minutely the recital of the sacred text. The accents served the cantillating or singing presentation as a type of musical notes." [248] It is true of antiquity in general that it made the transition from spoken to sung words with facility.[249] For Luther *singen und sagen* ("to sing and to say") are still closely knit.[250] The manner in which the charismatic (1 Cor. 14:16; *Didache*, 10, 6) or the bishop (*Didache*, 15, 1) spoke the prayer in worship was, very probably, not essentially different from the manner in which the leader in prayer prayed in the synagog. There is no doubt that songs were sung in the worship of the apostolic congregations. Here, too, we must inquire into the meaning of the combination of the words with the sung melody.

However, the problem "worship and art" is posed not only by this or by that detail of worship, but also by the fact that worship as a whole is a structure executed by man and designed as a symbolic form for a very definite content and meaning. When we spoke of the symbolic character of the form of worship and there established a flexible measure of appropriateness, we formulated concepts which also pertain to the work of art. When we pointed out the paradoxical union of restraint and freedom in the form of worship, we touched on a fact which is at least analogous to the fundamental law which is operative in those arts that may be conceived of under the viewpoint of play. Is only an analogy involved here? Or might worship in its execution be related to that childlike game which wisdom plays here on earth and yet also before God? (Prov. 8:29-31) [251]

These questions cannot be answered unless we indicate into which light art is moved by faith in the Gospel of Jesus Christ.

Art in the Beginning of All Things

"In the beginning was the Word, and the Word was with God, and the Word was God . . . All things were made through Him, and without Him was not anything made that was made" (John 1:1, 3). God said: "Let there be," "And it was so" (Gen. 1:6, 24). Every creature is what it is by the Word of God, which creates and sustains it. In their being, the creatures correspond to the creative Word. This correspondence to the Word is the creatural being's goodness and truth, which as such also radiate the beauty of the creatural being.[252] This correspondence to the Word lends the creatures a radiance that transcends their functional and purposive design. To be sure, the creatures are tools for God's work of preservation, but they are more than technical means. The world is not like a chest filled with tools. In this very word "more" something of this Word-nature appears which inheres in the creature and which determines the particularity of its being, with which the creature corresponds to the creative Word of God. Wherever this radiance, appearing in the Word-nature of the creatures, this inseparable union of their goodness, truth, and beauty, can be captured and exemplified in a work, there a work of art is born in the beginning of all things.

To do this requires man who is created in the image of God. The work of man can never be creative. But according to God's will, it must be oriented to the creature, it must adopt the creature in its creaturalness, foster it, cherish it, shelter and preserve it. Here God precedes man with a special work. God plants a garden on earth to serve as man's dwelling place (Gen. 2:8). The garden is the sign for the delivering, sheltering, and preserving of the hidden and true being of the creature. The garden is not merely a delimited sector of earth, although such a delimitation over against the cosmic expanse is also part of the garden's gift and benefaction. The garden is, above all, a parcel of earth that stands out in bold relief, a parcel of earth distinguished by God's special proximity, also a parcel of earth that was cultivated from the beginning, a veritable ennobled piece of ground. Here hidden possibilities are brought to the fore by a work, are brought into the light, and are thus realized. This garden is the dispensing center of the earth (Gen. 2:10-14). The entire world bears within it the potentialities of this garden. From this garden the entire earth receives quickening powers, which preserve it in its being-earth, in its fruitfulness, and which make it resemble the Garden of God, even if only remotely. The Garden of God is a sign for the *cultura* of this earth, in which also the work of art will find its place.

The work of man must succeed God's garden-work if God's garden, man's world, is to endure on the earth. God's garden-work resembles a directive for man's work on the earth. Wherever man sojourns, God wants the earth to be cultivated and developed into a world for man's abode. And this is to be achieved by the work of man, who takes over God's work, preserves, and protects it. (Gen. 2:15)

Within the framework of this commission to man the miracle of language, which is a work and which is art, takes place. The aloneness of man poses a problem for God Himself: a need, which He assumes and resolves. God creates the appropriate creatural counterpart to man, the creatural thou. And in the quest for this thou, the miracle of language is performed. In the finding of this thou, language itself finds its consummation.

Through God the beasts of the field and the birds of the air are drawn close to man. In the Garden they enter into his world; they are fit into it by man's appellative word (Gen. 2:19). In the appellative word man expresses the nature of the creature which he encounters. The original function of language as work, as art, was to state the God-wrought essence of the creature. The appellative word explains the being which is peculiar to each creature. In the appellative word this being of the creature is captured by means of a human work and in a manner close to man, and is thus drawn truly close to him. In that way this event, which takes place in the linguistic work of man, establishes communion between man and creature, and yet manifests the limitations of that communion. This word apprehends the creature's peculiar and true being, and places it in this new verbal mode of being closely and familiarly before man and thereby fits it as a real member into the world of man. Thus the appellative word creates nearness and familiarity, and yet leaves room open in this familiarity and nearness for that communion between I and thou, which infinitely transcends it and which completes the essence of man; this is a communion in which nearness and familiarity consummates itself in becoming one. Surveyed from this becoming-one, this communion, there is, to be sure, no note of lament, of sadness, of wild desire vibrating in the appellative word, but there is a quest, a seeking, yearning expectation which still awaits fulfillment.

The birth of the appellative word marks the birth of the work of art, which as such simultaneously embraces recognition of the true, creatural being. In the word of man, which is apt to express the God-created essence of a creature encountered by him, the echo of that creative Word through which this creature received and retains its peculiar substantial being reverberates on earth. When this word is spoken as a reverberating, earthly-creatural echo of the Creator's Word, the creatural being is secured among men and preserved in the disclosure of its own true being.

But this appellative word is still in quest of a final fulfillment in the ultimate communion, in which the I meets its thou and both become one. The miracle of language fulfills itself in the combination of words by which man is able to express who and what this God-given thou is (Gen. 2:23). Just as the creatural thou, which man encounters, infinitely transcends all other creatures in its correlation to man, thus the structural combination of words released in this encounter incomparably transcends the mere appellative word. Now the word becomes poetry, now it becomes a jubilant song. Now the appellative word evolves into a construction of words in metrical order and in playful freedom, in vibrating rhythm and melodious tone. From this verbal expansion the arts are born in their manifoldness, vitally united with the word and borne by its essence. In this word structure there is no longer any quest, but fulfillment itself, the fulfillment of the human being in its encounter with the God-appointed thou. Therefore there is in this word structure an infinite joy, expressed however, in the finite word without ever being expressed exhaustively. In this construction of words, expressing jubilation and yet objectively naming the thou, in the strict order of its construction, in the free play of its images, in the rhythmic movement accompanying and uniting with it, in the embellishing splendor which it radiates, in its elevation of story to song — in the union of all these elements, man's work of art fulfills itself. For here the creatural being of man, made in God's image, is captured and preserved, as encountered by him and disclosed to him, in the mirror of the word, which has attained fullness. In this word, equally pervaded by the fullness of the creatural being and the fullness of the arts, man's work of art fulfills itself.

In the beginning of all things, man's work of art is the echo on earth of God's act of creation and of God's Word of creation. In that way this work, the mirror of the Word-related, true being of the creatures, is simultaneously "a glorification" of God (Hein-

248

rich Vogel). To be sure, the creatures' being appears more resplendent when engaged by man's work of art, attaining a splendor which it lacked before. However, this work of art is not a glorification of the creature. Nor is it a glorification of man, who produces it. The work of the appellative word and the work of the never exhaustively related story about the communion in the thou are, to be sure, a necessary part of the essence of man's likeness to God. But all of these verbal works, together with the other arts accompanying them and uniting with them, glorify, even by their very existence and with their ultimate and real intent, the Creator, because they echo the Word of the Creator. Whoever by his work brings into focus the essence of the creature, which corresponds to the Word of the Creator and is therefore its true and peculiar essence, thereby glorifies Him from whom and through whom and to whom everything is that is. In the beginning of all things man's work of art is, at all events, praise of the Creator — even if it merely expresses the real essence of this granite, of this rose, of this dove, of this lion, to say nothing of the jubilating word which exultantly sings about who thou art and what thou art to me. Therefore, in the beginning of all things the work of art is an essential element in the worship of the prime creature; it is an agency for the glorification of the Creator. In the beginning of all things the work of art is the vessel in which man captures the glory diffused over creation, exhibits it, presents it to God as a thank offering.

Art in God's Rule of the World

The Garden of God is lost. The appellative word is lost.[253] The story of the communion in the thou, elevated to a bridal song of rejoicing, is hushed. The path leading back to the beginning is blocked to fallen man. He cannot slip by the cherubim with the flaming sword. And still the appellative word and the bridal song of rejoicing are so much a part of man's essence that he is henceforth constrained to look for that word and that song in every mature work of art. Art remains restive because the work of Eden is denied it. The art of fallen man will, even and especially in its greatest maturity, ever remain a quest for the appellative word and the bridal song about the thou. This restiveness may become suffering, may become torment.[254] Every mature work of art will be marked by this suffering. The fulfillment which is diffused over the work of Eden remains denied to the work of fallen man.

But is not every work of art rendered impossible now in fallen man's abode by the loss of the paradisiac work? Indeed, the tool, the implement, and the object of utility manufactured by it, that is, cloth, now seem to replace the work of art. God provided also for this new situation of man with a guiding act, which accompanied him into his new situation, so to say, as a directive. Man has forfeited his innocence. He bears shame on his body. Moreover, he must now go out into the inhospitable land, which is bereft of the protection and the beneficence of God's Garden. By reason of his shame and his destitution he stands in need of protective cover. God supplies him with this. God does not create this cover as a new creature by His creative Word; but He fashions it — similar to a craftsman — from a suitable material (Gen. 3:21), and now calls man's attention to this object as a new and important element of his new world. Man's world is no longer a garden, a park. To be sure, the fertile earth is still his world. But this earth bears thorns and thistles; this earth demands labor and sweat. The awesome travail of birth and the gruesome night of death hover over the earth. Of what use is the work of art to man in these circumstances? Cloth is what he needs here and, consequently, also the tools, serviceable implements which are entirely utilitarian, the wedge, the stone ax, the coat, the tent. Thus it is not art, but tools and the articles manufactured with them, that we find in the beginning of the history of fallen man.

But God's creating word remains operative in the life of man exiled from the Garden. The quest for the work of art is therefore ineradicable, no matter how obtrusive the tool has become. The person who is prone to be wholly engrossed in the world of tools, who is interested only in the utility of material, betrays his own essence. He is in danger of seeing and treating man himself only as material and thus of destroying human nature. To be sure, the discovery and the development of the tool marks an immeasurable force for progress in the history of man. But it was not this discovery and this development that kept the history of man within the human sphere. We know, where the immense, dynamic power of the tool presumes to rule alone, the history of man verges on the abyss of the nonhuman and on its death in the subhuman. Among the forces which have restrained the history of man from this abyss and from this death, the force with which man still strives for the work of art in the midst of his world of tools is not the least. In this force man discovers that room for free play was left him in his world of labor and toil. In this force man discovers that a free area is left him also for ornamentation in the utility of his material, yes, even in the utility of the tool with which he fashions his material.[255] The discovery of this free play and of this area for ornamentation was a token of mercy, without which man's humanity could not have been preserved. From play and ornamentation arises the work of art of fallen man.[256]

This work of art is subject to other conditions now than it was in the beginning of all things. A change in the creatural being, which must appear in the work of art, corresponds to a change in man's capability, of which we have already spoken. To be sure, God's word of creation still stands effectively and preservatively over the creatures. But the word-nature of the creatures is hidden more now than ever before. The destruction which the invasion of the corruptive forces wrought on the most sensitive spot of the cosmos, on man, is spreading to all earthly creatures. A curse rests on the earth because of man (Gen. 3:17). The futile, the vain, the transitory, the corruptible exercise their power over all creatures (Eccl. 1:1 ff.; Rom. 8:19 f.). Just because the creatures remain related to God's creative Word, there is a melancholy yearning stirring in them, which longs for release from the bondage of corruption. If the work of art today betokens a bit of the goodness and the truthfulness of the creatural essence, this is not only a memory of the relationship of the creatural essence to the Word of the Creator, but it also reveals some trace of the creature's suffering, which distorts it, and of the creature's yearning for a coming deliverance. But the work of art will testify chiefly, and especially, in its zenith, let us say in the Attic tragedy, of the deep fall of man, of his forlorn condition, of man's disrupted world.[257]

But in this very limitation the work of art can still display splinters and fragments of the true creatural essence. Amid the melancholy yearning for the lost, the sorrowful lament over the present, and the anxious awaiting of a still indescribable future, fallen man's work of art will bring to light, under God's rule of the world, a trace of the enduring word-relationship of the creature, and thereby disseminate a beneficent and relieving joy, which, though mingled with pain, warms and nurtures and preserves human existence. Even now the work of art manifestly transcends the mere offerings of the existing situation. It penetrates into the existing situation as into a mountain and brings from the hidden interior a bit of the real element to light. In that respect it is comparable to science, which in cognition also discloses a hidden element as a real element.[258] Together with science and the remaining institutional orders of community life, such as marriage, family, law, and state, art also contributes toward the preservation of the human side of man's existence and fills his gloomy confinement with a beneficent gloam, so that he can somewhat get his bearings and at least breathe amid the troubles, pains, problems, and gloom, and now and then even breathe freely.

The Forbidden Image

From its very beginning, art in God's rule of the world is in extreme jeopardy. And it succumbs to this danger almost throughout the length and breadth of pagan humanity and develops into a magical, sorcerous, tyrannically enslaving image, which is engaged in the service of a consuming and raging idol. In order to understand this peril to art and to comprehend how it could fall prey to this innate jeopardy, we must hear the Biblical account of the origin of the arts in the world of fallen man:

> Then the Lord said to Cain, "Where is Abel your brother?" He said, "I do not know; am I my brother's keeper?" And the Lord said, "What have you done? The voice of your brother's blood is crying to me from the ground. And now you are cursed from the ground, which has opened its mouth to receive your brother's blood from your hand. When you till the ground, it shall no longer yield to you its strength; you shall be a fugitive and a wanderer on the earth." . . . Cain knew his wife, and she conceived and bore Enoch; and he built a city, and called the name of the city after the name of his son, Enoch. To Enoch was born Irad; and Irad was the father of Mehujael, and Mehujael the father of Methushael, and Methushael the father of Lamech. And Lamech took two wives; the name of the one was Adah, and the name of the other Zillah. Adah bore Jabal; he was the father of those who dwell in tents and have cattle. His brother's name was Jubal; he was the father of all those who play the lyre and pipe. Zillah bore Tubal-cain; he was the forger of all instruments of bronze and iron. . . . Lamech said to his wives:
>
> > "Adah and Zillah, hear my voice;
> > you wives of Lamech, hearken to what I say:
> > I have slain a man for wounding me,
> > a young man for striking me.
> > If Cain is avenged sevenfold,
> > truly Lamech seventy-sevenfold." [259]

Just as the discovery and the development of tool and material transpired against the dark background of man's first fall, so the development of play and ornamentation into art again took place against the dark background of a second evil deed. In punishment man forfeits also the nourishing soil on which he stands. Fratricide is the deed from which that world of man grows which develops tool and material in an undreamed-of fashion, and which also makes play and ornamentation a complete work of art within the capabilities of fallen man. The event of murder changes this world anew for man. Murder portends an inhuman end of the history of man. This menacing, inhuman end can be checked only by the isolation of the person who has become a murderer. This isolation entails an impoverishment, another impoverishment touching the earth. Where murder has become possible, man is forced out to the extreme edge of possible human existence, to the place where the nourishing, firm soil of the field changes into the barren, shifting sand of the desert. And here at this boundary of field and desert, of life and death, and in the restless roaming over this perilous area, the work of art of fallen man arises.

As man peers into the desolate boundlessness and the deadly solitude of the desert, a desire for the enclosed city awakens in him. And the construction of the city gives birth to that art which in several respects may be viewed as the beginning, as the ἀρχή, as the first of the arts in the life of fallen man, the "primary art" of archi-tecture. To be sure, the city is unable to restore the nourishing soil to man. It remains akin to the desert.[260] Nor can the city reinstate the peace of free fraternal communion; it produces only a torpid and distorted image of this communion, the city-state, which by threat and application of force provides for a stopgap regulation of communal life within the periphery of its walls.

The contact with those chaotic forces of desolation which erupt in the heart of man and disfigure, outside of his ordered world, the face of the earth into a wilderness, engenders the longing for a work which bridles the menacing chaos and produces a cosmos of regulated order and harmony. Where the breath of death is felt, where man in desperation defends himself, with tool and material, against a challenge to his whole existence, there he simultaneously and fervently seizes upon the free area of play and ornamentation and fashions it into a work of art.

Fallen man's work of art, originating in the perilous borderland between nourishing field and deadly desert, reflects the rent that marks his entire existence. By reason of this rent, man's work of art is fractured art already in its production. It really appears only in pieces, which will never join into a whole, even though they search for each other as long as works of art are created.

The amazing development of the tool and its products is already accompanied by the increasing specialization of the craftsman. Man's knowledge becomes one-sided. No one masters everything any longer. Hardly any one is any longer able to do many different things. Each one is competent to do only one thing. This one-sidedness of man is, essentially, due to the impoverishment within which the work of art is born. No matter how excellent a work of art may be, it now shares in this impoverishment. It itself is inclined to one-sidedness. Here we find the builder of cities, there the musician, the sculptor, the poet — each one for himself. To be sure, they are related. They have the same ancestry. They are kith and kin. They will search each other out and find each other; they will, as long as they live, walk together. However, each one also stands independently alone and as such goes his own individual way and devotes himself to his own peculiar work. To be sure, arts search each other out; however, from their very beginning they also show a peculiar, highly dangerous countertendency: each one has a propensity to step out of the paternal-fraternal circle and to isolate itself, to become pure architecture, pure music, pure painting, pure poetry.

Where the tendency to purism, innate in the individual arts, gains the upper hand, the arts are threatened with their doom. Only so long as they are rooted together in their common ancestry do they have life. To be sure, each has its own life, but this is merely an indication of the mysterious wholeness of the work, which is lost on this earth for all times. Thus art enters into man's historical world as a multiplicity of separate arts, which must necessarily appear as an impoverishment in every work of every art, and which, furthermore, evinces a dangerous inclination toward death.

But the danger to art reaches beyond this. How is art to serve fallen man, who wanders about aimlessly in the danger zone between field and desert? Even so, under God's rule of this world, art is to preserve man's life as befitting a human being. Precisely for fallen man, art, in conjunction with science, law, state, marriage, is to be a means of orientation in his restless roaming. The work of art is to shine precisely for him in the power of the word-related, true, creatural being, which becomes manifest in him.

Now the question arises whether this man apprehends in the work of art the real and authentic light for the illumination of reality, or whether he beholds this light of art, the warrant for all that is genuine and true, in an entirely different light, as an escape from reality, as the light of a will-o'-the-wisp, of a visionary world, of a world of magic. Why was the art of fallen man born in that dangerous borderland between nourishing soil and deadening desert? More burdensome than the toil in the field occasioned by thorns and thistles is man's knowledge of the chaotic, unfathomable forces deep down in his own heart and on the face of the devastated earth. Is it possible that man could no longer bear the sight of the misery of devastation? Does he invent lute and flute and ornamentation artistically devised in order to fashion a world into which he can flee with his mortally wounded heart? Is it a Fata Morgana, which the human heart craftily publicizes as a saving oasis on the desolate face of the earth, to compensate for the loss of earth? Might the work of art succeed, after all, in replacing the Garden of God? Might art not heal the wound in the historical existence of man? Is there "redemption" in art?

Where this belief is affirmed, art loses its beneficent quality. Indeed, it strengthens man's sense of being, but in a manner that he loses the last bit of earth from under his feet. To be sure, the paradisiac light of glorification seems to flare up again. But what and whom does the work of art glorify now that it has broken through the protective boundary in which alone it can reveal real being?

The first person who again bursts forth into a glorifying song following that jubilation in the beginning of all things is, according to the Bible, Lamech, the first poet, the first in the genealogy of the arts. The rhythm, the mellifluous, euphonious word of song, is still the generating principle of the arts. In the beginning of all things the song glorified the thou, the communion of the I and the thou, in which the I and the thou become one for the conception of a child and the begetting of new life. But where the song comes into being in the historical existence of man, it has degenerated into a vindictive, vaunting, death-dealing song of the sword. This man Lamech vaunts himself, he puts himself into the light, into the light of a consuming fire. To be sure, the woman stands at the side of the man also in this glorification; however, not as his bride, but only as a foil for the ghastly self-praise, which must necessarily be vain boasting. The function God's mercy assigned to art for fallen man is here perverted into a horrible opposite. The glaring light of this work does not illumine the true creatural being, but it incites to further devastation. This light is a fire that consumes, it is no longer the spark of that pain-affirming joy that warms.

Where art becomes man's means for crushing the last bits of true creatural being that manifest themselves to him, where art becomes a blinding, consuming Fata Morgana, where it, instead of disclosing itself humbly and lovingly to the creature it encounters, is misused for the glorification of the I and has entirely lost its orientation to the thou, there man has lost the last crumb of the nourishing earth from under his feet. The decline in being has now approached the borders of absolute zero. Man is about to tumble into the abyss. In this moment a terrible fate befalls art: It enlists in the service of magic, of sorcery, of the "power" of the idol. Now the forbidden image is made, which is to restore the fullness of the lost being to fallen man by magic power.[261] Now the work of art is engaged — climax of ghastly perversion — in the service of the idol and becomes an idol itself.

The magic image and the idol image presuppose the might of the devil. True creatural being, which corresponds to God's creative Word in essence and quality, and the created spirit Satan, who from the beginning and on principle rebels against God, are separated by an infinite gulf. But it is part of the puzzling mystery of the Satanic powers to dazzle and delude with a show of true creatural being just where, because of their destructive influence, man's decline in being has progressed to the very borders of absolute zero. The riddle of this mystery inheres in the fact that there is, of course, no Luciferian truth and goodness, but indeed a Luciferian beauty. It was taken by violence from truth and goodness and thus is the victim of violence, but now, in the hands of the Satanic powers, it commits violent rape itself in the name of Luciferian beauty.

No matter how far our knowledge of man reaches back in time, it finds him abandoned to the magic image in earliest history soon after he crossed the threshold where he appears as man.[262] This image includes magic-cultic power over the object of the image, and it radiates this power. The ever bustling freedom of reality, withdrawing from man, is transfixed in this image, as it were. This image is "congealed reality."[263] It is concentrated dictatorial might. It is not the Word-nature, not the truthfulness of the being that appears in this image, but in this image man himself, in the power of the devil, aspires to the power of one who has being (*des Seienden*). The power of the one who has being is captured, as it were, in this image, and accordingly man employs this power for the tyrannical subjection of the world surrounding him. In place of the loving encounter in which the Word-conforming, and therefore truthful, being of the creatures is to reveal itself in the God-willed work of artistic man, the despotic, tyrannical exercise of power of magic-cultic enchantment now enters upon the scene. The peak of this wickedness is reached when the forbidden image presumes directly to capture the Lord of all creatural being, God Himself, and to hold His divine power in the clutch of man.[264]

It cannot be denied that the magic image and the idol image are able to radiate might with the help of the devil. But the effect of this might is necessarily and exactly the opposite of what a work of art must be. In the periphery of this power of images and idols a disclosure of the Word-relatedness of the creatural being through art and science is hardly possible any longer. In place of the illumination which the work of art was to provide for the world of man, man encounters that demonic darkness in which the true creatural being may be destroyed to the point where man slaughters man as a sacrifice to the idol. It is surely not coincidental, but profoundly rooted in the relationship between Creator and creature, that the truth of the creatural being remains deeply hidden where magic and idol reign, despite all display of man's might. The greater man's addiction to the power of the forbidden image, the deeper the darkness of the world in which he lives. Wherever the idol reigns, there man's cognition-geared thinking and his artistic activity will be grotesquely distorted.[265] The avenues to the Word-conforming, true creatural being are barricaded in the environs of the forbidden image. It is one of the great benefactions — outside of God's revelation of salvation — which God's kindness bestowed on fallen mankind that the destructive dominion of the idol was pushed back so far here and there — for instance, in Athens at the time of classical tragedy — that the reality of man's world begins to reveal itself to fallen man at least sketchily in science and in art.[266]

Art as a Result of the Encounter with the Gospel of Jesus Christ

"And the Word became flesh and dwelt among us, full of grace and truth; we have beheld His glory, glory as of the only Son from the Father" (John 1:14). The incarnation of the Eternal Word also affected art profoundly. Jesus Christ is the one true, eternal image of God in our midst, clad in our flesh and blood (Heb. 1:3; 2 Cor. 4:4; Col. 1:15). Therefore the magic-cultic image is plainly and simply the forbidden image. The magic image, the sacral royal image, the cultic idol image is shattered on Jesus Christ. For His sake the Old Testament already interdicts the magic and the idol image, in order, as it were, to leave room for the appearance of the Word and of the image of God in the flesh.[267] Also the art which, in idealistic diminution, presumes to produce the divine and the absolute as the prime cause of all things is broken to bits on Jesus Christ. Wherever art makes the claim that the deity itself appears in its work, the Christian faith can only repudiate it.[268]

But does not all art fail when it encounters the Christ-event? The Word became flesh, sin-laden, condemned, sacrificed flesh. Wherever God appears in the flesh, the cross stands erected. And where this one image of God in our flesh and blood is erected, there we find the countenance of this One inhumanly disfigured. "He had no form or comeliness that we should look at Him, and no beauty that we should desire Him" (Is. 53:2). Through this "form" of the suffering and dying God-man, art in God's rule of the world also enters a deadly crisis. The countenance of the Crucified discloses that humankind shut itself out from the light of the Word which shone for it in creation. Whoever is aware that man crucified the eternal Word of God in Jesus, knows that every immediate, childlike access to the Word-conforming, true being of the creature, also the enduring word-relatedness of the creature, is lost to man. Wherever art stands in the periphery of the Word of the Cross, it will be impossible for it to return either to a naively outspoken pagan sensualism or to a well-contrived pagan tragedy.

But is there any place at all for art under the cross? This question must be viewed in its pressing and threatening earnestness if we wish to recognize how art is possible under the cross. Under no circumstances is it possible in the manner in which it was realized by the pagan, who either erects the forbidden image at the peak of his artistic productivity or reaches into the void with an answerless question.

The judgment that is passed in the cross on us and our work procures our pardon. The Crucified is also the Risen One. In a peculiar harmony of contrasts, the Word of the suffering and dying Servant of God is juxtaposed to the prophetic word of the Messiah-King: "You are the fairest of the sons of men; grace is poured upon your lips" (Ps. 45:2). We will never be able to comprehend fully the intimate interrelation of Isaiah 53 and Psalm 45. The interrelation of the worst disfigurement and of the highest glory is by its very essence numbered among the mysteries of Jesus Christ. For the beauty which appears in Jesus Christ is the beauty of the complete obedience of the Son over against the Father. The beauty of this obedience, of this compliance, is already fused in a hidden way with the countenance of the Crucified, even though it first beams forth in a special measure of heavenly glory in the refulgence of resurrection at Easter. Thus, the cross does not decree the rigor of death on man, but it confers the gift of a new life. To be sure, Jesus' cross and resurrection involves a judgment on all the pagan possibilities and realities of art, but this judgment is infinitely surpassed by the disclosure of a new possibility of art, on which a reflection of the beauty of Jesus rests because it emulates His obedience.[269]

The work of art which is an encounter with Christ's cross and resurrection absorbs, first of all, that work of art which was to eventuate in God's rule of the world, and which did eventuate here and there at least fragmentarily in defiance of the dominion of idols. The work of art occupies a prominent place in the realm of the profane especially in the periphery of the Gospel. The work of art that follows the encounter with the Gospel takes up that melancholy recollection of what was lost, the mournful lament over the present situation, and the anxious, groping expectation of what lies in the future, placing them into the light of Jesus Christ.

In the incarnation of the Word, that Word appeared through whom all that exists came into being and through whom it is preserved. The beginning of all things is again brought close to us in Jesus. In the power of Christ's birth the closed Garden of Eden is again opened. In the power of this birth the exultant cry is verified: "The angel guards the gate no more!" Access to the true, the Word-conforming being of the creature is provided. In the incarnation of the Word, in the inhuman disfigurement of the Crucified by the curse of sin imposed on Him, the abyss of the lost condition, also the gruesome disfigurement of the creature by the powers of perdition, is so clearly revealed that its view would petrify us if this cross were not the cross of Christ. In the glory of the incarnate Word, which — transcending the paradisiac radiance of the beginning by far — beams forth especially at Easter, the promise of the coming eschatological change is distinctly inscribed over all creatures. The work of art which results from belief in the Gospel will itself be a sign for the eschatological *transitus* into which the creature is placed through Christ's cross and resurrection. This

work of art has beheld the creatural being in its in-being in the crucified and resurrected God-man. In this work nothing will be ignored,
neither the Word-nature of the creature as rooted in the beginning,
nor the creature's sin-wrought perversion, nor the divined radiance
of a future transfiguration. This work will, above all, indicate symbolically the movement into which the creature is transferred by Jesus'
cross and resurrection, the movement leading from the beginning,
passing through the lost condition, and approaching the final transformation and liberation.[270] A work of art endued with the grace to show
forth something of this in signs becomes, precisely in its profaneness,
an objective glorification of the Triune God and of the work of Jesus
Christ — solely by reason of the fact that it throws a clear light on the
state and condition of the creature in Jesus Christ.

The creatural being, as revealed through Jesus Christ, is the true
being. The work of art which brings this true being into view is for
that very reason the true work of art. Therefore art in the environs
of the word of the cross faces a new, final, end-time decision. The way
back into the pagan sphere is barred to it.[271] That is demonstrated in
an exemplary way by classicism and idealism.

The pagan aspects of this science and form of art cannot be overlooked; however, they do not constitute its essence. A relapse into the
pagan realm will not succeed. Science and form of classical and idealistic art are clearly a post-Christian phenomenon; and this "post" is not
a neutral designation of time, but it indicates the sphere of power in
which the artistic experience of classicism and idealism became possible. The decision which art in the environs of the word of the cross
confronts includes a critical decision of either — or: art either moves
toward the work which, as a result of the Gospel, becomes a sign for
the eschatological *transitus* of the creature which dawned in Christ,
or art enters the service of the Antichrist.

We sense the Antichristian possibilities only from afar, but we
cannot pass them over in silence. These end-time possibilities are
intimated in the mysterious Revelation of St. John (Rev. 13:17). Now
the forbidden image becomes the image of the beast from "the bottom-
less pit." The forbidden saying becomes a blasphemy of Christ. The
pagan myth becomes a prophecy of the Antichrist, which animates the
image of the beast. This art is not profane, but it belongs to the Antichristian cult which worships the beast. The tyrannical, consuming
might of the forbidden image will even be surpassed where the image
of the beast unfolds its might, and, despite the dazzling miracles of the

Antichrist, will conjure up the inhuman end of earth's history in the apocalyptic dissolution of all things.

By way of contrast, the art that tends toward the work stemming from the Christian faith will be in the service of God's rule of the world, even when unaware of this; for it contributes toward disclosing reality and toward the preservation of human existence as human. The fate of art in the post-Christian culture will certainly be dependent on the relationship between art and faith. The crisis of art, which must set in where the word of the cross demonstrates its power, can be comprehended only if conceived from the problematical situation which, as a result of the sermon on Christ, cleaves to post-Christian culture like a thorn in the flesh.

The work which depicts the creatural being as revealed to the view by Christ is the true work of art, because Jesus Christ Himself is the truth. Therefore the approximation to this work will be the most important objective measure for the evaluation of a work of art; however, not the only one. Not only what appears in a work of art, but also how that being appears, is decisive for the worth and the quality of a work. The exclusive feature of a work as a work of art lies in this very *how* of its appearance, in the form.

In the case of the time-bound play, the material for the form is the word of speech, the musically animated tone, and the gesture; in the case of space-bound ornamentation, it is composed of space outlined by construction of plastic form, of line and color. Added to these are the various combinations of these elements of form, the most important of which yield, on the one hand, the vocal song, and, on the other, the painted picture. When the being, disclosed through Jesus Christ, is a being in motion, a being in the eschatological *transitus,* a being in the history of God, then the time-bound elements of form will be found in a special affinity to the art made possible by the encounter with the Gospel.

But since the power of the end-time transformation is already effective in advance, also the space-bound species of art will receive a new significance in the environs of Christian faith as references to the time-transcending rest of contemplation, even though the rest of these space-bound works cannot as yet beam forth the eternal rest of the people of God, but will have to absorb and reflect the movement of the eschatological *transitus.* In the environs of the Christian faith the dispersion of the arts with their goal of puristic isolation will be held in check by a countermovement that strives for a fraternal alliance of the arts and points to their future, supermundane, and real union.

The central problem of the form of art is the peculiar dialog relationship, in which the form is a symbol of what it manifests. The art which results from the encounter with the Gospel also casts a very definite light on this problem. Where the creatural being, as disclosed by Christ, appears in this disclosure in the work of art, its character, which points away from itself and directs to something lying behind it, becomes of special significance in the symbolism of form. One may, perhaps, speak of a restrained humility of form, which does not clumsily and domineeringly stretch out its hand to devour that which makes its appearance but in keeping with the eschatological *transitus* — mindful of its own inadequacy — stands aside, content with remaining transparent in every respect, and prefers to approximate the symbolic cipher rather than to lose its directing character by egotistical concentration.

But precisely in this humble, deaconal position, the form is dignified to manifest the Christ-disclosed, eschatologically animated, creatural being in the new manner of the work of art, to make it shine forth, and thereby to endow it with repute and esteem. Precisely in the movement of humility, which inclines toward the severe symbolic cipher, a naively playful possibility of expression and a joyousness of expression may again be born from renunciation, an unconcerned, childlike playing before God the Lord, which is a mirror of the sonship of God delivered from the Law. Where that deaconal movement of humility and this movement of expression, released for happy play, unite in a mysterious balance, there the artistic form of art is fulfilled on this earth, because thus it so fittingly adapts itself to the creature's plan-of-salvation situation, to the "not yet" of the executed eschatological transition, and to the "however already" of the dawning re-creation.

Art in Worship

The salvation-event in worship engages the art which stems from the encounter with the Gospel for its service. That dawning eschatological *transitus* in which worship stands attracts that art which itself has become a sign of this *transitus*, and thereby assigns it a new task and places it into a new dimension. The fact that the form of worship is molded by art is closely related to the last things, which have their beginning in worship. The Spirit poured out over the congregation creates in it a reflection of the coming glory, brilliance, and beauty which is inseparable from the coming kingdom of God. "The eternal great beauty," which no tongue on earth can ever express (Johann Walter), by the work of the Spirit already casts its splendor from afar on the form of worship. Therefore we join Scripture in speaking of the loveliness and beauty of worship (Ps. 84:1; 27:4).[272] It surely betokens no arbitrariness of language when the New Testament uses the word which the Greeks applied to physical grace and to beauty of speech, χάρις, to signify the grace of God in Christ.[273] The grace of beauty and the *gratia Dei* are not unrelatedly juxtaposed, much less do they face each other hostilely.[274] Where the grace of God appears, an extravagant something, a rapturous something, also appears, which seeks the rapturous element of the work of art, finds it, attracts it, and makes it the vessel of its extravagant radiance. Art in worship is part of its pneumatic essense. Art in worship is numbered among the arrows that point to the ineffable beauty of the coming kingdom of the resurrection from the dead.

The phenomenon of pneumatic inspiration points in the same direction.[275] Luther perceived the marks of a Spirit-wrought inspiration in hymns, both in their words and in their melody. He commented on the sequence *Veni, sancte Spiritus, et emitte coelitus lucis tuae radium:* "The Holy Ghost Himself created this song, both the words and the tune." [276] According to Luther, also the song "Christ Is Arisen" was inspired by the Holy Ghost.[277] Such pneumatic inspiration, taking shape in the phraseology of a hymn and in its tonal structure, is an indication that the Spirit is not inimical to the work of art which serves Him, but that He Himself invests it with an end-time radiance.[278]

The dominant material in which art appears in worship is the word. From beginning to end, this word is the creatural agent for the salvation-event in worship. The question regarding the form of this word, the question regarding the vessel into which this word is poured, is decisive for what art in worship really is. This question is subdivided into two — the one regarding the text and the other regarding the melody of this word. Here we must note that these two seek each other and may again enter into a mysterious union, so that the melody, on its part, may become a symbolic vessel for the text. However, it is necessary first to consider the question regarding the form of the word as text, that is, the question regarding the pure form of speech as such.

Depending on the form given it, art will assert itself more decidedly at one time than at another in worship. In the hymn the text will be governed by the formative power of art. There are hymns the texts of which betray a good, craftsman-like aptitude rather than mature, creative art. It is important to recognize that no word voiced in worship is exempt from the obligation to function as the creatural means by which the Holy Ghost performs a saving work on man and by which He bears man's thankoffering before the throne of God.[279] Therein lies the singular responsibility which the proclaiming and praying church must exercise over against language. Linguistic uncouthness in proclamation and in prayer is not in keeping with the service which the word must render in worship. To be sure, the Holy Ghost is able to demonstrate His power also through debased speech. Even a particle of a word or even a wordless sigh may, admittedly, be a Spirit-wrought prayer in a special situation.

But the word voiced in worship is subject to a particular condition: It is not a word of proclamation on the part of an individual, but on the part of the congregation, not a word of prayer of an individual, but of the congregation, even when spoken by an individual. In 1 Cor. 14 Paul teaches that, by reason of its relationship to the congregation, the word in worship is subject to very special conditions of form. In proclamation and prayer, the word must be designed for service to the community.

Therefore this must be a well-molded word. The congregation as a whole must be able to move in its form, even though it is spoken by an individual.[280] When Paul names "intelligibility" in 1 Cor. 14 as the modus of the word serving the congregation, he surely does not mean to say that the word must be a subtly and elaborately contrived word. This is already shown by the fact that even the prophetic speech and laudation, yes, also the revelation of a special mystery in God's act of salvation, which Paul calls "apocalypse," is such an "intelligibly" spoken word. "Intelligibility" here manifests itself as a powerful form, which makes the word a Spirit-wrought word and yet, at the same time, a word, and consequently a work, consciously molded by man. The modus of "intelligible" speech reflects the work-character, and so the form-character, and so the community-character, of this word.

We must be seriously aware that no word of worship dare be excepted from being a form for the creatural means of God's redemptive activity, also not the word of the preacher. The element of art will recede decidedly, almost vanish, in the word form of the sermon, in contradistinction to the hymnic word, in the form of which it is dominant. And yet we cannot dispense with an element of art in the sermon. As we ponder this subject further, we will face the task of devising a doctrine of spiritual oratory. Why should not the art of well-constructed, appealing, purposeful speech, which strives to move heart and will, mind, and thinking with the power of the Word of God, be engaged by the work of the Holy Ghost?

The New Testament, perhaps especially the Letter to the Hebrews, shows us that this should indeed be done. Despite many formal analogies existing between an oratory marked by philosophical rhetoric and this spiritual eloquence, the latter will not try to excel by means of "plausible words of wisdom," which Paul terms a wisdom of this world, but it will be characterized by the weakness of the cross (1 Cor. 2:1-5). However, we should be aware that there may well be, under this presupposition, the charisma of a truly spiritual eloquence, conforming entirely to the "foolishness" of the Gospel, which must be effective to a greater or lesser degree in every sermon. This eloquence, engaged by the Spirit and molded by the Spirit, presents the form for the word of man through which God Himself performs His work on the hearer in the sermon. Subject to this law of form, also the sermon may bear the element of art.

Here a principle manifests itself which applies to all the arts in worship. A direct result of the subservient role of the arts in worship is a rule which may be expressed in the well-known words of Jerome: *Non vox canentis sed verba placeant.* ("Not the voice but the words of the singer must meet with approval.") [281] Thus the artistic word must never as such obtrude in worship; it must, rather, be so exclusively devoted to the subject it presents that it consigns itself to oblivion in the conduct of worship. In the moment in which, for example, the gift of eloquence becomes so conspicuous in the language of a sermon that attention is riveted to this language as such, this eloquence has ceased to be spiritual. Art in worship is the better, the less its character as art obtrudes and the more its character as art melts away in the function of a vessel that contains the creatural means of the pneumatic event.

What is true of the sermon also applies to prayer in worship, even to an extemporaneous prayer. To speak of an "eloquence," or even of a "rhetoric," of prayer seems repugnant to us. When applied to prayer, these terms assume a derogatory meaning. Without a doubt, the species to which these terms apply are degenerate forms of prayer. A closer scrutiny will tell us that also the congregational prayer is subject to the law of this subservient form and thus to similar criteria of form as the sermon. Respecting the form of prayer, especial thought must be given the fact that this prayer must serve as the verbal vessel of the entire congregation's prayer. Therefore the prayer in worship must most rigorously conform to the element of form to which Paul refers in 1 Cor. 14 when he speaks of "intelligible" speech. That does not exclude but, rather, implies that here especially the word form of the prayer is, in the final analysis, a gift. If any work of art can be produced only by virtue of a gift — the human effort involved notwithstanding, this must particularly be true of the art which serves in worship. That the text of a prayer may be a work of art in prose will be apparent to anyone who steeps himself in the collects of the old Roman sacramentaries or in those of Luther. To be sure, wherever affected and stilted phrases come to the fore, the work of art is virtually destroyed. Where an individuality thrusts itself to the fore, the community character of the form is obscured. Here, too, the good quality of the form will be reflected by the fact that the form is entirely forgotten in the act of worship and is completely absorbed in the content of the prayer.

When we examine the church's versifications of psalms and its hymns of praise, we immediately discover that the art of poetry is here engaged in the service of the words of worship. Just as oratory requires rhetoric, so poetry calls for poetics. As the rhetoric that is related to the form of the sermonic word has been widely neglected, so also the function of poetics related to the poetry employed in worship is taken note of by only a few.[282] We, too, can only point out that this function is meaningful and necessary, without attempting to solve it. The following reflections are to serve that purpose.

Why does the word of worship not forgo the form of poetry? Why does the congregation wait for a member to arise in its midst to contribute a psalm or a song to worship (1 Cor. 14:26)? Does this betoken only a formal, cultic element which Christian worship has in common with pagan cults, or is more than that involved here? Is it not possible that the necessity and the characteristic of poetry which serves in worship might derive directly from the essence of Christian worship?

The congregation is the sponsor of the worship service. That must become concretely manifest. Therefore the congregation must preach and pray as a whole and with one voice. And that can be done only if this joint preaching and praying is carried out in an order to which all adapt themselves (1 Cor. 14:40). Therefore such a word spoken by the congregation in common must be an orderly word. In the instance of rather brief acclamations, several fixed forms suffice for this function of order. But as soon as the content of the Gospel or of the laudation develops into several sentences, or as soon as the content expands in this or in that direction, it becomes necessary to find a form into which the whole congregation can, as it were, enter and move about in its activity of worship. That seems to be almost a technical basis in which the poetry serving in worship is rooted. This seemingly technical element must not be depreciated. Nothing less than the charismatic-prophetic character of the New Testament congregation and the power of order springing from the Holy Spirit are hidden behind this. Form as means for the common movement of the congregation joined into one body and form as manifestation of the regulating power of the Spirit — these two closely associated elements mold the word into poetry, as they lay hold of it in worship.

We must indeed bear in mind here that the word of worship fashioned by poetry need not necessarily have the form of a German hymn. Here it becomes apparent for the first time in our deliberations that art in worship, like all art, has a history, through which it is subject to a mutation of form and a mutation of style. We need but call attention to rhyme, an element of form which was as self-evidently absent from the songs of the apostolic congregations as it seems to be indispensable to the hymns of our congregations. The adherence of art to a style that changes with the history of civilization poses a serious problem for the organization of worship, which affects the musical, as well as the poetical, form of the word and asserts itself no less urgently in the layout of the church building. Worship must here guard against taking either one of two devious paths. The one is the archaization of the artistic style; the other is the complete surrender of the artistic style to the cultural situation of the day. In the former, the artistic style forfeits its function of service to the present-day witness; in the latter, the constancy, the continuity in the structure of worship as shaped by the arts is lost. In the process, strange reversals may turn up. The ardent champions of an allegedly witness-effecting style fail to notice that they are "archaizing" precisely by this zeal, since history has moved forward in the meantime and carried art forward with it. Those who revert to forms or adopt forms that impress us as archaically odd may thereby sometimes approach just the form which is an especially effective witness to the present.[283] The very nature of the church moves us to set up the principle that the word of worship, molded by poetical and musical art, is not supposed to manifest the ideal of a culturally conditioned, stylistic uniformity. The worship of the apostolic era already shows us that there obviously was room for two basic forms of style of the "song" in worship, the psalm stemming from Israel and the hymnic song, the ode (ὠδή), related to Hellenistic stylistic forms. The Magnificat and the Benedictus exemplify the Hebrew style of form; 1 Tim. 3:16 illustrates the Hellenistic form. Therefore the stylistic forms which mold the word in worship may be manifold; at one time the witness-character, slanted to the present, will predominate, at another the association with the fathers, oriented to the past. If we perceive the marks of pneumatic inspiration in some of the compositions of the fathers, we would indeed be ungrateful for these gifts, were we to discard them in the interest of uniformity of style. But it would likewise register contempt for spiritual gifts if the church would decline to avail itself of hymns that are born in the congregation today simply because they are new or because their artistic style will not fit into a traditional pattern.

Of course the question must be raised whether the poets in the congregation are cognizant of the demands that must be made of poetry, even with respect to form, which is to serve as proclamation or of contemplation of the Word, or as prayer and praise, in worship. Here the basic difference between spiritual poetry and the church song or church hymn must first of all be considered.[284] In the former the poet may and must express himself far differently than in the poetry designed for the worship service. To be sure, the poetry which serves the congregation in worship will well forth only from a faith that is personally embraced. But "the clear, solid purity, force, and universal validity of the testimony" (Rudolph Alexander Schroeder), which poetry suited to worship must display, is not frequently found within one generation. Church song and church hymn presuppose that the person of the *ekklesia* is speaking and singing in the person of the poet. When the I of the poet is absorbed, as it were, into the person of the *ekklesia* and thus a mysterious union between poet and *ekklesia* is effected, then that song and hymn comes into being in which the church again recognizes its own voice.

This universal validity of testimony required of the church's song and hymn points to a new element, which will always assure poetry a place in worship. We noted earlier that song and hymn are very closely related to profession.[285] The congregation needs a concise verbal form, which comprehensibly summarizes the basic element of the message of salvation and the central content of glorification. It is impossible for the congregation to have the entire text of Paul's Epistle to the Romans before it, but it may well be conversant with Luther's hymn "From Depths of Woe I Cry to Thee." We are tempted to speak of a pedagogical function of the hymn here. This designation indeed intimates what we have in mind, but it does not entirely cover it. In a tangible, forceful, and impressive form the hymn visualizes and presents the message of salvation, or individual, important segments of it. And the tangibility, forcefulness, and impressiveness of this form of expression is, not in the last place, also due to the fact that it is poetry.

But these reflections have not yet recognized the real basis and the true essence of the poetry which serves in worship. Poetry is not only metrical language but also elevated language. The poetry which serves in worship means to be song already in its linguistic form. If the congregation's worship is distinguished by the fact that the Holy Spirit is operative there in a special manner, then words will have to be voiced there in which a Gospel-wrought, pneumatic emotion assumes form in a special manner. Where the Gospel and the Holy Spirit are at work, man now already receives a bit of the joy that is no longer of this world. In this joy, saying turns into singing. In this joy even the linguistic form of the proclaiming and the praying word will exhibit that wonderful unity of melody and word which is characteristic of the psalm song of the *ekklesia*. The fact that the form of the word uttered in worship is message and melody in one is essentially due to the character of this worship as determined by the eschatological novelty of the Gospel. The victory over the death-dealing Law through the Gospel, the reception of salvation in Christ, the liberation through the Spirit, the anthropological, cosmological, and plan-of-salvation place in which the church's worship takes place on earth, the New Testament pneumatic character of Christian worship, the eternal praise of divine glory, which has its beginning in worship — all of this together makes the form of the word in worship turn into song and hymn.[286]

Our deliberations on this subject may well go a step further as they weigh the significance of the dawning of the last things in worship has for the poetical form of the word. The New Testament shows us that the verbal vessel of our language may disintegrate under the impact of the onrushing new eon. This takes place in the language of tongues, which is no longer speech, but which appears as babbling and outside the bonds of molded words. However, this speech of tongues is not the babbling of babes, but it is a mode in which the inexpressible verbal form of the heavenly world (2 Cor. 12:3; 1 Cor. 13:1) breaks into this human world of ours. Paul recognized this form of speech — which is no longer speech — only for the worship of the individual (1 Cor. 14). Despite the onrushing impact of the coming new eon, he adhered to the principle that only the "intelligible" word may serve in worship. But this rupture of intelligible speech in the speech of tongues shows us that the word will not remain unaffected by the approaching might of the kingdom of God. It, too, will be drawn symbolically into the future eschatological transformation of all things. Where that happens without destroying speech as speech, it becomes uniquely "elevated" when it is attracted by the future worship before God's throne as by a magnetic force, and in a sense it is elevated above and beyond itself and thus becomes elevated speech. This elevated speech is the speech of the heart, which is elevated to God by the Spirit. Here the hymn is born. The linguistic form of the church's hymn is a sign of the pneumatic eschatological elevation of speech. The hymn is still sung "intelligibly." It does not become the language of angels or of tongues, but its form of expression stands on the boundary line of rapture. At this very boundary line speech achieves its greatest force, its most lucid purity, its brightest radiance, its profoundest beauty. The fact that language endures this tractive force toward rapture and absorbs it as a tension factor without breaking up over it, is the miracle of the pneumatic inspiration from which the hymn is born.

The hymn is the form for the adoring, glorifying word of the congregation, in which its present participation in the ministry of the angels before God's throne is most distinctly manifested. In its hymnic culmination, poetry in worship is the sign which the coming eschatological transformation of all things already stamps upon speech without destroying it as such. Hymns are not born in a church which is ignorant of the onrushing impact of the last things and of the rapturous force of the Spirit. The bride who eagerly awaits the advent of her Lord will not be found without her bridal adornment also in her speech. And the church's bridal adornment in the realm of the word in worship is the work of poetry, which presents the church with the hymn. The hymn is part of the eschatological bridal form of the *ekklesia*.

These deliberations on the necessity and characteristic of poetry in worship are reflected in a study of the necessity and characteristic of music in worship.

Historically, the function of music in worship is traced to a point where we hardly look for it any longer today: to the reading of Scriptural passages. Not the poetry, but the "prose" of the sacred text first attracts the musical tone. When reading Scripture, the reader's voice must become the vessel for the voice of the prophets and apostles and, through them, for the voice of Christ Himself. In its form of expression, the voice of the reader must be a sign of the voice of prophets and apostles which it represents. And this formulation, in turn, illustrates how the basic law for art in worship is effective down to this detail. The reciting tone is the answer to the problem of form present here. There is no other means through which the proclamatory authority of this word, the extramundane origin of this voice, the sacredness of this text, and also the inviting, appealing nearness of its message could be witnessed to more distinctly in a symbol of sound than through the reciting tone. Even the factor of pneumatic involvement, without which the Gospel cannot be read properly in worship, is singularly manifested in this tone by the very economy of its forms, without thereby giving prominence to the individuality of the reader; the reciting tone, rather, keeps it pleasantly in the background. The relationship between word and tone is defined by the fact that the tone does not in the least hamper and curtail what the word wants to express, but leaves the word entirely free. In the reading of Scripture, the musical tone places itself at the feet of the sacred Word, as in a *proskynesis,* with the utmost humility and renunciation of any claim to importance of its own.

Something similar applies to the prose of prayer. But a new factor is added here. Prayer is a word spoken in common, and must therefore also be an especially ordered word. Such a joint and orderly word unites, compulsively, with the musical tone. The elementary function of music in worship consists in its ordering and regulating force. The word vested in musical tone exercises a stronger regulative power than the spoken word. [287] Even a congregation numbering thousands of members can, for example, pray the preces of the horary prayer jointly as with one voice when the words are carried along on the simple reciting tone provided for it.[288] This tone receives the multiplicity of the many into the oneness of the one mouth. Where the individual prays as the spokesman of the congregation, the musi-

271

cal tone also serves to accentuate the community character of this form of expression. The individuality of the praying person is completely absorbed by this tone. The recitation of the prayer in a musically bound tone is a clear indication that the praying person is the spokesman for the others.

The strongest root which music strikes in worship is identical with that from which poetry as song and hymn sprouts, namely, the New Testament joy of those justified by faith and the pilgrim's blessed hope, which is in the stage of the eschatological *transitus*. We cannot deal with the individual problems of musical organization that suggest themselves here. We shall attempt to indicate only the dogmatic component contained in a doctrine of music in worship.

Music in worship, too, is distinguished by its definitely diaconal position. For it serves exclusively the form of the word in worship. That is immediately seen when the musical tune is added to the words of song or hymn. The investment of these words with melody is demanded even by the form of the word. The word form of this poetry would be incomplete if the words were merely spoken; they insist on being sung. The word's real essence is first attained when it is seized by the musically animated tone. Since "a song involves a being native to two worlds," [289] this composition first achieves completion when its text is clad in melody. In song, poetic art and musical art embrace each other fraternally; however, in a manner in which music respects poetry's right of primogeniture, while the word in no way tyrannically enslaves music in this union but accepts its service as being freely and voluntarily rendered.

As music enters the service of a given word form and completes the tonal body of the word by means of melody, it underlines the factor of singing in the word's function of singing and saying. The singing tone issues, like the singing of the word, from the pneumatic joy of the Gospel, which is characteristic of the *ekklesia* of the New Covenant and, moreover, pervades the chief form of its worship. The combination of word and tone is part of the completeness of the joy of justification.[290] What Luther calls Musica, this combination of the word and musically actuated tone,[291] is a form of manifestation tailor-made for the Gospel. Where the doctrine of justification is recognized as the core of the Gospel, the Musica must, in the nature of the case, appear as a prominent factor in the practical arrangement of the makeup of worship.[292]

The joy born of justification is very closely connected with the anticipatory joy of hope. To be sure, the "new song" begins when the liberating and redeeming message of justification is accepted by faith. But the new song of the *ekklesia* is first fulfilled in the final consummation before God's throne (Rev. 14:3). It is very significant that Holy Scripture cannot envisage the final perfection of the *ekklesia*, indeed, the final perfection of the creature in general, without the singing of songs. The Musica is therefore necessarily part of the blessedness of the creature, it is part of the final perfection of the congregation — an eschatologically transformed Musica, to be sure, but one nonetheless which does not bear this name arbitrarily.

The Musica which is engaged here on earth in the service of the *ekklesia's* hymnic song, and which first materializes the hymn in its peculiar essence, is as such a reference to the coming perfection of our worship before God's throne. Despite the deep gulf between what will be one day and what is now, there is an objective correspondence between what the church does now as it sings hymns on earth and what it will one day do together with all angels and archangels before God's throne. The joy of the Gospel, vibrant in the Musica, is a reflection of the ineffable, future bliss. Worship as end-time mystery, worship as the hidden beginning of the last things, worship as the place in which the future joyful feast of the kingdom already becomes hidden presence, this worship, because of its pneumatic reality, calls for this Musica, which is based in God and which will one day be perfected in God, but which, in all weakness and imperfection, appears already here on earth in the worship of the believing and hoping congregation.

Thus the Musica, which lays hold of the word, and the word, which is clad in the Musica, become a sign of that peculiarly uncommon, unworldly, exuberant, overflowing element of Christian worship, which is something stupendous and something extremely lovely at the same time. If Jesus, the crucified and risen Lord, really vouchsafes the congregation His presence in worship through Word and Sacrament, if justifying grace and the re-creating Spirit are really active here, if the redeeming compassion of God and the radiance of His love really takes hold of the congregation of believers, then it is singularly appropriate to this pneumatic presence that the word joins hands with the Musica and the latter becomes the audible form in which the word appears.

If the last things really have begun to dawn with Pentecost, if men and women really speak prophetically in the assembled con-

273

gregation, then the Musica, which lays hold of the word and which serves the word, is surely not one of the least signs of this eschatological-pneumatic character of the *ekklesia*.[293] In the singing of the church there is an intimation of that pneumatic-prophetic exaltation, an intimation of that prophetic rapture which cannot be divorced from the essence of the *ekklesia* without dimming its eschatological nature. The very fact that the word appears in the audible form of the Musica merges the "intelligibility" of the word (1 Cor. 14) with its pneumatic exuberance into a union in which neither of the two essential elements is destroyed, but both wonderfully pervade each other.

This carries us to the last basis for this union of word and Musica. This word has, so to say, an inexpressible margin. This word, now expressed in the church on earth, has a movement within it which tends and strives toward the still inexpressible word of the heavenly world. This word of the church, together with the tones of all the creatures, shall one day be merged in the laudation of the angels. The tongue of man shall one day join with the tongue of angels. Therefore the word which is now uttered in the church on earth already has that invisible, but effectual, margin of the inexpressible. The sign of this margin, the sign of the coming communion of the human with the angelic speech, is seen in the fact that the proclaiming, thanking, and praising word of the earthly church appears in the audible form of the Musica. This is indeed a celestial, an angelic art. Therefore the eschatological coordination of human tongue and angelic tongue is suggested and indicated by this music of worship, which lays hold of the word and is held by the word.

Proceeding from these deliberations, we should try to establish the premises for the solution of the particular church-music problems of musical aesthetics, which are posed by the singular connection between word and music in the song of worship. First of all we will bear in mind here that, without detracting from the intimate association between word and music, music in worship — viewed from the redemptive function of the Word — still remains an element which is added to the word. Neither this being-added nor the mode and manner in which the music is added to the word is necessary for salvation. This implies that in this intimate association between music and word the former reverently and humbly accords the word appearing in it the liberty which it derives from God. But in that very way music, too, in its association with the word, receives and retains the freedom of its musical essence. Without prejudice to its diaconal position, it will materialize its own musical essence by this very attitude. Particularly where the Word of Holy Scripture itself is involved, will the Musica not presume in any way to press this Word into musical form. Musica may not and dare not fix the message of this word in advance. After all, to use a figure of speech of Origen, the eternal God Himself is mounted on this word issuing from the mouth of man.

Perhaps this explains the particular relationship between word and Gregorian chant, which so distinctly marks the latter as music appropriate to worship.[294] This does not mean to preclude that the congregation may also repeat the words of Scripture as they were heard, believed, and experienced by them, and as they are astir in their hearts. In the professing and glorifying song the word appears even more strongly than in repeated word of Scripture, for its is a word that has already penetrated ear and heart of the congregation. The musical form of this word may take that into account. The polyphonic motet and the song with its setting are able to do that. But also in these musical forms we must take heed that the content of the word is of prime importance and the manner in which the word is alive in the person expressing it is of lesser importance, whether a word directed to God or one directed to man is involved. It is precisely at this point that the musical form must resist the temptation to dim the message of the song or to veil it completely by an expression of subjective emotion.

Also the question regarding the relationship between the monosyllabic and the melismatic form of the individual tune should be drawn into the light of our theological discussion. The melisma, swinging out far on the monosyllable, may contain an especially impressive reference to that mysterious word-margin of the inexpressible. The element of the exuberance, of the overflowing fullness, is especially apparent here, particularly in the Easter Jubilus of the Alleluia. Here the Easter joy can already detach itself from the concrete single word and intimate in the musical tone as such and beyond all words — comparable in this to the speech of tongues — something of the fullness of the eschatological gift of salvation, overflowing the vessel of the word.[295] Do not some tunes of the Gregorian chant resemble a pneumatic breakthrough of the tune to the border of the angelic tongue? But this relative detachment of the singing voice from the word is possible only because the melismatic element remains bound to the monosyllabic element. Only in the confines of humble self-limitation, demanded by its relationship to the word, may the tune occasionally intimate symbolically that pneumatic rapture, which is not missing from the "intelligible" worship if it is really a worship in spirit and in truth.

A glance at this relative detachment of the musical tone from the word, which takes place here and there in the melody assigned to the word, suggests the question whether music may go beyond this and entirely detach itself in worship from the word and as wordless music become a constituent part of the church's worship. No one will deny that wordless instrumental music may and should serve and glorify God, just as any other independent work of art which springs from the encounter with the Gospel does. But one must not mix this worship of independent arts and of their independent works with the worship of the assembled congregation. This principle also applies when the independent work of art may be viewed, with respect to its function of glorification, as an immediate fruit of Christian faith. Therefore we do not consider it appropriate to present music which is detached from its association with the word as a component of congregational worship.[296] For instance, if the organ is playing independently, let us say during the distribution of the Lord's Supper, this playing should follow the form of the organ chorale. For the melody adopted in the organ chorale is related to certain texts, and thus, both for the musician and also for the congregation, it forms a bridge to the sung word, which in this instance finds a voice only in the accompanying song of the heart. This confinement of music in worship to word-bound music by no means precludes that the compositions played at the opening and at the conclusion of worship may, and perhaps as a rule also should, be independent musical compositions, which are entirely detached from a text. However, these compositions should not be heard in the course of the worship service.

Thus far our deliberations have shown that in worship the most prominent servants among the arts are the art of words and, in coordination with it, the art of music. The ministry of these arts is vital only in the administration of worship. Word and melody are not vital on paper, but only in the voice. The ever actual event-character of the verbal and musical arts corresponds to the event-character of Christian worship. However, there are also other arts involved in the administration of worship, to which this actual event-character is not peculiar. Their works are not vital only in the administration of worship, but exist also independently of this, also *extra usum,* in their physical form, even though these works first attain fulfillment of their purpose in the administration of worship. That applies to architecture and the plastic art.

Undoubtedly the appearance on the scene of these two types is more coincidental than this is true of the art of words and the art of music. The optical element manifestly does not have the same relevance to the salvation-event in worship as the acoustic element does. As we reflect how the plastic arts exercise their diaconal function in worship, we must remember that sight *(visio)* is a term that first becomes theologically significant for us in the development of the doctrine of the eternal bliss in the final consummation, when the history of salvation on earth terminates. The place of worship in the plan of salvation dictates that architecture and plastic art are not so closely related to it as the arts of word and music, which are joined to eventful and historical time.

The service which the plastic arts and their artistic patterns render in worship is based on the elementary fact that the administration of worship calls for certain implements. It is very characteristic of the worship of the *ekklesia* in the New Testament that it, compared with the Old Testament temple worship, is dependent on a minimum of such implements. It requires a Bible, a lectionary. Thus it engages the art of making books in the service of the Word of God. It requires a table, which is distinguished as the Lord's table. It requires the vessels for the celebration of Holy Communion. To set aside and properly equip a place in the house of worship for the proclamation of an individual to the congregation is dictated by practical considerations and simultaneously accords symbolic distinction to what happens in that place.[297]

The number of articles required to implement the worship service either because of practical need or because of objective relevance can be increased without much effort — down to the garb of the people who render special services in worship.[298] In our context it is important to recognize that these implements, since they are distinctly related to the worship-event, must be amenable to particular laws of form, which clearly reflect their relationship of service to the worship-event. This purpose is served by the ornamentation of these implements. Even their form as such must adorn them.

277

In the measure in which the ornamental element as such is conspicuous in the implement, in that measure the artistic element will also be conspicuous in the craftsmanship of this implement; for instance, in the antependia of the altar.

Undoubtedly, an element of free play is evident in ornamentation. However, genuine ornament is never an object of idle and empty play. With regard to the ornamentation used in worship, we must be warily intent on making it relevant to its special function. This ornamentation motif of which we are speaking here has more than an aesthetic basis, although ornamentation in worship also submits to aesthetic laws of form; yes, it does this especially in worship, in order to be a genuine ornament. This ornamentation motif has above all a theological basis. Very likely Wilhelm Löhe was the first to point out the analogy between the costly, pure ointment of Mary in Bethany and the ornamentation in worship.[299]

This ornamentation is not "superfluous"; it is superfluous only when compared with the bare utility of the implement. To be sure, this ornamentation is something "overflowing," as beauty in general manifests this element of overflowing. This overflowing element of ornamentation has, in the final analysis, its basis in the special presence of Jesus Christ, which eventuates in worship. The ornamentation corresponds to the celebration of a given event. The ornamentation must be a sign of the veneration of the present Lord. It is a sign of the joyous surrender of the congregation to its Lord. It is part of "the loving demeanor of the bride over against the Bridegroom."[300] Unless we take account of the real presence of Jesus in worship, this must appear as extravagance, just as Mary's ointment did to Judas.[301]

But we must not overlook the possibility that an arrangement of implements which appears deficient in ornamentation may, under certain circumstances, be an equally appropriate sign of the Lord's presence. For fashioning Communion ware and altars Wilhelm Löhe laid down the following important principle: "The closer to the elements and the heavenly gifts, the greater the simplicity; the more remote from these, the greater the ornamentation. . . . In the immediate proximity of the heavenly treasure, man takes off his shoes."[302] If this principle is taken seriously, the ornamentation in worship will show a peculiar restraint, a peculiar blotting out of the ornamentation motif. In a manner of speaking the ornamentation stands humbly afar; it is not aggressive, but expresses its function with a peculiar indirectness. The ornamentation adorns by possessing the adorning element as though it did not possess it. This very "possessing it as though it did not possess it" constitutes its peculiarity as ornamentation in worship.

Pictures in the house of worship transcend the ornamentation motif. Here the plastic art arrives at an independent development of its worship function. A deliberation on pictures in worship must first of all emphatically point out that the pneumatic present manifestation of the salvation-event through Christ's institution is bound exclusively to the means of the man-proclaimed Gospel and to the sacrament. A picture of Christ created by art or any other pictures of Biblical events or figures can never exercise such a function of self-manifestation. Christ's institution does not accord us the liberty to consider the picture a means of pneumatic communication with the object of the picture. Nor may we ever ascribe to the monogram of Christ, or to the sign of the cross, or to other symbols, the power of an effective representation of what these symbolize.

On the other hand, the believer is free to provide the place of worship with pictures and symbols for the sake of worship. However, we must absolutely refrain from trying to portray God the Father, even if we should assign only a pedagogical significance to His picture. If plastic art wishes to depict God the Father, it must confine itself to a purely hieroglyphic symbol. To be sure, the true, divine essence did assume human nature; but we must bear in mind that this was not done in the person of the Father, only in that of the Son. In view of this, the picture of Christ, also the sculptured representation of the crucified Christ, cannot be forbidden. Where the incarnation of the Son is taken seriously, the believer is at liberty to portray, also in a work of art, the image of Christ which he bears in his heart.[303] At times such a picture may even be a witness which wards off a docetic annihilation of the true humanity of Jesus Christ. Whatever is really creatural may also be portrayed; and Jesus is a true, creatural person, born of the Virgin Mary!

To be sure, the portrayal of the God-man, who in His humanity is also God's Son, and who is in possession of His glory even in His deepest humiliation, poses a basically insoluble problem for art. The problem first becomes soluble when this basic impossibility is recognized and acknowledged.[304] For then the idea of the portrayal of the God-man is thwarted in the work of art itself by the testimony that the God-man, the crucified Lord, is positively not "portrayable" in His humiliation and in His glory. The symbolic "picture" will replace the pictorial representation. The pictorial will itself pass over into the symbolic, into the cipher, so that countenance and body of the Crucified become but a remote symbol in the work of art for this countenance and body. Furthermore, it may seem quite appropriate to dispense also with this symbol-picture, this cipher-picture, and to erect the cross without the body.

These considerations will apply to all works of the plastic arts which wish to serve in worship. In these works the symbolically designative character of the pictorial art must be especially distinct. To be sure, this principle will be comprehended only when the function of the plastic arts in worship is clearly understood. These hardly have a didactic function in worship. We do not deny that Biblical events and figures are impressed on the mind by illustrative pictures. But in contradistinction to the illustration of a Biblical story, didactics must not be the original intention of the picture in worship. Rather, in this picture we find the concentration of a function which is performed by the entire place of worship as a work of art — in its form to be a symbolically designative agency for the pneumatic salvation-event in worship.[305]

The form of the house of worship does not bring about the redemptive presence of the Triune God; but it is a sign that this special redemptive presence of God eventuates in this place through Word and sacrament. The form of the house of worship does not enable the congregation to invoke the name of God, to pray, to praise, and to thank; but it is a sign that this turning of the creature to God through Word and Spirit eventuates here. Nor does the picture effect the pneumatic presence of the object pictured; but it points out that the story of salvation becomes present through Word and sacrament in the administration of worship. The picture must point out that the *communio sanctorum* becomes reality in the conduct of worship through the work of the Spirit. The picture must point out that this assembly on earth lives, in accord with Heb. 12:22 ff., in a real fellowship with the heavenly festive assembly of the Jerusalem above.

As the arrangement of the house of worship must reflect the word of Scripture: "My house shall be a house of prayer" (Luke 19:46; Is. 56:7),[306] so the picture in particular must assume the function of reminding the congregation that the pneumatic presence of the salvation-event becomes a reality in this place through Word and sacrament. Like the house of worship as a whole, the picture in this place will prove of special help to the congregation to concentrate on God and to meet the Word of God with a collected mind. But this picture will also be helpful in opening heart and mind for petition and praise to God. The ultimate and most decisive rule to be applied to the picture in the place of worship is expressed in the question: Can, must the Christian pray before this picture? The picture in worship surely fulfills its function if it aids in the proper pneumatic administration of worship; and not the least of these functions is that it be of assistance in prayer.

This function places the stamp of the symbolic on the picture. Here the picture may approximate the hieroglyphic cipher, so that the concrete, representational element recedes almost completely behind the picture's symbolic character. Here it is all-important that the picture, together with the arrangement of the building, presents an appropriate frame for what takes place in worship and thus really carries out the function of symbolic reference. Then also the recession of the representational concreteness will seem not only tolerable but also correct and appropriate. However, the picture becomes intolerable if the representational concreteness recedes or is covered up and the reference to the fact of the pneumatic real presence is not supplied.

It is understandable that the plastic art shies away from the task assigned to the picture in the house of worship. For a merely repristinating Byzantinism or any other reprise of style will not be of any help. Therefore absolute abstention from the picture, a whitewashed wall, may at times be a particularly impressive and artistic frame for the pneumatic event of the real presence. In certain situations this voluntary complete abstention may furnish the only fertile soil for a rebirth of the function of the plastic arts in worship. Then the whitewashed wall may one day be enlivened with an adornment or an inscription.[307] Then the ornamental symbol may arise with the ornament, and from the ornamental symbol the picture serving the church in worship may again emerge as a symbol of its bridal adornment. Abstention, which can afford to wait; humility, which stands afar; simplicity, which takes off its shoes and covers its head before the epiphany of the holy — in every historical situation this constitutes the origin of all arts which can truly serve in worship.

THE REALIZATION OF A UNIFIED SERVICE OF THE WORD AND OF THE SACRAMENT

We have become acquainted with several factors that operate in the implementation of the form of worship. But these have not yet brought the total form of worship into focus. That is the task confronting us now. In facing it, we shall confine ourselves to the chief form, the main worship service *(Hauptgottesdienst)*. For the two accompanying forms stemming from it do not involve such structural difficulties, touching the doctrine, as we meet in the implementation of the chief form.

The first difficulty concerns the relationship between the proclamation of the Gospel, insofar as this is carried out through the reading and the expounding of the prophetic-apostolic Word of Scripture, and the celebration of the Lord's Supper. When the Confessional Synod of the Evangelical church of the Old-Prussian Union in 1940 called attention to the fact that Holy Communion occupied an "unbiblical, stunted position" in our life of worship and suggested that approximately once a month the sacrament be administered not as an adjunct to and after the conclusion of the worship service but "within the congregational worship service," a critical situation was brought home to us which had been troubling many people for a long time. Since then we have become ever more aware that the Holy Communion practice of our church calls for a far-reaching reformation.

But how is the celebration of Holy Communion related to that proclamation of the Gospel which is carried out through the reading of Scripture and through the sermon? Is Holy Communion added to the oral sermon as an affirming and sealing pledge, comparable to a seal attached to a document? Does Holy Communion visualize the bestowal of the Gospel on the individual? Do I encounter the oral word of the Gospel in Holy Communion in a form in which it also becomes tangible and visible for a poor, weak person like me? All of these questions may be answered affirmatively, and these affirmative answers are not wrong. And yet they do not adequately define the relationship between the oral Gospel sermon and the celebration of Holy Communion.

The image of an attached seal might after all convey the impression that it is something merely appended to the actual epistle of God to mankind, the oral word, in order to allay our misgivings regarding the reliability of this epistolary word. Where the relationship of Holy Communion to the sermon is defined under the viewpoint of a bestowal of the redemptive gift to an individual, the danger is imminent that the spiritual event of Holy Communion is individualized, that it is, as it were, splintered on the individual. And, finally, when the visibility of the Word, in contradistinction to its audibility, is adduced in defining the relationship between sermon and Holy Communion, the institution of Holy Communion very easily appears as an accommodation of Christ to our sensuous-physical nature. Then the oral sermon, which addresses itself through the sense of hearing to the spiritual understanding, again appears as the actual form for the mediation of the Gospel — to say nothing of the dangerous crypto-Platonism and rationalism, which so easily ally themselves with this definition of the relationship between sermon and Holy Communion.

To define the relationship between the oral sermon and Holy Communion in a manner appropriate to the Biblical position, one must undoubtedly proceed from Christ's distinctive institution of Holy Communion. This institution does not exclude, but it includes, the anamnesis of Christ in the form of oral proclamation. When the congregation convenes in obedience to the command "Do this in remembrance of Me," it dare not neglect to carry out the apostolic anamnesis of Christ through the reading and the expounding of Scripture. That the Lord is remembered in this act also by means of the apostolic word and its exposition is part of the anamnetic character of Holy Communion. Therefore the execution of the apostolic anamnesis of Christ through the present oral proclamation forms an integrating component of that act of the congregation by which it fulfills Christ's command: "Do this in remembrance of Me!"

If we look for the essential feature in which the presentation and the exposition of the apostolic word merge into a unit with the rite of the sacrament, we will find it in the anamnesis of Christ. While the independent service which features the sermon derives chiefly from Christ's missionary command, and therefore must contain the missionary element that leads to Baptism and also the catechetical element which leads back to Baptism, and while the horary prayer serves chiefly the continual prayer of intercession and praise, the main form of the worship service, from beginning to end, is distinctly marked by Christ's command to His disciples: "Remember Me!" If the congregation knows what it is doing when it assembles for the main worship service, it stands ready to carry out the commemoration of Christ in the form assigned to the disciples by

Christ. And in this form, the anamnesis through the oral word and the anamnesis through the rite of Holy Communion are a spiritual unit from the beginning.

The anamnesis which is carried out in Holy Communion, however, retains its special, stringently exclusive character. Without detracting from the homogeneousness of the total form as the anamnesis of Christ, the worship service, as it passes over to the administration of the sacrament, presents a clearly perceptible caesura, which dare not be effaced. To be sure, the church makes itself accessible to the world as far as at all possible. The church admits those "who are outside" and also its own unconfirmed youth to the main form of its worship as far as at all possible. It permits all to partake of the intracongregational, edifying word of the anamnesis of Christ. But then Christ's institution obliges the congregation to draw a line of demarcation which delineates the exclusive character of the anamnesis carried out through the celebration of Holy Communion.

Consequently, the chief form of worship involves a progression, a movement, from the pure anamnesis of the Word to the anamnesis of the Meal. Those not yet able to take this step must be kept aware that something decisive is still lacking in their worship. The caesura of which we spoke must be made to appear as the interruption of an act which has not yet reached its end. But they who take the step from the pure anamnesis of the Word to the anamnesis of the Meal are aware from the very beginning that they are engaged in a unified anamnetic movement which first reaches its conclusion with the eating and drinking at the Meal. To them this entire worship is from the very beginning a Holy Communion worship service. Thus the uniformity of the chief form of our service dare not be seen in the statics of a geometrical figure, for instance, of an ellipse, or of two concentric circles. This uniformity is, rather, the undividedness of a motion. The uniformity of the service of Word and sacrament inheres in the dynamics of the one anamnesis of Christ, which is carried out in the apostolic Word and in the Lord's Supper, in a progression from the one to the other.

The recognition of this uniformity and the acknowledgment of this recognition in the spiritual life of Christians — that is the decisive procedure through which the chief form of the worship service is implemented as a unity of the service of Word and sacrament. The practical methods by which this unity is realized will vary with local

284

conditions. They cannot be discussed in detail here; however, the following basic considerations must be taken into account.

Our studies have shown us that the information that comes to us from the Gospel itself is the truly formative factor here. Therefore absolutely everything depends on having this recognition be wrought by the Gospel itself. Thus, to begin with, it is all-important that the shepherds of the congregation, who are responsible for proclamation and doctrine, learn from Scripture the true essence of worship, of the proclamation of the Word and of Holy Communion, and recognize their interdependence. Then it will devolve on them to lead the congregation assembled for worship to the same knowledge and acknowledgment by means of proclamation and indoctrination. Without the Gospel-wrought knowledge worship-life cannot be revitalized. Without this knowledge every attempt at reformation would spell nothing but unspiritual tyranny.

Furthermore, no congregation should dispense with the service which features only the sermon, not even on Sundays and holy days. The juxtaposition of these two forms will commend itself especially where the recognition of the oneness of the service of Word and sacrament has already pervaded an inner core of the congregation to a degree that this core will be unwilling to forego the total form of worship on any Sunday or holy day. This core will be ready to suffer any ordinary inconvenience and assemble at an earlier hour of the morning, thereby still leaving enough time for the sermon service in the forenoon. Those who regard the main form of the worship service as an integral part of Sunday or of a holy day will not wish to gather in the evening for the main service, but they will want to spend the whole day in the radiance of the concluded celebration, preferring the Easter-like morning to the evening.

But even with this timing, questions remain which reach into the area of doctrine. Such a question arises from the fact that participation in Holy Communion every Sunday is, as a rule, not yet possible for the individual Christian, even if he attends services every Sunday. Must he forgo his attendance in the main service if he does not wish to partake of Holy Communion? Must he, like one who is not admitted to the sacrament, leave the church before the administration of the Holy Supper? No! It is possible for the individual to join spiritually in the celebration of Holy Communion, even if he does not receive the body and blood of the Lord. The oft-repeated opinion that the celebration of the sacrament under these circumstances degenerates into a spectacle is foolish. This is not in keeping with the facts of spiritual life. Of course it goes without saying that there is no celebration of Holy Communion without the actual participation of communicants in the congregation. But when the sacrament is administered, then also those who do not eat and drink physically are able to join in the commemoration of the Christ. To be sure, they abstain from participation in an essential component of the commemorative event on that day; but the rite contains such a plenitude of other features in which also the noncommuning members can join. In addition to the distribution of the elements, we have prayer, praise, and the proclamation of the words of institution. To join in these cannot be denied anyone. The fact that the words of institution possess the quality of promise and thus also the quality of proclamation for all who hear them is basic to the knowledge of the Reformation doctrine of Holy Communion, which Christendom must never again abandon. He who abstains from the physical partaking is by no means excluded from that "eating" which is indispensable to the redemptive reception also of him who eats the food physically, i. e., for the acceptance by faith of Christ's testament, which is found in its full power and authority in the Word associated with the rite of Holy Communion. (John 6:35)

We dare not overlook the fact that the distribution of the elements is not at all devoid of a message for him who does not commune. It is an act of proclamation. It is an exposition of the words of Christ's testament executed through an act. Thus it is not a mute sign, but a sign that loudly proclaims the sacrificial love of the crucified Lord. Even that part of the sacrament's administration in which the noncommuning person seems to occupy a very marginal position is an event that enables his spiritual participation.

To be sure, such participation is hardly possible for one who rarely partakes of the sacrament. But he who communes frequently participates in the celebration even when he himself does not approach the Lord's Table; he does this in remembrance of the last Meal of which he partook and in anticipation of the next one of which he will partake. In such a recollection and in such an expectation he also gives ear to and joins in those prayers and laudations which relate to the reception of the Meal.

Finally, it is very important for the implementation of the chief form of the worship service that the relationship between confession and Holy Communion be properly understood. It is generally agreed today that the confession should not be placed between the sermon and the celebration of Holy Communion. Wherever that is still in vogue, the unified total form of the worship service, that of Word and Holy Communion, cannot be implemented. We cannot enter into the multiple problems of confession, of its order, and of its practice; however, the thesis that confession is an act of worship which requires its own independent order must be supported. A confession of sin as a confession of general guilt and a petition for forgiveness of sin may very well be combined with every form of worship. But confession with the definite, indicative absolution demands its own order.

In our context, the dogmatic question regarding the relationship of this confession to Holy Communion is, perhaps, still more important than a recognition of the liturgical independence of confession. In the minds of most evangelical Christians the partaking of the bread and wine at the Lord's Table presupposes that sins have been confessed and absolution has been received. If we recognize that the main service, which includes the celebration of the Lord's Supper, purposes regularly to assemble the entire congregation of the baptized and the believers, a question must suggest itself. As long as the evangelical Christian went to the Lord's Table but once, or at the most twice, a year the association of Holy Communion with preceding confession and reception of absolution did not pose a question. But as soon as a spiritual breakthrough to a more frequent and regular participation has taken place, the traditional association of reception of absolution and reception of Holy Communion becomes questionable. Only a reflection on principles which does not lose sight of the historical factors can prove helpful here.[308]

Luther contended for and achieved a rightful place for private confession with reception of absolution.[309] It cannot be insisted upon legalistically. Nor may it be connected with Holy Communion in a legalistic manner.[310] But the Holy Supper dare not be administered without the exercise of discipline. In the circumstances in which the Wittenberg Reformation had to be carried out, an examination of those who wished to receive Holy Communion was a necessary function of the ministry. To be sure, it cannot be said that a kind genius hovered over this institution and its history. This examination, announced by Luther as early as 1523,[311] was conducted in the form of a doctrinal test.[312] For the "intelligent people" one such examination sufficed for a lifetime. As a rule it was to be administered once annually.

In special cases it could be omitted entirely.[313] Unfortunately Luther used the expression "confession" after the year 1524 also as a designation for this examination; and this proved disastrous for the further development. In fact, this examination, when applied to the "simple" and "unintelligent," soon included also the confession of individual sins and the reception of absolution.[314] The Augsburg Confession bears this out in Art. XXV: "Confession in the churches is not abolished among us; for it is not usual to give the body of the Lord, except to them that have been previously examined and absolved." (*Confessio in ecclesiis apud nos non est abolita. Non enim solet porrigi corpus Domini nisi antea exploratis et absolutis*). The doctrinal test developed into an "individual preparation" [315] for Holy Communion. To be sure, the actual private confession with absolution remained independent and free. But this "individual preparation" was declared necessary in view of the simple folk.[316]

It goes without saying that this practice involved no end of difficulties. A doctrinal examination included confession of sin and absolution! Confession with absolution which may not legally be demanded was nonetheless combined with an examination which was regarded as irremissible for the "simple" and "unintelligent" communicants! The free element was here linked to the necessary and was thus deprived of its freedom! The pastor had to use his own judgment in differentiating between the "intelligent," who did not require this examination, and those who had to submit to it. The danger that social differences might play into this is obvious. Finally the obligatory nature of this examination also brought it about that the confession connected with it was regarded as a necessary precondition for participation in Holy Communion even when the examination was adjudged unnecessary.[317] Although Luther never made confession and absolution an obligatory condition for the reception of the sacrament, through this unfortunate development confession lost its independence implicit in Christ's institution and became "a sort of purification for the reception of Holy Communion." [318] Nor did that change when, in the course of the 18th century, this individual preparation was abandoned more and more and was replaced by the general confession current today. [319]

This reminder of the fateful history of our problem shows unmistakably that we have to keep two subjects apart in its solution: the necessary discipline in Holy Communion and the liberty in the use of confession and absolution. In support of that doctrinal examination, Luther established the rule that admission to Holy Communion should be dealt with in analogy to admission to Baptism: an interrogation touching on belief *(interrogatio de fide)* was to be conducted.[320] Indeed, if the baptized person was not subjected to such an interrogation on faith before his baptism, he must submit to it after his baptism and before his admission to Holy Communion. Here we find a root of confirmation. But confirmation includes, in the form of examination, that interrogation regarding faith. To be sure, this examination must be taken seriously. It must be recognized as a component of the administration of Holy Communion, namely, as a presupposition for the admission to the sacrament; and it must be treated accordingly. If this is done, its repetition is void as long as this admission is in force. However, we must not forget that this admission must be rescinded under certain circumstances, and that excommunication must be pronounced. If a Christian has sinned so that he, in accordance with the words of the apostle (1 Cor. 6:9 f.; Gal. 5:19-21; Eph. 5:5; Rev. 22:15), has forfeited his admittance to the kingdom of God, and impenitently persists in his vices, he must be excluded from the Holy Communion congregation until he mends his ways and repents. Now a renewed admission becomes necessary, which cannot be pronounced without a preceding pastoral interrogation, nor without confession and absolution.[321]

Thus we have cut the cord which ties the reception of Holy Communion by law and by custom to a preceding reception of absolution. It is surely true that we stand in great need of absolution. No line dare be written which questions this need or which minimizes the magnitude of this gift. But the reception of Holy Communion may be made absolutely dependent on a preceding confession with resultant absolution only when that ultimate boundary has been crossed, when a commandment has been transgressed which effects the exclusion from the living membership on the body of Christ. In all other instances I dare not demand of myself or of others that confession be made and absolution be received prior to the reception of the sacrament.[322] Of course, opportunity for confession must also be offered on, or better before, each Sunday or holy day on which Holy Communion is administered. But we must maintain the independence of confession over against Holy Communion and the independence of Holy Communion over against confession. When this independence is carried out in practice, the final obstacle is surmounted that obstructs the implementation of a unified form of the service of the Word and Holy Communion.

The Formulary of the Service

The formulary of the Agenda serves the implementation of the form of worship. The Agenda is the concretization of the dogma of worship. To be sure, the Agenda is more than a logical conclusion drawn from a presupposed dogmatic premise. The composition of the Agenda stems from a decision of the church. In this decision a number of circumstances have to be taken into consideration which could not yet be taken up in their concrete reality by the dogmatic tenet. But, on the other hand, dogma must be effective in the composition of the Agenda as the formative eidos, as the formative entelechy. This we want to demonstrate on the most difficult and sensitive point of the order of service, the form of the administration of the sacrament.

The total form of the main worship service will, if we take account of its historicalness, encompass the following parts: (1) the introductory Invocation, ending with the Collect; (2) the presentation and the acceptance of the prophetic and the apostolic Word, ending with the sermon-related hymn; (3) the Intercession and the Thankoffering of the congregation; (4) the sacramental rite in the narrower sense, beginning with the Salutatio and the Sursum corda and ending with the Distribution; (5) the concluding part of the service. For answers to questions arising from parts 1, 2, 3, and 5, the foreword to Christhard Mahrenholz's *Entwurf der Agende für evangelisch-lutherische Kirchen und Gemeinden,* 1951, may be consulted. However, in "the unquestionably very difficult segment of problems surrounding the Holy Communion liturgy between Sanctus and Distribution" many a question had to remain unanswered there.[323] This is where our deliberations set in.

The Words of Institution and Holy Communion Prayers

Already the form of the New Testament reports on the institution of Holy Communion is evidently molded by liturgical use.[324] But we are unable to determine the liturgical place that such a report occupied in the worship of the apostolic congregations. Nor is it possible to discover definitely from the New Testament what function such a Holy Communion report was to exercise in the administration of the congregational celebration of the sacrament. The only fact that can be unmistakably learned is that the evangelists and Paul and their congregations were absolutely convinced that their celebration of the sacrament was the Meal instituted by Christ in the night of His betrayal. However, the question whether the recitation of the words of institution effected the consecration of the elements was never put and therefore never answered. The church became aware relatively late of the function which the words of institution exercise in the administration of Holy Communion. Perhaps it was Augustine, who, in his discussions with the Donatists, made this discovery with regard to the Sacrament of Baptism, a discovery which was so basic for the later theological development of the Occidental doctrine of Holy Communion.[325] The words with which Christ instituted Christian Baptism appear in the actualizing form of the baptismal formula. And only these words and nothing more, not a prayer or any other item, constitute, in conjunction with the water, Baptism as the Baptism of Christ; they make Baptism a sacrament.[326] It is not surprising that this conception became the criterion also for the consecration in Holy Communion.

In the essays "On the Mysteries" and "On the Sacraments," ascribed to Ambrose and possibly genuine in content, the consecratory power of the words of institution are emphatically stressed.[327] In the latter essay the words of Christ are already sharply contrasted with the laudations and the prayers used in the administration of Holy Communion. No contributing function is imputed to the words of prayer in the consecration; the entire weight already rests on the words of institution, and the consecration is unmistakably bound to the words of Christ.[328] This doctrine, which characterizes the Occidental conception of consecration, "first began to develop in Merovingian-Carolingian times and initially on the soil of Gaul, that is, Franconia, and then gradually made its way." [329] In the ninth-century dispute on Holy Communion the importance attached to the words of institution grew noticeably. Paschasius Radbertus (died after 856) contrasts Christ's all-powerful and all-authoritative words of institution incisively with all other words and all other authorities. Only by means of His words does Christ in His omnipotence effect that bread and wine become His body and blood. "All else spoken by the priest or sung by the clergy is nothing other than laudation and thanksgiving, or pertains to invocations, prayers, and supplications of the believers." [330] The fully developed doctrine of transubstantiation stresses the exclusiveness of the authority due the words of Christ still more. This is clearly seen in Thomas of Aquinas: Just as all prayers are dispensed with in an emergency baptism and the Sacrament of Baptism is validly administered only by means of the act of baptism, so the Sacrament

291

of the Altar, too, may be administered validly when all else is omitted in the Canon of the Mass and only the words of institution are spoken, presupposing that the priest is really intent on doing what Christ wants to have done in memory of Himself. The omission of the prayers of the Canon merely signifies, in Thomas' opinion, an infraction of the ritual of the church (which he, to be sure, views as a grave sin), but not the annulment of Holy Communion as a sacrament.[331] For Luther, the might of Christ's words of institution disperses the entire Canon of the Mass. With an unprecedented, but obviously intended, radicalism he draws the final liturgical conclusion for the organization of the rite of the sacrament.[332]

> The "Sermon von dem neuen Testament," 1520, already contrasts the words of institution with the prayers of the mass (which we also found in Ambrose [?], Paschasius Radbertus, and Thomas) with an inexorable finality: "We must detach the mass entirely and completely from the prayers and the gestures, which were added to them by the holy fathers, and separate these as far as heaven is from the earth, so that this mass really remains nothing other than the testament and sacrament comprehended in the words of Christ. We must esteem any additional words over against the words of Christ as we esteem monstrance and corporal over against the host and the sacrament itself, which we regard merely as supplements for the convenient and proper administration of the sacrament." [333] Here prayers still appear as a vessel for the sacrament; but in the following years the might of Christ's words bursts this vessel asunder. Now the Roman Canon must submit to a type of exorcism, patterned after the formula of Baptism, as Luther adjures and expels it with the words: "Canon, yield to the Gospel and make way for the Holy Spirit, for you are a human word!" [334] While the words of institution are still flanked by the Preface on the one side and by the Pax Domini on the other in the *Formula Missae* of 1523, this, too, has been done away with in the *Deutsche Messe*.[335] The words of institution, in close association with the Distribution, are now projected above the entire act in solitary magnitude. Their divine might and majesty no longer tolerate any human words of prayer in their immediate proximity.

The dogmatic result of this development may be summarized thus: For Luther, the words of institution and the distribution of the elements constitute the Sacrament of the Altar. With regard to the emphasis on the power effective in the words of institution, Luther is the finisher of this Occidental doctrine, which dates back to Augustine, the doctrine of the exclusive power of the words of Christ in the administration of the sacrament.[336] This side of Luther's doctrine of Holy Communion was most clearly evolved in the years 1524–1529 during his disputations on this sacrament. The arguments advanced against Zwingli on the liturgically employed words of institution as a unit of words of authority and words of command, spoken in the person of Christ, are perhaps the clearest expression of Luther's conviction on this subject.[337]

The liturgical result may be summarized thus: Luther's *Deutsche Messe* points "in an unmistakable, terse form to the simple and the essential," which really makes Holy Communion Christ's Holy Communion.[338] That constitutes the incomparably strong witness-character of this order in the setting of the Reformation. This reduction to the one thing that is absolutely commanded in Holy Communion was a necessary act, a reformatory act, for the liberation of Christ's institution from the fetters of the Roman Canon.

To be sure, we must not overlook that also in Luther's *Deutsche Messe* the words of institution and the distribution of the elements are found in a very definite liturgical association, which must be noted in the dogmatic appraisal of this formulary. The words with which Luther introduces the words of institution are especially significant: "Accordingly, we want to administer and use the Testament in His name and by His command, employing His own words and saying: Our Lord Jesus Christ, in the night. . . ."[339] These introductory words demonstrate that the words of institution, together with the distribution of the elements, carry out the Christ-commanded commemoration here and now. Thus, we find the words of institution bracketed very closely with human words also here.

Furthermore, we must note that, according to Luther, the commemoration of Christ in Holy Communion necessarily includes thanksgiving. Therefore we dare not overlook the fact that also in the *Deutsche Messe* the administration of the Sacrament encompasses praise and thanksgiving in the Communion hymns. If we take for granted the consecration and distribution practice as recommended by Luther in this order, then thanksgiving and praise are so closely connected with the words of institution that they are even partially enclosed by them.[340] Also the preparative prayer is not missing from this order. It is found in the paraphrase of the Lord's Prayer, which clearly points to the imminent reception of the Lord's Supper.[341]

293

Even the "terse form" of the *Deutsche Messe* shows that the words of institution and the distribution of the elements are surrounded and accompanied by words which the church does not speak in the person of Christ, but in its own person. There are three wordgroups that stand out in bold relief: (1) the anamnetic incorporation of the present celebration into the context of the Christ-commanded institution; (2) thanksgiving and praise; (3) prayer in preparation for the reception of the sacrament. A development of these wordgroups in a form evolved from Luther's *Deutsche Messe* is certainly possible, especially in view of Luther's principles.[342] Under certain circumstances, such a new development may even appear imperative today, namely, because of the testimony which must always be included in the appropriateness of the form. We recognized the witness character of the *Deutsche Messe*. We will have to ask ourselves whether our situation today does not demand a different, a more highly developed arrangement of those elements which are also contained in Luther's order of the mass. We answer in the affirmative because of two closely connected reasons.

We spoke of the ecumenical obligation, to which the church is subject also in this very arrangement of its worship service. Today we perceive more clearly than the Reformers were able to do how the church's order of service has digressed from the pattern of Communion celebration plainly in evidence since Justin's day. As a type, this order may be in common use also among separated churches. It is still widely preserved in Christendom, though here and there in greatly decadent form. Within the framework of our ecumenical obligation, our fidelity to the position of the Reformation involves not only our negation of the heretical distortion of the original type but also our affirmation of its evangelical organization. Therefore we regard it effective testimony if the evangelical churches return, in a manner consonant with their doctrine and their tradition, to the ecumenical type of the sacrament's celebration, which is still clearly recognizable in Luther's *Formula Missae*.

The second reason which directs us in the organization of the rite of the sacrament is still more cogent. Luther himself repeatedly enunciated the principle that our form of the sacrament's administration must resemble the celebration of the sacrament in the night of betrayal as closely as possible.[343] But if "the simple institution of Christ" is an effectual prototype for the liturgical organization of the sacrament,[344] then this very principle must prompt the question whether the form in Luther's *Deutsche Messe* really and unsurpassably reflects the closest approximation to the instituting Meal of Christ. In order to clarify this question, we are obliged to go back a little further.

It cannot be disputed that Jesus prayed over the bread and, later, also over the cup at the beginning of the act of institution and before He stated what this bread and this wine were.[345] The evangelists report that Jesus in His role as head of the family of disciples regularly opened their meals with a prayer of thanksgiving (Mark 6:41; 8:6; Matt. 14:19; 15:36; John 6:11). In this He demonstrated something particular, something that was characteristic only of Him (Luke 24:35). The conviction that this prayer of thanksgiving bore a certain significance also for the food is not foreign to the Gospels. This is evident from Mark 8:7 (as Jesus gives thanks, He "blesses" the fish) and from Luke 9:16 (Jesus pronounces the blessing over the five loaves and the two fish). Perhaps also Matt. 26:26 and Mark 14:22 belong to this category.[346]

The apostolic congregations, too, scrupulously adhered to this Jewish custom of table prayer adopted by Jesus (Rom. 14:6; 1 Cor. 10:30; Acts 27:35). This table prayer has an axiomatic dogmatic significance. That is shown by the statement in 1 Tim. 4:3-5, which is important for our context. This passage is directed against false teachers, who were characterized by an asceticism that was either Jewish-legalistically, or Hellenistic-gnostically oriented: These people "forbid marriage and enjoin abstinence from foods which God created to be received with thanksgiving by those who believe and know the truth. For everything created by God is good, and nothing is to be rejected if it is received with thanksgiving; for then it is consecrated by the Word of God and prayer." [347] The food is "consecrated" by the table prayer. Through Baptism and faith the Christians belong to Christ. Thereby they belong to the new creation, "which the second Adam, Christ, brought about" (Rom. 5:12-21; 1 Cor. 15:45 to 49).[348] The table prayer extricates the food, which comes from God's good creation, from the sin-corrupted world of creation and assigns it to the new creation, in which all is very good again in Christ. This assigning, this hallowing, this consecrating is performed on the food by the table prayer. One phrase in this passage is deserving of special notice. This hallowing of the food is effected "by the Word of God and prayer." It is obvious that the word "prayer" here refers to the thanksgiving mentioned in verses 3 and 4, consequently to the Christian *berachah.* But what is here meant with "the Word of God"? Some regard it a reference to the creative word of the almighty God,[349] which is, indeed, effectual here and now. But it seems more reasonable to assume that it refers to a word actually uttered by the praying person and connected with the prayer. "It seems best to relate λόγος θεοῦ ('Word of God') to table prayers couched in Biblical phraseology." [350]

The hallowing or consecrating of the food by God's Word and prayer is of basic significance for an understanding of the organization of Holy Communion. Holy Communion is certainly a meal. In the New Testament the Christian *berachah,* the εὐλογία, is a necessary part of the meal. For the apostolic congregations Holy Communion is unthinkable without the hallowing and consecrating of the food "by the Word of God and prayer." This table prayer is typified by Christ's example. If the church is intent on doing what Christ did in instituting the Meal, it will not neglect the εὐλογία.

It is obvious that the apostolic congregations did not omit it. "The cup of blessing which we bless (ὃ εὐλογοῦμεν), is it not a communion in the blood of Christ?" (1 Cor. 10:16). The third cup in the Passover is called "cup of blessing." The special feature of the cup in the Lord's Supper is marked by the appended words "which we bless." The cup becomes the cup of Holy Communion by the εὐλογία spoken over it. And this εὐλογία is unquestionably prayer, glorifying, anamnetic prayer of thanksgiving. But this prayer directed to God simultaneously relates to the cup. For the cup is the object of the praise and the blessing. This also applies to the bread. The εὐλογία over the bread is contained in the breaking of bread. The bread becomes the bread of Holy Communion by virtue of this particular "breaking," which is inseparably connected with the glorifying prayer of thanksgiving (Mark 8:6; Matt. 15:36). In 1 Cor. 10:16 the εὐλογία even appears as the factor that virtually constitutes the sacrament as such. And this εὐλογία was indubitably prayer.[351]

We cannot say definitely in what manner Christ's words of institution were recited by the apostolic congregations in the administration of Holy Communion, but we can say definitely that, according to the apostolic testimony in the New Testament, the Holy Communion εὐλογία was spoken as a prayer over bread and wine. We can furthermore say definitely that, according to the apostolic testimony in the New Testament, this Holy Communion prayer, the εὐλογία, is an essential factor in blessing and hallowing the food as Holy Communion food. And, finally, we can definitely say that, according to the New Testament's testimony, "the first mass of Christ" — to borrow Luther's expression — is itself an example and effective archetype for these facts.

These facts, unmistakably derived from the New Testament, are of basic importance. We observed that Holy Communion can exist only in association with Christ's institution of the sacrament. But one of the signs of this association is the invocation of the name of Jesus Christ. Invocation of that name is prayer. No other action more appropriately characterizes this association with the institution, joined to the proclamation of the instituting words, than the invocation of the name of the Lord Jesus. The very fact that Christ's words of institution are joined with prayer moves them unmistakably into the association with the institution of the sacrament. Far from mutually excluding each other in Holy Communion, Christ's words of institution and prayer seek and attract each other. If the apostolic report on a profane meal is true, namely, that the food is "consecrated" by the Word of God and prayer, it is quite natural that the food in Holy Communion is consecrated in like manner. The Word of God, which consecrates the food as the food of Holy Communion, is Christ's word of institution. The prayer, which dare not be omitted according to apostolic testimony and the example of Christ, is the εὐλογία, "a prayer of thanksgiving in the form of a blessing and spoken for the purpose of blessing." [352]

Luther and the church of the Augsburg Confession insisted over against Rome on the integrity of Christ's institution. Therefore they rightly emphasized that, in addition to the words of institution, eating and drinking was a factor constitutive for the administration of the sacrament. But we ask: Was the εὐλογία of the Holy Communion accorded its rightful place in this, in keeping with the institution of Christ and the practice of the apostles? To be sure, the εὐλογία is not missing here. Its function is assumed by the words of institution. These place bread and wine under the εὐλογία of Christ. But the εὐλογία of the congregation celebrating here and now is not being expressed.

When Christ instituted Holy Communion, He spoke the εὐλογία as a prayer of thanksgiving. Also the apostles and the apostolic congregations recited the εὐλογία of the Holy Communion as a prayer of thanksgiving and of blessing spoken over bread and wine. Might not this apostolic interpretation of Christ's command "Do this!" be meaningful and binding also for us? If we, in agreement with the Formula of Concord, insist that obedience to the entire act instituted by Christ is necessary for a proper administration of the sacrament, and if the blessing of bread and wine is part and parcel of this entire act, then the form of blessing which conforms to the example of Christ and to apostolic testimony, and which, as blessing, is also thanksgiving, would seem to be highly appropriate to the required approach to the form.

If Christ's words of institution and the εὐλογία belong together, then the objection can no longer be raised that it is inappropriate if a prayer intervenes between the recital of the words of institution and the distribution of the elements. As expressed in 1 Tim. 4:5, the word of Christ and the prayer of thanksgiving belong together. Therefore the prayer joined to the words of Christ does not place the distribution, a necessary part of the sacrament, in jeopardy. It is decisive that the distribution actually takes place in the administration of Holy Communion. With a view to the concrete celebration taking place here and now, we may and must speak of an indissoluble connection between the distribution and the consecration. If no distribution follows the words of consecration in worship, then the consecration is, indeed, not realized. But we can by no means conclude from this that the distribution has consecrating power, nor that the consecration is made questionable if prayers or the Pax Domini are spoken after the words of institution.[353]

The Eucharistic Epiclesis as a Dogmatic and Liturgical Problem

In the εὐλογία spoken over bread and wine, the fully developed Eucharistic epiclesis (= invocation) is a prayer with a double content: for the descent of the Holy Spirit on bread and wine, to consecrate the food and make it body and blood of Christ, and for a salutary reception of the Meal's gifts of grace.[354] The second content of the prayer poses no dogmatic difficulties; for Christ's body and blood are received for salvation, for the remission of sin, and for a salutary participation in the pneumatic body of Jesus Christ only by a Spirit-wrought faith. It is most appropriate that not only the individual prays silently for the gift of a Spirit-wrought faith and for a salutary reception of the sacrament, but that also the Holy Communion congregation voices this petition collectively in the liturgical we. Therefore the dogmatic problem of the epiclesis converges on the question whether the first content of the prayer is legitimate. As we use the term epiclesis in the following discussion, we have only this consecration petition in mind. Is this petition in accord with Holy Writ? Is it in accord with Christ's institution? Is it a proper unfolding of what takes place in Holy Communion on the basis of Christ's institution? Or is it most inappropriate? Does it, perhaps, even harbor heresy?

Our conception of Christ's words of institution requires no further proof that the epiclesis is not necessary.[355] Where the consecratory function is ascribed exclusively to the epiclesis, as this is done by Cyril of Jerusalem (died 386?), Theodore of Mopsuestia (died 428), and the confessional writings of the Eastern church in the 17th century,[356] the fact is ignored that in the church's celebration of Holy Communion Christ's words are spoken "in His name and by His command," and are thus spoken as His own words. For the sake of Christ's honor we have to reject the opinion that the epiclesis is necessary for the administration of the sacrament, and that it alone effects the presence of Christ's body and blood. The really dogmatic problem of the epiclesis first arises when the decisive function of the words of institution in effecting the sacrament are not disputed and the epiclesis is viewed as an appropriate development of the consecratory event.

Chrysostom (died 407) may serve as an example of a proponent of this position. He teaches: Christ Himself is present in every Holy Communion celebrated by the church, and through His word He makes bread and wine become His body and blood. The priest pronounces the words of institution vicariously for Christ. The words: "That is My body," transform the elements in the power of God (μεταρρυθμίζει). Just as the words "Be fruitful and multiply" were spoken only once (Gen. 1:28), yet are not limited in their effective power by this "once," but show forth their effective power "throughout time" in our human nature, so also the words of institution were spoken only once by Christ, but in the church's Eucharist they are as effectual "from that day on until today and until Christ's return" as in that first Meal.[357]

Nonetheless the power of Christ's words does not abrogate the epiclesis. With his prayer, Elijah called down the fire from heaven upon altar and sacrifice (1 Kings 18). But that was only a precursory type for the miracle in the Eucharist, which far overshadows it. Here the priest calls not fire but grace down upon the sacrificial gifts by his urgent and assiduous prayer; not that the sacrificial gifts might thereby be consumed, but that they may enkindle the hearts of all and thus let them appear more lustrous than silver refined by fire. And this gift from above is none other than the Holy Spirit, who touches the gifts present there.[358]

Here the food is indeed consecrated "by the Word of God and prayer" (1 Tim. 4:5).[359] As with Chrysostom and Gregory of Nyssa (died 394), the emphasis may rest on the words of institution.[360] Or, a dogmatic balance may be established between the words of institution and the epiclesis, as is found in John Damascenus (died 749?).[361] Finally, occasioned by the polemical discussion with the West, the view of Cyril of Jerusalem gained predominance, and the epiclesis deprived the words of institution of their consecratory power.

For us the dogmatic problem of the epiclesis is posed by the type of doctrine espoused by Gregory of Nyssa and Chrysostom. Here we shall take no cognizance of the Eastern church's view on the "transformation" of the elements into the body and blood of Christ. As for us, we are firmly convinced by the words of Christ that bread and wine, which are body and blood of Christ in Holy Communion, convey to us for physical reception Christ's body and blood in the form of bread and wine. On the premise of this doctrine of Holy Communion, the dogmatic problem of the epiclesis may be formulated thus: If Christ Himself makes bread and wine in Holy Communion the bearers of His body and blood by His almighty and authoritative words of institution, is it appropriate in view of this — for it can impossibly be necessary — for the church to petition that this miracle may be wrought here and now in the present administration of the sacrament? In answering this question, we shall for the time being disregard the special content and the position of the prayer and try to clarify the question regarding the justification of a consecration petition in general, in order to discuss, subsequently, the special content and the position of this petition.

In this connection it will be of some importance that not only the first German mass, the influential *Evangelische Messe* of Kaspar Kantz, 1522, contains a consecration petition, which precedes the words of institution,[362] but also the liturgy of Pfalz-Neuburg, 1543, and, patterning after it, the Kassel Agenda of 1896.[363]

300

Pfalz-Neuburg

Lord Jesus Christ, Thou only true Son of the living God, who didst give Thy life into bitter death for us all and didst shed Thy blood for the remission of our sin, and who also hast commanded all Thy disciples to eat this same body and to drink this same blood and to remember Thy death, we bring these Thy gifts, bread and wine, before Thy divine Majesty and pray that Thou, through Thy divine mercy, goodness, and power, wouldst hallow and consecrate them and cause this bread to be Thy body and this wine to be Thy blood, and that Thou wouldst let them be blessings unto eternal life for all who eat and drink of the same, Thou, who with God the Father in the unity of the Holy Ghost livest and reignest now and in eternity.

Kassel

Almighty God, heavenly Father, who hast delivered Thy Son, our Lord Jesus Christ, into death, and hast ordained that His body and blood be our food unto eternal life, we bring these Thy gifts before Thy divine Majesty, Thy own from Thine own, and pray Thee to hallow and bless them through Thy divine mercy and power, that this bread and this cup may be the body and blood of our Lord Jesus Christ for all who eat and drink of the same, and that Thou wouldst let them be blessings unto eternal life for them, Thou, who livest and reignest with the Son and the Holy Ghost now and in eternity.

These prayers are undoubtedly a consecration petition. They approach an epiclesis also in content. Self-evidently, any thought of "transubstantiation" is absent here. Nor is the Holy Ghost mentioned in particular. However, the terms "divine mercy and power" may, as the fathers' usage of language shows, be substitutes for a specific mention of the Holy Ghost. — For the dogmatic problem of the epiclesis the anglicanizing suggestions of Bunsen and Abeken are less significant for us[364] than the deliberations of Ernst Sartorius and Theodosius Harnack. In his outline of the Holy Communion liturgy Sartorius accepts the cited Pfalz-Neuburg prayer and places it between the Sanctus and the words of institution. He supports this action with a reflection that will also guide us in our decision: "As surely as the consecration is not effected by the prayer of the minister but by the words of the Lord, so surely it is nonetheless fitting to petition Him for this." [365] Harnack inserts a "consecratory prayer" after the words of institution. The decisive phrases have also been borrowed from Pfalz-Neuburg, but expanded by an important addendum. This consecration petition is joined to the anamnesis. It reads: "Thus mindful . . . we place these gifts before Thy countenance, Thy own from Thine own, and pray Thee to hallow and bless them, and, through Thy divine goodness, mercy, and power, cause this bread, *in accord with the institution of our Lord Jesus Christ,* to be His body and this wine to be His blood. . . ." This is followed by a petition for the salutary reception of the fruits of Holy Communion, with an eschatological prospect.[366] How are these consecration petitions to be appraised?

It is true that the church pronounces Christ's words in Holy Communion in His person, in His stead. However, we must not forget that the church's authority to make this pronouncement is entirely a derived, transmitted, and bestowed authority. Jesus Christ is and remains the Lord of this Meal. The church remains a tool in His hand also when it acts in His person and in His stead; it remains His handmaid. The church's reliance on the unswerving faithfulness of its Lord and the inviolability of His testament dare not in any wise be weakened also with regard to the event of His real presence.[367]

But this confidence must never lose its pneumatic character and become carnal security. When the doctrine of the real presence is misused and in such a misuse induces carnal security in view of the presence of Christ's body and blood, Christ's testament, to be sure, is not invalidated, but the administration of the sacrament then degenerates into an unspiritual mechanism, which brings judgment upon the heads of those guilty of this. The sign that would ward off this carnal security with its devastating consequences is the church's petition in which it implores that, in the power of Christ's institution, bread and wine may become bearers of Christ's body and blood also now in this concrete celebration. A consecration petition, such as contained in the Pfalz-Neuburg order of service, is in keeping with the fact that the church always exercises its conferred authority and power to administer Holy Communion as a servant and never with self-assurance and arrogance. Such a consecration petition is an appropriate sign indicating that the Lord Himself is and remains the One who acts in Holy Communion. In that way it serves the honor of Christ.

But what about the content of the consecration petition? May it pray for the sending of the Holy Ghost upon bread and wine? Does such a prayer contain an intimation of a heretical pneumatology, a heretical doctrine of the Trinity? Might the epiclesis necessarily imply a denial of the *filioque?*

Whoever wishes to decide the question regarding the dogmatic justification of the epiclesis must give serious thought to the doctrine of the Holy Ghost. We do not presume to say that this doctrine has been unfolded by our church with adequate clarity and certitude. The dogmatic atrophy of this doctrine from which our church is suffering more than it is aware must necessarily prove a strong factor of uncertainty also in our deliberations on the epiclesis. However, the following might be affirmed on the basis of Biblical testimony.

The bread and wine which we place on the altar in the Lord's Supper are, as a natural fruit of the earth, a gift of the Creator, just as the bread in the kitchen and the wine in the cellar are. But something happens to these gifts of the Creator when they are used in Holy Communion. They are lifted out of their profane use, which, according to 1 Tim. 4:6, already calls for a "consecration" through the Word of God and prayer, and, engaged in a special and singular use, they become the means for the appropriation of Christ's body and blood. In analogy to the consecration of the food in 1 Tim. 4:5, this engagement must also be designated as a being-consecrated;[368] but this deals with a special type of consecration which is basically without analogy. If even the "natural" use of food by the Christian, who belongs to a new eon in Christ, includes, or better presupposes a being-consecrated of the food, then it is surely true, and true in a particular sense, of that wonderful reception of food which Christ Himself makes the means of effecting His presence. But he who consecrates is God the Holy Ghost! Of course, the works of the Trinity that relate to world and man and history and creature are undivided. And yet we ascribe certain divine works to a certain person of the Trinity; this we do on the basis of Biblical testimony and the knowledge of faith effected by it. And all that deals with hallowing and consecration, all that relates to the creature's reception into the dominion of God, down to the resurrection of our bodies from the dead — all that is a work peculiar to the Holy Ghost.

Do not venture to say that the Holy Ghost occupies Himself only with man or even only with the spiritual side of man! Even the doctrine of creation refutes that. Even the omnipresence of God in the living creatures is not without the Holy Ghost and His working on the creatures. That is intimated in Gen. 1 and Ps. 33:3 and expressed in Ps. 104:29 f.[369] The work of the Spirit is universal also in the re-creation. For we are waiting for a new heaven and a new earth (2 Peter 3:13) as surely as we hope for the eschatological transformation of our bodies by the life-giving Spirit (1 Cor. 15:45). But this universal work of the Spirit is rooted in His work on the crucified Lord when He raised Him from the dead. (Rom. 8:11)

The doctrine of the Holy Ghost reveals that it is the Spirit, who in creation, in preservation, in justification, in regeneration, in final consummation opens the door to God for the creature who finds this door locked to God's nearness, to His work, to His life; that it is the Spirit who gains access to Him and makes God's work effective on and in the creature. That applies also to bread and wine in Holy Communion. In 1 Cor. 10:3 f. Paul shows that the consecrated Eucharistic food is associated with the Spirit: The food which conveys Christ's body and blood to us for our physical reception is not devoid of the Spirit, by whom it is hallowed, made accessible, and furnished for this service; the food in Holy Communion is permeated by the Spirit, it is βρῶμα πνευματικόν.[370] Therefore the petition for the descent of the Holy Spirit upon bread and wine in Holy Communion as such involves no unscriptural doctrine.

But the relevance of this petition goes further than that. Luther's and the Lutheran Church's doctrine of Holy Communion has shown unmistakably that the real presence may not be construed as an "impanation," as a locally delimited entering of Christ's body and blood into the elements. That would be an insupportable rationalization of the end-time mystery which takes place in Holy Communion. But Luther, too, recognizes in the doctrine of the real presence that Christ in the condescension of His compassion again submits to conditions in Holy Communion which are in a way analogous to His incarnation.[371]

But in the Son's assumption of the flesh we behold the work of the Holy Spirit (Luke 1:35; Matt. 1:18). The *unio hypostatica* between the deity and the humanity of Christ does not take place without the Spirit's coming to the creature, without His singling out the creatural for a union with the divine, without His hallowing it and consummating the union. In Holy Communion, the *unio sacramentalis* between the earthly bread and Christ's sacrificial body, glorified in eschatological consummation and in divine-pneumatic

304

derestriction, is involved; the sacramental union between the creatural wine of this earth and Jesus' covenantal blood, shed on the cross and eternally present in eschatological freedom before God's throne (Heb. 12:24), is involved. Nor is the bond of this union effected without the particular cooperation of the Holy Spirit, who, from His inner-trinitarian origin, is the binding bond, and who in His work in the plan of salvation again and again proves Himself the bond which assembles, joins, and unites. Therefore it is most appropriate to ascribe the work of uniting the food with the body and blood of Jesus in Holy Communion to the ministry of the Holy Spirit.

But the consecration prayer may be a petition for the descent of the Spirit on the creatural means of the real presence of Christ's body and blood for another, a final and surely decisive reason: In their essence Christ's body and blood are not separated from the Spirit, but are themselves, as it were, thoroughly pervaded by the Spirit (Pneuma). From His origin in the body of His mother Mary, Christ's humanity was begotten by the Spirit. The Man Jesus is bearer of the Spirit unlike any prophet, any apostle, any Christian, but as only the end-time Redeemer of the world can be (Mark 1:10 f.). Jesus' humanity is derestricted for the essence and work of the Spirit through the eschatological transformation, effected in Him at Easter in the resurrection (Rom. 8:11), so that the Lord and the Spirit are one in "dynamic identification" (2 Cor. 3:17; 1 Cor. 15:45). Therefore, as Luther untiringly affirmed in His doctrine of Holy Communion over against Zwingli, the flesh of Christ is a Spirit-flesh, a God-flesh, which is flesh and Spirit in one.[372]

Between Pentecost and Christ's return the hidden epiphany of Jesus' humanity takes place in the outpouring Spirit. During this interim, the outpouring Spirit is Himself the hidden epiphany of the humanity of Jesus, in which and with which He, the God-man, effected our salvation, in which and through which we receive salvation. Therefore we may teach: Where the epiphany of Jesus' body and blood eventuates in the bread and wine of Holy Communion in a hidden but real manner, the Spirit is present as the decisively cooperating bearer of this epiphany. Therefore it may not be construed as an unscriptural conception of the Gospel or as a detraction from Christ's honor when the consecration prayer implores the Holy Spirit to descend upon the creatural means, which are, by virtue of Christ's institution, bearers of His body and blood in Holy Communion.

The last question posed by the epiclesis pertains to its place

305

within the Holy Communion liturgy. Here the dogmatic problem simultaneously becomes a liturgical one in the narrower sense. We recognized that the words of institution spoken in Christ's stead are, by the power of Christ, the means of consecration in Holy Communion, in the entire act commanded by Christ. The work of the Spirit on bread and wine takes place simultaneously with this event, in which bread and wine, by virtue of Christ's institution, become bearers of His body and blood. Here the work of the Spirit enters the work of Christ, ministering and mediating. May this simultaneousness and this cooperation of the Spirit's work, dependent on Christ's institution, be expressed by the position of the epiclesis in the liturgy? The simultaneousness cannot be expressed. Our language is bound to the before and the after. The liturgical language, too, must express simultaneous events in a succession of sentences. Only the proximity of the epiclesis to the words of institution can intimate that both the implored work of the Spirit and the real presence of Christ take place in one pneumatic "now."

May the epiclesis be placed before or after the words of institution? In the Eastern church its position following the words of institution and the anamnesis has prevailed. But liturgical documents from Egypt prove that originally it was placed before the words of institution there.[373] If the εὐλογία together with the words of institution may be conceived as a whole, which is carried out in a single pneumatic "now," then the question regarding the sequence of the liturgical acts seems inconsequential. Then the position of the epiclesis after the words of institution and the anamnesis might follow the tripartite schema which underlies the Apostles' Creed and the Nicene Creed. Obviously the grouping "Father-Son-Spirit" determined the structure of this prayer already with Hippolytus. The epiclesis following the words of institution and the anamnesis may be viewed as an anamnetic presentation of Pentecost, in which it accords with the plan-of-salvation nature of this event that its presentation is executed in the form of a petition for the Spirit.

One may also interpret the position of the epiclesis in the Eastern church thus: In the consecration the work of the Holy Spirit is only cooperative and performed on the background of the institution of Christ. The work of the Holy Spirit on the elements is done on the foundation of the instituting words of Christ. If one tries to conceive of this cooperation of the Spirit, this dependence of the Spirit's work on the work of Christ, under a temporal aspect and

306

to express this with a sign, one is inclined to have the words of Christ precede the epiclesis also in time.[374]

But the epiclesis theology of the Eastern church shows that this very postposition of the epiclesis may foster very serious errors. The moment the epiclesis is no longer viewed as a unit comprehended in a pneumatic "now," and the chronological sequence of individual elements appears important, the content of the postposed epiclesis must question or even contest the consecratory power of Christ's words. This engenders that epiclesis theology which predominated in the Eastern church during the 17th and 18th centuries. We do not dispute that the Eastern church can overcome this erroneous development from the basis of its own tradition, without altering the position of its epiclesis. But a consecration petition following the words of institution is no longer possible for the Occidental churches. Since the work of the Spirit does not complete the work of Christ in the consecration, but only accompanies it cooperatively, an epiclesis petitioning for consecration must stand, in our Western tradition, before the words of institution, if it is to be used in any form whatsoever. We cannot ignore the importance which history still has in the plan-of-salvation period between Pentecost and Christ's return. That also applies to the worship service — without detracting from its pneumatic character. To be sure, the redemptive event of Christ's cross, together with the exalted Lord, is found in the spaceless and timeless, eschatological, sovereign liberty of God's kingdom. But the church is not yet in the kingdom of God, as Christ is. Therefore the events of historical time are still so important to the church that its praying, too, is determined by it. Is not every petition of the church geared to future fulfillment? May the church on earth disregard the coming of what it prays for? Manifestly, it is restrained from doing that so long as it prays in its worship service: "Thy kingdom come." This prayer urges the church to take the course of history, the time of history, seriously also in its worship. Where that is done, the dimension of the future, which opens in every petition, is irreconcilable with an epiclesis prayed after the words of institution.[375]

Anamnesis as Prayer

We observed that the main worship service comprising proclamation of the Word and Holy Communion is, as a whole, already an anamnesis. We also recognized that prayer is a pneumatic dimension which encompasses and supports the worship service as a whole.

Despite this, individual acts protrude from this "total dimension" of worship as special acts of prayer. Should not also the anamnesis of Christ in the entire anamnetic event of Holy Communion project at one point as a special act? Should prayer and anamnesis not pervade each other here? We noted that the εὐλογία of Holy Communion is a very appropriate development of the memorial which Christ instituted. This εὐλογία is in fact the proper place where the congregation prayerfully declares before God that it is remembering here and in this act what was done for it by God in Christ. With these words of prayer of the expressed anamnesis of Christ the congregation, standing before God's throne, hides itself, as it were, in the Christ-event. With these words of prayer it appears before God's throne as a congregation which has been received into Christ's cross, resurrection, and ascent into heaven, and is, as such, not only hidden but also sheltered with Christ in God.

With regard to this anamnesis it must be our critical concern absolutely to avoid every intimation that the congregation on its part is offering God the sacrifice of the cross, which is present in Holy Communion.[376] We shall also not deal here with the congregation's offering of self to God, a thought that is current in the Anglican liturgy. Here we must behold the memorial of Christ's sacrifice in its character of immeasurable grace, free from any alloy. The presentation of our offering must not be intermingled with the anamnesis of Christ's offering. Where Christ's presentation of His sacrifice eventuates, it surely behooves us to silence any declaration of sacrifice on our part.

The Eucharistic Prayer in Outline

The doctrine of worship and its form culminates in the attempt to express how the church should pray over bread and wine in the administration of Holy Communion. In this attempt we must focus our attention on the following guidelines:

1. In accord with the example of Christ, the church should not only pronounce Christ's words of institution over bread and wine, but it should also pray in words of grateful, anamnetic praise and thus carry out the εὐλογία, the "consecration" of bread and wine. The customary Preface is only the beginning of this εὐλογία, which demands a continuation following the Sanctus.

2. The words of institution constitute the absolutely enjoined component of the consecration of bread and wine in the sacrament.

They should project prominently in their special, absolutely decisive function. The musical tone of their recitation may also contribute to that end.

3. Preceding Christ's words, a consecration prayer is possible and appropriate. The prayer taken from the Pfalz-Neuburg order of service may serve as a pattern. It was adopted and followed also by Sartorius, Harnack, and by the Kassel Agenda of 1896.

4. It is most appropriate to join the spoken anamnesis to the words of institution.

5. The petition for the salutary reception of the gifts of grace in Holy Communion should not only be left to the individual, but should also be expressed by the congregation in the liturgical We. This petition is included in an anamnesis of Pentecost; for the special feature of the Pentecostal anamnesis is petition for the present coming of the Spirit.

6. It is very much in keeping with what is done in Holy Communion that the congregation prays for the perfection of the body of Christ and for return of Christ.

7. The εὐλογία of the Lord's Supper, which begins with the Preface, is best concluded with the Lord's Prayer. The Pax Domini, which follows this, forms the bridge to the distribution of the elements, which begins with the Agnus Dei.

The wording of the prayer which is properly placed between the Sanctus and the Lord's Prayer and encompasses the words of institution is granted only to those who administer the Sacrament of the Altar more frequently than the writer of these lines is able to do. As a final word on the doctrine of worship we here submit to the reader's scrutiny an outline for such a prayer patterned after Theodosius Harnack. It outlines the type of prayer required at this point in the celebration of the sacrament. However, the suggested wording must be subject to revision by the Holy Spirit, who operates in the congregation assembled about Word and sacrament.

After the Preface has been prayed and the Sanctus chanted, the congregation shall continue to pray, through the ministry of the pastor, as follows:

Praise be to Thee, holy Father, inscrutable, eternal God, together with Thy only-begotten Son, the Image of Thy essence,

309

and to the Holy Spirit, who unites in the perfect communion of love from eternity to eternity.

We laud Thee that Thy goodness hath created heaven and earth and hath fashioned us men in Thy image. We thank Thee that Thou hast borne us sinners, who deserved Thy wrath, with great forbearance and patience and still preservest us. Above all, however, we praise and magnify Thy tender compassion which sent Thy beloved Son Jesus Christ into our flesh, to restore Thy image to us and to redeem us from sin and from death and from the powers of darkness and to bring us home to Thee. Assembled in His name and in His memory, we pray Thee for His saving presence in this sacred Meal. We place this bread and this wine, Thy gifts, before Thy countenance, heavenly Father, and pray Thee to consecrate and to bless them through the power of the Holy Spirit, that this bread be the body of our Lord Jesus Christ and this wine be His blood, as we now administer His own Testament according to His command:

OUR LORD JESUS CHRIST, THE SAME NIGHT IN WHICH HE WAS BETRAYED, TOOK BREAD; AND WHEN HE HAD GIVEN THANKS, HE BRAKE IT AND GAVE IT TO HIS DISCIPLES, SAYING, "TAKE, EAT; THIS IS MY BODY, WHICH IS GIVEN FOR YOU. THIS DO IN RE-MEMBRANCE OF ME."

AFTER THE SAME MANNER ALSO HE TOOK THE CUP WHEN HE HAD SUPPED, AND WHEN HE HAD GIVEN THANKS, HE GAVE IT TO THEM, SAYING, "DRINK YE ALL OF IT; THIS CUP IS THE NEW TESTAMENT IN MY BLOOD, WHICH IS SHED FOR YOU FOR THE REMISSION OF SINS. THIS DO, AS OFT AS YE DRINK IT, IN REMEM-BRANCE OF ME."

Therefore we recall before Thee, Lord, heavenly Father, the redemptive suffering and the life-giving death of Thy dear Son Jesus Christ, our Lord. We profess and praise His victorious resurrection from the dead and His mighty ascension into Thy heavenly sanctuary, where He, our High Priest, ever represents us before Thee with the one, all-sufficient sacrifice of His body and blood, given and shed for us on the cross, and present to us in the mystery of this sacred Meal.

We thank Thee for the bread of life and the cup of salvation, for the remission of all our sins, for the new birth of our lost life, for the infinite fullness of the future glory, which Thou offerest to us through Jesus, Thy Servant. Eternal glory and thanks and praise be to Thee for Thy mercy.

We implore Thee to send down upon us the Holy Spirit, who quickens. Sanctify and renew us in body and soul. Grant us the faith that saves so that we may receive the true body and true blood of Thy Son with thanksgiving and unto our eternal salvation. And as we all are one body in Christ Jesus, our Lord, through the communion of His body and blood in this sacred Meal, gather Thy elect from the ends of the earth into Thy holy people. Let us endure patiently to the end. For Jesus' sake deliver us from the terrors of the Day of Judgment, and cover us with His righteousness when that day dawns, so that we, together with all other believers, may celebrate, united with Him, the nuptial feast of the Lamb in His kingdom, which has no end. Hear us as we pray in His name and with His words:

OUR FATHER WHO ART IN HEAVEN, HALLOWED BE THY NAME; THY KINGDOM COME; THY WILL BE DONE ON EARTH AS IT IS IN HEAVEN; GIVE US THIS DAY OUR DAILY BREAD; AND FORGIVE US OUR TRESPASSES, AS WE FORGIVE THOSE WHO TRESPASS AGAINST US; AND LEAD US NOT INTO TEMPTATION; BUT DELIVER US FROM EVIL.

The congregation concludes the prayer saying:

FOR THINE IS THE KINGDOM AND THE POWER AND THE GLORY FOREVER AND EVER. AMEN.

NOTES

FOREWORD

1. *Works of Martin Luther, The Philadelphia Edition,* Vol. VI (Philadelphia: Muhlenberg Press, 1932), p. 84.
2. Ed. by K. F. Müller and Walter Blankenburg, pp. 84—361.
3. *The Book of Concord,* trans. and ed. Theodore G. Tappert (Philadelphia: Muhlenberg Press, 1959), p. 342.
4. Ibid., pp. 375—379.
5. Ibid., pp. 425—426.
6. Ibid., pp. 426—428.
7. E. g., in "The Holy and Blessed Sacrament of Baptism," "The Blessed Sacrament of the Holy and True Body of Christ, and the Brotherhoods," and "A treatise on the New Testament, that is, the Holy Mass," *Luther's Works,* Vol. 35, ed. E. Theodore Bachmann (Philadelphia: Muhlenberg, 1960), pp. 29—111, Luther makes only occasional and passing remarks. In "The Adoration of the Sacrament," *Luther's Works,* Vol. 36, ed. Abdel Ross Wentz (Philadelphia: Muhlenberg, 1959), pp. 292—293, Luther makes a concession to common usage and links worship with "having faith" *(anbeten, ehrbieten).*
8. The first three of these were translated by Paul Zeller Strodach and the fourth by A. Steimle in *Works of Martin Luther, The Philadelphia Edition,* Vol. VI.

CHAPTERS

1. On the following, cf. *Theologisches Wörterbuch zum Neuen Testament* (hereafter cited as ThWNT), ed. Gerhard Kittel and Gerhard Friedrich (Stuttgart: W. Kohlhammer, 1933—), IV, 58 ff., and the literature cited there. Consult the respective commentaries with regard to the quoted Scripture passages.
2. Cf. ThWNT, III, 155 ff.
3. Cf. G. Bornkamm, "Die Häresie des Kolosserbriefs," *Theologische Literaturzeitung* (ThLZ), 73 (1948), 11 ff., and *Das Ende des Gesetzes* (Munich, 1952), pp. 139 ff.
4. Luther's comment on 2 Thess. 2:4 is informative. When the Antichrist "exalteth himself above all that is called God, or that is worshiped, so that

he as God sitteth in the temple of God" [KJV], this is a sign of "the rule of the Antichrist in Christendom, by which he gets his commandment to be esteemed more highly than God's commandment and service" (WA *Deutsche Bibel*, 7, 254 f.). Worship, inclusive of worship "in church," is thus rooted in God's Word. The Antichrist places his word over against God's Word as the sovereign, binding power and thereby begets the anti-Christian worship which is based on "human doctrine."

5. Cf. ThWNT, IV, 221 ff. and in addition to the literature mentioned there: E. Raitz v. Frentz, S. J., "Der Weg der Liturgie in der Geschichte," *Eph. liturg. Anal. hist.-asc.*, 55 (1941), 74—80.

6. In later antiquity "liturgy was a word as generally current as the word taxes is today." (O. Casel, ΛΕΙΤΟΥΡΓΙΑ — MUNUS, *Oriens Christianus*, III, 7 [1932], 289.)

7. Erik Peterson, ΕΙΣ ΘΕΟΣ, Göttingen, 1926 (*Forschungen zur Religion und Literatur des Alten und Neuen Testaments*, New Series, 24), p. 178; similarly, E. Raitz v. Frentz, p. 76. Differently, R. Meyer in ThWNT, IV, 225, lines 42 f.: ". . . the very general concept of serving is applied to the cultic relationship to the gods." However, this conception may be questioned, especially since "the very general concept of serving," which is discussed on page 224, as a rule still clearly shows that the respective service is performed in an overlapping organic or legal communion.

8. Egyptian conditions might have acquainted the translators with the cultic use of *leiturgia*. Cf., e. g., A. Deiszmann, *Bibelstudien*, Marburg, 1895, pp. 137 f., and Friedrich Preisigke, *Wörterbuch der griechischen Papyrusurkunden*, II (Berlin, 1927), 12 f. Strathmann, on the other hand, regards it as more probable that "the old, official, political-technical usage was ringing in the ears" of the translators (ThWNT, IV, 228 f.). But the strict cultic use of the word *leiturgia* in the Septuagint rather suggests, in agreement with Debrunner (ThWNT, IV, 229), a polemical contrasting of the true, God-revealed "service" with the service rendered the idols.

9. In ThWNT, IV, 233, lines 35 ff., Strathmann voices a different view. In his opinion, Acts 13:2 is the first passage "which shows us the application of this important Old Testament cultic term to the purely spiritual Christian worship service, even though this may involve only a small prayer-fellowship of leading men." However, it seems very doubtful that Acts 13:2 actually means to spiritualize an Old Testament cultic term and apply it to the worship of the *ekklesia*. Under no circumstances does Acts 13:2 support the Eastern Church's later adoption of the word *Leiturgia* for its worship services and specifically for the Eucharist. See pp. 19 f.

10. In Phil. 2:17 τῆς πίστεως is an objective genitive; the Philippians do not offer their faith, but their faith is offered as a sacrifice by Paul through a *leiturgia*.

11. Thus Bengel already commented on this passage: "Paul rejoices over the anticipated spilling of his own blood as if it were the wine customarily sprinkled and poured out at the base of the altar of sacrifice."

12. ThWNT, II, 270, lines 37 ff.

13. Cf. Wilhelm Hahn, *Gottesdienst und Opfer Christi. Eine Untersuchung über das Heilsgeschehen im christlichen Gottesdienst* (Berlin, 1951), p. 34. Hahn would like to construe "this absence of a term which clearly defines and delimits the Christian worship service in the New Testament" as an indication "that the boundaries between worship and the other phases of

congregational life in early Christendom were fluid." However, we must consider here that it is just these other phases of the congregation's life that may be described with terms bearing a cultic stamp, whereas the same terms cannot be applied to the activity of the congregation assembled for worship. What happens in the worship service is an eschatologically new experience, and the newness of it cannot be expressed by the "spiritualization" of a given cultic term. On the question of spiritualizing, cf. Hans Wenschkewitz, *Die Spiritualisierung der Kultusbegriffe* . . ., Angelos Supplement 4, 1932.

14. Cf. Wilhelm Hahn, pp. 29—33, where the following thesis is elucidated: "In early Christendom, the worship service is not dissolved into ethical obedience and faith in action, for surely the entire life of a Christian must be worship. Rather, the congregation's assembly for worship occupies the all-determinative position in the life of early Christendom and rules and sustains all the rest of the life and activity of the congregation and the Christian."

15. *Ekklesia* is the people of God of the end time in the New Covenant. At all events, it refers to the specific "congregation" and the "church" as a whole at one and the same time.

16. This expression may be permitted for reasons of clarity, although it contains a tautology inasmuch as "assembly" is surely the most important meaning of the word ἐκκλησία.

17. It may be assumed that also James 2:2 has the assembly of the Christian congregation in mind. With regard to this and the term *synagoge* in its Christian application, cf. M. Dibelius in Meyer's *Kommentar* (1921) and the literature cited there, p. 124, n. 3.

18. Cf., e. g., Hermas, Mandatum XI, 9—14; Dionysius of Alexandria in Eusebius, *Historia ecclesiastica*, VII, 9, 2.

19. It is significant that Luther again translates the word *synagoge* (Rev. 2:9; 3:9) with *Schule* ("school"), whereas he chooses the word *Versammlung* ("assembly") in James 2:2. On the other hand, he consistently translates *ekklesia* with *Gemeine* ("congregation"), even when the word refers to a gathering of the *polis*, as in Acts 19:32, 39 f.

20. Cf. Stephanus, *Thesaurus Graecae Linguae*, VII, σύναξις. This is based on an aorist συνάξαι, which is not used in classical Greek (Luke 3:17). In pre-Christian times the word σύναξις was employed very rarely. Thus the church is obviously adopting a new coinage, corresponding to the newness of its situation implicit in its history of salvation. In the church's usage of language, the word σύναξις is first found in Origen. In Cyril of Jerusalem it is already firmly established. See the evidence in J. M. Hanssens, S. J., *Institutiones liturgicae de ritibus orientalibus*, II, Rome, 1930, pp. 25 f.

21. Cf. J. A. Jungmann, S. J., *Missarum Sollemnia*, I, 222.

22. Note the emphasis on this term in Apol., XXIV, 79.

23. Cf., e. g., the beautiful expression in Cyril of Jerusalem, *Catechetical Lectures*, 18, ch. 24; J. P. Migne, Series Graeca (MSG), 33, 1044: 'Εκκλησία δὲ καλεῖται φερωνύμως διὰ τὸ πάντας ἐκκαλεῖσθαι καὶ ὁμοῦ συνάγειν. ("The church is rightly called *ekklesia*, because it calls forth all men and assembles them in one place.")

24. To be sure, Pseudo-Dionysius Areopagita (around 500) already divorced the meaning of "*ekklesia* — assembly" from the term *synaxis*, which he uses for the Eucharist. He uses *synaxis* synonymously with *koinonia (communio)* and interprets it as the fellowship with the Head Christ, mediated to the individual Christian through the Eucharistic communion. It is not the Christians

who are brought together as *ekklesia*, but the communicant is united with the Savior by God through the sacrament. Cf. *De eccl. hier.*, III, 1 (MSG, 3, 424): To be sure, each sacrament leads our fragmented life to a uniform divineness (ἑκάστης ἱεροτελεστικῆς πραγματείας καὶ τὰς μεριστὰς ἡμῶν ζωὰς εἰς ἑνοειδῆ θέωσιν συναγούσης). But in the final analysis this unifying power derives from the Eucharist, which effects the bringing together and the uniting (συναγωγή) of the consecrated with the "One." Pachymeres (13th century) aptly explains this *synaxis*-concept of Pseudo-Dionysius in his paraphrase, MSG, 3, p. 452 B thus: *Synaxis* by no means refers to the assembly of the people (congregation), as some at present declare, but to the union and communion with God (τὴν πρὸς θεὸν συναγωγὴν καὶ κοινωνίαν). Similarly, 488 A.

25. Cf. ThWNT, III, 726 ff.

26. On the question regarding the worship character of these meals cf. Rudolf Stählin, "Die Geschichte des christlichen Gottesdienstes," *Leiturgia*, I (Kassel, 1954), 8 and 13 f.

27. Behm in ThWNT, III, 729, line 19. Outside the New Testament, "breaking of bread" is nowhere used in connection with the worship service. Cf. J. M. Hanssens, II, 23.

28. Cf. R. Stählin, p. 13, and the essay by O. Cullmann mentioned there. Gerhard Kunze also fully concurs with this thesis of Cullmann. Cf. *Monatsschrift für Pastoraltheologie* (MPTh), vol. 40 (1951), pp. 120 f. Also cf. G. Bornkamm, *Das Ende des Gesetzes*, p. 113, n. 2.

29. Also Clement, Letter 44, 2, uses *leiturgia* to designate the official ministrations of the bishops.

30. Cf. L. Eisenhofer, *Handbuch der katholischen Liturgie*, I (1932), 5. Hanssens, II, 33—36; E. Raitz v. Frentz, p. 78.

31. Cf. Du Cange, *Glossarium mediae et infimae Latinitatis*, II, 404b, and J. A. Jungmann, I, 221.

32. To be sure, the heathen who "fear God" (σεβόμενοι [τὸν θεόν]) are called *colentes [Deum]*: Acts 13:43; 16:14; 17:4; 18:4.

33. This view does not do justice to the phenomenon of the pagan *cultus;* however, it is widespread. Cf., e. g., Franz Rendtorff, *Die Geschichte des Gottesdienstes unter dem Gesichtspunkt der liturgischen Erbfolge*, 1914, p. 6. Also G. Kunze, "Gottesdienst nach evangelischem Verständnis," *Calwer Kirchenlexikon*, I (1937), 733b, still takes the same view; cf. MPTh, 40 (1951), 313. G. van der Leeuw begins to overcome this viewpoint in *Phänomenologie der Religion*, 1933, especially in par. 50: "Sacrifice," pp. 327 to 337; cf., e. g., pp. 331 f.: "The sacrifice, particularly the sacrifice of gifts, has now moved into a far wider context. It is no longer a commercial undertaking with the gods, corresponding to one carried on with man; it is no longer homage to God, such as is paid to princes. But it is a disclosure of a blessed source of the gifts. One gives and one receives, and it is impossible to say who is really the donor and who the recipient. Both share in the mightiness of the donated objects. Consequently, the donor does not occupy the center of the action, nor does the recipient, not even when he is a god or a godlike being. The center of the sacrificial act, the center of power, is the gift itself. It must be given, that is, it must be put into motion. . . . Instead of the rationalistic *do ut des*, we must say: *do ut possis dare*, I give you power so that you might have power and so that life does not stagnate for want of power."

34. G. van der Leeuw, p. 334.
35. E. Raitz v. Frentz, pp. 78 f., cites three places in which λειτουργός in the profane usage is translated with *liturgus* (in the *Codex Theodosianus*, in Firmius Maternus, and in Martianus Capella). *"Liturgia* is not used in the religious sense as a substitute for *cultus* or *sacra."* The reference to Augustine, *Enarrationes in Psalmos*, on Ps. 135(136):2 J. P. Migne, Series Latina (MSL), 37, 1757, proves that *liturgia* is here regarded as a Greek word and not as an adopted foreign word: "If therefore nowhere in the divine Word the holy angels are found to be referred to as gods, I think the best reason is that by that name men may not be induced to pay to the holy angels that ministry and service of religion which in Greek is called *liturgia* or *latria."* It was the scholarly work of Humanism that first captured the word *liturgia* for the West. In 1558 a writing by the Roman Catholic mediation-theologian Georg Cassander appeared under the title *Liturgica*. This was followed by Jacob Pamelius' *Liturgica Latinorum* (1571). Thus, the word *liturgia* was first introduced as a technical expression.
36. Cf. the many examples cited in the work by O. Casel mentioned in note 6 above.
37. Cf. R. Stählin in *Leiturgia*, I, 34 f., and the literature mentioned there.
38. Cf. Du Cange, VII, 448 ff., and RE³ [*Realencyklopädie für protestantische Theologie und Kirche*, 3d ed. (1896—1913)] VII, 7.
39. *Latreuein* is reproduced once (Rom. 1:25) by *servire* (together with *colere*, designating the pagan cult), once (Acts 26:7) with *deservire* (designating Israel's zealous, legalistic service to God).
40. Cf. Grimm's *Deutsches Wörterbuch*, II, 115, under "dienst."
41. Large Catechism, I, 16.
42. Ibid., III, 84.
43. Calvin uses the word *cultus* without any hesitation for the adoration of God encompassing all of life. But he seems to be hesitant about applying the same term to the congregation's assembly for worship. In the foreword to *La Forme des Prières et Chantz Ecclesiastiques*, 1542 (*Corpus Reformatorum*, 34, 166 ff.), he is obviously at pains to create a term for "worship" in the narrow sense, one which relates to the language of the New Testament. Thus he speaks, for example, of *les assemblées qui se font, tant le Dimanche que les autres iours, pour honnorer et servir Dieu* ("the assemblies which meet both on Sunday and on other days to honor and serve God"); or *noz assemblées spirituelles* ("our spiritual assemblies"); *l'assemblée Chrestienne* ("the Christian assembly"); or *les fideles, quand ils convienent au Nom de Jesus Christ* ("the faithful assembled in the name of Jesus Christ"); or *quand nous convenons en son Nom* ("when we come together in His name"). As in the New Testament, the concept of "assembly," or of "coming together," stands in the foreground. But Calvin, too, was evidently unable to fashion a fluent expression for colloquial speech by means of these paraphrases.
44. "Wörlitzer Predigt" (1532), WA 36, 354, 4 ff.
45. Cf. note 33. On the concept of the phenomenon manifesting itself, cf. G. van der Leeuw, *Phänomenologie*, p. 634 ff.
46. According to 1 Peter 3:18—4:6, also the victorious invasion of Christ into the realm of death might serve this confrontation; this is underscored especially by 4:6. This invasion of Christ has forever engraved its mark into the realm of the dead. That this mark becomes a kerygmatic confrontation with

Christ for those who died after Christ but never came in contact with the Gospel in this life, in some manner entirely foreign to the historical conditions of this life, can neither be disputed categorically nor be maintained as dogma.

47. Cf. my lecture "Der Ersterschaffene als Gottes Ebenbild", *Evangelische Theologie* (EvTh), 1951—52, pp. 298 ff. Cf. also E. Sartorius, *Über den alt- und neutestamentlichen Cultus* (Stuttgart, 1852), pp. 1—25; K. Barth, *Kirchliche Dogmatik*, III 1 (2d ed., 1947), particularly pp. 240—258; Luther, *Genesis-Vorlesung*, 1535 ff., particularly on Gen. 1, 26 ff., WA 42, 41 to 87; *Luther's Works* (St. Louis, 1958), 1, 55 ff.

48. E. Sartorius, p. 17.

49. Words of prayer and praise addressed to God can by no means be disclaimed for the prime creature. But since he still stands before the eschatological transformation of his physical existence, of his *vita animalis,* and since he consequently also stands under the commandments of God, which instruct him with regard to activities relative to the creatures, this oral prayer to God involves a special, time-filling, concrete act.

50. G. v. Rad, *Das Alte Testament Deutsch*, 2, on Gen. 2:1-3.

51. K. Barth, III 1, p. 242.

52. Cf. F. Delitzsch, *Commentar über die Genesis* (Leipzig, 1872), p. 109: "The blessing and hallowing must not be viewed from the perspective of the Mosaic legislation, as though it meant to say that God blessed in the future for that reason, etc. . . . The σαββατισμός of the Creator shall become the σαββατισμός of the creature; therefore He makes this day a perennial source of refreshment through His blessing and invests this seventh day by means of His hallowing it with a special glory for the creature here at the dawn of history."

53. The particular character of this day is also associated with the fact that God expects those special acts of prayer and praise not only from the individual but also from the people, planned from the beginning in the union of man and woman.

54. Cf. K. Barth, III 1, p. 255: "In the creaturely realm there is actually a correspondence to the day of rest observed by God and a repetition of it. As God with His rest following His work reserves to Himself His freedom for direct action and work, the possibility of His immediate self-witness, so man, too, must not be completely absorbed by his work; he, too, must pause at regular intervals — manifestly for the express purpose that he, on his part, may be ever free and accessible for that immediate self-witness of God, 'that you may know that I, the Lord, sanctify you' (Ex. 31:13; Ezek. 20:12). The very thing that would necessarily happen according to A. Ritschl's theology dare not come to pass: that man's life become one single workday of 'Weltanschauung and morality.' It is precisely this workday that is delimited by the 'day of the Lord.' And it is significant that this term may designate both the day of the epiphany and of the judgment of Jehovah, which terminates this eon (the Day of Judgment) and also this Sabbath. Furthermore, this Day of the Lord bears a particular name, whereas the others are not especially designated in the language of the Old Testament but, as is evident already from the report in Gen. 1, are differentiated only by numbers and are thus merely pre-days of this one day." — Note that the liturgical books of the Roman Catholic Church follow the same rule. Ordi-

narily, only the first day of the week bears a special name: *Dominica.* The remaining days are designated only with numbers: *Feria* II, III, etc.

55. WA 42, 80, 4; 110, 18 ff.: *Hoc verbum erat Adae Evangelium et lex, erat eius cultus, erat servitus et obedientia, quam poterat Deo in ista innocentia praestare* (*Luther's Works,* 1, 146: "For Adam this Word was Gospel and Law; it was his worship; it was his service and the obedience he could offer God in this state of innocence."). — Could it be accidental that, in view of the *status innocentiae,* "Gospel and Law" appear here in this sequence? Cf. WA 42, 79 ff. also on the following reflections.

56. WA 42, 71, 41, to 72, 4 (*Luther's Works,* 1, 94).

57. WA 42, 80, 19—34 (*Luther's Works,* 1, 105—106). This Sabbath-like laudation and thanksgiving of the paradisiacal man even has a "form," a liturgical "formula," which it follows! Ps. 148 and 149, in which sun, moon, stars, fish, and dragons are exhorted by man to praise God, are viewed as *quandam formam talis gratiarum actionis* ("a onetime formula of such thanksgiving").

58. On the extravagance of this worship, cf. the beautiful comment of Luther, WA 42, 71, 31 (*Luther's Works,* 1, 94): "Adam was created, *ut quasi ebrius esset leticia erga Deum* ('that he was, as it were, intoxicated with rejoicing toward God')."

59. Prior to Christ's birth, suffering, and death, there can be only signs among men to indicate that this one God-pleasing worship will one day come to earth and that it is already redemptively effective as seen from this future event.

60. Cf. the renunciation formula of the Baptism liturgy: *Abrenuntias satanae? Abrenuntio. Et omnibus operibus ejus? Abrenuntio. Et omnibus pompis ejus? Abrenuntio.* ("Do you renounce the devil?" "I renounce him." "And all his works?" "I renounce them." "And all his vanity?" "I renounce it.")

61. I refer the reader to the respective elaborations in the manuals on the theology of the Old Testament. To date Old Testament studies have not yielded a comprehensive monograph on the cultus in the Old Testament.

62. That does not exclude, but it includes, that God, even before Israel's election, had His witnesses among men who lived from the promise of His gracious coming. Gen. 4:26; 5:24; 6:8 ff. point that out. However, God's history with mankind receives its particular Messianic character with Israel's election.

63. With regard to the following, see the magnificent and profound insight which Fr. Delitzsch presented in his *Genesiskommentar* (Leipzig, 4th ed., 1872), pp. 227—284. Also see the important paragraph 40 in L. Köhler, *Theologie des Alten Testaments* (Tübingen, 1947), pp. 104—112. An important sector in this series of problems is treated by Martin Schmidt, *Prophet und Tempel. Eine Studie zum Problem der Gottesnähe im Alten Testament* (Zollikon-Zurich, 1948).

64. H. Wenschkewitz, "Die Spiritualisierung der Kultusbegriffe" (Angelos-Beiheft 4), 1932, p. 37, points to a tradition "according to which the second temple was entirely devoid of the Schekhina." To be sure, the words of Jesus in Matt. 23:21 presuppose the presence of God in the temple.

65. Cf. H. Wenschkewitz, p. 38.

66. L. Köhler, p. 170: "To make intelligible" here means to elucidate the elementary, history-of-religion sense. The history-of-salvation understanding cannot be brought about only by a history-of-religion elucidation.

67. P. 176. With regard to the placating odor, cf. Gen. 8:21; furthermore, the numerous passages in Leviticus and Numbers, where Luther translates *süszer Geruch* ("sweet odor") (see the concordance). Ezek. 5:13 is basic for the idea of placation.

68. W. Eichrodt, *Theologie des Alten Testaments*, I (Berlin, 1948), p. 74.

69. These facts were entirely overlooked by L. Köhler when he supplied the caption "Die Selbsterlösung des Menschen" for Israel's sacrificial service (p. 169). But W. Eichrodt, p. 73, writes: "As we know, the sacerdotal law attaches great importance to the fact that the atonement is provided and commanded by God Himself, and it anchors its effect in this divine order . . . Reconciliation does not depend on the plenitude of offerings and on the artistic composition of effective rites, but on the obedient performance of what the God of the covenant Himself has ordained for the maintenance of the covenant. That also eliminates any thought of a special meritoriousness inherent in the sacrifice; the sacrifice-apparatus, too, is the graciously bestowed gift of the God of the covenant, which affords man scope for making confession and for making amends."

70. Cf. W. Eichrodt, I, 213.

71. Cf. L. Köhler, pp. 171 ff., on the distinction between gift offering and communion offering.

72. Cf. H. Wenschkewitz, p. 93.

73. With regard to this and the following, cf. especially E. Lohmeyer, *Kultus und Evangelium* (Göttingen, 1942), pp. 33 ff.

74. E. Lohmeyer, pp. 34 f.

75. H. Wenschkewitz, p. 94.

76. Cf. E. Lohmeyer, pp. 44—51, for a convincing analysis of the story of the purification of the temple. The quotation is found on p. 48.

77. For the exegetical problems posed by these passages, consult, in addition to pertinent commentaries, especially H. Wenschkewitz, pp. 97—101; Ph. Vielhauer, *Oikodome* (diss. Heidelberg, 1939), pp. 63—70; E. Lohmeyer, pp. 76—79; W. Hahn, *Gottesdienst und Opfer Christi*, 1951, pp. 51—57; ThWNT, IV, p. 887, line 30, to p. 889, line 3; V, p. 141, lines 14—38.

78. In the apocryphal Ebionite Gospel (E. Hennecke, *Neutestamentliche Apokryphen* 2d ed., 1924, p. 45, No. 14) the following words are attributed to Jesus: "I have come to abolish sacrifices, and if you do not cease sacrificing, the wrath (of God) will not depart from you." These words, indeed, contain some truth. The epiphany of the Messiah does abolish the Old Testament sacrifices. On the other hand, it may be significant that these apocryphal words are not found in a canonical Gospel. The abolition of the sacrifices which Jesus effects must be understood, basically, as fulfillment. The Old Testament sacrifices are abolished only by being absorbed, as it were, into the sacrifice of Jesus. In Jesus' words recorded in Matt. 12:6: "Something greater than the temple is here," this plan-of-salvation relationship obtains a clear formulation, especially in Schlatter's commentary (1929), where he declares that "μεῖζον includes what the temple procures for the congregation, but surpasses it by that which Jesus gives it."

79. Cf., e. g., B. O. Michel, *Das Zeugnis des Neuen Testaments von der Gemeinde*, 1941, p. 56: "It seems that not only the οἰκοδομήσω of Matt. 16:38 and Mark 14:58 but also the σῶμα-conception point directly to the Easter-event, for through the 'new resurrection from the dead arises the temple of

His body' in the Johannine sense (John 2:20), and also in the synoptic sense (Mark 14:58)."

80. Ph. Vielhauer, p. 69.

81. Cf. especially 1 Peter 2:24; Eph. 2:11-22; also Rom. 7:4 fits into this context. Cf. furthermore the exposition of these passages in the chapter that is basic for the doctrine of worship in W. Hahn: "Die Teilhabe am gekreuzigten und auferstandenen Christusleib," pp. 50—73. In this section the following thesis is exegetically expounded in detail: "The body of Christ, sacrificed on the cross and raised from the dead at Easter . . . already encompasses the church" (p. 50). With a view to Rom. 7:4 and 1 Peter 2:24, the author declares: "In both events the dying of all of us is included in the death of the body of Jesus, and from this inclusion in the death of His body issues a new life for us" (p. 51). Also the thesis formulated on p. 59, stating that the "body of Christ" is in Paul's mind basically "the crucified body of Golgotha, in which the church already knows itself created and into which it knows itself incorporated," points in the same direction as our reflections do. Cf. furthermore p. 61: "This dying and rising of Christ, which create the new temple of God, already comprehend the entire temple which grows from it, the new congregation of the Spirit. . . . The new church and congregation is present in nuce in Christ's death and resurrection." Also cf. Heinrich Schlier, "Die Kirche nach dem Brief an die Epheser," in Beiträge zur Kontroverstheologie, I, pp. 84 f.: "The mythos of the heavenly first man, who comes down from heaven and collects the souls into his body and returns them to the pleroma, enabled our letter to apprehend and unfold the subject matter which it wants to clarify: that the church actually has its origin in the body of Christ, and that means in the physical and bloodily crucified body of Jesus Christ, which as such receives the redeemed into itself and bears them to God. . . . The mythos afforded the possibility to conceive of the Man Jesus, who is the Christ, as Him who in His being includes the being of the other men, re-presents them in Himself. . . . This body of Christ on the cross, this concrete, physical body of the Redeemer stretching to the heaven on the cross, who accords mankind reconciliation with God in Himself, is already potentially or also virtually the body of the church composed of Jews and Gentiles." — Perhaps it is immediately clear that this exposition by Hahn fundamentally approaches Schlier in his exposition of Eph. 2:14-16. That is of special interest, since Hahn arrived at his conclusions without any knowledge of these statements by Schlier.

82. The adherents of the so-called consistent eschatological interpretation of Jesus' proclamation, which was presented very impressively by A. Schweitzer, are of the opinion that Jesus expected the immediate breakthrough of God's kingdom to come with His death. They say that Jesus expected that His death would immediately bring about the factual end of this world and the factual re-creation of the new world of God. Thus He had expected no history of the world beyond His death, but the immediate eschatological transformation of all conditions, the immediate and complete presence of the kingdom of God. The fact that the church, placed into this earth's history, appeared on the scene instead of the kingdom of God, is said to have been contrary to Jesus' proclamation and expectation, as this church itself is here placed into sharp contrast to the kingdom of God. It may be assumed that this position is overcome today, even if it may still have isolated proponents. The most recent New Testament studies have clearly recognized the hidden presence of the kingdom of God in Jesus' person and work; they have further-

more elaborated that the church and God's kingdom are not two mutually exclusive realities but rather that the earthly church itself is an eschatological entity and includes a charismatic presence of God's kingdom. Finally it has become evident that the Messiah and His people, Christ and the church, are closely allied, and that in accord with Christ's conviction a certain period of time would elapse between His death and His early return in which His disciples would be gathered about Holy Communion as the eschatological congregation of the Christ. Among the more recent investigations of the problem dealing with the church and the kingdom of God in the New Testament cf. O. Michel, *Das Zeugnis des Neuen Testaments von der Gemeinde,* 1941, especially pp. 26—30, and W. G. Kümmel, *Kirchenbegriff und Geschichtsbewusztsein in der Urgemeinde und bei Jesus,* Zurich-Upsala, 1943.

83. Here it must be noted that God Himself acts in all that the church as such does. Just as the church is the work of God, it is also a tool in the hand of God.

84. Cf., e. g., W. G. Kümmel, pp. 27 ff.

85. But as Christ in His glorified corporeity is here also seen by His disciples, these Easter epiphanies are simultaneously a prototype of that final epiphany of Christ, of His Parusia, in which all the world will behold, must behold, Him in His glory. Insofar the coming of God's kingdom is already visibly placed before the disciples in these epiphanies.

86. John 20:22 is no "substitute" for Pentecost! In contradistinction to Pentecost, Christ Himself is visibly present in John 20:22. But the characteristic feature of Pentecost's gift of the Spirit consists in the very fact that Christ is really present in it without standing visibly in the midst of His own.

87. Cf. the following section on the anthropological place of worship.

88. Cf. E. Käsemann, "Kritische Analyse von Phil. 2, 5-11," ZThK, 47 (1950), pp. 349 f. and p. 359: "With this hymn the Christian congregation on earth, as it were, joins by way of response in the homage of the principalities in the divine throne room."

89. Begetting, conception, and gestation are here included in the term "birth."

90. Here a dogmatic deliberation on original sin might be necessary.

91. The heathen who are not reached by the message of Jesus Christ before their death are, to be sure, under the wrath of God, but for the sake of Jesus Christ they are also under the patience of God. Cf. n. 46 above on the question whether 1 Peter 3:18—4:6 intimates that after death also these heathen might perceive an echo of Christ's descent into hell and thus encounter also a kerygmatic form of Christ.

92. Cf. my lecture "Grundlegung der Tauflehre" in P. Brunner, "Aus der Kraft des Werkes Christi" (*Kirchl.-theol. Hefte,* IX), Munich, 1950.

93. Here it becomes clear that the questionable state of our confirmation practice casts its deep shadows on the worship of the church. The latter will first recover when the basic root from which it develops in its practice, confirmation, becomes sound. The exigency of the worship service is fundamentally the exigency of confirmation. As long as Baptism is not reflected practically in confirmation with regard to its power to set apart from the world and to implant into the *ekklesia,* little of the spiritual exigencies of our congregations in general and of their worship exigencies in particular will change. The sharp and incisive bounds of early Christian Baptism and of the saving power of these bounds dare not be wiped out by a baptism-and-confirmation prac-

tice. As long as the church itself by its practice contributes essentially to the obscuration and blurring of the Baptismal bounds, the basic root of its worship exigency will not be removed. On the other hand, a recognition and a beginning of a spiritual breakthrough of what really takes place in worship will also stress the significance of the Baptismal bounds in doctrine and practice.

94. Cf. E. Peterson, "Von den Engeln," *Theologische Traktate*, 1951, pp. 360, 376, 381; K. Barth, *Kirchliche Dogmatik*, III, 3, p. 565.

95. Cf. E. Peterson, pp. 333 f.; K. Barth, III, 3, p. 545.

96. Cf. the text of the Preface: "Therefore with angels and archangels and with all the company of heaven we laud and magnify Thy glorious name, evermore praising Thee and saying: Holy. . . ." This formulation implies that the worship of the angels precedes that of the church, that it serves as a pattern, and that it is superior to the worship of the church. At the same time it reflects that God already incorporates the worship of the church, in answer to its petition, into the worship of the angels, vouchsafing an invisible and yet real communication between celestial and terrestrial worship.

97. Also cf. K. Barth, III, 3, p. 540: "It first happens in heaven and then on earth that God is praised by the creature, that He finds His creatural correspondence and witnesses. He found them in heaven before He found even a single one on earth. There they live for Him in profusion and perfection, even when there are seemingly, or really, but a few on earth, and when these all are but poor witnesses. And because His kingdom comes from there to here, provision is made that He will always have many and true witnesses also here in those who come here with Him from there, namely, in the existence of His strong angels who are active and present in their full number, willingness, and readiness, also where the earthly creature falls behind both in the quantity and quality of its praise, and in view of whom the seemingly or really sad state of affairs on earth may never and nowhere be adjudged unbearable and hopeless." Furthermore p. 552: "Wherever the praying congregation of saints is found on earth, there the angels, too, are found (1 Cor. 11:10). And where the angels are, there are, as these are turned toward the earth, also — and therefore the golden bowls in their hands — the prayers of the saints."

98. W. Hadorn, *Die Offenbarung des Johannes*, 1928, on 5:13.

99. Is. 44:23. German translation according to B. Duhm, *Das Buch Jesaia*, 4th ed., 1922.

100. Ps. 96:11-13. German translation according to H. Gunkel, *Die Psalmen*, 1926. Ps. 98:7-9 presents a parallel.

101. H. Gunkel comments with regard to the quoted prophetic passages and the psalms he is about to mention: "The prophets speak of the future, the psalmists of the present." (Gunkel-Begrich, *Einleitung in die Psalmen*, 1933, p. 36)

102. Ps. 19:2 f. German translation according to Gunkel's Commentary.

103. Does this difficult verse 3 state that the mysterious, extravagant language of the cosmos contains "no words, no speech," that its sound is not heard with our physical ear (thus Gunkel)? Or does it mean to say in accord with the translation current since the Septuagint that this wonderful speech of the cosmos is heard in all the languages of humankind despite its "soundlessness" (thus Weiser in AT Deutsch, Vol. 14)? On the basis of v. 4 it must, of course, be said that this cosmic voice fills all the earth. It is equally certain

that this voice is not one of the historical languages. Rather, this cosmic language transcends all national languages, it is truly ecumenical: εἰς πᾶσαν τὴν γῆν ἐξῆλθεν ὁ φθόγγος αὐτῶν καὶ εἰς τὰ πέρατα τῆς οἰκουμένης τὰ ῥήματα αὐτῶν. In the ecumenicity with which this voice transcends the national tongues it is related to the voice of the church, which by no means elevates one of the national languages to the status of a sacred language but enters all languages and thus pervades them all.

104. German translation according to Gunkel's Commentary. — In N. P. Kondakov, "L'icone russe," II (Prague, 1929), Plate 97, a Russian icon of the 17th century from the Russian Museum is depicted, which presents a most impressive commentary on our psalm. The icon is called: "Praise the name of the Lord!" It portrays the exalted Lord as the recipient of the cosmic liturgy united with the liturgy of the church. Obviously, the painter adapted the icon down to its details to Ps. 148. But this icon also expresses most strikingly the basic thought of our deliberations on the cosmological place of Christian worship. I am indebted to Prof. L. A. Zander of the Sergius-Institut in Paris for this information. (A reproduction of this icon forms the frontispiece for *Leiturgia*, I.)

105. B. Duhm, on Is. 44:23.

106. H. Gunkel's Commentary, on Ps. 118.

107. K. Barth, *Kirchliche Dogmatik*, III, 3, pp. 538 f.

108. Ibid., III, 2, p. 206.

109. Shakespeare, *The Merchant of Venice*, V, 1, quoted in a German translation (A. W. v. Schlegel) by Gunkel in his exposition of Ps. 19:4.

110. Here we call attention to Luther's comment, which moves Ps. 148 back into the Garden of Eden (cf. n. 57 above). Adam has the authority to exhort the earthly creatures to praise God only because he faces them as their master by God's commission. Therefore the nonhuman, earthly creature will arrive at the fulfillment of its worship only by man's leadership in the praise of God.

111. Cf. Anders Nygren, *Commentary on Romans*, trans. Carl C. Rasmussen (Philadelphia, 1949), pp. 335 f.

112. Cf. Luther's Large Catechism, II, 54 f.

113. Cf., e. g., Justin, *Apology* I, 65.

114. Cf. P. Graff, *Geschichte der Auflösung*, I, 213 ff.

115. Cf. the Gregorian Christmasday collect for the second mass: . . . *qui nova incarnati verbi tui luce perfundimur* (". . . as the new light of Thy incarnate Word is shed upon us, . . .").

116. Apol., XXIV, 18.

117. Ibid., 25.

118. Ibid., 33.

119. Ibid., 18.

120. E. Sartorius, *Über den alt- und neutestamentlichen Cultus*, 1852, pp. 51 f. and 117 f.; Th. Harnack, *Praktische Theologie*, I (1877), pp. 267 ff., 413 ff., et passim; C. A. G. von Zezschwitz, *System der praktischen Theologie* (Leipzig, 1876), pp. 30, 60 ff., 132, 250, 259 ff., et passim.

121. WA 49, 588, 15—18. In Rörer's transcript Luther's words read: "ut da hin gericht, ut nihil in ea fiat quam ut ipse nobiscum loquatur per verbum et nos per orationem et lobgesang" (ibid., 4 f.). Cf. furthermore the Large Cate-

chism, I, 84; lecture on Genesis, WA 43, 564, 6—18; Lecture on the Gradual Psalms, WA 40, III, 90, 10—102, 4.

122. Cf., e. g., P. Althaus, *Das Wesen des evangelischen Gottesdienstes*, 2d ed. (1932), pp. 22 f.

123. This danger is clearly seen in K. Handrich, "Das Wesen des Gottesdienstes," EvTh., vol. 1949/50, p. 369.

124. The Erlangen liturgical studies have always been very sensitive to this in-each-other of the two sides. Cf. E. Sartorius, p. 52; Th. Harnack, pp. 268 f., 415.

125. M. Doerne, "Grundlagen und Gegenwartsfragen evangelischen Gottes-dienstes," *Musik und Kirche*, 14 (1942), p. 63.

126. Cf. J. Horst, "Proskynein. Zur Anbetung im Urchristentum nach ihrer reli-gionsgeschichtlichen Eigenart," *Neutest. Forsch.*, III, 2 (Gütersloh, 1932), especially pp. 186 f., 193 f., 199 f., 273 f.

127. Cf. P. Brunner, "Schrift und Tradition," *Schriften des Theol. Konventes Augsb. Bekenntnisses*, Pamphlet 2 (Berlin-Spandau, 1951).

128. Cf. N. A. Dahl, "Anamnesis. Mémoire et Commemoration dans le christi-anisme primitif," in *Studia Theologica* (1947), pp. 69 ff.

129. O. Schmitz, *Die Bedeutung des Wortes bei Paulus* (1927), p. 28.

130. Cf. Luther, Large Catechism, II, 38 f.

131. Th. Harnack, p. 417.

132. Cf. H. Asmussen, *Die Lehre vom Gottesdienst* (Munich, 1937), pp. 58 ff., especially pp. 61 f.

133. Cf. Th. Harnack, p. 432: "Reduced to its core," the sermon "is a great, gen-eral absolution, and its sacramental character is rooted in this circumstance."

134. WA 18, 202, 32—203, 2; 203, 27—204, 4.

135. WA 12, 213, 7—11.

136. That the Lord wants to be "with me" (Gen. 26:3) is "the simplest and yet the most perfect expression of the fact" that the blessing of the Lord is meant for me. Cf. ThWNT, II, p. 754. The peace of the Lord, which the *Pax Domini* lays on the congregation, is also the last word in the Aaronic blessing.

137. W. Foerster on Luke 10:5 f. and Matt. 10:13 in ThWNT, II, 412.

138. WA 43, 524, 32 to 525, 26: Neque vero haec benedictio inanis tantum sonus verborum est, aut verbalis quaedam imprecatio, qua alius alii bona dicit et comprecatur, ut cum dico: Det tibi Deus sobolem pulchram et morigeram. Haec verba sunt tantum optativa, quibus nihil alteri confero, sed tantum exopto, estque benedictio pure eventualis et incerta. Haec vero benedictio Patriarchae Isaac est indicativa et certa in futurum. Non est exoptatio, sed donatio boni, qua dicit: Accipe haec dona, quae verbis promitto. . . . In scriptura sancta autem sunt reales benedictiones, non imprecativae tantum, sed indicativae et constitutivae, quae hoc ipsum, quod sonat re ipsa largiun-tur et adferunt. Cuiusmodi etiam nos in novo Testamento habemus per sacerdotium Christi, quod est nostra benedictio, cum dico: accipe absolu-tionem peccatorum tuorum. Si dicerem: utinam essent tibi remissa peccata, utinam esses bonus et in gratia Dei: aut precor tibi gratiam, misericordiam, regnum aeternum et liberationem a peccatis, haec charitatis benedictio dici posset. Sed benedictio promissionis et fidei et praesentis doni haec est: Ego absolvo te a peccatis tuis in nomine patris et filii et spiritus sancti, hoc est, reconcilio animam tuam cum Deo, aufero a te iram et indignationem Dei, et

constituo te in gratiam, do tibi haereditatem vitae aeternae et regnum coelorum. Ista omnia sunt potestatis praesenter et vere tibi donantis, si credis, quia non sunt opera nostra, sed Dei per ministerium nostrum. Non igitur benedictiones imprecativae sunt, sed collativae. . . . Iudaei nimis frigide has benedictiones tractant, tantum enim accipiunt eas more humano et modo optativo: non in definitiva sententia: Benedictio vero talis sententia est, quae definit et concludit aliquid, *ein entlicher spruch oder urtheil.* — "But this benediction is not a mere empty sound of words or a kind of wordy prayer by which one person wishes and prays down blessings upon another, as when I say: 'May God grant you handsome and obedient children.' These are only wishful words, by which I confer nothing on another person but only express a wish, and this is merely a probable and uncertain benediction. But this benediction of the patriarch Isaac is definite and sure for the future. This is not a wish for a blessing but a bestowal of it, in which he says: 'Receive these gifts which I promise in words.' . . . In Holy Scripture, benedictions are realistic; not merely wishful, but definite and effective, for they present and bestow in actual fact the very thing that is named. This type we, too, have in the New Testament through the priesthood of Christ, for this is our benediction when I say: 'Receive the forgiveness of your sins.' If I said, 'Oh, that your sins might be forgiven; oh, that you might be good and under God's grace; I pray for grace, pity, the eternal kingdom, and release from your sins': this could be called the benediction of love. But the benediction of promise, faith, and the actual gift is this: 'I absolve you from your sins in the name of the Father and of the Son and of the Holy Spirit, that is, I reconcile your spirit to God, I remove from you the anger and wrath of God, I establish you in grace, I give you the inheritance of eternal life and the kingdom of heaven.' All these gifts are a matter of ready power and belong truly to Him who gives them to you, if you believe, because they are not our works but works of God through our ministry. They are therefore not blessings prayed for but blessings bestowed upon you. . . . The Jews treat these blessings too coldly, for they receive them only in the manner of men and the wishful manner, not in the decisive sense. But a benediction is a judgment which makes definite and establishes something, a final, decisive sentence or judgment."

Also cf. E. Stauffer, "Zur sakramentalen Bedeutung des kirchlichen Segens" in *Viva Vox Evangelii, Festschrift für H. Meiser* (Munich, 1951), pp. 324—334.

139. H. Holzinger's comment is significant, "Numeri," *Kurzer Hand-Commentar zum Alten Testament,* ed. K. Marti (Tübingen and Leipzig, 1903), p. 29, on Num. 6:27: "Indubitably verse 27b expresses the opinion that the priestly blessing is not only intercession, but that it, somewhat akin to the absolution of the Catholic priest, has exhibitive significance," as if the exhibitive conception of the Absolution and the Blessing were not of central significance for Luther's theology.

140. Note the pertinent formulations of Th. Harnack, p. 436: "To be sure, the receipt and the result of the blessing presuppose subjective conditions, but where these are present, they do not first make the blessing exhibitive. It is that already per se by virtue of divine power. But they are the condition without which one is not only unable to receive the exhibited salutarily, but without which it is also converted into its opposite, because God's Word and promise always operate critically."

141. Th. Harnack, p. 481.

142. To mention only a few hymns which mark the psalm hymn of the New Covenant particularly clearly as bearers of the proclamation of the Word, we select the following in the EKG: Nos. 1, 15, 17, 21, 47, 76, 77, 132, 239. Self-evidently, also among the *Psalm-Lieder*, Nos. 176—200, outstanding examples of the proclaiming song are found. As proof that the charisma of psalm poetry is not extinct at present, we refer the reader to Nos. 14 (Klepper), 35 (Müller-Osten), 133 (R. A. Schröder).

143. Cf. his essay: *Die drei Symbola oder Bekenntnis des Glaubens Christi*, 1538, WA 50, 262—283, especially 265, 39 ff.

144. Ibid., 263, 9 ff.: "It is . . . a fine symbol or confession (whoever the author may be) fashioned into a song, which is adapted not only for the confession of the true faith, but also for praising and thanking God."

145. The fact that Luther placed the Agnus among the hymns of praise (WA 30, II, 615, 3—6) can be explained in view of this element of hymnic form. Luther, too, evidently has the hymnic relative clause in mind, when he says in the passage in question: "Therefore it clearly sings about Christ and praises Him for bearing our sin; and with beautiful and few words it mightily and charmingly sets forth the memory of Christ." Cf. Th. Knolle, *Die Eucharistiefeier und der lutherische Gottesdienst* (Erlangen, 1939), p. 29.

146. Letter of Clement, Ch. 59. The passage is all the more significant since Clement does not quote a fixed formula here but concludes his letter to the Corinthians in the manner in which he was wont to pray in the worship service following the sermon. The hymnlike part is significantly an expansion of the address in the prayer and reads: ". . . who hast opened the eyes of our heart that we may know Thee,

    The only Most High in the heights,
    The Holy One, resting in the sanctuary,
    Who subdues the pride of the haughty,
    Who brings the designs of the heathen to naught,
    Who kills and saves and creates life,
    The one Benefactor of the spirits and God of all flesh,
    Who peers into the abyss,
    Who watches over the works of man,
    The Helper in danger,
    The Savior in despair,
    The Creator and Guardian of every spirit,
    Who peoples the nations on earth
    And from among all hast elected those who love Thee," . . .

Regarding this text, cf. Ed. Frh. von der Goltz, *Das Gebet in der ältesten Christenheit* (1901), pp. 197 ff.

147. *Kollekten-Gebete für die Sonn- und Feiertage des Kirchenjahres* (Neuendettelsau: Luth. Lit. Konferenz Deutschlands, 1951), Nos. 5, 6, 7, 39. The hymnic relative clause is found in more than 70 of the 129 collects in this pamphlet.

147a. Cf. *Agende für evangelisch-lutherische Kirchen und Gemeinden, Das Ordinarium*, prepared by the Luth. Lit. Konferenz and the literary committee of VELKD (Berlin, 1952), pp. 68 f.

148. Cf. N. A. Dahl, *Anamnesis*, p. 82, note 1, and p. 86, note 1.

149. According to N. A. Dahl, pp. 85 f., the "proclaiming" in 1 Cor. 11:26 is carried out in the "consecrating" of the bread and the cup. Also cf. J. Schniewind's conception of this passage in ThWNT, I, 70, 22 ff.

150. Cf., e. g., E. Molland, *Das paulinische Evangelion* (Oslo, 1934), p. 59; G. Friedrich, ThWNT, II, 717, 13 ff.

151. 1 Cor. 3 and 4 clearly show that the apostle, his colaborers, and his successors may be viewed collectively in the service of proclamation and of doctrine as incumbents of the same office. Cf. also Melanchthon, "Tractatus de potestate papae," 10 f.

152. G. v. Rad, *Das formgeschichtliche Problem des Hexateuchs* (1938), pp. 25 f.

153. A. Weiser, *Die Psalmen,* I (1950), pp. 12 f. Also cf. pp. 14 f. The details of many a question in this matter may still remain unsettled, but the decisive knowledge regarding the function of the sacred Word to bring into the present and to witness to the story of salvation, may be regarded as assured. Also cf. W. Marxsen, "Repräsentation im Abendmahl?" in MPTh, 41 (1952), 72 f.

154. Pesachim, X, 5, quoted in P. Billerbeck *Kommentar zum Neuen Testament aus Talmud und Midrasch,* IV, 68.

155. W. Marxsen, p. 72.

156. Cf. R. Asting, *Die Verkündigung des Wortes im Urchristentum* (1939), pp. 742 f.

157. Large Catechism, II, 38 f.

158. O. Schmitz, p. 17.

159. R. Bultmann, *Theologie des Neuen Testaments* (Tübingen, 1938 ff.), pp. 297 and 303.

160. Large Catechism, II, 38.

161. O. Schmitz, p. 18.

162. Cf. Luther, *Auslegung deutsch des Vaterunsers für die einfältigen Laien* (1519), WA 2, 113, 35 ff.: "Now you see what the facts are regarding this daily bread, that Christ truly is this bread. But He is of no use to you, nor can you avail yourself of Him unless God changes Him into words, so that you might hear Him and thus know Him. For what does it help you that He sits in heaven or that He is in the form of bread? He must be dissolved, prepared, and changed into words through the internal and external word; see, that is, then, truly God's Word. Christ is the bread, God's Word is the bread, and yet a thing, a bread. Then He is in the word and the word is in Him, and to believe in the same Word means to eat the bread. And he whom God grants this lives eternally."

163. J. Jeremias, *Die Abendmahlsworte Jesu,* 2d ed. (1949), p. 112.

164. Cf. E. Lohmeyer, *Das Evangelium des Markus* (Göttingen, 1947), pp. 302 to 310, especially pp. 308 f. This basic thought of Lohmeyer was already expressed by Th. Zahn, *Das Evangelium des Matthäus,* 4th ed. (1922), p. 695, on Matt. 26:29: "The food and the drink which He [Jesus] has now prepared for His disciples, without partaking of it Himself, no longer reflects the character of the previous table fellowship of Jesus with His disciples, nor does it bear the character of their future communion in the kingdom of glory, but it belongs, both in its character and in its idea, into the time of the separation between Jesus' death and His parousia. It is a meal of the congregation that is waiting for its Lord."

165. Cf., e. g., the proofs in J. Jeremias, pp. 108—111.

166. Cf. K. G. Kuhn, "Über den ursprünglichen Sinn des Abendmahls und sein Verhältnis zu den Gemeinschaftsmahlen der Sektenschrift," EvTh, vol. 1950

to 51, pp. 508—527, especially pp. 510 and 514 f. Kuhn's statement "that the much debated question: Was Jesus' last meal a Passover meal, or was it not? is not at all relevant to the interpretation of the significative words and of Holy Communion" seems correct to us. On the other hand, the conclusion on p. 520 does not sound plausible. If Mark 14:22-24 presupposes the framework of a fellowship meal, then Jesus' institution is also in this event a recasting of a meal which is already molded ritually, and which as such points to a repetition.

167. J. Jeremias, p. 115.
168. See the references in J. Jeremias, p. 116. N. A. Dahl stresses, p. 73, that the commemoration played a large role already at Jesus' time also in the synagogal liturgy. See above all the informative material in Bo Reicke, *Diakonie, Festesfreude und Zelos,* Uppsala-Wiesbaden, 1951. Bo Reicke considers it very probable "that Jesus Himself spoke of His anamnesis in the last night" (p. 261).
169. Cf. J. Schniewind, ThWNT, I, 70, 22 ff.
170. N. A. Dahl, pp. 82; 85 f.
171. Cf. R. Otto, *Reich Gottes und Menschensohn* (Munich, 1934), pp. 253 f.; and above all K. Galling, "Hesekiel," *Hdb. z. AT,* 13 (Tübingen, 1936), pp. 16 ff.; W. Rudolph, "Jeremiah," *Hdb. z. AT,* 12 (Tübingen, 1947), p. 110; also V. Herntrich, "Der Prophet Jesaja," *AT Deutsch,* 17 (Göttingen, 1950), pp. 154 f., on Is. 8:18.
172. Very likely R. Otto was the first to call attention to this connection of Jesus' institution of Holy Communion with the cultic anamnesis of Israel and Jewry. He did this in his essay "Vom Abendmahl Christi," which appeared in the *Christliche Welt* in 1917 and was reprinted in *Sünde und Urschuld* (Munich, 1932), pp. 96—122. Here and there these elaborations by Otto require many a correction; but his insights regarding the anamnesis-event, pp. 106 f., 113, 117, 120 f., may really be termed a prophetic anticipation of the results of an investigation which, in detail, is still in progress today, the basic thought of which (rendering the salvation-event present through cultic anamnesis) may be assumed, however, as firmly established.
173. R. Otto, *Reich Gottes und Menschensohn,* p. 255.
174. R. Otto in *Sünde und Urschuld,* p. 121.
175. It is perhaps an enduring fruit of S. Mowinkel's statements in *Psalmenstudien,* II, which, in other respects, are surely problematical and unclear, that he showed the association of the eschatological expectation with the cultic event.
176. Cf. Bo Reicke, pp. 177 ff.
177. J. Jeremias, p. 105; Th. Zahn, pp. 697 f.
178. E. Lohmeyer, *Das Evangelium des Markus* (Göttingen, 1937), p. 306, against Jeremias, who, to be sure, retains the application to the food, but looks for a *tertium comparationis* to stand mediatingly between bread and body, wine and blood (". . . with the bread the fact that it is broken, with the wine it is the red color," p. 106). Thus Jeremias again reverts to an effective symbolic act.
179. W. G. Kümmel's assertion (Lietzmann-Kümmel, "An die Korinther I, II," *Hdb. z. NT,* 9 [Tübingen, 1949], p. 182) that Paul used the words "the body of Christ" unexceptionally in the sense of the "mystical" body of Christ, the congregation, and that he used "body of His flesh" when he meant the earthly body of Christ (Col. 1:12) is hardly tenable in the face of Rom. 7:4. The

attempt to place the "mystical" body of Christ over against the historical body of His flesh might in any case be problematical. No one will question that there is a difference between Christ's historical body of the flesh and His transformed and divinely derestricted resurrection body with regard to the mode of its being. But this difference does not eliminate the identity. Through the pathway on which God walked from Good Friday to Easter the "historical" and the "mystical" body of Christ are one also for Paul. Cf. W. Hahn, *Gottesdienst und Opfer* (Göttingen, 1951), pp. 58 f., 64, 68, 73. Cf. also H. Schlier, *Die Kirche im Epheserbrief* (1949), pp. 85, 87 ff. Therefore the contrasting of "partaking of the Lord's Supper" and "partaking of the elements," stressed by W. G. Kümmel, which reflects his contrasting of Christ's mystical body and His historical body of the flesh, is untenable. Paul's doctrine of Holy Communion cannot be summarized in the following sentence: "The participation in the Lord's Supper, and not the partaking of the elements, makes the Christian a real partaker of the body of Christ (Kümmel means: of the "mystical" body of Christ) and of the effect of His death for His congregation" (Kümmel, p. 182). It is surely true that the participation in the Lord's Supper and in particular the partaking of the Eucharistic food confirms the Christians ever anew as members of Christ's body, which they became through Baptism (1 Cor. 12:13), and ever makes them as such members in the structure of Christ's body, and thus actually ever builds the body of Christ itself. It is also true that participation in the Lord's Supper, which includes partaking of the Eucharistic food, permits the Christians actually to share in the redemptive effect of Christ's death. But it is not true that these statements adequately describe Paul's doctrine of Holy Communion. In spite of everything Paul did not delete Jesus' words referring to the cup even in his interpreting and expanding doctrine of Holy Communion (1 Cor. 11:27). The latter cannot be formulated without the inclusion of the words relative to the cup. The partaking of Jesus' blood, mediated by the drinking of the cup, undoubtedly includes, as a gift of grace, participation in the redemptive effect which Jesus' death has for the congregation; however, it cannot be confined to it, but it is participation in the blood of Jesus itself which was shed for us. Whoever receives the Eucharistic food in the Lord's Supper "in an unworthy manner" is guilty not only of Christ's "body," which constitutes itself in Holy Communion, but also of His blood (1 Cor. 11:27). On this point the essay by E. Käsemann, "Anliegen und Eigenart der paulinischen Abendmahlslehre," EvTh, 1947/48, pp. 263—283, which W. G. Kümmel cites in corroboration of his idea, is manifestly more penetrating. Page 274 asserts, relative to 1 Cor. 11:27, that bread and body of the Lord and that cup and blood of the Lord are identical here "in a mysterious manner." In view of the end of v. 29, it does not seem possible for E. Käsemann "to refer τὸ σῶμα (the body) to anything but the element in Holy Communion" (p. 277). It is surely correct to say — and E. Käsemann does not deny this — that the presence of this body includes the presence of the *ekklesia*-body and therefore must also include the agape and all that pertains to a "worthy" reception. But that does not eliminate the real connection of the bread with Jesus' death-body and of the wine with Jesus' sacrificial blood. It is therefore surprising to hear W. G. Kümmel declare that it is wrong to assume that the Christian, according to Paul, "receives the blood in the wine, the body of the Lord in the bread (p. 181. Lietzmann, especially also H. Seesemann). Cf. G. Bornkamm, "Zum Verständnis des Gottesdienstes bei Paulus," in "Das Ende des Gesetzes, Paulusstudien" (EvTh, Vol. 16 [1952], pp. 119 ff., especially p. 121: "Christ's body, which was given into death and which we receive, makes us, as the recipients, the σῶμα (body) of the congregation."

180. J. Jeremias, p. 105.

181. This was recently stressed again by W. Marxsen, in his dissertation on "Die Einsetzungsberichte zum Abendmahl," pp. 204, 210.

182. Cf. E. Gaugler, "Das Abendmahl im NT," especially p. 45, in W. Marxsen, p. 203.

183. Cf. J. Jeremias, p. 105.

184. H. Sasse, "Das Abendmahl im NT," in *Vom Sakrament des Altars* (1941), p. 69.

185. Luther rightly questioned the presence of Christ's body and blood in the Roman private mass, because a decisive element of conformity to the institution is absent there: distribution and meal. Cf. the proofs in H. Grasz, *Die Abendmahlslehre bei Luther und Calvin* (Gütersloh, 1940), p. 107. In the Roman mass, in which the congregation communes, Luther perceived Christ's institution still preserved, although in a distorted form, and therefore he did not dispute the real presence there. Cf. H. Grasz, p. 109.

186. Cf. P. Brunner, *Aus der Kraft des Werkes Christi* (1950), pp. 45—47. The affirmation of the Formula of Concord (S. D., VII, 83) also remains basic: "The command of Christ: 'This do!' (which embraces the entire action or administration in this sacrament, that in an assembly of Christians bread and wine are taken, consecrated, distributed, received, eaten, drunk, and the Lord's death is shown forth at the same time) must be observed unseparated and inviolate."

187. The statement that bread and wine are not Christ's body and blood *extra usum* is correct. But it is wrong to limit the *usus* of the sacrament to the act of distribution and reception. The *usus* is the entire act conforming to Christ's institution. In this act, the real presence has a concrete duration, also according to Luther, both before and after receipt of the "consecrated" food. Cf. H. Grasz, p. 109 f.: "There can hardly be a doubt that Luther recognized a real presence *ante* and *post sumptionem.*" Also the Formula of Concord declines to confine the *usus* to the oral consumption (S. D., VII, 85 f.).

188. Cf. the letters to Simon Wolferius in Eisleben of July 4 and 20, 1543, in WA *Briefe*, 10, 336 ff. and 347 ff.; also H. Grasz, pp. 113 ff.

189. Cf. the text quoted by H. Grasz from Th. Kolde, *Analecta Lutherana* (1883), p. 223.

190. E. Lohmeyer, p. 304. Also see T. F. Torrance, "Eschatology and the Eucharist" in *Intercommunion,* ed. D. Baillie and J. Marsh (London, 1952), pp. 303—350. This important treatise first became available to me during my revision of the text. In numerous points the view of T. F. Torrance coincides with our own attempt to clarify the salvation-event in Holy Communion. Especially in the plan-of-salvation conception, and thus in the eschatological conception, of the sacrament is there far-reaching agreement. Admittedly, in the doctrine of the real presence the agreement is sadly interrupted.

191. Cf. Bo Reicke, *Diakonie, Festesfreude und Zelos in Verbindung mit der altchristlichen Agapenfeier,* Uppsala-Wiesbaden, 1951.

192. Cf. Bo Reicke, pp. 186 f.

193. This insight is gaining ground more and more. Cf., e. g., E. Schweizer, "Das Abendmahl, eine Vergegenwärtigung des Todes Jesu oder ein eschatologisches

Freudenmahl?" in *Theol. Zeitschrift*, 1946, pp. 81 ff., where "the absolute necessity of belonging together for both types of Holy Communion" is stressed (p. 100). The treatise of Bo Reicke cited above also clarifies the close relation of these two points, especially on pp. 244 ff. and 291 f.

194. Cf. E. Käsemann, EvTh., 1947/48, pp. 273 f.; G. Bornkamm, *Das Ende des Gesetzes*, p. 112; Bo Reicke, pp. 264 ff. and 278 ff.

195. Cf. the proofs in J. Jeremias, p. 118.

196. Cf. W. Marxsen, MPTh, p. 71.

197. O. Michel in ThWNT, IV, 678, 26 f.

198. Here we have tried to pick up the factor of truth contained in the quite untenable explanation which J. Jeremias, pp. 115—118, assigns to Jesus' anamnesis-command (". . . so that God might remember me"). At the same time we have penetrated to the boundary line where a deep gulf separates our doctrine of Holy Communion from the Roman Catholic Church's doctrine of the sacrifice of the mass. Where a presentation of the one-time and nonrepeatable sacrifice of Jesus Christ on the cross by the church — that is to say, concretely by the priest — is taught, where, accordingly, Holy Communion is conceived of as a sacrifice offered by the church through the priest and is thus presented to God, there, in contradiction of the apostolic Word, the intercessory act of Christ is identified with the intercessory act of the church, and Christ's honor is impugned.

199. Cf. H. Lietzmann, *Messe und Herrenmahl* (1926), p. 257.

200. H. Sasse, *Vom Sakrament des Altars*, p. 60.

201. Cf. G. Bornkamm, "Das Anathema in der urchristlichen Abendmahlsliturgie," in ThLZ, 1950, col. 227. In revised and expanded form, this essay appeared in the aforementioned "Paulusstudien" of the author's *Das Ende des Gesetzes*, pp. 123 ff.

202. On this doctrine of the effects of Baptism, cf. P. Brunner, "Die evangelischlutherische Lehre von der Taufe," *Luthertum*, Pamphlet 4 (Berlin, 1951), especially pp. 39 f.

203. Cf. G. Bornkamm, *Das Ende des Gesetzes*, p. 122: to distinguish the body means "to apprehend the meaning of the sacrament correctly, namely, to conceive of Christ's body as His body given for us, which unites the recipients into the body of the church and thus makes them responsible one to the other."

204. Cf. p. 119.

205. Cf. the elaborations of W. Elert on "Das liturgische Wir" in *Das christliche Ethos* (Tübingen, 1949), pp. 467 ff., especially p. 470.

206. Cf. the numerous proofs in Köhler-Baumgartner, *Lexicon in Veteris Testamenti libros* (Leiden, 1948 ff.), under "jadah," pp. 363 f. While the Vulgate may use the same word *(confiteri)* for "to confess sins" and "to praise God," corresponding to the Hebrew, Luther must choose a special word for the second meaning: as a rule he expresses this with *dem Herrn danken* ("to thank the Lord").

207. On the concept of confession in the New Testament cf. O. Michel in ThWNT, V, 206 ff., especially 210, 36 ff.

208. With regard to the term Acclamation, cf. especially E. Peterson, ΕΙΣ ΘΕΟΣ, 1926.

209. Cf. F. Kattenbusch, "Die Entstehung einer christlichen Theologie" in ZThK, NF, Vol. 11 (1930), pp. 161 ff.

210. The claim that the Sanctus first becomes a hymn of praise on the lips of the monks, and is merely acclamation on the lips of the congregation (Cf. E. Peterson, "Von den Engeln," *Theologische Traktate*, p. 356), can surely not be reconciled with the New Testament concept of the *ekklesia*.

211. In the mass-liturgies of the Eastern Church, the Sanctus, sung by the choir, is designated as the "Hymn of Victory." Cf. Storf-Schermann, "Griechische Liturgien," *Bibl. d. Kirchenväter*, Vol. 5 (1912), p. 104 ("Jakobusliturgie"), p. 178 ("Markusliturgie"), p. 246 ("Chrysostomusliturgie"), p. 269 ("Basiliusliturgie").

212. On this concept of theology cf., e. g., Cyril of Jerusalem, *Mystagogic Catechesis*, V, ch. 6 (MSG, 33, 1113). Eusebius, *Church History*, V, 28, 4—6 (ed. Schwartz, p. 500); ibid., X, 4, 70 (ed. Schwartz, p. 882). In addition to note 209, cf. E. Peterson, "Von den Engeln," *Theol. Traktate*, pp. 371 ff., and R. Schneider, "Vom Wesen der ostkirchlichen Eucharistie," *Die Ostkirche und die russische Christenheit*, ed. E. Benz (Tübingen, 1949), pp. 149 f.

213. J. Horst, *Proskynein*, p. 311.

214. J. Horst, p. 236.

215. J. Horst, pp. 199 f. and 273 f.

216. Cf. Luther, *Vom Anbeten des Sakraments des heiligen Leichnams Christi* (1523), WA 11, 443 ff., especially 447.

217. Ibid., pp. 445 f.: "Worship is not a function of the mouth but of the whole body. It is to bow the head, bend the body, fall on the knees, prostrate oneself, and so forth, and to do such things as a sign and acknowledgment of an authority and power; just as people bow in silence before secular princes and lords. . . . From this understanding of outward worship you will also understand what Christ meant by true spiritual worship. It is the adoration or bowing of the heart, so that from the bottom of your heart you thereby show and confess yourself to be this subordinate creature. For from this you see that true worship can be nothing else than faith, or faith's sublimest activity with regard to God. . . . But where worship is offered from the heart, there follows quite properly also that outward bowing, bending, kneeling, and adoration with the body." — Relative to the last remark, P. Althaus may also be consulted, "Von der Leibhaftigkeit der Seele" in *Universitas* (1952), pp. 915—921. These deliberations are important for the understanding of the outward mien and deportment in worship. According to Althaus, this deportment is more than an "expression" of some inner emotion. Cf. p. 916: "The term 'expression' does not cover the intimate and essential relationship which often exists between the psychic-immaterial and the physical. It does not mean that a psychic event, already 'finished' in itself, only 'emerges' in corresponding physical attitudes or motions, but it means that this event first becomes entirely real and that it is entirely present in the physical. And it does not first 'express' itself with a view to someone else, to whom a psychic attitude or motion is to be imparted, but it expresses itself for the sake of its own self. From itself it strives for embodiment. For this relationship of the physical to the psychic-immaterial the term 'expression' says far too little. We must replace it with the term 'form'; in many instances the physical is the form of the psychic-immaterial, in which the latter first fully comes into its own." Cf. the applications of this principle on p. 917: "Thus also the inward feeling of reverence before men, before the king, before the master, before old people, before the parents tends to take physical form. It is not indifferent to it whether or not it becomes physi-

cal." — "If it is allowed to follow its immediate urge and is not hindered by other considerations, the heart's submission to God seeks the physical act of kneeling. With this it does not intend to express anything — again we would have to ask: For whom? — , but it wishes to be complete, wishes to be entirely itself. Only in the humble posture of the body the psychic attitude finds its full human reality."

218. Vilmos Vajta, *Die Theologie des Gottesdienstes bei Luther* (Stockholm, 1952), conveys a good picture of this, especially his presentation of Luther's critical analysis of the Roman mass under the perspective of *beneficium* and *sacrificium*, pp. 43—113. This important and comprehensive monograph appeared when the printing of the present treatise was practically concluded. I am happy that I can at least call attention to his work, which is basic for the investigation of Luther's doctrine of worship. Vajta's book (XIX and 375 pages) and my treatise came into being entirely independently of each other. Therefore a comparison between the two may prove informative in more respects than one. Vajta's book contains a large number of parallels especially to our Chapter C. Compare, for example, the chapter "Das Wort und die Werke Gottes" in Vajta's book, pp. 122—134, with our elaborations on "Das Heilsgeschehen in der Wortverkündigung," pp. 207 ff. ("The Salvation-event in the Proclamation of the Word"), in order to learn how closely our doctrine of the proclamation of the Word, taken from Scripture, is related to Luther's doctrine. Aside from many details, it is particularly the chapter "Glaube (Freiheit) und Liebe (Ordnung) im Gottesdienst," pp. 316—349, that shows many contacts with our dogmatic argumentation for the form of worship. Furthermore, the total conception of worship as "work of God" and as "work of faith" (Vajta), or as "service of God to the congregation" and as "service of the congregation before God" (cf. pp. 122—125) have very much in common. For a further conversation on the doctrine of worship it might prove fruitful to investigate how those elements of our doctrine of worship which — compared with Vajta's presentation — seem to be "new" at first glance over against Luther's doctrine, really relate, on the one hand, to Luther's theology of worship and, on the other, to the doctrine of Scripture.

The dogmatic bases on which Luther's criticism of the Roman mass rests, have now been set forth clearly by Ernst Bizer in his treatise "Römisch-katholische Messe und evangelisches Abendmahl" in *Ecclesia semper reformanda* (Ev. Theol. Sonderheft, 1952), pp. 17—40. In a certain respect, this is a reply to Erwin Iserloh, "Der Kampf um die Messe in den ersten Jahren der Auseinandersetzung mit Luther," *Katholisches Leben und Kämpfen im Zeitalter der Glaubensspaltung* (*Vereinsschriften der Gesellschaft zur Herausgabe des Corpus Catholicum*. Pamphlet No. 10), Münster i. W., 1952.

219. This should be noted also today. The Lord's Prayer is no profession to be recited in common.

220. A conspicuous document on the contention for the eschatological freedom of worship, especially germane to the New Covenant, is Luther's writing *Wider die himmlischen Propheten, von den Bildern und Sakrament* (1525). We select the following statements from it (WA 18, 211, 12 ff.): "Christ's kingdom does not consist in external things, places, times, persons, works. . . . It is not bound to a special place, as though it had to be there and nowhere else, as they do who do not leave our conscience free, but bind it to particular places, works, and persons. As He Himself, Christ, and His kingdom are not bound to any place or external thing, so also everything that belongs to

His kingdom is free and unfettered; as, for example, the Gospel, Baptism, the Sacrament, and the Christians."

221. The basic texts are found in CA VII, XV, XXVI, and XXVIII and in the corresponding sections of the Apology. The decision of the Formula of Concord (X) also belongs into this context.

222. The elaborations on pp. 234—236 must be considered here.

223. The great reduction to what is absolutely enjoined for the worship of the *ekklesia* was very impressively explained by Luther in the beginning of his *Sermon von dem Neuen Testament, das ist von der heiligen Messe* (1520), WA 6, 351 f.: 1. "The less law, the more justice; the fewer commandments, the more good works." 2. "Another result of many laws is that many sects and divisions in the congregations arise from them." In Christ's institution these viewpoints are noted in a unique manner: "Christ, in order to prepare for Himself an acceptable and beloved people, which should be bound together in unity through love, abolished the whole law of Moses. And that He might not give further occasion for division and sects, He appointed in return but one law or order for His entire people, and that was the holy mass." For Luther, the holy mass instituted by Christ is only the rite of the Sacrament of Holy Communion, consisting of "thanksgiving to God and the administration of the Sacrament." One must compare the entire section in its context.

224. Cf. pp. 139 ff.

225. We must note that the Spirit proceeds from the Father as well as from the Son *(filioque)* not only with regard to the intratrinitarian origin. Also the Pentecostal outpouring of the Spirit upon the church proceeds from Christ: The exalted Messiah Himself received the promised Spirit from the Father and poured Him out. The Lord Jesus, who traversed this earth, and the Spirit, poured out on the church, are so closely associated that one may say on the basis of a "dynamic identification" (Windisch): The Spirit is the effectual epiphany of the Lord Jesus in His congregation (2 Cor. 3:17). Therefore the freedom, which this Spirit grants, can never run counter to the will of the incarnate Word.

226. How difficult it sometimes is to pursue a consistent course in this matter is illustrated by the changing fate the elevation experienced in the Lutheran worship of the 16th century. Cf. P. Graff, I, pp. 191 f.

227. These reflections also apply to the relationship between the prayer prescribed in the Agenda and the improvised prayer. Basically, the former may be regarded only as a type of prayer suggested by this or that occasion, but not as a legal-ritual form. That does not imply any disparagement. The pastor will, of course, avail himself of this type of prayer in worship. Only when the wording of the Agenda prayer has become so vital in the praying person as to render the Agenda quite superfluous as a prop for his memory, may he be carried beyond the fixed wording of the prayer. Furthermore, special occasions may necessitate alterations of, or additions to, the prayer supplied by the Agenda.

228. In his preface to the *Deutsche Messe*, 1526, Luther pointed out that this movement toward a uniform worship service should come to pass especially within the freedom of the believers that conforms to the Gospel. Cf. WA 19, 73, 6 ff.: "It would be well if in every jurisdiction public worship were uniform and neighboring towns and villages observed the same ceremonies as the city." Luther is obviously motivated by the viewpoint that the people

who communicate and associate with each other in their daily walk of life should find the same order of divine service everywhere. If this principle had been applied to our modern conditions and taken into account in time, then a greater effort would have been made toward achieving such a uniformity in the Evangelical churches of Germany before the advent of the problem posed by the fugitives, which so painfully revealed the disparity of the liturgical order in these churches.

229. Cf. R. Stählin in *Leiturgia*, I, 13 f. and 22. With regard to the roots of the early Catholic form of the sacramental rite in the Pauline congregations, we point especially to H. Lietzmann's disclosure (*Messe und Herrenmahl*, pp. 178—181) of the intimate relationship between the liturgy of Hippolytus and the worship service of the apostolic era.

230. However, we must oppose the demand that Baptism must be administered in the main service. If this is done amid the congregation assembled for the main service, then the proper time for this is before and not anywhere within this service. Then the Introit and the Credo, under certain circumstances also the Gloria, may be dropped. In a service with sermon, Baptism may also be performed at the end of the service before the blessing is spoken.

231. We may ponder the question whether or not a fourth form may be found, pointing in the same direction as Luther's famous "third form" of worship (WA 19, 75). This form would be marked by a decisively charismatic nature. Free Gospel testimony and free prayer would be in the foreground. But also this form is a service of the Word in view of what takes place in it, if the proclamation of the Word with the prayer accompanying it is the focal point. If prayer were to predominate, then this service would be parallel to the horary service. If Holy Communion is also celebrated in this service, then it corresponds to the main service. Thus, touching the subject matter, we really find no new type of a form of worship here, but only a difference in the mode of administration, which may manifest itself in each typical form mentioned by us.

232. That it is not proper for a woman to conduct a worship service in which the whole congregation is assembled, and that she should not preach in such a service and administer Holy Communion, poses too far-reaching a subject for us to enter upon here.

233. H. Schlier has correctly emphasized (ThWNT, I, 164 f.), with reference to Col. 3:16 and Eph. 5:19, that, in contradistinction to the words which the apostle transmits in his missionary proclamation and then in his doctrine, the congregation instructs and admonishes itself mutually and alternately in its hymns: "The spiritual song of the church is the word of Christ, voiced in worship in the form of alternate and mutual exhortation."

234. Cf. H. A. Köstlin in RE³, 19, 466.

235. Cf. *Leiturgia*, I, 26, 35, 38.

236. Cf. *Kirchenbuch für die Vereinigte Evangelisch-protestantische Landeskirche Badens*, I (Karlsruhe, 1930). The themes mentioned above are taken from that Agenda.

237. Cf. *Deutsche Messe*, WA 19, 97, 3: "I want to stress this point, however, that this paraphrase and admonition be made in formal or prescribed words or be formulated in some definite manner for the sake of the common people. We cannot have one man do it one way today and tomorrow another man do it some other way, everybody showing his art and confusing the people, so that they can neither learn nor abide by anything. What chiefly

matters is the teaching and guiding of the people. Here it is necessary, therefore, to limit our freedom and keep to one form of such paraphrase and admonition, particularly in one church or congregation by itself, if, to retain its liberty, it will not follow the form used by another." These words retain their significance for fixed forms of prayer, even if we no longer emphasize their didactic factor with Luther but have in mind the congregation's joint spiritual use of prayer.

238. Cf. the literature references in Rietschel-Graff, *Lehrbuch der Liturgik* (Göttingen, 1951), p. 52, par. 9: "Der Kultus und die Kunst."

239. For Th. Harnack, cf. his basic par. 6: "Die Bestimmung der Kunst zum Dienst im Cultus" in his *Praktische Theologie*, I, pp. 289—304; for Rietschel, cf. the chapter in his book mentioned in n. 238 above.

240. Alfred Bäumler's "Ästhetik," appearing in *Handbuch der Philosophie*, published by Max Dessoir, Vol. I (1934), affords a preliminary view of the history of aesthetics. Eduard v. Hartmann's *Die deutsche Ästhetik seit Kant* (Berlin, 1886) is basic for its more recent history. The present efforts in aesthetics and philosophy of art seems to be characterized by two factors: by its ties to medieval philosophy and by Heidegger's attempt to penetrate to a new foundation. For the former we mention the following works: Jacques Maritain, *Art et Scholastique* (Paris, 1920); Theodor Haecker, *Schönheit. Ein Versuch* (Leipzig, 1936); Adolf Dyroff, "Ästhetik des tätigen Geistes" (*Deus et anima, Archiv für christliche Philosophie und Dichtung*, Vols. II and III), published posthumously by W. Szylarski (Bonn, 1948). An outstanding document for a new basis for the philosophy of art, which, to be sure, still awaits clarification, is Martin Heidegger's treatise "Der Ursprung des Kunstwerks," in *Holzwege* (Frankfurt a. M., 1950), pp. 7—68. The question, decisive for the theologian, whether truth appearing in a work of art is creatural or not, manifestly still remains open here. This question no longer remains open in the study by Wilhelm Weischedel, "Die Tiefe im Antlitz der Welt. Entwurf einer Metaphysik der Kunst," *Philosophie und Geschichte*, 73/74 (Tübingen, 1952), which is related to Heidegger but unfortunately goes far beyond him in this matter. Although we find important analogies to our own convictions in this significant treatise, we disagree with Weischedel's reflections in their deification of the truth as it appears in a work of art. The most essential theoretical accomplishment emerging from aesthetical science itself might be found in Paul Frankl's *Das System der Kunstwissenschaft* (Brünn and Leipzig, 1938), a work distinguished by the methodical stringency of phenomenological deduction.

241. For us the most important theological attempt to do justice to the phenomenon of beauty and art is found in the little treatise by Heinrich Vogel, *Der Christ und das Schöne* (Stuttgart, 1947). On the other hand, the ethics of art, which Leo Fremgen has submitted under the title *Kunst und Schöpfung* (Gütersloh, 1942), hardly comes into consideration for our studies. Prior to Vogel, Edmund Schlink had already expressed some basic thoughts on a particular area in his treatise "Zum theologischen Problem der Musik," in *Sammlung gemeinverständlicher Vorträge*, 188 (Tübingen, 1945; 2d ed., 1950). Rene H. Wallau, *Die Musik in ihrer Gottesbeziehung* (Gütersloh, 1948), purposes to take up the problem suggested by Schlink but fails to progress beyond him in the theological interpretation of music. However, it is very significant that Karl Barth has again taken up the problem of divine beauty within the framework of his doctrine of God's eternity and glory (*Kirchl. Dogmatik*, II, 1, pp. 732—752). Following in his steps, Eduard

Buesz attempts to advance "to a theological concept of beauty" in his trial lecture, which appeared under the title "Zu einem theologischen Begriff des Schönen" in the *Theologische Zeitschrift* (Basel, 1951), pp. 365—385. But it seems to me that the question still remains open, whether from the concept of beauty evolved there, we can arrive at a theological interpretation of a work of art which corresponds to the Word of God and also does justice to the historical facts.

242. For the area of the plastic arts, Hans Sedlmayr's *Verlust der Mitte* (Salzburg, 1948, 4th ed., 1951) may be adduced, although with reservations. In spite of all the questions that may be directed to the basic conception and to individual theses of the author, this book has the merit of clarifying the fact that the artistic decision, basic to the history of art, evinces in its ultimate meaning a component which is related to the Christian faith and can be made perceptible only from it.

243. Cf. H. Freiherr v. Campenhausen, "Die Bilderfrage als theologisches Problem der alten Kirche," ZThK, 1952, pp. 33—60.

244. Cf. above all Luther's *Wider die himmlischen Propheten, von den Bildern und Sakrament* (1525), WA 18, 80, 21 ff.; 82, 21 ff.; 83, 9 ff. — H. Preusz, *Martin Luther, Der Künstler* (Gütersloh, 1931), affords rich material on Luther's position over against the arts. Cf. also the continuing interpretation of this subject in H. Freiherr v. Campenhausen's "Luthers Stellung zur bildenden Kunst," in *Kunst und Kirche*, 1940, pp. 2—5. Cf. also Luther's basic utterance in the preface to the hymnal of 1524, WA 35, 475, 2 ff. On Luther's theological interpretation of music, cf., in addition to Preusz, mainly Chr. Mahrenholz, *Luther und die Kirchenmusik* (Kassel, 1937). — One might compare, e. g., Question 98 of the Heidelberg Catechism or the fourth chapter of the Second Helvetian Confession with these to discover that a "different spirit" prevails here.

245. Cf., e. g., the form analysis of the Ephphatha pericope, Mark 7:31 ff., in E. Lohmeyer's Commentary, p. 149. According to Lohmeyer, vv. 32-35 and v. 37 belong to the original form of this story. In this form the report shows a very clear articulation. Its word form is a perfect vessel for its message, and therefore may be regarded as art. Similar observations can be made of many pericopes and passages of the Gospels. Note, e. g., what E. Gaugler's *Das Abendmahl im Neuen Testament* (Basel, 1943), p. 10, says on Mark's report on Holy Communion: "Mark's report excels by reason of a hardly surpassable simplicity. There is not a superfluous word; there is no word for mere stylization. As much appears repressed as expressed. Only the most necessary is recorded. And yet all that is really important seems to be mentioned. For that very reason, we suppose, its structure reflects that great art which is possible only with such great objectivity." — E. Buesz also treated the question (p. 375) how the writings of the Biblical witnesses in their total form are peculiarly related to their testimony.

246. For the performance of the psalms, cf. Gunkel-Begrich, *Einleitung in die Psalmen*, pp. 65, 123 f., 175 ff., 266 f., 273, 279, 316, 368 f., 394, 411, 455 f.

247. Cf. B. Gemser, *Sprüche Salomons, Hdb. z. AT*, 16 (1937), p. 14.

248. Gesenius-Kautsch, *Hebräische Grammatik* (Leipzig, 2d ed., 1909), par. 15.

249. Cf. H. Schlier in ThWNT, I, 163, 28 f.

250. When Luther speaks of the transmission of the Gospel by the congregation, he often employs the term *singen und sagen* ("singing and saying"). The best-known illustration for this is found in the first stanza of his *Kinderlied*

auf die Weihnacht Christi ("From Heaven Above to Earth I Come"). Also cf. the texts cited in nn. 286 and 290. How closely melody and text blend into one for Luther is shown, for example, by the fact that he, during those critical weeks of 1530 on the Coburg, wrote not only the words of Ps. 118:17 (Vulgate version) on the wall, but also added the notes of the Gregorian antiphon to the words. Cf. WA 35, 535 f.

251. Cf. Friedrich Buchholz, *Musik und Musiker in der christlichen Gemeinde*, Pamphlet 1 of *Lemgoer Beiträge zur Musik* (Regensburg, 1952), pp. 30 f.

252. The Hebrew word for good also means "pleasant, beautiful, friendly," so that it does not mark too great a departure from the Hebrew text when the Septuagint translates this with καλός in Gen. 1, especially since καλός may also mean "serviceable, excellent." Cf. ThWNT, III, pp. 539 ff., especially pp. 545 f. It must be said that whatever corresponds to the creative Word and will of God must for that very reason in essence possess a particular and by no means apparent beauty. Might that which "corresponds to the will of God" not be the root of creatural beauty in general?

253. Nietzsche obviously was definitely aware of the metaphysical insufficiency of our words, when he wrote in the fragment "Über Musik und Wort," 1871 (*Kröners Taschen-Ausgabe*, I, 234 f.): "The multiplicity of languages immediately implies that word and thing are not completely and necessarily identical, but that the word is a symbol. But what does the word symbolize? Surely only concepts, whether conscious or, mostly, unconscious concepts; for how might a word-symbol correspond to that innermost essence, the images of which we ourselves together with the world are? We are acquainted with that core only as concepts, we are familiar with it only in its figurative utterances; moreover, there is nowhere a bridge which might lead us directly to it." In the beginning of all things the appelative word is this "direct bridge," which leads us to that "innermost essence," of things, to that "core," which is not a mere concept but constitutes the word-nature of the creature, through which it is what it is.

254. Cf. the profound words of Baudelaire: "When an outstanding poem brings tears to the eyes, these tears are no evidence of joyful exuberance, but they rather witness to a startled melancholy, to a nervous inveighing, to a nature, which, consigned to this imperfection, would fain occupy a revealed paradise already here on earth" (quoted from *Jean Cocteau — Jacques Maritain, Der Künstler und der Weise*, published in a German translation by K. Eschweiler, Augsburg, n. d. [1927?], p. 69).

255. Cf. E. Dennert, *Das geistige Erwachen des Urmenschen. Eine vergleichend-experimentelle Untersuchung über die Entstehung von Technik und Kunst* (Weimar, 1929). For our purpose Dennert's information on pp. 181 ff. is especially interesting, where he shows that the oldest and best-known stone tools of the paleolithic period already reflect a sound geometric sense of form, adding well-proportioned forms to the pure utility of the tool.

256. It is very significant that Paul Frankl, *Das System der Kunstwissenschaft*, pp. 502 ff., arrives at the same result in his deduction of the arts. Note the following basic conclusion on p. 503: "All works of art are aesthetic works, consequently, either ornament or play, thus either only-ornament or only-play, or they are profane, theoretical, sacral works, which become also-ornament and also-play by means of the aesthetic conformation of the free remnant."

257. Because the Greek tragedy, with its "chilly blast of horror" (R. A. Schröder),

reveals something of the forlornness and desperation of human existence, it appears to us as the most mature work of pagan art. Cf. the convincing words with which R. A. Schröder has characterized it in "Kunst und Religion," *Die Aufsätze und Reden,* I (Berlin, 1939), 423 f.: "It seems as though the Deity had from the very beginning placed a terrible gift of fate, as a counterbalance, into the cradle of this inexpressibly endowed people, the gift of all-coveting, all-consuming thought. We find instances already in Homer, from whom the Attic tragedy borrowed not only many of its materials, but also the tensions of its world-image. And this thought, thrusting forward, in conformity with its nature and its fate, into the void and ending in the void, discovered at the extreme verge of the Greek soulworld nothing but the shadow of its own impotence, the Moira, the Ananke, the blind, chaotic fate. And thus the tension of the Greek tragedy is a tension from abyss to abyss, from the abyss of an indefinite and undefinable horror above and without to the abyss of a heart within, of the heart that may no longer be sure of itself. — The Sophoclean saying that only the unborn may be accounted happy, remains, all in all, the final word of the Greek tragedy." Cf. also the author's "Collected Works," Vol. 3 (Berlin and Frankfurt a. M., 1952), p. 252.

258. It would pose a charming task to show how this theologically supported interpretation of the work of art and its function is reflected in expressions of the artists themselves. I call attention especially to Goethe's short essay of the year 1789 on "Einfache Nachahmung der Natur, Manier, Stil." It develops the following basic thought: "As simple imitation is based on a tranquil existence and a loving present, as the manner apprehends a phenomenon with an easy and capable mind, thus style rests on the deepest foundations of cognition, on the essence of things, insofar as we are permitted to recognize it in visible, tangible forms." This movement of imitation by way of manner to style is manifestly identical with the movement which leads to the fully evolved function of the mature work of art. Is this objective movement not also mirrored again and again in the history of art? Does not Goethe's differentiation formulate divinatorically also a historical course in the history of art in the 19th and 20th centuries? When Cézanne sees the essence of painting in the fact that the painter charms the sense perception of a given moment into the painting (*réaliser une sensation;* cf. Haecker, *Schönheit* [1936], p. 50), this art, according to Goethe's interpretation, would still have to be designated as manner. Here the creating subject with its momentary, sentient feeling occupies the foreground. The artist who occupies this position "invents a manner for himself, creates a language for himself, in order to express in his way what he apprehended with his soul" (Goethe). Here the proper omission, an almost irreparable error in thinking, becomes the essential means of this artistic language. The transition from manner to style — these terms understood in Goethe's sense — might be illustrated by van Gogh. When Goethe speaks of style, he thinks of the acme of a work of art. Not only a characteristic and characterizing omission is involved here, but also the recognition of something that is concealed in the phenomenon as such. With regard to style, it is not a matter of expressing "the conspicuous, the dazzling" (Goethe) of the phenomenon, but here it is a matter of beholding — Goethe's reflections obviously tend in that direction — the hidden Eidos (in the Aristotelian sense of the word), which, to be sure, can never be recognized without the concrete, perceptible object. *So seh' ich in allen die ewige Zier* ("In all

340

things I see the eternally bright"). These words taken from the "Türmerlied" (*Faust*, II, 5, 11296 f.) move the interpretation of a work of art as style into the range of a theological explanation.

259. Gen. 4:9-12; 17-24. Also see the German translation of G. v. Rad in *Das Alte Testament Deutsch*, II (1949), 83 and 89.

260. Is it not an essential mark of a city, no matter where it is located, to lose the fertile and nourishing soil from under its feet and to approach the growing desert? It is surely not a mere coincidence that the ornament, the purely ornamental, is characteristic of rural mechanic art from the earliest time down to the present. To have the mature work of pictorial art arise from pure ornament manifestly requires that dangerous border zone between fertile field and wilderness, which must not only be defined geographically but also culturally, and in this sense is a distinctive mark of an urban existence.

261. Note that the forbidden image is accompanied by the forbidden song, the magic formula. In antiquity, *carmen* designates not only prayerful invocation, but not infrequently the devilish antitype, the magic incantation. Cf. F. J. Dölger, *Sol Salutis* (2d ed., 1925), pp. 108 f.

262. The lively discussion that was waged for several decades over the interpretation of the cave pictures of the Paleolithic period might now be conclusively decided in the sense of the magic image. For a short summation of the results of this discussion see Friedrich Behn, *Kultur der Urzeit*, I, *Die vormetallischen Kulturen*, Slg. Göschen, 564 (Berlin, 1950), p. 41: "Since it is one of the primitive human conceptions and elementary ideas (from which, e. g., also Islam's prohibition of images stemmed) that possession of a picture confers power over the depicted object and the ability to achieve mysterious effects on it, it was assumed that consummate skill in the exercise of that artistic activity acquired similar magic power over animals, that it assured and increased the yield of the hunt, lured the game, aided its propagation, and the like. . . . Animals first appear on the walls as they begin to migrate or to become extinct. Thus the mural pictures are neither chronicles of the hunt nor the issue of a pure artistic urge, but they are means to thoroughly material ends. The symbolic signs of killing and capturing game, often found on or beside the forms of animals, i. e., spears, or hands, which express the wish still more eloquently, belong to the same category of thought. Some of the animals show wounds made by spear or arrow; the animal was killed symbolically, which is another side of the picture's magic."

263. H. van Oyen, "Zur Frage der christlichen Kunst," *Theologische Zeitschrift*, 1951, p. 437. The formula quoted above follows van der Leeuw.

264. With regard to the duration of the magic image in the historical time of man, cf. the summation in the first chapter of Hubert Schrade's *Der verborgene Gott. Gottesbild und Gottesvorstellung in Israel und im alten Orient* (Stuttgart, 1949). This chapter bears the caption "Der Bildglaube in Vorderasien und in Ägypten" (pp. 13—23). Cf., e. g., the following significant statement: "Before our present views of a picture began to dominate, the peoples regarded it not as a mere copy and semblance but as something very real, as something vitally effectual. The miracle of pictorial representation loomed so great to them that they viewed the image even for that reason as vibrant and vital and assumed that it had absorbed the essence and the powers of the one portrayed. It was assumed this was

the same person once more, a kind of double. The portrayal appeared as a mysterious process of life capable of genuine magic" (pp. 13 f.).

265. This is, perhaps, most strikingly exemplified in the pre-Columbus cultures of Central America, in which the dominion of idols found its most horrible development. There is a deeply hidden but powerfully effective and essential connection between the dominion of idols and the stagnation and congealment of art into mask and caricature.

266. In "Kunst und Religion," *Die Aufsätze und Reden,* I (Berlin, 1939), p. 423 (also in *Gesammelte Werke,* III, 251 f.), R. A. Schröder shed some light on the connection between the spirit-culture of Athens, which was hostile to idols and in that sense "atheistic," and the maturest art of Greece, the Attic tragedy. From an entirely different point of view and from different premises, Andre Malraux's *Psychologie der Kunst,* I: *Das imaginäre Museum* (Baden-Baden, 1949), pp. 80 f., disclosed the connection between those gods of Greece "which were more vital as hypotheses than as forces of fate" and the radical advertence of art to the profane: "Despite a formal evolution, in which Egypt had from century to century ever more affirmed its rigid order of death and of the celestial bodies, and Assyria its order of blood, art after all was nothing more than the pictorial expression of an answer which every culture had already once for all given to fate; persistent questioning, Greece's very own voice, hushed this Tibetan litany within some fifty years. . . . Greek art was the first to appear as profane."

267. With regard to the Old Testament prohibition of images, G. von Rad's remarks in *Verkehr und Forschung,* 1952, pp. 178 f., where he reviews H. Schrade's book (see n. 264 above), merit our special attention: "The subject of the prohibition of images cannot be understood if explained from the perspective of the conception of God. It, of course, does not purpose to make a religio-philosophical statement on how God is (that one should envisage Him as supermundane or immaterial), but on how He reveals Himself. Whereas pagan antiquity attributed to images a transparency of the world of the gods and regarded them capable of illustrating the divine, the prohibition of images denies that Jehovah is revealed in man-made images. This is surely also an expression of His power, but chiefly of His freedom and hiddenness, inasmuch as Jehovah does not permit man to proclaim His person so statically and visually." — We may be permitted to add: In the plan-of-salvation connection between the Old and the New Covenant, the Old Testament's prohibition of images keeps a space free, as it were, for the coming, end-time, and only self-incarnation of God in Him who is the eternal image of the Father, and who becomes bodily present in the kairos of the end-time consummation, in Jesus.

268. W. Weischedel clearly recognized that in *Die Tiefe im Antlitz der Welt,* pp. 67 ff. ("Kunst als Offenbarung des Göttlichen"). The theologian must agree with the philosopher when the latter writes: "The assertion that the divine is revealed in art stands and falls with the idea that the divine is conceived as the profundity of the world. That is emphatically denied by the Christian conception of God." Weischedel senses that "the supermundane God, who as a person addresses man" can make His appearance in this world only "in the human form of the Redeemer." Weischedel regards the idea that God appears also "in the cultic sacrifice" as Christian doctrine. This error is based on the element of truth that the means of grace, Word and Sacrament, can also be conceived as means of the hidden epiphany of Jesus Christ. But for the Christian faith, art can never be the means of

the epiphany. In this respect Weischedel is correct. In this sense the theologian can only concur with Weischedel in his answer to the question whether there can be a Christian art. With reference to this Weischedel writes: "The question is not whether the subject is Christian or non-Christian, but whether art in its essence, in this circumstance that the absolute appears as a thing of the world in it, may be Christian. That must be denied. There is no art springing from the spirit of Christianity which is really in earnest." One can only be grateful to Weischedel for these statements. But his statements crumble when the profundity of the world, appearing in the work of art, is not the absolute, the divine, but the being "corresponding to" the creative word and thus the true creatural being, which, by reason of this correspondence and truthfulness, also possesses goodness and beauty. Would the metaphysics of art designed by Weischedel not gain also in philosophical strength of deduction, if it could resist the charm and attraction of Schelling's and Hegel's aesthetics? Is the creature as such not profound enough to contain truth, creatural truth, creatural beauty, creatural beauty in profundity? Or might the secret of the creatural be completely hidden to philosophical reason? The fact that with Heidegger the question regarding creaturalness of the truth that appears in a work of art may still be open rates his philosophy of art essentially higher than Weischedel's.

269. On the subject of Christian art, cf. Th. Haecker, "Christentum und Kunst," in *Hochland,* 1939, Pamphlet No. 6, reprinted in *Opuscula* (Munich, 1949), pp. 415—447; H. Gürsching, "Kirche und Kunst. Versuch einer Wertbestimmung auf den Trümmern des 19. Jahrhunderts," in *Zeitwende,* 1948, pp. 511—528; H. van Oyen, "Zur Frage der christlichen Kunst," *Theol. Zeitschr.,* 1951, pp. 423—445.

270. That this may happen in art, might have been surmised even by Baudelaire, when he wrote: "In poetry and throughout it, in music and throughout it the soul captures some of the refulgence which shines beyond the grave" (quoted by J. Maritain in *Der Künstler und der Weise,* p. 69). The deceased painter Walter Timmling comes very close to our view when he says: "The beautiful that we experience through our ears or our eyes is always a reminder of the Garden of Eden, a reflected light issuing from there and a longing drawing us to eternal bliss" ("Prolegomena zur Theologie der Künste," MPTh, 1949, p. 74).

271. Cf. R. A. Schröder, pp. 416 ff. (*Gesammelte Werke,* III, 244 ff.), where he clarifies the statement "that within the period of historical time in which we are now living, within the world which we may and must call our own, no poet and no artist is conceivable who might not, in a certain sense, be called a Christian poet and artist." — To be sure, the phenomenon of the antichristian apostasy should be incorporated into this view. Thus Schröder's statement should be delimited by supplementing: — unless poet and artist place their talents into the service of the antichristian powers.

272. Here we may also think of Ps. 27:4, even if the Hebrew text does not speak "von den schönen Gottesdiensten des Herrn" [Luther's translation of Ps. 27:4, literally translated: "of the beautiful worship services of the Lord." RSV: "the beauty of the Lord."]. The poet desires to behold the loveliness, the graciousness, the friendliness of the Lord. But this gracious loveliness and charm manifest themselves, for Ps. 84 and Ps. 27, in the worship, where it can be "beheld," so that also the form of worship receives a reflection of this loveliness and charm.

273. Also the Old Testament contains illustrations, perhaps especially Ps. 27:4.

The word for the *Huld* of God (*Huld* = "graciousness, favor, benevolence, kindness"), which the poet would like to behold, also signifies loveliness which pleases. The same fact is reflected in the relationship between the German words *Huld* and *hold*.

274. Th. Haecker took note of that in *Schönheit*, 1936, pp. 44 ff.

275. The general phenomenon of artistic inspiration is penetratingly described by Nietzsche in "Ecce homo," Kröner pocket-edition of his works, Vol. 11, pp. 350 f. The special phenomenon of pneumatic inspiration, which is possible only in the church, must be distinguished from this. The New Testament recognizes the reality of such an inspiration also for art used in worship. The songs, referred to in Eph. 5:19, demonstrate that. They are called "spiritual songs" because they are inspired by the Pneuma. Cf. H. Schlier, ThWNT, I, 164, 18 ff. On the phenomenon of pneumatic inspiration also cf. the passages quoted from Luther in the following notes.

276. WA TR 4, No. 4627.

277. WA 46, 315, 12: "The Holy Ghost inspired him who composed this song." Luther believed that also the text of the Christmas song *Ein Kindlein so löbelich* could be traced to the working of the Holy Ghost: "To be sure, the Holy Ghost must have taught the writer of this song to sing thus" (WA 17, II, 306, 31). Cf. H. Preusz, *Martin Luther, Der Künstler* (1931), pp. 92 f.

278. Here the decisive reason for the rights of liturgical tradition come into view. The pneumatic inspiration in which a hymn is conceived is surely not identical with the inspiration which makes a person an apostle or a prophet. Cf. the humor with which Luther relates, in the preface to his exposition (1530) of Ps. 111 (WA 31, I, 393, 15 ff.), his attempt to rewrite this psalm into a hymn: "In fact, I intended to write a new and special hymn on this psalm. But the Holy Spirit, the greatest and best Poet, had already composed better and finer hymns, namely, the precious psalms, to thank and praise God. Therefore I gave up my wretched and worthless poetry." Nor is a hymn composed by pneumatic inspiration a canonical text, comparable to the words of the Bible. But within the realm of art in worship, such a work born of pneumatic inspiration may serve as a guide for this art. Therefore it will appear as a formative factor in the church's worship far beyond its own form- and style-restricted time; it will become part of the permanent stock of its liturgical tradition.

279. The announcements (*Abkündigungen*) can, to be sure, be mere communications, which do not come under the conditions discussed here.

280. This principle applies, appropriately, to all arts that are employed in worship.

281. Augustine was keenly aware of the danger that the hearer might abandon himself to the aesthetic form as such. Cf. his deliberations on psalm chanting in *Confessions*, X, Ch. 33. There we also find a statement akin to that of Jerome: *moveor non cantu, sed rebus quae cantantur* ("I am moved not by the singing but by what is sung"). To be sure, also the reverse takes place occasionally; but it should not: . . . *mihi accidit, ut me amplius cantus quam res, quae canitur, moveat* (". . . it happens to me that the singing moves me more than what is sung"). The danger formulated here from the viewpoint of the subject must also be banished in consideration of the characteristic of the work of art itself that serves in worship. Under this viewpoint see the informative remarks of Augustine, loc. cit., on the distinction between the chanting of the psalms under Athanasius in Alexandria and that under Am-

brose in Milan. For an interpretation of the passages quoted from Augustine, cf. Heinz Edelstein, *Die Musikanschauung Augustins nach seiner Schrift "De musica"*, phil. diss., Freiburg (1929), p. 126, where an attempt is made to fit this decidedly diaconal position of music in worship into the change to which Augustine's view on music was subject.

282. R. A. Schröder numbers among these few. Cf. his fine treatise *Die Kirche und ihr Lied*, Berlin, 1937. This essay contains important elements of the poetics of the hymn.

283. Cf. H. Gürsching, "Kirche und Kunst," *Zeitwende*, 1948, p. 523: "Moreover, nowhere can the future relationship of art to the church be divined better than in the area of music. . . . The way backward from harmony to counterpoint and to the psalm tone suddenly opens up as a way forward; one can easily determine, how, in which ways, and to what degree 'new art' bursts forth from 'old art' also liturgically."

284. With regard to this difference cf. R. A. Schröder, *Die Kirche und ihr Lied*, pp. 19 ff.

285. Cf. pp. 139—140, 207, 210—211.

286. Luther presented these facts in the foreword to the Babst Hymnal, 1545, most clearly and pithily. We select the following sentences (WA 35, 476 ff.): "In the Old Testament under the law of Moses worship was very difficult and burdensome, for the people had to offer so many and various sacrifices from all they possessed, both from their home and their fields. The people, being indolent and miserly, were loath to do this; or they did everything for reasons of temporal enjoyment. . . . But where there is such a lazy or unwilling heart, there can be either no singing at all or at least no good singing. If one is to sing, heart and mind must be cheerful and happy. Therefore God abolished such indolent and unwilling worship. . . . Now there is a better worship in the New Testament, to which the psalm (96) refers here: 'O sing to the Lord a new song! Sing to the Lord, all the earth!' For God gladdened our heart and mind through His dear Son, whom He gave for the redemption from our sin, death, and devil! Who sincerely believes that cannot do otherwise than to sing cheerfully and joyously about it, so that others may also hear it and gather about. But he who does not sing about this, gives evidence that he does not believe and does not belong into the new and joyful Testament, but under the old, lazy, morose Testament."

287. Cf. H. Henche, *Die gottesdienstliche Aufgabe der Kirchenmusik* (Gütersloh, 1951), p. 13, with regard to this elementary regulative function of music in worship.

288. That was the surprising and happy experience of that great congregation that had gathered from all parts of the world for the convention of the Lutheran World Federation in Hanover at the end of July 1952, as it assembled for matins and vespers.

289. R. A. Schröder, *Die Kirche und ihr Lied*, p. 8.

290. Cf. Luther, "Vorrede zum Septembertestament," 1522, WA DB, 6, pp. 2, 4: "*Euangelion* is a Greek word which means: good message, good tidings, good report; people speak and sing about this and rejoice over it. Similarly, when David defeated the mighty Goliath, the good news, the comforting tidings, were disseminated among the Jewish people, apprising them that their terrible enemy was slain, that they were liberated, and that joy and peace were restored to them, all of which prompted them to sing and leap with joy. Thus this *Euangelion* of God and new Testament is good news and

tidings, spread throughout the world by the apostles, telling about a real David, who contended against sin, death, and devil, vanquished them, and thus redeemed, justified, quickened, and saved, without any merit of theirs, all who were captive to sin, tormented by death, and overwhelmed by the devil, and in that way brought them peace and returned them again to God; they sing about this, they thank and praise God for this and rejoice eternally, if they at all believe that firmly and remain constant in faith."

291. The Musica which becomes theologically significant for Luther is obviously in a large measure — if not exclusively — melody combined with words.

292. In this connection the following reference, found in J. Maritain's *Der Künstler und der Weise*, p. 93, deserves attention: Around the year 1070 a converted Jew from Morocco, the rabbi Samuel of Fez, wrote an apology about the arrival of the Messiah as having already taken place *(De adventu Messiae praeterito)*. As a significant sign he stresses the fact "that the prayer-song has passed from the synagog to the church; the latter alone sings the new and universal song the prophets long for." — And, indeed, the church, which lives from the Messianic fulfillment, being a praying church, is also a singing church.

293. The prophetic-charismatic character of the *ekklesia* and its spiritual song are, according to Eph. 5:18 f., closely allied. In the old church the church's hymn is understood as a prophetic utterance. With regard to this, see the text quoted by F. J. Dölger, *Sol salutis* (Münster, 2d ed., 1925), pp. 132 f., from *Confessio Cypriani*, 17: "Thereupon we went into the church, where one could see the choir which resembled a choir of celestial men of God or a choir of angels, intoning a song of praise to God. They added a Hebrew word to each verse as with one voice, so that one was inclined to believe that they were not a number of men, but one rational being, a unit, emitting a wonderful sound, which the deceased prophets thus again proclaimed as a prophetic word through the living." Also cf. A. Dohmes, "Der pneumatische Charakter des Kultgesanges nach frühchristlichen Zeugnissen," in *Vom christlichen Mysterium* (Düsseldorf, 1951), pp. 35—53. The application Luther makes of 2 Kings 3:15 in his doctrine of the Musica fits into the comparison of the hymn with a prophetic voice. Again and again this text appears in his statements on the Musica. Cf. the passages in H. Preusz, p. 125. For Luther, this text is almost a *sedes doctrinae;* it is a basic passage for his point of view. That is also demonstrated by the fact that it found a place in the poetical *Vorrede auf alle gute Gesangbücher, Frau Musica,* 1538; here we read (WA 35, 485, 7 ff.):

> Zum göttlichen Wort und Wahrheit
> Macht sie das Herz still und bereit,
> Solchs hat Eliseus bekannt,
> Da er den Geist durchs Harfen fand.

[Freely translated: "Music hushes the heart and prepares it for the divine Word and truth. Elisha acknowledged that when he found the Spirit by playing on a harp."]

294. In a masterly fashion, Fr. Buchholz described this peculiarity of the Gregorian chant also from the viewpoint of musical aesthetics. Cf. *Musik und Musiker in der christlichen Gemeinde* (Regensburg, 1952). The description of the Gregorian chant, found in Buchholz's essay *Vom Wesen der Gregorianik,* 1948, pp. 36 f., seems especially informative to me for the unique diaconal position which Gregorian chant occupies over against the word: "What the chant accomplishes with near perfection cannot be described better than

346

with the words with which the Master of Offenbach characterized, in an analysis of the book of pericopes by Henry the Second, the powerful form of the initials of this Codex: 'that they express without describing, that they stand at a distance and present no image, and yet are so fervid and intense.' Do we not in these words virtually hear the melodies resound, which must be numbered among the most magnificent and pretentious products of human music? Indeed, because of this fervor and simultaneous standing-afar, the chant merits the honorable name of liturgical music above all other extant forms of music." — Buchholz's statement on "the inner relationship between music and its words," pp. 33 ff. of this essay, seems to me to be one of the most important characterizations of Gregorian chant to date.

295. In his *Enarrationes in Psalmos,* Augustine repeatedly and beautifully described how the melody, when sung, detaches itself from the word syllables in consequence of exuberant joy and soars forth in a free cantilena. He employed the observation made during harvest or vintage, when the singers of happy songs are so carried away with their joy that this can no longer be expressed with words. "They turn away from the word syllables and resort to the tone of jubilation. For this tone is an indication that the heart is pregnant with something it cannot express. To whom is this tone of jubilation more appropriate than to the inexpressible God? For He whom you cannot fully express is inexpressible. And if you cannot express Him fully and yet dare not keep silent, what else remains for you to do than to jubilate, than that the heart rejoices without words and the immeasurable joy be no longer confined by the bounds of words?" Accordingly, to sing in the jubilus means *verbis explicare non posse, quod canitur corde* ("not to be able to express in words what is being sung in the heart") *(Enarr. in Ps. XXXII;* MSL, 36, 283). Also cf. *Enarr. in Ps. XCIV;* MSL, 37, 1213: *Quid est jubilare? Gaudium non posse explicare, et tamen voce testari, quod intus conceptum est et verbis explicari non potest: hoc est jubilare* ("What does it mean to sing in a jubilus? It means not to be able to express your joy, and yet with your voice to give evidence of what is felt in the heart and cannot be expressed in words. That is singing in a jubilus."). The heavenly joy is of a type "that we, indeed, cannot express in words." — We on our part say: The melisma of the jubilus is the symbol of the borderland of the inexpressible encountered by the word of thanks and praise, it is a sign of the Johannine "joy," the pneumatic fullness of which causes the earthly vessel of words to overflow. — The passages from Augustine could easily be multiplied. Cf., e. g., also *Enarr. in Ps. XLVI;* MSL, 36, 528. On the passages quoted, H. Edelstein remarks, p. 127: "Here music is taken exclusively as mediator and expression of Christian piety, and thus its function as an autonomous cultural object is overcome. How alien this piety and its integrated music is to antiquity's view of music is apparent from the fact that this new music abandons the rhythmical structure, founded on its ties to words and their division into short and long syllables, a feature which was the essential structural element of all music of antiquity." We should note how this new music, detached from the ancient verse and its rhythm, is enabled by this very surrender of the rhythmic structure to serve the words of prose in the reading of Scripture, in the psalmic song, and in prayer.

296. On this point we disagree with A. Stier, *Der Dienst des Kirchenmusikers* (Kassel and Basel, n. d.), p. 25. We need hardly emphasize that our point of view is not born of "puritanical narrowmindedness." Evidently the more recent church music is developing very vitally "in the direction of a still

stronger liturgical obligation, which finds expression especially in the plenitude of the cantus firmus settings of the hymn and in the music of the Ordinary and the Proper. Thus the church music attends in ever-growing measure
to its liturgical function and clearly demonstrates that it purposes to be, first
and foremost, music of the worship service" (K. F. Müller, "Die Leipziger
Kirchenmusiktage vom 10.—16. Juni, 1952," *Musik und Kirche*, 1952,
p. 143).

297. Cf. Luther's words quoted by P. Althaus in *Das Wesen des evangelischen
Gottesdienstes*, 1932, p. 43, from WA 42, 72, 17: *Hodie in templis habemus
altare, propter communionem Eucharistiae, habemus suggesta seu cathedras
ad docendum populum. Haec non necessitatis tantum causa, sed etiam
solennitatis facta sunt* ("In our churches today we have an altar on account
of the communion of the Eucharist, and we have platforms or pulpits for
teaching the people. These have been built not only for necessity's sake but
also for solemnity's sake."). This distinction and association between *necessitas* and *solennitas* is reminiscent of the two sides that must be distinguished
in the architectural problem of church construction. *Necessitas* corresponds
to the technical-rational side, which grows from the practical needs, *solennitas* corresponds to the particular artistic side of the problem, according to
which the spacial form becomes a symbolic reference to the hidden pneumatic event of worship. In fact, *necessitas* and *solennitas* are the two poles for
the services expected of architecture and the plastic art with regard to the
house of worship and its equipment.

298. On the question of liturgical vestments, cf. W. Lotz, *Das hochzeitliche Kleid*
(Kassel, 1949), where also important materials for denominational information is presented.

299. Cf. the dictation "Vom Schmuck der heiligen Orte," which Wilhelm Löhe
used for the instruction of the deaconesses in Neuendettelsau, in the edition
of the Johannes Stauda Verlag, Kassel, 1949, p. 11. In the valuable notes
(p. 56.), the editor, A. Rickert, points out that Rupert von Deutz (d. 1135)
saw the ornamentation of the sacred vessels symbolized in the anointing of
Jesus by the "woman who was a sinner" (Luke 7:37).

300. Rudolf Schäfer in P. Althaus, p. 43.

301. Therefore Löhe is correct when he writes to Pastor Meurer on June 17, 1865:
"The richer the sacramental life, the more warranted are interest in paraments and parament societies. Without sacramental life, the occupation with
paraments is apparently a mere tinkling cymbal, hollow and empty. . . .
Therefore all interest in paraments should issue from an increasing enthusiasm for a sacramental life and its blessings." Quotation according to A.
Rickert, p. 45.

302. In the cited letter of June 17, 1865. There Löhe applied this principle to the
fashioning of the cup used in Holy Communion and to the altar. However,
a far wider significance for this principle must be acknowledged.

303. Cf. Luther, WA 18, 83, 6 ff.: "Thus I know for certain that God wants us to
hear and read His work, especially the suffering of Christ. But if I am to
hear it or ponder it, I must inevitably envisage it in my heart. Consciously
or unconsciously, when I hear Christ, a picture of a Man hanging on the
cross is sketched in my heart, just as my natural face is outlined in the water
as I peer into it. Now, if it is not sinful but good that I have Christ's picture
in my heart, why should it be sin if I have it in my eyes? Especially since

the heart is considered superior to the eyes and is thought of as contaminated less with sin than the eyes, for it is the true residence and dwelling of God."

304. If the following statements of Karl Barth, *Kirchliche Dogmatik*, II, 1, 751, are referred to the attempts to portray Christ's face in art, we can agree with them: "No other face tells simultaneously of the human suffering of the true God and of the glory of the true Man. That is exclusively the function of the face of Jesus Christ. — And that is the crux of every attempt to portray this face, the mystery of the painful story of the picture of Christ. This could and can be only a painful story. Precisely the suffering God and the triumphing Man — these precisely in their oneness! — precisely the beauty of God, which is the beauty of Jesus Christ, no human art should presume to reproduce. And the only, but urgent, wish that we want to address at this point to all Christian artists, no matter how well-meaning, talented, and genial they may be, is finally to abandon this unhappy attempt — for the sake of God's beauty." The question whether Christ's face could not be presented in symbolical portrayal was obviously not considered by K. Barth.

305. Cf. the principles underlying the arrangement of the worship space of the evangelical churches, proposed in 1951 at the Rummelsberg Convention: The place of worship must not only be functional, but it must at the same time "bear witness by its form to what is taking place in and amid the congregation assembled for worship." (Cf. the text of the Rummelsberg principles in G. Langmaack, "Der gottesdienstliche Ort," *Leiturgia*, I, 409 ff.).

306. Was this considered in the Rummelsberg principles? They do not adequately express that "what is taking place in and amid the congregation assembled for worship" must not be construed only as "proclamation," but that it also encompasses the special service of the congregation before God in prayer and praise.

307. Luther's foreword to the collection of funeral hymns, 1542 (WA 35, 480, 17 ff.), already shows that Scriptural passages written on the wall may belong to the adornment of a place of worship. Cf. also the interesting remark on a combination of picture (altar picture!) and copy of Scripture in WA 31, I, 415, 23 ff.

308. On the historical development of our problem, cf. Klaus Harms, *Die gottesdienstliche Beichte als Abendmahlsvorbereitung in der evangelischen Kirche, ihre Geschichte und Gestalt* (Schriften der pommerschen Gesellschaft zur Förderung evangelisch-theologischer Wissenschaft), Greifswald, 1930. To be sure, the practical suggestions of the author are not practicable for us.

309. His writing *Von der Beicht, ob die der Papst Macht habe zu gebieten*, 1521 (WA 8, 138 ff.), is basic for this.

310. *Formula Missae et Communionis*, 1523 (WA 12, 216, 31 ff.): *De confessione vero privata ante communionem sentio, sicut hactenus docui, esse eam scilicet nec necessariam nec exigendam, utilem tamen et non contemnendam* ("Concerning private confession before Communion, it is my opinion — and so I have always taught — that it is obviously not indispensable, nor ought it to be demanded, but that it is useful nevertheless and not to be despised.")

311. Maundy Thursday Sermon, 1523 (WA 12, 477, 20 ff.): "I will let it pass once more this year that every one go [to Holy Communion] in accord with his own opinion. But in the future we must provide that no one be admitted to the Sacrament before he is questioned and before we ascertain the attitude of his heart, whether he is informed regarding its essence and why he is receiving it."

312. Cf. *Formula Missae,* WA 12, 215, 18 to 216, 7. The doctrinal examination referred to the following points: What is Holy Communion? What does it confer? For what purpose do communicants wish to receive it? If possible, the words of institution should be recited. With this examination cf. also Erich Roth's *Die Privatbeichte und die Schlüsselgewalt in der Theologie der Reformatoren* (Gütersloh, 1952), pp. 56—59. Roth construes the doctrinal examination as a form in which "the key of knowledge" (Luke 11:52) is employed. This key consists of the ministry of teaching, preaching, and pastoral care, "by which the people are to be brought to knowledge, that they may learn and know how they must serve God and be saved" (WA 30, II, 491, 20; cf. Roth, p. 56). "This *exploratio* is not understood if it is fit into the pedagogical plane of a purely academic examination" (Roth). We have to agree with Roth's criticism of the conception of the *exploratio* which Albr. Schönherr submits in *Lutherische Privatbeichte* (Göttingen, 1938), pp. 17 ff. According to Roth, p. 59, also Klaus Harms should have considered the common factor, which combines the doctrinal examination and the private confession on the basis of the relationship between the key of knowledge and the binding and unbinding key. — However, in our opinion, an almost unbearable tension remains between the imposition of the examination and the freedom of private confession, if examination and absolution are combined into one act.

313. Cf. WA 12, 215, 29 ff.

314. Cf. Kl. Harms, pp. 46 ff.

315. Klaus Harms uses this expression for the interrelation of examination, confession of individual sins, and reception of absolution, which has become characteristic of this act.

316. Cf. the *Unterricht der Visitatoren an die Pfarrherren* in the second edition of Luther in 1538 (WA 26, 216, 20 ff.): "No one shall be admitted to the sacrament unless he has previously been to see the pastor. The latter shall inquire whether he rightly understands the sacrament, whether he is in need of counsel otherwise, or whether he is a person of whom one knows that he is well informed about everything. For if the pastor or preacher himself, who occupies himself with this daily, wishes to go to the Sacrament without confession or examination, he shall not herewith be forbidden to do that. The same may also be said of other intelligent persons who are able to instruct themselves, lest such confession develop into a new papal constraint or binding custom; this shall and must be a matter of freedom to us. And I, Doctor Martin, myself go [to Holy Communion] several times without prior confession, in order not to bind my conscience with this custom; and yet I again avail myself of confession and do not want to be deprived of it, especially because of the *absolutio* (i. e., because of God's Word). For the young and untrained folk must be trained and treated differently than the understanding and experienced people." Cf. also p. 220, 11 ff. In this connection, also note the following testimony of Luther with regard to his personal experience in *Vermahnung zum Sakrament,* 1530 (WA 30, II, 617, 34 ff.): "I shall cite my own experience here as an example for all who will be warned, so that they may learn what a cunning rogue the devil is. Several times I had resolved to go to the Sacrament on this or on that day. But when that day arrived, my zeal had vanished, or some obstacle presented itself, or I felt myself unworthy. This prompted me to say: 'All right, I will do it a week from now.' The next week found me just as unworthy or just as beset by obstacles. 'All right, I will do it next week.' These weeks grew

so in number that I was in danger of getting entirely away from it and of not going to the sacrament at all. But when God gave me the grace to perceive the devil's knavery, I said: 'Is it what we want to do, Satan?' Then be gone with your and my worthiness!' And I tore myself away and went to the Sacrament, also several times without previous confession (which is not my habit otherwise), to spite the devil, especially since I was not aware of any grave sin."

317. Kl. Harms, pp. 64 f.

318. Ibid., p. 66.

319. Ibid., pp. 107 ff.

320. WA 12, 215, 18 ff.

321. The relationship between Baptism and Holy Communion, absolution and Holy Communion, Holy Communion and excommunication, and confession of the excommunicated and Holy Communion calls for a new dogmatic study. Here an especially difficult problem is presented by the hidden self-exclusion from the Holy Communion congregation, which the baptized member decrees against himself when he annuls his membership in Christ's body and forfeits his inheritance in the kingdom of God by committing the sins mentioned as examples in 1 Cor. 6:9 f.; Gal. 5:19-21; Eph. 5:5. Even E. Bizer's meritorious demarcation over against the Roman Catholic "solution" of these questions (pp. 34—37, especially p. 37) has, in my opinion, not yet clarified the basic dogmatic problem hidden in the background.

322. Cf. Martin Kähler, *Die Sakramente als Gnadenmittel* (Leipzig, 1903), pp. 76—82, especially p. 80: "If I may not go to the Lord's Supper without it (absolution), I must already have beforehand what it is to offer me. If I may not seek the communion with the Lord's body and blood without it, then I may not receive the pledge until I have assured myself in advance of the gift and received this gift guaranteed me by that very pledge. — That is not a clarifying presentation, but a confusing obscuration."

323. Cf. Ch. Mahrenholz, p. 61.

324. Cf. e. g., E. Gaugler, *Das Abendmahl im Neuen Testament* (Basel, 1943), pp. 10 f., especially the comment on M. Dibelius and K. G. Goetz, p. 11, n. 1. According to Gaugler, "a slight influencing" of the text through liturgical employment may "hardly be questioned" also with regard to the text of Mark. A study of Paul's report in 1 Cor. 11:23-26 shows "that it bears a far more reflective, a more liturgical stamp than that of Mark" (p. 17).

325. Cf. P. Drews, "Epiklese", RE, 3d ed., V, pp. 410 f.

326. Augustine, *Tract. in Joan. ev.*, 80, 3; MSL, 35, 1840: "Why does not Christ say (John 15:13): 'You are clean through Baptism by which you are washed,' but: 'by the Word which I have spoken to you'? Answer: because it is the Word which cleanses also in the water! Remove the Word, and what is the water other than mere water! Join the Word to the element, and then the sacrament is effected; this, too, is, as it were, a visible Word."

327. On the question of genuineness, cf. B. Altaner, *Patrologie* (Freiburg, 3d ed., 1951), p. 334.

328. *De mysteriis*, 9; MSL, 16, 424 f.: "The sacrament which you receive is effected by the words of Christ. If the words of Elijah were able to draw fire from heaven, should not the words of Christ be able to change the peculiar quality (*species*) of the elements? Regarding the works of the whole world you read: 'And God said, and it was so; He commanded, and they were cre-

ated.' And the words of Christ, which had the power to create from nothing, to create from what was not, should they not be able to change what already is into something that it was not before? . . . The Lord Jesus Himself says: 'That is My Body.' Before the consecration with the heavenly words, another peculiar quality is spoken of [namely, bread]; after the consecration, the body is proclaimed. He Himself says: 'My blood.' Before the consecration a different object is mentioned [namely, wine]; after the consecration the blood is proclaimed." — *De sacramentis,* IV, 4; IV, 5; V, 4; MSL, 16, 458—462; 463; 471. We select the following statement from IV, 4; MSL 16, 458 f.: "How can that which is bread be Christ's body? By means of the consecration! But in which words, in whose speech does the consecration consist? In the words and in the speech of the Lord Jesus! For all that is said prior to this by the priest offers praise to God and renders intercession for the people, for the kings, and for the others. But at the point where the Holy Sacrament is effected, the priest no longer employs his own speech but the speech of Christ. Thus the speech of Christ effects this sacrament."

329. Kurt Goldammer, *Die eucharistische Epiklese in der mittelalterlichen abendländischen Frömmigkeit* (Bottropp), p. 57.

330. Paschasius Radbertus, *De corpore et sanguine Domini,* 15; MSL, 120, 1321 f. These deliberations already remind one very much of the position which Luther took in the *Sermon von dem neuen Testament* in 1520. Goldammer comments on the cited passage: "This sentence might have been written by Luther himself" (p. 63).

331. Cf. *Summa theologica,* III, q. 78, a. 1, obj. 4; ad 4.

332. Th. Knolle most recently showed this exemplarily in his treatise "Luthers Reform der Abendmahlsfeier in ihrer konstitutiven Bedeutung," *Schrift und Bekenntnis,* Hamburg, 1950.

333. WA 6, 367, 19 ff.

334. *De abroganda missa privata,* 1521, WA 8, 448, 27 f.

335. Cf. the contrasting of these in R. Stählin, "Die geschichte des christlichen Gottesdienstes," *Leiturgia,* I, 58 f.

336. With regard to the emphasis on the distribution as a necessary feature for the integrity of Christ's institution, Luther is found in the sharpest contrast to medieval times. Cf. Thomas, *Summa theologica,* III, q. 78. a. 1. ad 2: Eating and drinking do not belong to the substance of the form of the sacrament, but only to a certain completion of the sacrament.

337. Cf. chiefly *Vom Abendmahl Christi, Bekenntnis,* 1528, WA 26, especially pp. 282—288.

338. Th. Knolle, p. 18.

339. WA 19, 96, 26 ff. and 97, 15. Note that in the liturgical execution 97, 15 is immediately joined to 96, 28.

340. Cf. WA 19, 99, 5—11.

341. Note above all the introductory words of the paraphrase (WA 19, 95, 22 f.) and the interpretation of the entire passage in Th. Knolle, pp. 16—18.

342. From the very beginning Luther indicated in his *Deutsche Messe* that it should "not be imposed as a law" (WA 19, 72, 3—10). Nor should the *Formula Missae* be abolished by the order of the *Deutsche Messe* (ibid., 75, 1 ff.). Cf. also the references to Luther's *Vermahnung zum Sakrament des Leibes und Blutes Christi,* 1530, WA 30, II, 614 f., in Th. Knolle, pp. 18 f.

343. Cf. *Ein Sermon von dem neuen Testament*, 1520, WA 6, 355, 3 ff.: "The more closely our masses resemble the first mass of Christ, the better they indubitably are, and the further removed from it, the more unreliable they are." Also see the remaining passages mentioned in Th. Knolle, p. 6, n. 9.

344. WA 6, 355, 12.

345. Referring to the bread, Mark and Matthew use the word εὐλογεῖν, Paul and Luke use εὐχαριστεῖν. Also Mark and Matthew designate Jesus' prayer spoken over the cup as εὐχαριστεῖν. εὐλογεῖν immediately brings to mind the Jewish table prayer spoken at the beginning of the meal, which was a *berachah*, a prayer of thanks and praise. Here εὐλογεῖν means to speak the prayer of thanks and praise as a table prayer.

346. Cf. W. Bauer, *Wörterbuch zum Neuen Testament* (Berlin, 3d ed., 1937), Col. 537, s. v. εὐλογέω. According to Bauer, the object must here be supplied from the context.

347. Cf. above all the exposition of this passage in J. Jeremias, *Die Briefe an Timotheus und Titus (Das Neue Testament deutsch, 9)*, 1934, which, in the main, hits the mark.

348. Ibid.

349. E. g., A. Schlatter and J. Jeremias.

350. M. Dibelius, *Die Pastoralbriefe (Lietzmanns Handbuch zum Neuen Testament*, 13), 2d ed., 1931. A table prayer such as Luther adopted for his Small Catechism does not seem out of the question here. Cf. *Bekenntnisschriften*, 1930, pp. 522 f. Here the Word of God is a psalm passage. This is followed by a prayer which also petitions for the "consecration" of the gifts. Such a very old form of prayer is in complete agreement with 1 Tim. 4:3-5.

351. It is possible that also 1 Cor. 14:16 f. belongs into this context. It does not seem unlikely to me that Paul here had particularly the εὐλογία of Holy Communion in mind: "If you utter the εὐλογία with the spirit [i. e., by speaking in tongues], how can he who is in the position of an outsider [i. e., one who is unfamiliar with speaking in tongues] say the 'Amen' to your thanksgiving [εὐχαριστία]? Why, he does not know what you are saying! You may be uttering a splendid prayer of thanksgiving [εὐχαριστεῖν], but the other person is not edified." Could it be coincidence that the same terms are used here which occur in the reports on Holy Communion: εὐλογεῖν and εὐχαριστεῖν? Unquestionably a prayer of the worship service is involved here, in which the amen of the congregation is considered a necessary part. Furthermore, we must note that the εὐλογία of the Holy Communion was a free prayer for a long time, which, although it was prayed "with the mind" (1 Cor. 14:19), nevertheless was regarded as a Spirit-wrought "improvisation" and was therefore perhaps fixed with regard to type but not with regard to wording. This extemporaneous εὐλογία of Holy Communion is, according to *Didache*, 10, 7, a pneumatic expression of the prophetic gift. All of that suggests that εὐλογία is used in a pregnant sense in 1 Cor. 14:16: "to pray the εὐλογία of the Holy Communion."

352. Th. Harnack, *Praktische Theologie*, I, 444. Cf. the entire section on pp. 443 to 447. Here basic insights are expressed, which, if they had been adopted and spiritually appropriated and absorbed by the evangelical church, had long ago led to a liturgical reorganization of the rite of the sacrament.

353. The last sentences refer to Th. Knolle, *Luthers Reform der Abendmahlsfeier*

in ihrer konstitutiven Bedeutung, pp. 12 ff. When Knolle emphasizes that the words of institution consummate the consecration "only in immediate and indissoluble association with the distribution" (p. 14), I can agree with him only if this immediateness and indissolubility refer to the concrete celebration of Holy Communion taking place right now. But if the immediateness and indissolubility are to mean that the consecration becomes questionable if words of prayer intervene between the words of institution and the distribution, then this conception of Christ's institution must be opposed.

354. Cf. the articles "Epiklese" by P. Drews, RE, 3d ed., V, 409—414; S. Salaville, DThC, V, 1, pp. 198—300; F. Cabrol, DALC, V, 1, pp. 142—184; J. Brinktrine, LThK, III, 724. Among the older literature deserving attention is L. A. Hoppe, *Die Epiklesis der griechischen und orientalischen Liturgien, und der römische Consekrationskanon* (Schaffhausen, 1864). Fr. Heiler, *Urkirche und Ostkirche* (Munich, 1937), pp. 256—262, presents a good introduction to the subject. To the enumeration of literary sources mentioned there (p. 257), may now be added the work by K. Goldammer, mentioned in n. 329.

355. See p. 291.

356. Cf. Fr. Heiler, pp. 257 ff.

357. *Homilia de proditione Judae,* 1, 6; MSG, 49, 380; *In 2. Tim. homilia,* 2, 4; MSG, 62, 612.

358. *De sacerdotio,* III, 4; MSG, 48, 642.

359. This form "by God's Word and prayer" is used since Origen (*Matthäuserklärung,* ed. E. Klostermann, 1935, p. 57, line 21; *Die griechischen christlichen Schriftsteller,* Vol. 40; *Origenes, Werke,* Vol. 10) to express the interrelation of the words of institution and the epiclesis in the consecration, e. g. in Gregory of Nyssa, *Oratio catechetica magna,* 37, 3; MSG, 45, 97. Cf. L. A. Hoppe, p. 232.

360. For Gregory of Nyssa cf. *Or. cat.,* 37, 3; MSG, 45, 96 f.: "We rightly and reasonably believe that at this point, too, the bread, consecrated through the Word of God, is transformed into the body of the Word of God. . . . As the apostle says (1 Tim. 4:5), the bread 'is consecrated by the Word of God and prayer.' It does not gradually change into the body of the Word by eating, but it is immediately re-created into the body of the Word, as was said by the Word Himself: 'This is My body.' " — Note the double meaning of the term "word" here: the word spoken over bread and wine in the Eucharist, and Christ as the Word of God. Manifestly, these two meanings are not to be divorced in the present text; rather, they pass over into each other.

361. Johannes Damascenus takes his cue from Chrysostom, when he (*De fide orthodoxa,* IV, cap. 13) compares the words of institution, similarly to Luther in *Vom Abendmahl Christi Bekenntnis* (WA 26, 282 f.), with the words of creation in Gen. 1 and Ps. 33. But for him the Spirit is the power which renders the words of institution effectual here and now. To be sure, now, too, the earth produces vegetation by virtue of the divine words of command in Gen. 1:11; however, to do this, rain is necessary! Thus in every Eucharist until the Day of Judgment the statement of His words: That is My body, that is My blood, becomes reality by Christ's omnipotent words of institution. But here Johannes Damascenus continues with a weighty "and": "And through the epiclesis, like a rain on the new planting, comes the overshadowing power of the Holy Spirit." Thus if we ask with regard to the miracle of the Eucharist, as Mary did with regard to the miracle of the

incarnation: 'How can this be?' we must answer, according to Johannes Damascenus and in analogy to Luke 1:35: "The Holy Spirit invariably supervenes and effects what transcends words and imagination." Cf. MSG, 94, 1140 f. — That opens the path to a practical and dogmatic predominance of the epiclesis over Christ's words of institution. Nikolaus Kabasilas (1290 to 1371) points to this path in his profound interpretation of the Greek liturgy of the mass. He emphasizes that the words of institution are spoken in the liturgy only as a narrative recital; the epiclesis first actualizes the power of these words for the present celebration of the Eucharist. Cf. MSG, 150, 425 ff. and Fr. Heiler, pp. 260 f.

362. Cf. "Die evangelische Messe von Kaspar Kantz," 1522, in Julius Smend, *Die evangelischen deutschen Messen bis zu Luthers Deutscher Messe* (Göttingen, 1896), pp. 73—78. On p. 75 the Preface and Sanctus are followed by the "significant caption" (Smend): "Now the Evangelical mass first begins." This caption corresponds with Luther's conception in *Sermon von dem neuen Testament*. Now a consecration petition follows immediately, which leads over to the words of institution: "O most gracious Father, merciful, eternal God, help that this bread and wine become and be for us the true body and the innocent blood of Thy dear Son, our Lord Jesus Christ, who on the day before His Passion took the bread. . . ." J. Smend comments on p. 79 that it is a mistake to "regard the old consecration petition, here merely assuming German form, as a proof of continuing Roman superstition." On the effect of the Kantz mass, cf. Smend, pp. 72, 83 ff., 152 ff. The consecration petition is also found in a Strasburg order of service (Smend, p. 132, note), of the year 1524. This petition was also taken directly from the Kantz mass into the Worms order of service: "Form und Ordnung der euangelischen deutzschen Messen, wie sie zu Worms gehalten wirt" (without year; not in Smend). Cf. the sparse data on this in *Lutherbibliothek des Paulusmuseums der Stadt Worms* (Darmstadt, 1922), Preface, p. XIX. For this reference and also for the photostat of this order of the mass I am indebted to the Rev. Dr. Germer in Worms. The Rev. Bishop (ret.) Stählin first called my attention to this order. This *Wormser Messe* still requires a closer liturgical-scientific study. Its singular importance consists in the fact that it probably is the only Evangelical German mass of the Reformation period that created a canon prayer which is in full agreement with Evangelical doctrine and yet adheres closely to the early-church type of εὐλογία with consecration petition, anamnesis, and a prayer for a blessed reception. I hope to be able to enlarge on this German Evangelical mass on another occasion.

363. Cf. P. Graff, "Die Epiklese in reformatorischen Ordnungen," MGkK, 1940, pp. 133—138; G. Kunze, "Kennen reformatorische Ordnungen die Epiklese?" Ibid., pp. 138—140.

364. Cf. P. Graff, p. 137.

365. E. Sartorius, *Über den alt- und neutestamentlichen Cultus* (1852), p. 267.

366. Th. Harnack, *Praktische Theologie*, I, 630 f. This outline is closely related to Harnack's fundamental elaborations, ibid., pp. 443—447.

367. Nor through the currently much cited *ubi et quando visum est Deo* ("where and when it pleases God") in CA, V, which, as CA, V shows, must be said with regard to the Spirit's power to kindle faith, but may not be applied to the effecting of the real presence. See p. 193.

368. Cf. Th. Harnack, *Praktische Theologie*, I, p. 444: "εὐλογεῖν signifies to bless, to invoke and appropriate God's blessing with thanksgiving and prayer, to

consecrate and to hallow, so that εὐλογεῖν, εὐχαριστεῖν, and ἁγιάζειν (Matt. 26:26, 27; Luke 22:17, 19; 1 Cor. 11:24; 1 Tim. 4:5) are synonyms, which express the form, the content, and the purpose of blessing. The εὐλογία is, accordingly, a prayer of thanksgiving in form, spoken for the purpose of blessing." Ibid. p. 445: "The essence of the εὐλογία must be defined in accordance with 1 Tim. 4:4, 5: ἁγιάζεται γὰρ διὰ λόγου θεοῦ καὶ ἐντεύξεως; for Holy Communion belongs to the category of meals, specifically, of sacred meals, and the blessing is a table prayer in a higher sense."

369. With regard to this, cf. the elaborations s. v. πνεῦμα in Cremer-Kögel, *Biblisch-theologisches Wörterbuch*, 11th ed., 1923, p. 940, where it is said of the Spirit of God that He is "the life-principle of the creature, which has God in it and which shows itself creative . . . the point where God and the creature meet."

370. Cf. Cremer-Kögel, p. 955: "This concerns food and drink produced by special divine act, which distinguishes them from other victuals." By way of elucidation, Cremer-Kögel refers to the content of the Pneuma-concept, mentioned in the preceding note. On the relationship between Pneuma and the food in Holy Communion, also cf. E. Käsemann, "Anliegen und Eigenart der paulinischen Abendmahlslehre," *Ev. Theol.*, 1948, pp. 267 f. — In answering the question whether the Eucharistic epiclesis of the Eastern Church has any Scriptural basis, we dare not automatically ignore John 6:63. The interpretation of this passage by A. Schweitzer, *Die Mystik des Apostels Paulus*, 1930, pp. 354 f., may be questioned. But we must note that A. Schweitzer draws the same viewpoint from John 6 that underlines the epiclesis of the Eastern Church. Relative to John 6:61-63 he writes: "The solution of the riddle by a reference to the Spirit, from whom alone life issues, consists in the fact that it is the Spirit, who unites with the bread and the wine of the Eucharist and transforms them into the flesh and blood of the Son of man, which convey the power of resurrection. . . . In the word concerning the Spirit, who alone quickens, the Logos-Christ thus retracts nothing of what He said before, but only explains how it happens that bread and wine are flesh and blood of the Son of man in the Eucharist."

371. According to Luther, we are as close to the Lord through the physical and spiritual eating and drinking in Holy Communion as Mary was who bore Him, as the shepherds were, who beheld Him, as Simeon was, who carried Him in his arms: WA 23, 193, 1—13. Cf. H. Grasz, *Die Abendmahlslehre bei Luther und Calvin*, 1940, p. 106: "Since the real presence was viewed in the closest association with God's condescension in the incarnation, it finally did not seem extraordinary that the heavenly gifts of Holy Communion in a way made themselves amenable to the conditions of this world."

372. Cf. WA 23, 201 ff.; 349 ff.; 367 ff.; 375 ff.; 26, 349 f. Also P. W. Gennrich, *Die Christologie Luthers im Abendmahlsstreit*, 1930, pp. 76—79.

373. Cf. R. Stählin, *Leiturgia*, p. 29, and H. Lietzmann, *Messe und Herrenmahl*, 1926, pp. 74—76.

374. Cf. L. A. Hoppe, *Die Epiklesis*, pp. 320 f.

375. These last statements contain the dogmatic criticism of the attempts to renew the epiclesis of the Eastern Church within the churches of the Augsburg Confession. The most important attempts of this kind in Germany are Fr. Heiler, *Deutsche Messe* (Munich, 2d ed., 1948), p. 30, issued on behalf of the "Evangelisch-ökumenische Vereinigung des Augsburgischen Bekenntnisses," and K. B. Ritter in conjunction with K. F. Müller, *Ordnung der Messe*

(Kassel, 1950), p. 36. Also the position of the consecration petition in Th. Harnack's outline, mentioned on page 301, comes under this criticism. In the meantime K. F. Müller has indicated that the position of the epiclesis after the words of institution appears problematical also to him. Cf. his treatise "Die Neuordnung des Gottesdienstes in Theologie und Kirche," in *Theologie und Liturgie* (Kassel 1952), p. 300, where he raises the critical question "whether an epiclesis referring to the elements and following the *Verba testamenti* is possible according to the Lutheran conception and rite, without entailing a fixation of the consecration factor." To raise this question is to answer it in the negative.

376. These allusions are avoided neither in the order of service of Fr. Heiler nor in that of K. B. Ritter. Cf. Heiler, p. 29: "We proclaim Him who had compassion with our frailty our pure, holy, unspotted Sacrifice. And thus we offer Thee, in conformity with His will, that which is Thine from that which is Thine: the bread of eternal life and the cup of imperishable salvation. Graciously look upon the all-sufficient sacrifice which Thy Son offered one time on the cross for the sins of the whole world and which ascends ever and ever with pleasing savor before the countenance of Thy sublime Majesty." Cf. K. B. Ritter, p. 36: "Cleansed and reconciled by His blood, we joyously enter the sanctuary and approach the throne of Thy grace with this pure, holy, all-sufficient sacrifice, with which He, our High Priest, ever represents us before Thee." On the other hand, the canon of the *Wormser Deutsche Messe*, mentioned above (n. 362), exemplarily avoided every allusion to a sacrificial offering. Now K. F. Müller, too, has correctly called attention to the problem (*Neuordnung*, p. 301) posed by Ritter's phrase "with this pure, holy, all-sufficient sacrifice": "And yet we are concerned about this 'with' in the anamnesis found in Ritter, because it fails to express unmistakably that our action is God's action, that all *actio* is *passio*, that an identification of God and man and a cooperation remain excluded, that where we do something, something is done to us by God."

SCRIPTURE INDEX

361

SUBJECT INDEX